Friedrich Nietzsche

Twayne's World Authors Series

German Literature

David O'Connell, *Editor*

Georgia State University

TWAS 857

FRIEDRICH NIETZSCHE
Courtesy of the German Information Center.

Friedrich Nietzsche

Robert C. Holub

University of California, Berkeley

Twayne Publishers
An Imprint of Simon & Schuster Macmillan
New York

Prentice Hall International
London Mexico City New Delhi Singapore Sydney Toronto

Twayne's World Authors Series No. 857

Friedrich Nietzsche
Robert C. Holub

Twayne Publishers
An Imprint of Simon & Schuster Macmillan
866 Third Avenue
New York, New York 10022

Library of Congress Cataloging-in-Publication Data
Holub, Robert C.
   Friedrich Nietzsche / by Robert C. Holub.
     p.   cm. — (Twayne's world author series : no. 857. German
literature)
   Includes bibliographical references and index.
   ISBN 0–8057–4595–5 (alk. paper)
   1. Nietzsche, Friedrich Wilhelm, 1844–1900. I. Title.
II. Series: Twayne's world author series : TWAS 857. III. Series:
Twayne's world author series. German literature.
B3317.H57   1995
193—dc20   95–6028
                                                  CIP

10 9 8 7 6 5 4 3 2 1

Printed in the United States of America

For Jost, Teacher and Friend

Contents

Note on Sources   *ix*
Preface   *xi*
Chronology   *xiii*

Chapter 1
Nietzsche's Life   1

Chapter 2
The Fanatic Philologist   14

Chapter 3
The Pedagogical Reformer   34

Chapter 4
The Scientific Dilettante   55

Chapter 5
The Social Observer   79

Chapter 6
The Genealogist of Morals   102

Chapter 7
The Anti-Theologian   128

Chapter 8
The Great Anticipator   149

Notes and References   *165*
Selected Bibliography   *175*
Index   *183*

Note on Sources

Parenthetical citations from Nietzsche's texts correspond to the following editions. In some cases the translation was modified for the sake of accuracy to the German original.

AC   *The Antichrist,* in *The Portable Nietzsche,* trans. Walter Kaufmann (New York: Viking, 1954), 565–656.

ADH   *On the Advantage and Disadvantage of History for Life,* trans. Peter Preuss (Indianapolis: Hackett Publishing, 1980).

BGE   *Beyond Good and Evil,* trans. R. J. Hollingdale (Harmondsworth: Penguin, 1973).

BT   *The Birth of Tragedy,* in *The Birth of Tragedy and the Genealogy of Morals,* trans. Francis Golffing (Garden City, N.Y.: Doubleday, 1956), 1–146.

BW   *Nietzsche Briefwechsel,* ed. Giorgio Colli and Mazzino Montinari (Berlin: Walter de Gruyter, 1975–84).

CW   *The Case of Wagner,* in *The Birth of Tragedy and the Case of Wagner,* trans. Walter Kaufmann (New York: Vintage, 1967), 153–92.

D   *Daybreak: Thoughts on the Prejudices of Morality,* trans. R. J. Hollingdale (Cambridge: Cambridge University Press, 1982).

EH   *Ecce Homo,* trans. R. J. Hollingdale (Harmondsworth: Penguin, 1979).

GS   *The Gay Science,* trans. Walter Kaufmann (New York: Vintage, 1974).

GM   *The Genealogy of Morals,* in *The Birth of Tragedy and the Genealogy of Morals,* trans. Francis Golffing (Garden City, N.Y.: Doubleday, 1956), 147–299.

HA   *Human, All Too Human: A Book for Free Spirits,* trans. R. J. Hollingdale (Cambridge: Cambridge University Press, 1986).

SB   *Sämtliche Briefe,* ed. Giorgio Colli and Mazzino Montinari (Munich and Berlin: Deutscher Taschenbuch Verlag and Walter de Gruyter, 1975–84).

SE   *Schopenhauer as Educator,* trans. R. J. Hollingdale, in *Untimely Meditations* (Cambridge: Cambridge University Press, 1983), 125–94.

SW   *Sämtliche Werke. Kritische Studienausgabe,* ed. Giorgio Colli and Mazzino Montinari (Munich and Berlin: Deutscher Taschenbuch Verlag and Walter de Gruyter, 1967–77).

TI   *Twilight of the Idols,* in *The Portable Nietzsche,* trans. Walter Kaufmann (New York: Viking, 1954), 463–563.

W   *Werke: Kritische Gesamtausgabe,* ed. Giorgio Colli and Mazzino Montinari (Berlin: Walter de Gruyter, 1982–).

Z   *Thus Spoke Zarathustra,* in *The Portable Nietzsche,* trans. Walter Kaufmann (New York: Viking, 1954), 103–439.

Preface

The thought of Friedrich Nietzsche has consistently been described, by himself and by subsequent commentators, as untimely. Nietzsche himself fostered this view with both direct statements and, indirectly, through imagery and suggestion. The first set of works that Nietzsche composed after his *Birth of Tragedy* was entitled *Untimely Meditations,* and in one of the last books he completed before the outbreak of insanity, the autobiographical *Ecce Homo,* he observed in obvious reference to himself, "some are born posthumously" (*EH* 69). The image of the lonely thinker isolated from his times and his contemporaries is reinforced in Nietzsche's most poetic and most celebrated work, *Thus Spoke Zarathustra,* in which the prophetic titular hero is often depicted alone with his thoughts in the mountains, or else surrounded by a group of disciples who misunderstand his visionary message. In *Ecce Homo,* Nietzsche advanced the following claim: "The disparity between the greatness of my task and the *smallness* of my contemporaries has found expression in the fact that I have been neither heard nor even so much as seen. I live on my own credit, it is perhaps merely a prejudice that I am alive at all?" (*EH* 33). This stylization as an isolated, misunderstood, and untimely thinker shaped much of Nietzsche's vast reception as well. Subsequent generations, believing that they have finally comprehended the essence of his philosophy, have frequently viewed him unhistorically as their contemporary. As we shall see in the final chapter of this book, Nietzsche has been recruited for many diverse causes in the cultural, political, and philosophical realms. In almost every case, however, Nietzsche's own characterization of his untimeliness has been accepted without much controversy.

The following study of Nietzsche disputes this claim of untimeliness. The thesis I will present is that Nietzsche can be best understood not as the great anticipator of later epochs, but as the great participator in his own epoch. Obviously his thought has been fruitful for subsequent writers and thinkers; his enormous impact is an empirical fact. But during the 20 years in which he wrote most of his works, Nietzsche was responding to discourses of his time, and his involvement in these discourses has usually been underestimated. Involvement, of course, does not always mean agreement; in a number of important instances

Nietzsche was "untimely" to the extent that he took issue with dominant trends or with the accepted wisdom of his age. Even when his engagement with his contemporaries was adversarial, however, he was entering into a dialogue with their thought and writing. Unfortunately, in this sort of introductory work I can elucidate only a few of the many connections between Nietzsche and the discourses of the nineteenth century; a more complete examination of the myriad threads that tie Nietzsche to his times will be the task of a more detailed and extensive scholarly work that I intend to write over the next few years. Nonetheless, I do hope to show here that various of Nietzsche's positions on topics ranging from education to ethics, from the natural sciences to social movements, and from cultural revitalization to the critique of religion were outgrowths of a nineteenth-century context. The connections that bind Nietzsche to his time are more numerous than scholars, in particular American scholars, have previously seen. Despite the extraordinary and provocative way in which he expressed his views, many of the positions he actually advocated make sense only within the time in which he wrote. In general I conceive this monograph as an affirmation that Nietzsche's discourse is congruent with the discourses circulating at his time.

I am indebted to the University of California at Berkeley for support while I was researching and writing this book. Various graduate students in the German department assisted me with my research, and I would like to express my gratitude to Karen Six, Karin Svenmo, and Marianne Fieweger for their contribution to my work. Parts of this manuscript were read by Jost Hermand and Renate Holub, both of whom supplied useful suggestions for improvement. Finally, I want to thank David O'Connell for his patience and his careful reading of a manuscript he received piecemeal over an almost two-year period.

Chronology

1844   Birth of Friedrich Wilhelm Nietzsche on 15 October in Röcken, Prussian Saxony to the pastor Karl Ludwig Nietzsche and his wife Franziska, née Oehler.

1846   Birth of Elisabeth Nietzsche on 10 July.

1849   Death of Karl Ludwig Nietzsche on 30 July.

1850   Nietzsche family moves to cathedral city of Naumburg.

1855   Nietzsche enters school associated with the cathedral.

1858   Accepted at prestigious boarding school Schulpforta, where he receives classical education.

1864   Matriculates at Bonn University to study theology and classical philology.

1865   Transfers to the University of Leipzig, where he becomes Friedrich Ritschl's favorite student. First acquaintance with the philosophy of Arthur Schopenhauer.

1866   Friendship with Erwin Rohde.

1867   First publication in classical philology. Enters military service in October.

1868   Riding accident in March leads to discharge from military on 15 October. First meeting with Richard Wagner in Leipzig in November.

1869   Appointed to special professorship in Basel in classical philology (January). Awarded doctorate by Leipzig (23 March). Gives up Prussian citizenship. Holds inaugural lecture on "Homer and Classical Philology" (28 May). Meets colleagues: historian Jacob Burckhardt and the theologian Franz Overbeck.

1870   Professorship regularized. Public lectures on "The Greek Music Drama" (18 January) and "Socrates and Tragedy" (1 February). Serves as orderly in Franco-Prussian War with Prussian army; contracts dysentery and diphtheria.

1871   Granted leave of absence from Basel due to ill health.

1872   Publication of *The Birth of Tragedy* (January). Series of five public lectures on education. Present at laying of foundation stone for Bayreuth opera house (22 May). Meets Paul Rée.

1873   Publication of first *Untimely Meditation: David Strauss, the Confessor and Writer.*

1874   Publication of second and third *Untimely Meditations: On the Advantage and Disadvantage of History for Life* and *Schopenhauer as Educator.*

1875   Meets Heinrich Köselitz (Peter Gast). Elisabeth moves to Basel and sets up home for herself and her brother.

1876   Publication of fourth *Untimely Meditation: Richard Wagner in Bayreuth.* Attends first Bayreuth festival (July). Granted one-year sick leave from University. Lives in Sorrento with Rée and Malwida von Meysenbug. Sees Wagner for last time.

1877   Returns to Basel and resumes teaching. Lives with Elisabeth and Gast.

1878   Publication of *Human, All Too Human,* which finalizes break with Wagner.

1879   Second volume of *Human, All Too Human* (Assorted Opinions and Maxims). Resignation from professorship due to ill health; granted pension. Travels in Switzerland, then to Naumburg.

1880   Publication of *The Wanderer and His Shadow.* Travels to Riva, Venice, Marienbad, Naumburg, Stresa, and Genoa, where he spends the winter.

1881   Publication of *Daybreak.* Travels to Recoaro and Riva with Gast; alone to St. Moritz and Sils-Maria. Winter in Genoa.

1882   Publication of *The Gay Science.* Meets Lou Salomé in Rome at the home of Malwida von Meysenbug (May). Returns to Naumburg; visits Berlin and Tautenburg, where Lou joins him. With Lou and Rée in Leipzig (October). Break with Lou and Rée; leaves for Rapallo (November).

1883   Publication of *Thus Spoke Zarathustra,* parts one and two. Death of Wagner (13 February). Travel to Genoa, Rome,

Sils-Maria, Naumburg, Genoa, and Nice. In Naumburg learns of Elisabeth's engagement to anti-Semite Bernhard Förster.

1884   Publication of *Zarathustra,* part three. Stays in Venice, Sils-Maria, Zürich, and Nice.

1885   Publication of *Zarathustra,* part four (published privately). Travel to Venice, Sils-Maria, Naumburg, and Nice. Marriage of Elisabeth and Förster, who leave for colony in Paraguay.

1886   Publication of *Beyond Good and Evil.* Stays in Naumburg, Leipzig, Genoa, and Nice.

1887   Publication of *The Genealogy of Morals.* Travel to Sils-Maria, Venice, and back to Nice.

1888   Publication of *The Case of Wagner.* Stays in Turin and Sils-Maria; return to Turin in September. Composition of last sane writings.

1889   Publication of *Twilight of the Idols.* Collapses on street in Turin (3 January). Retrieved by Overbeck. Enters clinic at Basel (10 January); transferred to clinic in Jena (17 January). Förster commits suicide in Paraguay after embezzling colony's funds.

1890   Franziska Nietzsche takes her son to Naumburg, where he remains in her care. Elisabeth returns from Paraguay.

1892   Plan for first edition of Nietzsche's published works (discontinued after volume five), edited by Gast, but arranged by Elisabeth, who then returns to Paraguay.

1893   Elisabeth returns from Paraguay for good.

1894   Founding of Nietzsche Archive.

1895   Publication of *The Antichrist* and *Nietzsche contra Wagner.* Elisabeth acquires all rights to Nietzsche's writings.

1896   Archives transferred to Weimar.

1897   Death of Nietzsche's mother; Elisabeth takes Nietzsche to Weimar.

1900   Death of Nietzsche (25 August).

1901   First version of *The Will to Power* (second edition 1906).

1908   First publication of *Ecce Homo.*

Chapter 1
Nietzsche's Life

Friedrich Wilhelm Nietzsche was born on 15 October 1844 in the small town of Röcken in the German state of Saxony.[1] Considering his later deprecatory attitude toward Germany and the Prussian monarchy, it is an irony of history that he was named for the Prussian king Friedrich Wilhelm IV. Responsible for this christening was Nietzsche's father, Karl Ludwig Nietzsche, a Protestant minister with some musical talent, who had received the parish in Röcken because he had made a favorable impression on the king when he served as tutor to the Duke of Saxe-Altenburg. Nietzsche's mother, Franziska Oehler, came to Röcken in 1843, when she was 17, to be the 30-year-old Karl Ludwig's bride. Her father was also a pastor, in the village of Pobles, located about an hour away from Röcken. When she entered the Nietzsche household, it was well populated with women. Karl Ludwig's mother Erdmuthe and his two stepsisters Rosalie and Augusta were already in residence, and less than two years after Friedrich's birth another female joined the group, Nietzsche's sister Elisabeth, who in later years would play a central role in Nietzsche's life, but an even more important part in establishing her brother's reputation, especially in Germany. The atmosphere in this pastor's home was Lutheran, strict, monarchical, and conservative. The most significant event for the family occurred in July of 1849, when Karl Ludwig, who had evidently suffered for years from a mild form of epilepsy and had experienced a nervous breakdown a year earlier, died from what was diagnosed at the time as a softening of the brain. Throughout his life Nietzsche was haunted by the thought that he had inherited the same genetically transferred disorder that killed his father. Barely five years old, Nietzsche had lost his father, and a year later his baby brother Ludwig also died. Thereafter Fritz, as he was called at home, lived surrounded almost exclusively by women: his mother, his sister, his grandmother, and his two maiden aunts.

After Karl Ludwig's death, the extended family, under the dominant influence of grandmother Erdmuthe, decided that they should leave Röcken and settle in the cathedral city of Naumburg. Although by today's standards Naumburg hardly qualifies as a metropolis, it was

1

quite a change from the small village that Fritz had inhabited for the first six years of his life. A city of some 15,000 inhabitants, Naumburg had a relatively large upper-middle class consisting of lawyers, church officials, and bureaucrats, and Erdmuthe's connections soon established the Nietzsche household in these circles. Nietzsche had attended a village schoolhouse in Röcken, but his educational possibilities were expanded greatly by the move to Naumburg. He first enrolled in the local elementary school, where he began to learn Greek and Latin, and was soon recognized as a precocious child. In 1855 Nietzsche continued his education when he was accepted into the *Domgymnasium*, a private preparatory school connected with the cathedral. Already in these early years we find two features that would persevere throughout his life: a voracious appetite for learning and reading, and a frail constitution that frequently disabled Nietzsche for long intervals of time.

Because of his considerable abilities Nietzsche was offered a scholarship to attend perhaps the most celebrated high school in all of Germany: Schulpforta. Located about four miles from Naumburg, Schulpforta was a boarding school renowned for its high level of academic achievement. Its graduates included such notable writers and scholars as the poet Friedrich Klopstock, the romantic author Novalis (Friedrich von Hardenberg), the philosopher Johann Fichte, Friedrich and Wilhelm Schlegel, central figures in German romanticism, and the noted historian Leopold von Ranke. At Pforta Nietzsche received the rigorous classical training that would catapult him into an academic career. He attended the school for six years and was acknowledged as one of the best students. The anecdote usually produced to prove his precocity involves Nietzsche's difficulties with his mathematics teacher. Evidently he failed mathematics during his final year, but when the teacher, a man named Buchbinder, suggested that Nietzsche not be allowed to graduate, he was berated by his colleague Wilhelm Corssen, who supposedly stated: "Do you wish perhaps that we allow the most gifted student that the school has had since I have been here to fail?" Buchbinder relented, and Nietzsche was allowed to graduate.

Nietzsche kept up with his old friends in Naumburg as well, and he was active in forming a small artistic-literary group called *Germania*. This title, of course, was a sign of the times; at this point in his life Nietzsche, like most Germans of his generation, was an ardent nationalist. Perhaps most significant about his activities during the mid-1860s, however, was that he had already begun to supplement his strictly academic activities with more general cultural concerns. By the time

Nietzsche graduated from Pforta, he had produced a remarkable body of both creative and scholarly writings—considering that he had not yet celebrated his twentieth birthday. After graduating from Pforta in 1864, Nietzsche studied at two German universities. At the University of Bonn he concentrated on classical philology after beginning as a theology student. At Bonn Nietzsche also attended classes in art history, church history, political science, and theology. He was a member of the student club or *Burschenschaft* "Franconia," and although he seems to have enjoyed the comradery, he resigned after a few months. From his letters it seems that his resignation had to do with lack of funds, and perhaps also with a desire to concentrate a bit more on scholarly pursuits and a bit less on carousing. At Bonn he also fought a duel, receiving a scar for his efforts. According to his close friend Paul Deussen, while at Bonn Nietzsche also visited a brothel, but left after playing the piano. Because Nietzsche's later insanity is frequently attributed to a syphilitic infection, Deussen's account has been considered significant and controversial.

At about this time the classical philologists at Bonn were embroiled in a bitter feud. The two main adversaries were Friedrich Ritschl and Otto Jahn, and the conflict between them became so enormous that it was known throughout Germany as the "Bonn philology war." The result of this life-and-death struggle in academia was that Ritschl resigned his position in Bonn and accepted a professorship at the University of Leipzig. Most biographical accounts claim that Nietzsche, who was working with Ritschl, followed him to Leipzig. But the letters from this period indicate that Nietzsche had made his decision about transferring to Leipzig before Ritschl had announced his intentions of going there. It seems that Nietzsche was persuaded by friendship and perhaps by the proximity of Leipzig to Naumburg. It is interesting that most commentators have believed what Nietzsche wrote to his mother—namely that he was going to Leipzig because of Ritschl—when he clearly stated in a letter to Carl von Gersdorff that he had decided to transfer to Leipzig only after Gersdorff had announced his matriculation, and that Ritschl's decision came later and strengthened his resolve to leave Bonn. In any case in 1865 we find Nietzsche in Leipzig continuing his studies and becoming increasingly involved with scholarly work in classical philology.

Perhaps more important for his intellectual progress during these university years was the influence of two figures: Arthur Schopenhauer and Richard Wagner. Since we will have occasion to deal with Wagner briefly in chapter 2 with regard to *The Birth of Tragedy,* it is more important here to say a few words about the guiding philosophical influence of Schopenhauer on the young Nietzsche. Although Schopenhauer belongs biographically to the first half of the nineteenth century, his influence is clearly a phenomenon of the 1850s and 1860s. His philosophy is a mixture of strict Kantianism with a thick coat of pessimism. So strong was the hold of Kant on Schopenhauer that it is said that he even took on the manners of his idol, taking walks with a poodle at a regular time in the afternoon.

Schopenhauer maintained Kant's distinction between a Thing-in-Itself (noumenon) and Things-for-Us (phenomena), which are objects of our perception, but he equated the former with *will,* as opposed to *ideas,* which relate to the phenomenal world. Hence the title of his most famous work, *The World as Will and Idea,* is meant to encompass these two halves of the Kantian polarity noumenon and phenomenon: will and ideas. What Schopenhauer meant by will may not be that clear, especially since we know will only by its external or phenomenal manifestations. It is important that we do not conceive of will as something individual; it is not simply what a person wants. Rather, like Hegelian spirit, it is a metaphysical notion that is supra-individual.

Ultimately this will, which is the essence of the world, was described by Schopenhauer as an unreasonable, irrational power. The world is the externalization of this power, and Schopenhauer believed that to live in the world is to suffer. Our dealings with the phenomenal world do not lead us to happiness: according to Schopenhauer epistemology has only a practical function. The only way to achieve happiness is to satisfy somehow the blind, irrational force in each of us. Happiness was thus for him something negative, the absence of pain, the cessation of desire. It is impossible to reach a total state of happiness, because the will can never be satisfied. If it were satisfied, it would lead to boredom and ennui, not happiness. With this in mind Schopenhauer outlined two main paths to temporary and tentative happiness: (1) aesthetic observation and contemplation—here one loses oneself in the object, which leads to a momentary annihilation of the ego or individuality; and (2) ascetic denial of all human drives, wishes, and desires. This second manner of negating the will suggests a turn to nothingness or Nirvana, and it is no coincidence that Schopenhauer was one of the first Europeans to incorporate into his philosophy what he understood of Eastern philosophy.

Schopenhauer's notions of will and idea, as well as his emphasis on suffering and sublimation, had a great deal of influence on Nietzsche, and we will see him preoccupied with various Schopenhauerian motifs and issues throughout his life, at first as a disciple, but later, increasingly, as a critic or reviser. During his school years, he delved often into Schopenhauer's works and obviously shared this reading with several of his friends who were similarly inclined. Schopenhauer was very likely the only modern philosopher whose works Nietzsche knew thoroughly. Although well acquainted with Greek and classical philosophers, it appears that most of Nietzsche's knowledge of medieval and modern philosophy came from secondhand sources. Significantly, his library evidences no texts of such renowned philosophers as Descartes, Leibniz, Spinoza, or Hegel. In any case, for the young Nietzsche Schopenhauer was less a philosopher in the academic sense of the word than a cult figure: reading his correspondence, we soon recognize that Schopenhauer was a cause for Nietzsche and his friends to which one owed allegiance. An adherence to Schopenhauer was the shibboleth for the small, exclusive circle to which Nietzsche belonged. What makes this adherence to Schopenhauer even more odd is that one can make a fairly convincing argument that Nietzsche never really shared wholeheartedly in the pessimism that was perhaps the outstanding feature of Schopenhauer's work. Thus Nietzsche's turn away from Schopenhauer was pre-programmed; his rejection of his philosophy is consistent with predilections that were apparent even when he was professing to be a loyal disciple.

In 1867 Nietzsche had to interrupt his studies for compulsory military service. He appears to have had mixed feelings about the military despite the positive remarks he later made about war and the exercise of power. At times he expressed his desire to go into the army; at other times he seemed to consider it more of a bother than anything else. When he finally did enlist, he was assigned to the cavalry, and it is reported that while falling off a horse during a training exercise, he hung onto the saddle from underneath the mount and whispered: "Schopenhauer, help me now." His tour of duty did not last very long. Evidently not a very accomplished horseman—although to judge from his letters, he felt otherwise—he sustained an injury to his chest while riding in March of 1868, was declared unfit for further duty, and was sent home to recuperate.

After recovering from his injury, in the fall of 1868 he first made the acquaintance of Richard Wagner and his wife Cosima, who quickly became his intellectual mentors and a kind of surrogate family. Early in 1869 he heard the astonishing news that through Ritschl he had received an *außerordentliche Professur* (special, full professorship) in

classical philology at the University in Basel. Although the University in
Basel was known for hiring young professors and was something of a
temporary stopover for recent doctorates who later moved on to academic careers at more prestigious German universities, this was still a great
honor for someone so young.

Nietzsche was only 24 years old at the
time, and the appointment was quite unusual since he had completed
neither his dissertation nor his *Habilitationsschrift* (a second major work
written after the dissertation), nor had he published very much in his
field at all.[2] Nietzsche, who had planned to spend 1869 in Paris studying
natural sciences, postponed his trip to France and accepted the position.
In order to teach in Basel he was compelled to renounce his Prussian citizenship, and since he never became a citizen of Switzerland, he
remained something like a man without a country for the rest of his life.
In May of 1869 he delivered his inaugural address in Basel on "Homer
and Classical Philology."

Nietzsche remained professor at Basel for 10 years, from 1869–79,
lecturing on a variety of themes in the area of classical antiquity and
philology. Perhaps the most notable acquaintance he made during those
years at Basel was Jacob Burckhardt, the famous professor of art history
and author of one of the most celebrated books on the Italian renaissance. During this period Nietzsche also made regular visits to see the
Wagners, who lived in Switzerland during the early 1870s. In 1870,
when the war that eventually led to Germany's unification broke out
between Germany and France, Nietzsche requested and received permission to enlist in the German army. He was allowed to serve as a medical
orderly, since the Swiss did not want to appear partisan to either France
or Germany. Again his military service ended infelicitously. While tending to the sick and wounded, Nietzsche contracted diphtheria and
dysentery and instead of attending to the ill, he was forced to recuperate
himself.

This fact is conveniently forgotten or repressed in the "Critical
Backward Glance," written for the second edition of the *Birth of Tragedy*
(original in 1872) in 1886. In this preface of sorts Nietzsche makes no
reference to his volunteering for military service in the Prussian army,
nor to the illnesses that compelled him again to cut this service short.
Instead, he makes it appear as if his first book-length project simply runs
parallel to the Franco-Prussian war. "While the thunder of the battle of
Wörth was rumbling over Europe, a lover of subtleties and conun-
drums—father-to-be of this book—sat down in an alpine recess, much
bemused and bedeviled (which is to say, both engrossed and detached) to

pen the substance of that odd and forbidding work for which the follow-ing pages shall now serve as a belated preface or postscript" (*BT* 3). Nietzsche cites further parallels with the battle of Metz and with the peace treaty at Versailles that ended the conflict. Obviously the reader is supposed to consider Nietzsche's work of comparable importance to that of the German army. His preoccupation with the origin of Greek tragedy and the possibility of its reemergence in modern times is likened to the grand struggle for empire and the unification of the Second Reich. Even in his early years Nietzsche was not one to shy away from grandiose comparisons with his work.

As the 1870s progressed, Nietzsche became increasingly dissatisfied with his philological career. In 1873 he applied for a recently vacated position as a philosopher at Basel, even though his training in philosophy was not very extensive. His idea was to give his own position to one of his close friends, Erwin Rohde, who was at that time in a temporary profes-sorship at the university in Kiel. Although Nietzsche continued on the faculty in Basel until 1879—with frequent leaves for illness in the second half of the decade—his contributions to classical philology were few, espe-cially if we, like the classical philologists of Nietzsche's era and our own, discount *The Birth of Tragedy*. This book, which will be treated in detail in the next chapter, is simply not very philological in its methods or content. An odd mixture of classical philology, half-baked enthusiasm for Schopenhauer, and Wagner veneration, Nietzsche's only book-length con-tribution to his field after his appointment to full professor was greeted by his colleagues with a mixture of disdain and perplexity.

His three major theses—the first concerning the rise of tragedy from a coupling of Dionysian and Apollonian principles (I–X), the second concerning the demise of tragedy due to Socratic or rational thinking (XI–XV), and the third regarding Richard Wagner as the renewer of tragic art in Germany (XVI–XXV)—seem implausible, overstated, and inappropriate: there is little philological evidence to support the first two, and the third seems to be an arbitrary and tendentious cultural intervention rather than a scholarly proposition. For the most part, *The Birth of Tragedy* went unnoticed by classical philologists; it was easy to overlook it since it did not appear in a scholarly or philological press or series, but rather with Wagner's publisher Ernst Wilhelm Fritzsch. The few who did read it apparently did not think much of it. Nietzsche man-aged to persuade Rohde to write a positive review, but this was an isolat-ed favorable reaction. Moreover, the review appeared in an unscholarly periodical, the *Norddeutsche Allgemeine Zeitung,* because it had been rejected by two more reputable journals that dealt more specifically with literary or philological issues. The only stir it did cause was the result of a negative review by a young classical philologist, Ulrich von Wilamowitz-Moellendorff. Wilamowitz was also a graduate from Pforta—he was four years younger than Nietzsche—but, unlike the professor at Basel, he was someone who would later be acclaimed as one of the outstanding scholars of his age. Wilamowitz was asked to write a review of the book by Rudolf Schöll, who was a student in Bonn under Ritschl and Jahn during the philologists' war—he completed his dissertation in 1865—and who later taught as a *Dozent* (something like a lecturer) in Berlin. Schöll's motive for asking Wilamowitz to write the review was probably petty vengeance. When the classical philologist in Basel, a man named Wilhelm Vischer-Bolfinger, stepped down in 1867 after 31 years of service to enter city government, a new philologist was needed. Vischer wrote to eminent scholars for nominations for his own successor. Ritschl apparently mentioned Nietzsche in an extremely favorable light at the top of his recommendations, and did not even include Schöll, who was also his student, in the letter. Thus, as Wilamowitz's biographer wrote, Schöll sought to even the score with both Ritschl and Nietzsche: "Schöll saw in the brilliant, passionate Wilamowitz the instrument provided by providence to wreak vengeance with no risk to himself on a detested rival and a faithless teacher, who had preferred an inferior."[3]

Wilamowitz's review appeared in a pamphlet entitled "Philology of the Future" (*Zukunftsphilologie*), and the substance of his attack is a refutation of the connection between Euripides and Socrates, which plays such an important role in Nietzsche's work. The Nietzschean camp responded with a letter from Wagner, printed in the *Norddeutsche Zeitung*; and Rohde, who had evidently written his first review more out of friendship than conviction, was finally bullied into rebutting Wilamowitz—a rebuttal (*Afterphilologie*: Sham Philology) that only discredited him further as a classical philologist and probably delayed his appointment to a regular position. The reaction of other scholars to this dispute was at most mild amusement; nothing from them appeared in public. In private most thought Nietzsche's position was nonsensical, and even today, when Nietzsche's name has achieved a greatness in non-philological circles that far outstrips that of Wilamowitz, one would be hard pressed to find a scholar of classical Greek who believes Nietzsche's response more accurate and faithful to the sources than Wilamowitz's. Although Wilamowitz was not always right, nor Nietzsche always wrong, it is fair to say that Wilamowitz has held sway among philologists, even if Nietzsche's views have proved to be more stimulating for subsequent generations of intellectuals and philosophers.[4]

Nietzsche was somewhat disappointed at the faint response his first book received, but it only served to confirm his growing suspicion that he was ill-suited to his academic career. As a result, instead of writing on classical philology and ancient civilization, Nietzsche turned to issues involving the critique of contemporary German culture. As a pedagogue Nietzsche had good reason to be concerned with matters of culture and education, and, like many of his contemporaries, he was a severe judge of the gymnasium and university system as they existed. As we shall see in chapter 3, his scathing criticisms of education and the university, evidenced in a series of lectures he gave in 1871, as well as in later aphoristic remarks, make fascinating reading, but they are often misunderstood. Nietzsche's position was not one that advanced democracy in the educational institution, but rather one that promulgated greater elitism and restrictions. He was not appalled by the conservative academies that existed during his time, but by their democratization and their concomitant decline.

Ironically enough, Nietzsche trumpeted the same line in the nineteenth century that the recently deceased Allan Bloom propounded in *The Closing of the American Mind* (1987). Although Bloom considered Nietzsche to be responsible or at least partially responsible for the breakdown of values in the American educational system and advocated a return to more traditional notions of education, the early views of Nietzsche and Bloom are strikingly similar: both advocate a conservative curriculum based on ideals of classical learning. Nietzsche's educational and cultural criticism did not come from the left—that position was occupied by the Socialist party and by the friends of Karl Marx and Friedrich Engels in Germany. It came instead from the right, from an elitist and non-egalitarian notion of the civilization process.

Thus if we examine Nietzsche's works of cultural criticism that appeared during the next few years, we will see that he not only abandoned classical philology, but also assumed a veneer of unorthodox conservatism not uncommon for Germany of the 1870s. The irony of the four *Untimely Meditations,* which appeared over the next few years, is that they were so timely. Certainly they were directed against a smug, philistine intellectual attitude, but they were hardly as unusual as Nietzsche and his later disciples would want us to believe. Indeed, the very gesture of appearing to be "untimely" was perhaps the most timely attitude during the ostentatious period of German history following the defeat of France. Nietzsche thus took aim at items that were high priorities for many others as well. His first meditation is a critique of David Strauß, a Hegelian and author of the important work *Das Leben Jesu* (1835); Nietzsche had been an enthusiastic reader of Strauß a few years before and appreciated his critique of religion, but now the Straußian attitude seemed too smug and content. The second meditation, which we will examine in more detail in chapter 3, is entitled *Advantage and Disadvantage of History for Life* (1874), and deals with the right way and the wrong way to educate students in a historical manner. The third and fourth meditations deal with Nietzsche's heroes: *Schopenhauer as Educator* (1874) is the title of the third meditation—as we have seen there was a veritable Schopenhauer vogue among young intellectuals at this time— and the fourth appeared as *Richard Wagner in Bayreuth* (1876)— Nietzsche had been present at the laying of the cornerstone for the famous Festspielhaus (opera house) in Bayreuth in 1872. Only in hindsight can we begin to see in this last meditation from the mid-1880s the beginnings of Nietzsche's disenchantment with his mentor.

After these essays, Nietzsche settled down into a genre that was more suited to his proclivities for the apodictic statement and clever turn of phrase. *Human, All Too Human* (1878 and 1879), *Daybreak* (1881), and *The Gay Science* (1882), often looked at as part of Nietzsche's middle period, are all aphoristic. In these works Nietzsche continued his critique of culture, but he appeared to move closer to a validation of the natural scientific method. In 1879 Nietzsche resigned from his teaching position at Basel—he had already taken a leave of absence in 1876—and lived on a small but adequate pension from the university. The reasons for his retirement at age 34 were probably complex. No doubt he was tired of teaching classical studies, which he had not pursued in a scholarly vein for almost a decade. Added to this was his physical condition, which had been rather poor even when he was a student at Pforta. Headaches and chronic stomach problems, the former possibly caused by eyestrain, made him uncomfortable in his position. He spent most of the next decade in cities in northern Italy, where he lived in boardinghouses during the winter, and in Sils-Maria in the Engadine region of Switzerland during the summer.

During this period his eyesight worsened significantly, but Nietzsche continued to read and write as much as his physical condition allowed. Indeed, some of his most enduring writing stems from the 1880s. The publication of what many consider his major work, *Thus Spoke*

Zarathustra: A Book for Everyone and No One, took place during the years 1883–85. Structured as an immense parody of the Bible, *Zarathustra* is divided into four books, most of which contain short parabolic statements about or from its hero. Here is where such notions as the last man, the superman, and eternal recurrence, all topics of chapter 4, are expounded. The year 1886 saw the publication of *Beyond Good and Evil,* another collection of parables, and in the following year, in order to clarify some of the ethical postulates in this text, he published the more essayistic work *The Genealogy of Morals* (1887). These last two works, with their emphasis on morality and their fierce rejection of the Judeo-Christian tradition (the central concerns of chapters 6 and 7), are generally viewed as part of Nietzsche's final period.

Perhaps the crucial biographical occurrence during the last decade of his conscious life was his relationship with Lou Salomé. The daughter of a deceased Russian officer, Louise von Salomé had left St. Petersburg, accompanied by her mother, after an unhappy love affair with a married man and traveled to the West, where she enrolled for courses at the University of Zurich, one of the first universities to admit women. Ill health, however, compelled her to leave Switzerland, and on her journey through Italy she met Paul Rée at the home of Malwida von Meysenbug. Both were close friends of Nietzsche. Malwida, a nineteenth-century feminist and the author of *Memoirs of an Idealist,* had become acquainted with Nietzsche when they were both Wagnerians. Rée, a Jewish scholar who wrote several books on ethics and psychology, had come to Basel in the spring of 1873 and soon became one of Nietzsche's most trusted companions. Indeed, he had just left Nietzsche and traveled to Rome, where he met Lou in Malwida's salon in March of 1882. Nietzsche soon arrived as well, and, like most of the men Lou met, including Rée, Nietzsche became infatuated with her. What is unclear from the documentation we possess is whether Nietzsche conceived the 21-year-old Russian woman as a lover, a wife, or a disciple—or perhaps a combination of the three. In the following intense months there arose something of a competition between Nietzsche and Rée for Lou's affection—or at least for her attention. Complicating the situation for Nietzsche was Elisabeth, whom Nietzsche engaged to accompany Lou to the opening of *Parsifal* in Bayreuth, and whose prudish self-righteousness and sisterly jealousy brought her into immediate conflict with the daring, emancipated Russian. The whole affair ended badly for Nietzsche. The "holy trinity" of Rée, Nietzsche, and Lou was eventually reduced to a pair with Nietzsche being the odd man out.

The significance of this episode for Nietzsche's life is threefold. With regard to Lou, Nietzsche again failed to attract and secure a female companion. During the 1870s Nietzsche had been persuaded by Malwida and others that he needed a wife, but despite the best efforts of friends to serve as matchmakers and an occasional halfhearted proposal of marriage, Nietzsche had failed to find the right woman. Lou, who was probably looking more for intellectual stimulation and introductions to important people than for a lasting relationship, was at least intellectually suited for Nietzsche, and her departure from Nietzsche's life signaled an end to thoughts of matrimony and, as we shall see, a decisive turn against women and women's emancipation in his works. With regard to Rée it meant the end of a friendship and the increasing isolation of Nietzsche with his work. Nietzsche did retain relationships with Franz Overbeck, the professor of religion in Basel, and with the composer Heinrich Köselitz, whom he called Peter Gast and who faithfully copied many of Nietzsche's manuscripts for publication, but during the 1880s he existed increasingly in seclusion from intellectual comradery. Finally, with regard to his sister, the affair with Lou had brought out the vicious pettiness in her character. The familial bond could no longer bridge the disparity of their worldviews; with Elisabeth's marriage to the anti-Semite Bernhard Förster in 1885 and her move the following year to Paraguay, where Förster hoped to start a pure German colony, the two siblings grew ever more distant from one another. Lou may have served as an inspiration for Nietzsche and inspired parts of *Zarathustra,* but the lasting effects of her entrance into, and precipitous exit from, Nietzsche's life were only the confirmation of his own self-imposed loneliness.

In the final years of his productive life, Nietzsche continued to write at a feverish pace, even though he was constantly plagued by headaches, impaired eyesight, and stomach disorders. In some of his works one can already detect a slight indication of the insanity to which he would eventually succumb, or at least an intensification of monomaniacal tendencies. During the final two years of his life he composed a series of shorter and seminal works: *The Case of Wagner* (1888) and *Nietzsche Versus Wagner* (1895) carry out an analysis and critique of the composer and, by extension, a self-criticism of Nietzsche's earlier views. *Twilight of the Idols* (1889) and *The Antichrist* (1895) both touch on a wide range of topics, but they are centrally concerned with the history of religion and morality. *Ecce Homo,* published posthumously in 1908, is one of the strangest autobiographies ever written. Perhaps because of his deteriorating mental health, these works mix brilliantly formulated diatribes with apparently ludicrous exaggerations. An illustration of the strange and provocative nature of Nietzsche's late thought are the titles of the four sections of *Ecce Homo*: (1) Why I am so wise; (2) Why I am so clever; (3) Why I write such excellent books (in this section he discusses and evaluates his own writings in chronological order); (4) Why I am a destiny.

On 3 January 1889 Nietzsche collapsed on a street in Turin, where he had been residing since the fall of 1888. It appears that he had tried to intercede when he witnessed a horse being beaten. In tears and lamentation he threw himself on the neck of the animal and lost consciousness. He was obviously suffering from a severe mental breakdown. The cause of his insanity has never been determined with any degree of certainty. Some have claimed that it was due to syphilis contracted either as a student in Bonn or Leipzig or during his brief stints in the military. Others have attributed Nietzsche's mental deterioration to the disease that evidently claimed his father's life and other members of his father's family. The last few letters we have from him indicate the extent of his insanity: he signed his correspondence either with the name "Dionysus" or with "the Crucified One." He claimed that he had created the world; he wrote to the king of Italy, addressing his remarks to his dear son Umberto; he stated that Wilhelm, Bismarck, and all anti-Semites had been eliminated. In one of his last letters he stated that he would rather be a professor at Basel than God.

After a few days Nietzsche was retrieved from Turin and returned to Basel by his friend Franz Overbeck. He entered a clinic on 10 January, but there was apparently no hope for a recovery. A week later he was transferred to a clinic in Jena, and in 1890 he was released into the custody of his mother, who moved with her son back to Naumburg. In 1893 Nietzsche's sister Elisabeth Förster-Nietzsche returned from Paraguay, where she had been trying to straighten out the affairs of the German colony established there by her former husband.[5] In 1894 she established a Nietzsche archive, which she relocated in Weimar in 1896; thereafter she dedicated herself to public relations on behalf of her insane brother. In 1897 Elisabeth acquired all legal rights to her brother's writings, and after their mother's death in the same year, she brought her brother to Weimar as well. By the time Nietzsche died on 25 August 1900, his reputation had already begun to spread across Germany, Europe, and the world. Eventually, in the twentieth century, he would become one of the best-known writers and philosophers of the nineteenth century.

Chapter 2
The Fanatic Philologist

From his earliest published essays in 1868 until at least the mid-1870s, Nietzsche's thought was significantly influenced by classical philology and by his enthusiasm for the music of Richard Wagner. Classical philology, of course, with a concentration on ancient Greece, was the subject that Nietzsche had studied most extensively at Pforta and at the Universities of Bonn and Leipzig, and it was because of this training and expertise that he was appointed to a professorship at Basel. This was the only area in which Nietzsche was expert in an academic sense. Although he is widely known today as a philosopher, his training in that area was rather minimal: aside from certain areas of Greek philosophy, he knew only the works of Schopenhauer with any thoroughness. His training in the classics, by contrast, was quite extensive. Because he abandoned his philological pursuits rather early, there is some question as to how proficient he was at his chosen profession. From the volume of philological work that he left behind, it is difficult to make an evaluation of how his reputation would have fared if he had remained active in the field.[1] Most professional philologists—both in his era and in subsequent times— believe that he could have made valuable contributions, and at least some of the work he published was of high quality. On the other hand, because he produced so little or perhaps because he became a philological apostate, he is rarely accorded any mention in histories of classical philology. The summary judgment on Nietzsche as philologist—at least in the context of philology in nineteenth-century Germany—is that he was a scholar who never lived up to his immense potential.

Nietzsche's enthusiasm for Wagner developed slowly. At first he expressed indifference or mixed feelings toward Wagner's work. But by the fall of 1868, he seems to have gained an appreciation for him, possibly influenced by his reading of Schopenhauer and by the more general acceptance of Wagner's music in Schopenhauerian circles. In his letters to friends he wrote about Wagnerian opera with enthusiasm and admiration. The final stage in his conversion to Wagnerian discipleship occurred when he made the composer's personal acquaintance. Evidently Wagner had heard of Nietzsche's enthusiasm for him through a mutual friend, and on Wagner's initiative a meeting was arranged. Nietzsche's correspondence to his closest friend, Erwin Rohde, gives us some indication of what this meeting meant to him. He wrote that he had assumed he was being invited to a larger gathering. Much to his surprise, however, the afternoon meeting at the home of the Brockhaus family consisted of "no one except the immediate family, Richard Wagner and us." Evidently Wagner played for them from the *Meistersinger,* and they discussed together their mutual admiration for Schopenhauer. Nietzsche described Wagner to Rohde as a "fabulously vivacious and fiery man who speaks very rapidly, is very witty, and livens up this sort of very private gathering." Friendly relations must have been established almost immediately, since Nietzsche referred to him in his letter as "Richard." A further indication of their intimacy is that Wagner read to Nietzsche from his autobiography, and when his young visitor was leaving, he shook his hand warmly and invited him back for further discussions of music and philosophy (*SB* 2: 335–42).

The effect on Nietzsche of Wagner as a person and of the cult around Wagner can hardly be exaggerated. The early, non-philological works of Nietzsche cannot be imagined without the composer, who was directly or indirectly inspirational for almost everything Nietzsche published until 1878. Large parts of the *Birth of Tragedy* were about Wagner, and the entire essay was understood—to an extent, correctly—as a promotion of his operas. The *Untimely Meditation* on (and against) David Strauß was written largely because of Strauß's support for one of Wagner's musical rivals in Munich for the post of conductor (*Kapellmeister*); Wagner was probably using Nietzsche as a tool for revenge because Strauß had opposed him. *Schopenhauer as Educator,* although not about Wagner, is an essay on the important philosophical link between Nietzsche and Wagner. And *Richard Wagner in Bayreuth,* presented to Wagner at the opening of the Bayreuth Festspiele in 1876, is obviously celebratory in character—although the attentive reader can already detect many of Nietzsche's later objections. In his private life Wagner assumed a prominent place almost immediately. Two months after his first meeting with Wagner, Nietzsche wrote to Rohde about him with a veneration that would last well into the mid-1870s: "I have extreme confidence that we can agree entirely about a genius who appears to me like an insoluble problem, and whom I make new efforts to understand year in and year out: this genius is Richard Wagner." For Nietzsche Wagner was the "living illustration" of what Schopenhauer meant when he used the word genius, and it is evident that his worship of Wagner went hand in hand with his adherence to Schopenhauer (*SB* 2: 352). In his correspondence during the next eight years Nietzsche would frequently allude to his visits to Wagner's home, the plans for Bayreuth, and Wagnerian music.

As a professor Nietzsche carefully separated his philological writings and academic activities from his enthusiasm for Wagner. But in his first monograph and perhaps most famous work, *The Birth of Tragedy from the Spirit of Music* (1872), he made a valiant effort to harmonize what seem like irreconcilable demands in both content and style. What makes Nietzsche's *Birth of Tragedy* a fascinating work, however, is not its Wagnerian pretentions nor its relationship to classical philology in Nietzsche's time, but the brilliance with which the young Nietzsche dealt with his topic. Indeed, it is a work of impressive breadth. Ostensibly about ancient Greece and the origins of tragedy in the development of the chorus, it is also a plea for a restoration or rejuvenation of European culture in the late nineteenth century, a piece of propaganda for Schopenhauer's philosophy, and an acclamation of Richard Wagner, his music, and his ideas. Like a symphony, it may be divided into three distinct movements. The first concerns the rise of tragedy and involves the notions of the Dionysian and the Apollonian. The second deals with the decline of tragedy and the concomitant rise of a Socratic way of thought. The third movement, which is taken up in the final 10 sections, advocates a return to the tragic worldview through the advent of Richard Wagner, a recuperation of the musical foundation upon which tragedy rests.

From this schematic summary of the work, at least one thing should be evident: the birth that is included in the title is not a very exact metaphor. It seems to fit for the origin of tragedy, which can be conceived as a unification of two tendencies. But the work also shows us another, perhaps more important birth: the birth of the Socratic, the realist, the Alexandrian, as Nietzsche variously called it; and this birth did not result from the unification of two, but rather from the genius of one. We can easily see from the preface of 1886 that this second birth—not thematized by the title—was far more important for Nietzsche. By 1886 Nietzsche no longer emphasized the Apollonian side of the dual nature of tragedy; what counted at this late date was the Dionysian, viewed as the driving force behind tragedy, and, indeed, behind our being in the world. History does not progress or change very much by the amalgamation of the Dionysian and the Apollonian; it simply reaches a point of resolution. With the introduction of the Socratic, on the other hand, we come to an opposition that propels history forward, or rather, downward. Indeed, the Socratic initiates history itself as conscious activity. But contrary to our expectations, Nietzsche did not envision this change to be beneficial to humankind. Rather, the downfall of tragedy is itself thematized in the text as a tragic fall from a lofty height. Without the coda of the Wagnerian final sections this work would present us with a most pessimistic view of the fall of humankind from an aesthetic pinnacle.

Apollonian and Dionysian

The Birth of Tragedy is perhaps most famous for its introduction and explication of two terms that Nietzsche placed at the very foundation of Greek tragic art: the Apollonian and the Dionysian. The first of these terms, the Apollonian, is associated initially and consistently with dreams. It is interesting to note that the way in which Nietzsche referred to dreams in 1872 seems closer to the way Freud used it less than three decades later in his famous study *The Interpretation of Dreams* (1900). For the dream is not identified with fantasy or delusion or imagination, but rather with appearance, image, and Gestalt. It is the basis of all pictorial arts, of any creative process whereby images are produced, and it is therefore an attribute common to every human being. "The beautiful appearance of the worlds of dreams, in the production of which every man proves himself an accomplished artist, is a precondition not only of all plastic art, but even, as we shall see presently, of a wide range of poetry" (*BT* 20). The Apollonian relates in particular to the eye, to the visual, to appearances, and in some ways it is proximate to the sphere of the phenomenal in Kant or the *Vorstellung* (idea or representation) in Schopenhauer. This association is furthered by the suggestion that it is somehow related to illusion, since illusion involves something that appears to us in the mind's eye, something that takes definite and limited form, something that is determinate, yet not the thing in itself. It is in this sense that Nietzsche also wrote about the *principium individuationis,* for this principle operates precisely as a limiting of chaos, as a cutting out from the flux of phenomena some limited and individual portion. The Apollonian is thus a kind of representational principle, something that allows something else to appear. It seems to function without its own content and is likened at various points to form itself.

But the Apollonian also has two other important fields of association. First, at the close of the second section Nietzsche referred specifically to the "Apollonian consciousness" (*BT* 28) that veils the Dionysian; it would seem that the Apollonian is at least a form of consciousness, if not related to consciousness itself. Second, we may have a better grasp of the Apollonian if we recognize that Nietzsche repeatedly claimed Homer to be the prototypical Apollonian artist. These references limit and define the scope of the Apollonian in a number of ways: (1) The Apollonian is not necessarily related to the rational or the Socratic, as some writers have claimed—although in his notebooks this distinction is less rigorously maintained. In *The Birth of Tragedy,* at least, it is ancient and archaic, pre-logical and prior to writing. At one point Nietzsche likened it to Friedrich Schiller's category of the naive, since both express a direct, unmediated, non-reflective relationship to nature. (2) It is capable of existing in artworks without the Dionysian. By contrast, the Dionysian does not seem to be able to constitute a work of art without the Apollonian. Another way of saying this is that art can consist of pure form, but not of a content that is without form. (3) The Apollonian principle is manifested equally well in words or in forms.

In some sense we may think of the Apollonian as an aesthetic category derived from the stereotypical view of Greece found in the writings of Johann Joachim Winckelmann: it is the embodiment of that "noble simplicity and tranquil grandeur" (*edle Einfalt, stille Größe*) that became the clichéd image of Greece in the Grecophilic period that lasted in Germany from the middle of the eighteenth century until the end of the nineteenth century, when Nietzsche himself overturned that tradition with works such as *The Birth of Tragedy.* This image of Greece, captured prototypically in Greek sculpture with its perfect forms and in the epic poems of Homer, constituted the basis for such works as Hegel's aesthetics, where we find Greek art to be the most perfect embodiment of the world spirit—before it manifested itself more perfectly in religion and then in philosophy. Nietzsche's association of Homer with the Apollonian artist or tendency indicates both his indebtedness to his predecessors and his differences from them. And the area in which he differs from them most is in adding another element to the Apollonian tendency that always threatens to shatter the tranquil greatness of the quondam ideal of ancient Greece.

That element, of course, is the Dionysian, which is first introduced as intoxication in contrast to the Apollonian dream. In common parlance, dream and intoxication are usually not considered opposites, and in some ways they are very similar: both are states in which logic does not prevail, and in which the individual does not have control. The contrast Nietzsche develops is thus not one between logic and illogic, or reason and irrationality, but between different kinds of pre-logical interactions with the world. To better understand the Dionysian we must consider its further associations with a kind of original situation in which a primeval unity of humankind exists. What Nietzsche appears to have in mind is a frenzied, instinctive, unconscious unity; his discussion is characterized by a distance or distancing from the typical images of the Enlightenment, and by an endeavor to counter these images with something more instinctual. "If one were to convert Beethoven's 'Pacan to Joy' into a painting, and refuse to curb the imagination when that multitude prostrates itself reverently in the dust, one might form some apprehension of Dionysian ritual" (*BT* 23).

Friedrich Schiller's "Ode to Joy," written in the 1790s and used by Beethoven in the 1820s in his ninth symphony, is here removed from its original association with the ideals of the Enlightenment. Nietzsche cites this tradition in an altogether different way. He is not interested in the affirmation of freedom or liberation, as much as he is in the loss of individuality. If the emancipatory bourgeois tradition of Schiller and Beethoven emphasized the brotherhood of humankind, then Nietzsche is emphasizing another line in Schiller's poem: "Seid umschlungen Millionen" ("Be intertwined you millions"). The notion of humanity becomes in Nietzsche's Dionysian interpretation an image of the chaotic circumstance in which individuation has not yet occurred. The Dionysian refers us to a condition that is more profound and divine, one in which the human sings and dances, and has become one with others. In contrast to the Apollonian, where each human being becomes an artist; here each human being becomes an artwork (*BT* 24).

The Dionysian also has more forbidding moments. It is associated, for example, with oblivion and self-forgetting. It is also likened to a subconscious or unconscious reality inaccessible to the human mind, and it is not too farfetched to consider it an early formulation of what Freud would later refer to as the "id." In this threatening aspect it reminds us of the cruelty and absurdity of existence, of the seemingly pointless suffering in human existence and the torments of life on earth. The Dionysian in this regard resembles closely the Schopenhauerian philosophy under whose sway Nietzsche composed this essay, a sway that he opposed later in the preface from 1886. At that later date he wished he could have affirmed life despite its ultimate meaninglessness; in the earlier work, the justification for existence assumed—again in reliance on Schopenhauer—only an aesthetic form. These "terrors and horrors of existence" that are identified with the Dionysian are captured best by the saying attributed to Silenus, Dionysus' companion. When asked by King Midas about man's greatest good, Silenus supposedly replied: "Ephemeral wretch, begotten by accident and toil, why do you force me to tell you what it would be your greatest boon not to hear? What would be best for you is quite beyond your reach: not to have been born, not to *be*, to be *nothing*. But the second best is to die soon" (*BT* 29).

This tale, which Nietzsche repeats for his reader, provides a clue concerning the frightful view of human existence associated with the Dionysian. In this quality it is definitely opposed to or at least on a different plane than the Homeric, which is captured by a much different attitude toward life. Prototypical for this worldview is Achilles' reply to Odysseus, when the latter visits him in Hades, that he would rather be the poorest slave on earth than the king of all the underworld. The Dionysian is not necessarily a negation of life—in Nietzsche's view it is rather a realistic appraisal of existence—but it is certainly far from the affirmation that Homer places in his hero's mouth. Moreover, the manner in which Nietzsche refers to the Dionysian also suggests that this horrible and loathsome reality embodied in the god of wine and intoxication is something that is always concealed from us, something hidden, something that perhaps we need to hide so that we avoid the confrontation with our miserable existence. It is therefore certainly not a coincidence that Nietzsche refers to the veil of Maya, alluding here, as his mentor Schopenhauer did, to Eastern philosophy, and in particular to Hindu myth and the illusory nature of all existence: "In the Dionysian dithramb man is incited to strain his symbolic faculties to the utmost; something quite unheard of is now clamoring to be heard: the desire to tear asunder the veil of Maya, to sink back into the original oneness of nature; the desire to express the very essence of nature symbolically" (*BT* 27).

From this exposition of the Apollonian and the Dionysian it should be obvious that it would not be most accurate or productive to conceive the terms as principles that are diametrically opposed. While it is true that the Dionysian is different from the Apollonian in each's respective association with individuation, at various points they are shown to be mutually conditioning principles rather than binary and antagonistic terms. It would thus be inaccurate to identify the Apollonian and the Dionysian with traditional terms of antagonism such as the objective and the subjective. Indeed, the distinction between the Dionysian and the Apollonian antedates all subject-object dichotomies, which are, rather, a product of Socratic thought and rationality.

At one point Nietzsche explains in more detail why the subjective is an inadequate category to encompass what he means by the Dionysian. With regard to the first lyric poet, Archilochus, Nietzsche asks: "Isn't he—the first artist to be called subjective—for that reason the veritable non-artist?" (*BT* 37). What Nietzsche means by this is that since art is defined by its ability to externalize or present something external, pure subjectivity and artistry are incompatible. The solution to this apparent contradiction involves a recasting of what we consider to be the subjective nature of lyric poetry, since Nietzsche suggests that the commonplace assessment of lyric as an expression of subjectivity is a distortion. The lyricist, like the musician, is not externalizing some fundamental core of his own being, but rather the ground of being itself. "The artist had abrogated his subjectivity earlier, during the Dionysian phase: the image which now reveals to him his oneness with the heart of the world is a dream scene showing forth vividly, together with primeval contradiction and primeval pain, the primeval delight of illusion. The 'I' thus sounds out of the depth of being; what recent writers on esthetics speak of as 'subjectivity' is a mere figment" (*BT* 38).

A true lyric poet must thus partake in the Apollonian (image and illusion) in order to express the abyss of being; but he himself is merely a conduit for something that escapes superficial subjectivity: "It is through the reflections of the 'I' that the lyric poet beholds the ground of being" (*BT* 39). Thus we do not really hear from Archilochus the individual when we read the lyrics of Archilochus; we are not interested in the subjective desires and dreams of a single person: "The man Archilochus, with his passionate loves and hates, is really only a vision of genius, a genius who is no longer merely Archilochus but the genius of the universe, expressing the pain through the similitude of Archilochus the man" (*BT* 39–40). The lyricist, like the musician, partakes in what we might call a Dionysian universalism: he expresses a core truth of fundamental being in the guise of images drawn—in the best of cases—from the Apollonian.

Far from being the "subjective" part of tragedy, the Dionysian is therefore radically non-subjective. Nietzsche makes it clear that the subject-object distinction, which Schopenhauer and a whole line of previous aestheticians before him had used to divide different genres into objective (epic) and subjective (lyric), is an invalid way of evaluating aesthetic phenomena. In true art there is no subjective element, if one means by subjective an individual contribution. The reason for this is that "the subject—the individual bent on furthering his egoistic purposes—can be thought of only as an enemy to art, never as its source" (*BT* 41). The subject is only a medium through which art passes, a medium through which the "true subject" expresses its redemption (*BT* 41).

Art is thus not created for us, as much as we might think this is the case. We are neither the originators nor the purpose for great art. Rather, we ourselves are the reflexes. Nietzsche is rather emphatic on this point: "For better or for worse, one thing should be quite obvious to all of us: the entire comedy of art is not played for our own sakes—for our betterment or education, say—nor can we consider ourselves the true originators of that art realm; while on the other hand we have every right to view ourselves as esthetic projections of the veritable creator and derive such dignity as we possess from our status as art works" (*BT* 41–42). It would appear that the truth of tragedy, the Dionysian basis of that genre, informs us about the entire comedy of art. And that truth is that we are not the source of art, but its effects. We, as anti-subjective mass, in Dionysian celebration and frenzy, are ourselves projections of a far more powerful and primitive source. Consciousness of art and knowledge in general are of no use in a comprehension of art. We fool ourselves when we believe we are able to stand outside of art objects (which is what we ourselves are) and take them into our consciousness; we are no more able to comprehend ourselves or to comprehend art, Nietzsche states, than painted soldiers are able to comprehend the battle into which they are painted. As knowers, that is, as epistemological subjects distinguishing objects from subjects, we can never comprehend the aesthetic realm, which alone explains the world. As epiphenomenal manifestations of fundamental urges, the most important of which is the Dionysian, we struggle with the world of representations and illusions.

Nietzsche derived for us therefore a notion of tragedy as a genre that fruitfully combines a Dionysian, anarchic, formless, frightful force with an Apollonian form or appearance. With this conception—and in the tradition of genuine philology—he could then reexamine the literature on tragedy and show where it was flawed. He was particularly keen on looking at the misunderstanding of the chorus. Since Nietzsche conceived of a Bacchanalian revelry at the basis of tragedy, and viewed the action on stage as a secondary effect of a mass phenomenon, he could not very well validate theories of the chorus that claimed it was an ideal spectator or a representative of the Athenian people on stage. In the course of his comments we can see clearly his anti-democratic bias. The explanation of the chorus as a prototypical democratic form meets with disdain, not only because Nietzsche believed that it did not correspond to the true origins of tragedy, but also because democracy itself is something he could never admit to his beloved Greece. "We would consider it blasphemous, in the light of the classical form of the chorus as we know it from Aeschylus and Sophocles, to speak of a 'foreshadowing' of constitutional democracy, though others have not stuck at such blasphemy. No ancient polity ever embodied constitutional democracy, and one dares to hope that ancient tragedy did not even foreshadow it" (*BT* 47).

Likewise, the notion that the chorus embodies an ideal spectator commenting on the tragic action was an absurdity to Nietzsche. Since Nietzsche believed that tragedy originated in the chorus, how could the chorus be an ideal spectator? A spectator without something to look at would be ludicrous. Nietzsche was much more inclined to see value in a third suggestion, one offered by Friedrich Schiller. In the introduction to *The Bride of Messina* (1803) Schiller had likened the chorus to a wall shielding the tragedy from the real world. Nietzsche agreed with this interpretation—although for reasons that Schiller might have rejected—since he felt that the chorus, and indeed tragedy in general, leads us to a state in which we forget ourselves and the world; it is metaphysical solace for us, as it was for the Greeks. The chorus itself is "the projected image of Dionysian man" (*BT* 54). Individuals and individuality are effaced; we become something other than what we are; we project ourselves outside of ourselves. Originally the action on stage was itself mere projection of the chorus, a person stepping momentarily outside the frenzied mass to act out a role. The truth of the chorus is thus Dionysian, and Nietzsche's view of tragedy can perhaps be summarized best as "the Apollonian embodiments in which Dionysus assumes objective shape" (*BT* 58–59).

Before turning to the conflict between the Socratic and the tragic, which prefigured Nietzsche's mature worldview and constituted the actual opposition in *The Birth of Tragedy,* we should not overlook some disturbing images occurring in the ninth section. Nietzsche begins with an interpretation—or better a reinterpretation—of the shibboleth of "serenity" in Greek art. What earlier generations have labeled "serene," Nietzsche contends, is simply the Apollonian coating over the horrific Dionysian reality. Earlier commentators have thus been only partially correct in their evaluation of Greek tragedy. But Nietzsche soon turns to more troubling issues. In commenting on Aeschylus' play *Prometheus* and Goethe's ode of the same name, he claims that the image of the defiant creator, eternally suffering for his defiance, is not only tragic, but prototypical for Aryan art. "The legend of Prometheus is indigenous to the entire community of Aryan races and attests to their prevailing talent for profound and tragic vision" (*BT* 63).

By contrast the Semitic peoples are characterized by the myth of the Fall. Nietzsche concedes that the two myths are related—"like brother and sister"—but there can be little doubt which myth is superior. The Aryan myth is masculine, active, and noble. The Semitic myth is female, passive, and tainted by curiosity, deception, suggestibility, and concupiscence. The Aryan race—which encompasses both the Greek and the German—is thus opposed at some fundamental level to the Semitic race. What is disturbing about this discussion is not simply that the stereotypes Nietzsche bandied about here had such awful consequences in the real existence of human beings in the twentieth century, but also that Nietzsche exhibited here—and throughout much of his work—the unfortunate tendency to think and express himself in typological or stereotypical categories.

Socratic Consciousness

In contrast to the Apollonian and the Dionysian, the most important figures in the final chapters (sections 11–15) of the original *Birth of Tragedy*—the chapters on Wagner were added later, perhaps as an enticement for Wagner's publisher Fritzsch—are two mortals, whom Nietzsche raises to mythological status. The kind of profound intuition found in the Apollonian and Dionysian unity is subverted with the advent of the reflection associated with the Socratic consciousness and the dramaturgy of the playwright Euripides. Because the epoch in which tragedy flourished was so short-lived and the reign of "Socratic consciousness" has been so long and oppressive, one might even contend that the most important subject of the *Birth of Tragedy* is really the *death* of tragedy and the concomitant birth of historical and rational thought and representation. Nietzsche initially approaches this issue by way of the theater. An important sign of the fall of tragic art was Euripides' introduction of mundane existence into tragedy when he brought the spectator onto the stage. In contrast to the older tragedians, who presumably were conduits for Dionysian profundity, Euripides is condemned for placing before the public "the true replica of actuality" (*BT* 70). The "actuality" Nietzsche refers to here is everyday reality, and this is made clear by his subsequent discussion. "Through him the common man found his way from the auditorium onto the stage. That mirror, which previously had shown only the great and bold features, now took on the kind of accuracy that reflects also the paltry traits of nature" (*BT* 70).

What kind of change has taken place in tragedy from Sophocles and Aeschylus to Euripides? In the first place, the common man and, with him, common everyday reality, have been represented on the stage. In earlier tragedy the spectator was allowed to glimpse the Dionysian mysteries through the dream images of Apollo. Now the spectator finds himself the object of representation. Second, the mirroring function of art has been altered significantly. In earlier tragedy it was not necessary to be accurate to empirical reality; accuracy in Nietzsche's tragic conception was a moot point. What was essential was the combination of effects. Now, however, accuracy or fidelity is fundamental. Indeed, even the unsuccessful parts of creation, those features that are no longer grand or worthy of images, are represented. In essence, Nietzsche accuses Euripides of doing precisely what many of the best artists and writers did in his own era: turning to realistic portrayal of social reality.

Euripides, however, is only the agent of a more powerful force, a demon who goes by the name of Socrates. The "new contradiction" in Western culture—or perhaps the first contradiction, since the Apollonian and the Dionysian worked in tandem—is the Dionysian and the Socratic (*BT* 77). It is significant that Nietzsche formulates it in this fashion, because the term he omitted is obviously the Apollonian. Why is this the case? The reason is that the Apollonian was always conceived as medium, as that force through which the Dionysian finds expression. Thus the Dionysian is more fundamental, more basic, more primary. This is occasionally shown in other passages in the *Birth of Tragedy*, for example, in section 14, when Nietzsche states that the essence of tragedy can only be interpreted "as a manifestation and imaging—or concretization—of Dionysian conditions, as the visible symbolizing of music, of the dreamworld of a Dionysian intoxication" (*BT* 89). We should recall that the connection of the Dionysian with the tragic was more original in Nietzsche's thought as well, appearing in the "The Greek Music Drama," while the Apollonian was added somewhat later.[2] In general in *The Birth of Tragedy* both the Dionysian and the Apollonian are accorded more or less equal billing on the tragic stage, but the discrepancy between the two becomes obvious during the next two decades, when the Apollonian receded into the wings, receiving only scant mention in Nietzsche's works, while the Dionysian occupied the entire spotlight. It is not coincidental that Nietzsche did not sign his last, half-crazed letters with the name of Apollo, but with the name of Dionysus.

The Socratic and the Dionysian, in different forms and with different emphases, in fact, can be said to be the content of Nietzsche's entire philosophy until his mental collapse. Neither tendency or elemental force is restricted to the sphere of aesthetics—in fact Nietzsche most often referred to Euripides' dramatic practice as an application of aesthetic Socratism (*BT* 79). Socratism, which occupied most of Nietzsche's writings as the philosophical attitude that must be criticized, rejected, and overcome, is a complex phenomenon extending to all areas of human existence. In art its main feature is an adherence to what we might call for convenience "realism," that is, to copying appearances, rather than capturing essences, to portraying the things of the world as they exist for us, rather than the things in itself (to put the matter in Kantian terms), and to dealing with representations, rather than with the realm of the will (to use Schopenhauer's formula). The essence of this aesthetic theory, according to Nietzsche, is clarity and comprehensibility; the motto he ascribed to it is: "Everything must be reasonable for it to be beautiful" (*BT* 79).

But it is obvious that these artistic precepts are only one branch of the Socratic. Immediately after quoting this motto, Nietzsche provided the parallel statement for morality: "Only one who knows is virtuous." And, as we shall see in chapter 6, this moral dimension of Socratism, particularly as it manifests itself in the Judeo-Christian religion, occupied Nietzsche's thought throughout most of the second half of the 1880s. The key to the Socratic, however, appears to be epistemological, even in this early work about art and tragedy. In each of the mottoes that Nietzsche produced, understanding and knowledge play a central role. Although Nietzsche's critique of traditional epistemology was complex, at its most fundamental level it entailed questioning conceptual thought in the broadest sense, and, in particular, scientific thought, which is a manifestation and logical outgrowth of the conceptuality Socrates introduced to human culture and its particular outgrowth in the nineteenth century. Socrates and his less-focused counterpart Dionysus are thus the names that stand for incompatible worldviews, not just incompatible aesthetic principles.

The Rebirth of Tragedy

That this initial discussion of tragedy had to do with current cultural issues in the nineteenth century may not have been obvious even to Nietzsche's original readers. Although Nietzsche relied heavily on popular texts such as Schopenhauer's philosophy and Wagner's works rather than on more reputable, ancient source material, it might appear from the discussion in the first 15 sections of *The Birth of Tragedy* that the Baseler professor of philology was investigating purely the academic topic of the origins and demise of Attic tragedy. The cultural imperative becomes clear, however, in the final 10 sections. Here Nietzsche speaks openly about a "rebirth of tragedy" and locates the possibility for this rebirth in contemporary German society. Not surprisingly the two persons identified most closely with this cultural project are Schopenhauer and Wagner. In a lengthy citation from Schopenhauer's *The World as Will and Representation,* Nietzsche demonstrates how his notion of the Dionysian was derived from his predecessor's discussion of the power of music. For Schopenhauer music differs from other art forms in that it is not a copy of phenomena in the external world, but a direct reflection of the will itself. Concepts and images are by comparison impoverished vehicles since they cling only to superficial manifestations; they are able to provide only reflective access to the world. Music, as "language of the will," supplies direct and intuitive access to a more fundamental reality.

The proximity of this discussion to Nietzsche's thesis is evident: "music incites us to an allegorical intuition of Dionysian universality; it endows the allegorical image with supreme significance" (*BT* 107). Music is thus intimately linked with the creation of myth, and in particular with the creation of the tragic myth, which speaks in allegorical form of Dionysian knowledge. Because of these insights into the nature of music and its connection with the "Dionysian" will, Schopenhauer is a herald of the renaissance of tragic art, the philosophical prophet of a neo-Hellenic revival.

It is Richard Wagner, however, who is assigned the cultural task of reintroducing tragedy to European culture. To do so he must overcome more than two millennia of Socratic or theoretical hegemony in Western societies. Socrates, responsible for the introduction of reflection, reason, and the sciences, was also the most fervent opponent of myth. In propagating individuality, rather than universal myth, in favoring imitation of external appearances over the unmediated reflection of the essence, in promulgating a metaphysics of optimism and progress instead of the sobering recognition of the eternal abyss, theoretical culture had pushed Dionysian-based tragedy to the margins and introduced its own, impoverished notion of art. What is interesting in the final sections of *The Birth of Tragedy* is that Nietzsche does not content himself with an aesthetic discussion, but widens his horizon to include explicitly other dimensions of the Socratic worldview. Identifying a Socratic perspective on life with an Alexandrian culture, Nietzsche sketches a central social contradiction for the nineteenth century: "Alexandrian culture requires a slave class for its continued existence, but in its optimistic view of *Dasein* [life, being, or existence] it denies the necessity for such a class; therefore it is headed for a horrific annihilation once the effect of its seductive and palliative slogans concerning the 'dignity of man' and the 'dignity of labor' have exhausted itself" (*BT* 117). Such comments on the social structure of nineteenth-century society are rare in Nietzsche's early work, but they became more frequent in his writings, starting with *Human, All Too Human.* Here it is necessary to note only that the Socratic, the Alexandrian, the theoretical, and the optimistic worldview relate not only to epistemological and aesthetic phenomena of the past, but to social and political dimensions of Nietzsche's own times.

Wagner thus represents an overcoming that has significance beyond the aesthetic sphere, although his chief impact is located squarely in the artistic realm. In the context of this work and of German culture, Wagner is the hope for a new Dionysian spirit. As Nietzsche had indicated earlier, "un-Dionysian" tragedy emerges with "newer drama," by which he meant Euripidean tragedy and all works that substitute a "deus ex machina" for "metaphysical consolation"; but in these last sections of *The Birth of Tragedy* he extends the Socratic to contemporary culture. The Socratic spirit, he maintains, manifests itself most typically in "the culture of the opera." In contrast to Wagnerian opera, which reunites the Dionysian with the Apollonian, traditional opera evidences all the deficiencies of Alexandrian art. Chief among its shortcomings are the superficial attachment of music and verse, and the abrupt alteration between partially sung declamation in the recitative and more lyrical musical passages.

The irony of this development is that the inventors of the recitative believed that they were resuscitating the primordial power of ancient Greek music. "Here we view the internal becoming of opera, that genuinely modern genre. In it, art satisfies a powerful need, but a need that is unaesthetic: a longing for the idyll, a belief in the primordial existence of artistic and good men" (*BT* 122). Nietzsche identified the recitative with optimism, with humanism, and with a faith in idyllic reality and the goodness of the human soul. It bases itself on the false presumption that words are necessary for genuine art, and that they must be understood by the audience. In Nietzsche's view such presumptions ultimately lead to horrible demands for equal rights, such as were seen in the socialist movement of his era. In its very essence, therefore, the culture of opera is antithetical to the tragic: it is "the birth of theoretical man, of the critical layman, not of the artist" (*BT* 123).

The correction to the "operatic" tendency comes from the "Dionysian foundation of the German spirit" as it has been manifested in the progression from "Bach to Beethoven, and from Beethoven to Wagner" (*BT* 127). In the midst of a culture characterized by superficiality and rationality, music preserves the purity of a genuine aesthetic drawn from the tragic Greek worldview. Nietzsche's vision vacillates between utopian and nostalgic perspectives. On the one hand, he indicates that the future will bring a new type of Dionysian culture, a rebirth that will surpass and condemn the Socratic, operatic, Alexandrian manifestations of the present. At that point all cultural, educational, and civilatory achievements of contemporary Germany would one day have to account for themselves before the incorruptible judge Dionysus (*BT* 128). On the other hand, this rebirth was cast as a return to a former greatness.

> For us, who stand on the watershed between two different modes of existence, the Greek example is still of inestimable value, since it embodies the violent transition to and struggles for a classical form of suasion; only that it is as if we were living through the great phases of Hellenism in reverse order and were at this very moment moving backward from the Alexandrian age into an age of tragedy. And the feeling is alive in us that the birth of a tragic age is for the German spirit only a return to itself, a blessed recovery of its true identity, after it had been compelled for a long time to exist in servitude to monstrous, external, and intrusive forces, which forced its helpless barbarity of form upon it. (*BT* 128)

As projection into the future or retreat to a golden age in the past, the rebirth includes two important features. First, it is conceived as a renaissance that is unique to Germany and, in particular, as an emanation of the tradition of German music. Second, Germany is intimately connected with ancient Greece; indeed, it is the modern successor of the Dionysian heritage in the ancient world. The stage is set—rhetorically and historically—for the entrance of Wagner. After German classicism failed to reintroduce the true spirit of Greece, after Schopenhauer has shown us the correct philosophical path, and after German music has developed as a Dionysian force, Wagner can now fulfill the role of reintroducing an authentic tragic culture to Germany and to all of Europe.

Considering the preparatory work that Nietzsche did to place Wagner and his oeuvre at the center of cultural aspirations for the Second Reich, his treatment of Wagner is rather understated. Although there was no doubt that Nietzsche was writing in support of the Wagnerian cultural mission, his name and his operatic works appear rather sparingly. In the most sustained discussion of a Wagnerian work, Nietzsche cites *Tristan and Isolde* as evidence that a Dionysian work of art must employ the Apollonian in order to achieve aesthetic perfection. His contention is that we would be unable to bear the pure Dionysian without its Apollonian gestalt:

> To these genuine musicians I direct my question: Can they conceive of a man who could experience the third act of *Tristan and Isolde*, without the aid of either word or image, purely as an overwhelming symphonic movement, without exhausting himself in the overstretching of his soul's pinions? How is it possible for a man who has placed his ear on the very heart chamber of the world-will and felt the unruly lust for life rush into all the veins of the world, now as a thundering torrent and now as a delicately foaming brook—how is it possible for him to remain unshattered? (*BT* 127)

With this illustration of Wagner's opera, Nietzsche demonstrates again his thesis concerning the necessary merger of the Apollonian and the Dionysian. He suggests, as he has throughout, that the Dionysian would be unbearable alone, that Dionysian wisdom must be mitigated by Apollonian deception or appearance. Music, which represents Dionysian art in its purest state, requires the Apollonian veil supplied by words and images. The question of which tendency prevails is answered variously. At one point Nietzsche appears to confirm an Apollonian victory, but he quickly reverses himself and speaks of the prevalence of the Dionysian in the tragic effect. At this point in his development it seems that on the whole he affirms a perfect union: "Dionysus speaks the language of Apollo, but Apollo, finally, the language of Dionysus; thereby the highest goal of tragedy and of art in general is attained" (*BT* 140). And this fortunate coincidence of the two divine principles governing aesthetic excellence, whose first occurrence was in ancient Greece, is uniquely identified with the artistic creations of Richard Wagner.

The Synthesis Undone

The task of the present, which Nietzsche mixed with some rather conventional appeals to German patriotism in the wake of the Franco-Prussian war and to Richard Wagner's operatic theories and practices, is to recapture the former Dionysian state of affairs. Because of Wagner, therefore, Nietzsche was able to combine his own academic studies—or at least some aspects of them—with his own enthusiasm for contemporary music and culture. But this synthesis of interests was a fragile one, and it did not last for very long. The reason for this is that the two interests soon proved to be irreconcilable. The philological world of nineteenth-century Germany was simply unable to validate Nietzsche's work, and Nietzsche himself must have recognized that, apart from his friend Rohde, his effort to infuse philology with cultural relevance had been a dismal failure. The choices that Nietzsche encountered were thus fairly limited: If he wished to continue with his professional career at the university and further his academic reputation, he would have to abandon his efforts to mix scholarship of the ancient world and celebration of Wagnerian opera. If he wished to contribute to the cultural renaissance he identified with Wagner and his cult, he would have to refrain from the scholarly conventions and pretensions that accompanied his education and profession. In the short run, as evidenced by the *Untimely Meditations,* he chose to restrict his published writings to Wagnerian propaganda, while maintaining his scholarly standards only in his official duties as a professor at Basel. In the long run, however, he abandoned both parts of his early project when he broke with Wagner in 1876 and resigned from his academic post in 1879.

Both his philological background and his fanaticism for Wagner continued to play a part in his writings long after they had ceased to be the driving forces in his life. The break with Wagner was fraught with ambivalence, and it was perceived differently by the two parties involved. There is evidence in Nietzsche's writings, even in the overtly laudatory *Richard Wagner in Bayreuth,* that he increasingly harbored misgivings about Wagner's cultural project. But Nietzsche did not act upon his private doubts until he attended the opening ceremonies of the Bayreuth opera house in the summer of 1876. Writing in *Ecce Homo,* Nietzsche excoriated everything about Bayreuth. He claimed that he was horrified by the other patrons, who evidently did not share his enthusiasm for the lofty cultural goals he had formerly associated with Wagner's works. Wagner, in his view, had been "translated" into German; Bayreuth was proof that he had been seduced by the philistine atmosphere of the Second Reich. It is quite possible that Nietzsche was also disappointed by the rehearsals and performances he attended, and offended because Wagner, who was the center of attention, obviously devoted more time to his more prominent guests than to the philology professor from Basel. Nietzsche, in short, had numerous reasons to interpret the entire occurrence as a betrayal of friendship and of their common cultural mission. No matter what the reason, Nietzsche used Bayreuth as a pretext to separate himself from his former mentor. Wagner appeared at first to have been rather puzzled by Nietzsche's behavior and could not understand why Nietzsche had reacted so unfavorably to the festivities. Obviously he did not immediately recognize the severity of the strain on their relationship. Two years later, however, the composer must have understood that something was amiss, since Nietzsche failed to respond when he sent him a copy of *Parsifal.* Wagner was miffed and gradually seems simply to have ignored and forgotten his wayward disciple. From the evidence we possess the break was much more momentous for Nietzsche, and we should not forget that while Wagner was a celebrated public figure at the pinnacle of his career, Nietzsche was a relatively unknown academic whose "philosophical writings" had received their chief notoriety because of their association with the circle of Wagner enthusiasts.

Psychologically the break with Wagner was a chapter in an oedipal struggle with a father figure. In subsequent remarks Nietzsche treated Wagner harshly, but also demonstrated at times reverence and respect for his accomplishments. In terms of cultural theory Wagner gradually came to represent a specific type of European artist who failed to overcome the decadence and nihilism surrounding him and therefore proved himself unable to redeem European culture. The fact that two of Nietzsche's final works—*The Case of Wagner* (1888) and *Nietzsche Contra Wagner* (1895)—focused on his former mentor indicate the lasting power and the significance of this relationship for Nietzsche. As Nietzsche himself wrote in the former work: "To turn my back on Wagner was for me a fate" (*CW* 155).

Nietzsche's continuing affiliation with philology was of a much different nature. Only one philological writing appeared after the publication of *The Birth of Tragedy,* and although Nietzsche continued to lecture at Basel on a variety of classical topics, his interest in academic research and publication quickly diminished. What remained with him from his classical studies was above all an ideal of Greek culture and society, particular in the pre-Socratic era.[3] As we shall see in the next chapter, a paradigm informed by the Greek world was an essential element in Nietzsche's pedagogical reflections, but even when he lost interest in educational reform, he maintained a positive view of the ancients. Indeed, Nietzsche occupied a pivotal position in the long German tradition of Grecophilia (love of Greece).[4]

While most of his predecessors in the eighteenth and nineteenth centuries, however, praised the ancients for their ideal of beauty, ethics, and politics, Nietzsche lauded Greece for its emphasis on strife, conflict, and hierarchy. In contrast to Johann Joachim Winckelmann's famous formula of "noble simplicity and tranquil grandeur," Nietzsche portrayed a Greek society—perhaps more accurately—as the site of struggle, inequality, and injustice. As Nietzsche wrote in *Twilight of the Idols* (1888): "To smell out 'beautiful souls,' 'golden means,' and other perfections in the Greeks, or to admire their calm in greatness, their ideal cast of mind, their noble simplicity—the psychologist in me protected me against such 'noble simplicity,' a *niaiserie allemande* [German simplicity or foolishness] anyway" (*TI* 559). As an aftermath of his philological activity, Nietzsche thus composed a new chapter in the Western reception of Greece, reevaluating the values of the idealist heritage. This new set of values, derived from his iconoclast views of Greece, remained foundational for his cultural project long after he had relinquished hope for Germany and Wagner to produce a neo-Hellenic renaissance in the nineteenth century.

Chapter 3
The Pedagogical Reformer

The second large theme that occupied Nietzsche's thoughts during the early and mid-1870s was education and the educational system. That Nietzsche was concerned with schools and universities is really not very surprising: outside of his brief stints in the military in 1867–68 and 1870 he had been either a student or teacher at a high school or university since he enrolled in Pforta in 1858. Furthermore, his concern with education was intimately connected with his cliquish and—at times—fanatic enthusiasm for Schopenhauer and Wagner. The reason for this has much to do with the German notion of *Bildung*. Translated often as "education" and connected intimately with the goals of the German educational system, *Bildung* actually refers to a general acculturation that may or may not be achieved through formal institutions. *Bildung* relates to the culture of a society as much as it does to its system of training and instruction, and Nietzsche was certainly not alone in measuring the achievements of Germany in the 1870s by examining the quality of *Bildung* among his peers. *Bildung* thus forms a bridge between culture and pedagogy, and these latter two notions are intimately connected in the German mind; even today the ministry in charge of education is most commonly called the "cultural ministry" (*Kultusministerium*). In devoting himself to the spread of Schopenhauer's philosophy and Wagner's music, Nietzsche was convinced that he was promoting a rejuvenation of German culture. In criticizing the present condition of the schools—in particular those devoted to higher education—and in suggesting the necessity for a reorientation, he was affirming a cultural objective consonant with his philosophical perspective.

Criticism of the Educational Institution

Nietzsche's critique of education was also connected with his philological activities since he relied heavily on the ideal of *Bildung* acquired from his classical studies. According to Nietzsche, the Germans should model themselves after the Greeks; they should emulate the *Bildung* that characterized that society; and the educational system should serve to facilitate this cultural/pedagogical project. What this means is elucidated most extensively in several writings from the early and mid-1870s. However, Nietzsche's critique of his contemporaries and his suggestions for reform were articulated with particular clarity in the unpublished lecture series "On the Future of Our Educational Institutions."[1] Delivered from January to March in 1872 in the hall of the university museum in Basel as public and popular events—not university and academic discourses—these five lectures were his first sustained effort after completing *The Birth of Tragedy*.[2] By all accounts they were a huge success.[3] According to Nietzsche approximately 300 people attended each lecture, and this enthusiastic response probably contributed to his initial intention to publish them as a small volume.[4] Although he eventually decided that they were not ready for dissemination in print, the notions Nietzsche developed in them are echoed often in his subsequent writings. These lectures, therefore, provide great insight into perhaps the most important facet of Nietzsche's early professional life and cultural concern, and despite his resignation from the teaching profession in 1879 and his increasing pessimism with regard to educational reform, he never significantly altered his views on the centrality of *Bildung* as a measure for the greatness of a society.

On the most general level Nietzsche opposed two tendencies of his time. The first, reflected in the enlightenment demand for "universal education," called for an extension of *Bildung* into ever-widening circles of society. Responsible for this widening of the educational system, according to Nietzsche, was the German state, which thereby endeavored to subsume culture and education as *Bildung* under its auspices. Here Nietzsche was making reference to the proliferation of public high schools and the generally increased access to education during the latter part of the nineteenth century. We should note, however, that the extension of *Bildung,* to which Nietzsche referred pejoratively, hardly reached the lower classes in any form. The second tendency that Nietzsche deplored was the narrowing and weakening of *Bildung.* Although the *Gymnasium* continued to grow and prosper, the *Realschule,* a practically oriented high school without extensive training in the classics, had gained increasing legitimacy; eventually a graduate of a *Realschule* could even gain admission to a university. To an educational purist this tendency appeared as a watering-down of requirements. To oppose these tendencies Nietzsche simply propounded their opposites: to counter the widening of *Bildung* he posited a narrowing; instead of the decreasing and weakening of the curriculum, he demanded a concentrating and strengthening of requirements. What Nietzsche proposed, therefore, in its most general terms was a system of exclusive and rigorous education very much like the one he had experienced. Only in this way, he believed, could German culture be truly saved and served.

The five lectures detail specific aspects of his plan to counteract the "barbarism" of contemporary pedagogical institutions in Germany. They are framed as a modification on Socratic dialogues. Nietzsche portrays himself as a young student at Bonn, who goes with a friend (and a servant) on a late summer day to practice shooting pistols.[5] Arriving at the edge of a forest, the friends encounter an old man accompanied by a dog and a younger companion. The older man, who is referred to as "the philosopher" and who is very likely modeled on Nietzsche's image of Schopenhauer, convinces the friends to cease their shooting and to cede their rights to this area to him. The remainder of the lectures purport to record various conversations conducted by the philosopher with his companion and with Nietzsche. In the first of these discussions the persona of Nietzsche and his friend are especially concerned about the endeavor of the state to exploit its youth and to turn them into useful civil servants. To counter prevailing state instrumentalization of education they have determined not to think about a profession and thus preserve an autonomous sphere in which *Bildung* can occur. The philosopher, however, uncovers the social source of their discomfort with the educational system. Institutions of learning, he contends, are being ruined by the democratic tendency. We have lost sight of the simple fact that the purpose of educational institutions should be to foster genius; the population at large should not have contact with them at all. After the companion repeats the critique of widening and weakening that Nietzsche had broached in the introduction, the philosopher again returns to social roots, rejecting the enlightened demand for "universal education" of the masses as a barbarity.[6]

The institution centrally responsible for the failure of the German educational system is the *Gymnasium,* and the philosopher supplies his audience with several areas in which it is deficient. Perhaps the most important of these was its purported neglect of the German language. According to Nietzsche, in an age of "newspaper-German," it is essential that the *Gymnasium* compel "the maturing, noble and talented youth" to develop elegance in his own language, and this should be accomplished with strict linguistic training if necessary (*SW* 1: 675). This demand for improved and more stringent instruction in German actually reflected

Nietzsche's own feeling, expressed frequently in early letters, that he had not received adequate instruction in his mother tongue. Instead of offering a purely practical training in the use of the German language, the *Gymnasium* is criticized for emphasizing German as an object of historical and academic learning. German is treated like a dead language rather than an opportunity for action and life. Moreover, the typical essay assignment in German—an autobiographical composition—stands in direct contrast to the implicit deprecation of originality and the discouragement of creativity.

What is missing for Nietzsche, therefore, even in the purported "classical education" of the *Gymnasium*, is a proper appreciation of the ancients, not as deceased authors and bookish knowledge, but as a tradition that is relevant and truly genial. The neglect of German and the trivialization of the classics are ultimately blamed on a decline in the German spirit to the point where culture and *Bildung* are identified with second-rate authors and composers. In a slight concession perhaps to his own educational experiences, Nietzsche—through the figure of the philosopher—begrudgingly concedes that a dry and formal scholarship is slightly preferable to the complete disintegration of learning into journalistic pseudo-culture. But he concludes that only the "renewal and purification of the German spirit" (*SW* 1: 691) can lead to a genuine revitalization of the pivotal institution in the educational system, the German *Gymnasium*.

Although the *Gymnasium* continues to be a central concern for the philosopher and his auditors, the conversation soon shifts to examine what the companion calls the "metaphysics of genius" (*SW* 1: 700). At the heart of this metaphysical proposition is the notion that the current system of education is unnatural. The reason for this is that it panders to the masses. Authentic *Bildung* is aristocratic by nature; only the interference of the state, under the influence of an unhealthy Hegelian philosophy, has led to the subordination of genuine cultural and pedagogical objectives under government. The result has been the proliferation of educational institutions and of teachers, and the concomitant distortion and leveling of educational goals. The primary target of this critique, articulated most forcefully by the philosopher, is the notion of *Volksbildung* (education for the people). *Volksbildung*, like universal education, is advocated by those who want "saturnalia of barbarity" and "fetterless freedom" while opposing the "sacred order of nature." The philosopher leaves no doubt concerning his disdain for the promoters of such an unnatural and demophilic pedagogy.

They are born to serve and to obey, and every moment during which
their creeping or grallatorial or lame-winged thoughts are active only
confirms what kind of stuff they're made of and what trademark they
have branded on them. *Bildung* for the masses cannot be our goal, but
rather *Bildung* for the select few, for people equipped for great and
durable works: we know very well that the judgment of posterity concerning the status of *Bildung* among a given people will be based solely
on those great, lonely heroes of the time, and that it will be evaluated
according to the manner in which these heroes are recognized, promoted,
honored, or segregated, abused, and destroyed. (*SW* 1: 698–99)

Volksbildung is thus the very antithesis of authentic *Bildung*. It seeks to
reverse the "natural hierarchy in the realm of the intellect" (*SW* 1: 699),
to arouse the masses from a slumber that is their true lot, and thereby to
destroy the noble and natural goal of promoting genius. Instead of
"breeding great leaders," the educational system, under the auspices of
the State, nurtures the pretension of culture and deceives the masses into
thinking that they can find their way with their own devices.

From his criticism of universal education and *Volksbildung* it might
seem that Nietzsche would have advocated a reduction in the more practically oriented training found in the *Realschule*. In fact, however, his
position was more complex. Nietzsche did not reject the *Realschule*;
rather, he was disturbed that the alternative to the *Realschule,* an institution that would foster a genuine and superior culture, did not exist.
Through the mouth of the philosopher he extols the virtues of imparting
practical knowledge: "Do not think, my friends, that I want to detract
from the praise of our *Realschulen* and advanced high schools: I esteem
the places where one learns mathematics properly, where one masters the
language of commerce, where one takes geography seriously, and where
one girds oneself with the astounding insights of natural science" (*SW* 1:
716). At the same time, however, he detects a leveling in the educational system that is perhaps the direct reflection of the recent regulations
permitting university attendance from the *Realschule.* "If it is true, that in
general the *Realschule* and the *Gymnasium* in their present goals are so
much in accord, and only differ from one another in nuances, so that we
can expect soon full equality before the forum of the State, then we are
completely without one species of educational institution: the species of
institution responsible for *Bildung*" (*SW* 1: 717).

In general, Nietzsche considered that there are two proper levels of
schooling and two distinguishable institutional structures. On the first,
students are trained in the spirit of the "survival of the fittest" (*SW* 1:

713) for the "struggle for existence" (*SW* 1: 714) and for overcoming the "depravities of life" (*SW* 1: 715); in these institutions students learn what they need for their individual careers and for life in the economic, social, and political order. The second type of institution, whose exact curriculum and goals are never delineated precisely, would be responsible for the propagation of culture. In this capacity it would not concentrate on the individual's integration into society, but rather the greatness associated with genius. Indeed, Nietzsche indicates that the production of a genius and his work is predicated on a cleansing of all traces of the subject so that the end result is a "reflection of the eternal and unchanging essence of things" (*SW* 1: 729). In Germany only the first type of institution exists; Nietzsche and the philosopher, in thematizing the institutions of *Bildung* (*Bildungsanstalten*) are therefore advocating pedagogical structures for the future.

In the first four lectures Nietzsche has his philosopher discuss issues primarily related to general education and high schools (*Realschule* and *Gymnasium*). Only in his final lecture does he broach the topic of university training. The philosopher's auditors, university students from Bonn, believe that the *Gymnasium* prepares its pupils for independence; for them the essence of university education is self-sufficiency in learning and research. But the philosopher cannot concur with this generous assessment. In a scathing attack on contemporary higher education, he rails against a system where students are reduced to ears that listen to the mouths of their professors and hands that write down what their professors say. This "akroamatic teaching method" (from the Greek *akroaomai,* to listen to), which we might consider overly restrictive, is actually criticized for allowing "academic freedom." Nietzsche's point is that students, bound in an external and superficial fashion to their professors, can pick and choose what they want to learn. The professors, for their part, are allowed to lecture on what they deem appropriate. Although the State oversees the "purpose, aim, and content of the strange speech and auditory procedures" (*SW* 1: 740), the entire arrangement appears too artificial and arbitrary. The philosopher therefore alludes with approval to other epochs which implanted "compliance, discipline, subjection, and obedience" while staving off "every presumption of self-sufficiency" (*SW* 1: 740–41).

Academic freedom, as conceived by Nietzsche, is deleterious to university education because it does not instill the proper respect for the highest cultural achievements. Consequently philology reigns supreme, and generations of uninspiring and uninspired professors reproduce without any concern for philosophy and art (by which Nietzsche means primarily Schopenhauer's philosophy and Wagner's music), both of which are barred from the modern university. The results are "degenerate and distracted men of culture" (*SW* 1: 746) who incline toward journalistic endeavor or dry academics with useless scholarship. Real university education, according to Nietzsche's philosopher, "begins with the opposite of everything that one now praises as academic freedom, with obedience, with subordination, with discipline, and with servitude" (*SW* 1: 750). True learning and culture flourish only under a regime of military-like discipline.

The Limits of the Historical Paradigm

Nietzsche's continued concern with problems of education and *Bildung* is reflected in his subsequent published writings as well. Indeed, pedagogical concerns are an important subtext of his *Untimely Meditations,* a series of essays that appeared in four volumes from 1873–76. Particularly important for education is the second *Untimely Meditation, On the Advantage and Disadvantage of History for Life* (1874). Composed quickly from November of 1873 to early January of 1874, it was part of Nietzsche's turn away from philological studies and toward more general cultural concerns, including the education of Germany's youth. Much of the latter part of *Advantage and Disadvantage* deals with this topic in a rhapsodic fashion. Indeed, at least the last seven of the 10 sections in the essay consist of remarks directed at institutions and assumptions in contemporary German society. The work thus appears to be dichotomous in structure: the first part, in sections 1 through 3, presents an abstract parsing of two sets of categories. We first encounter a discussion of three types of human being—the historical, the unhistorical, and the superhistorical—followed by a consideration of three approaches to historical material: the monumental, the antiquarian, and the critical history. Thereafter we find the aforementioned extended and sometimes rambling, albeit much more spirited, diatribe against the present age, organized loosely around five "dangers" listed at the start of the fifth section. Although Nietzsche does return briefly to his original considerations at the close of the work, the work is apt to leave the impression of disunity in tone and purpose. What nonetheless unites this essay is a theme common to both the conceptual sections and the sections of critique: the pernicious character of "historical" education.

Nietzsche begins his treatise on historical education with a familiar distinction. The question he implicitly poses is what characteristic or characteristics separate human beings from animals. The typical nineteenth-century answer to this question would probably have been "consciousness." Important for Nietzsche is not simply consciousness, but other, related matters such as forgetting, happiness, dissimulation, honesty, and truth.[7] In one of the most amusing passages in the work he implores us to consider the herd grazing in the field, suggesting that these animals have no sense of history. They are "enthralled by the moment" and are therefore neither melancholy nor bored. The human predicament is to long for this blissful state, yet at the same time to reject it: the human being "is proud of being human and not an animal and yet regards its happiness with envy because he wants nothing other than to live like the animal, neither bored nor in pain, yet wants it in vain because he does not want it like the animal" (*ADH* 8).

In other words, the human being would like the same result that animals achieve—freedom from pain and boredom, happiness and contentment with life—but we cannot give up consciousness, nor do we want to. The animal is happy, but not conscious—at least not historically conscious and therefore it does not have a memory of happiness, a consciousness of happiness, or even a mechanism to express this happiness. Or, as Nietzsche puts it, in a more playful fashion: "Man may well ask the animal: why do you not speak to me of your happiness but only look at me? The animal does want to answer and say: because I always immediately forget what I wanted to say—but then it already forgot this answer and remained silent: so that man could only wonder" (*ADH* 8). Consciousness in Nietzsche is a barrier to fulfillment, a hindrance to the implicit goal of human existence: happiness.

The difference in consciousness between animals and humans, phrased in terms of forgetting and memory, leads to the central distinction in this important initial section of the essay. The human being who cannot learn to forget and remains attached or chained to the past lives a historical life. The animal lives unhistorically and is therefore happy, but happiness is not the only characteristic associated with an unhistorical existence. A further important feature is the existence of a certain primitive and unreflected honesty. The animal, Nietzsche claims, does not know how to dissimulate; it cannot pretend to be something that it is not; it cannot deceive. The animal is thus like the child, who likewise lives unhistorically, and Nietzsche hypothesizes that the reason the adult human being is moved upon seeing a herd of animals or a child has to do with the memory of a lost paradise. The curse of the child is that it will grow up; a necessary part of education and socialization is for the child to learn the fateful phrase "it was," which serves as a constant reminder that existence is basically "a never to be completed imperfect tense" (*ADH* 9). The only escape from this situation is death, which of course brings the "longed-for forgetfulness," but also robs us of the present. From the perspective of death, then, existence "is only an interrupted having-been, a thing which lives by denying itself, consuming itself, and contradicting itself" (*ADH* 9). Thus we are presented with an unusual dilemma: humankind is condemned to historical existence, but this very historical consciousness robs us of happiness and fulfillment.

In most of the remainder of the first section Nietzsche drops his comparison between the animal and the human being and places the opposition between historical and unhistorical life within the human being. He indicates that we can achieve a temporary happiness if we seek to imitate the animal and live unhistorically. Indeed, the sine qua non for happiness is the capacity to forget or, expressed academically, the ability to live unhistorically—at least temporarily. It is also the prerequisite for action. At various points, in fact, Nietzsche declares that the human being must live both historically and unhistorically, that both are necessary "for the health of an individual, a people and a culture" (*ADH* 10). The historical element that he admits as necessary, however, is limited insofar as it must contribute to "life." Since he repeatedly declares that the unhistorical is necessary for life, his limited concept of the historical appears to approach its very opposite, and Nietzsche's work therefore flirts continuously with contradiction. On the whole, however, there is no doubt, even in this section where balance seems to be the watchword, that the unhistorical is far more important for happiness. Only by shrinking our horizon to a point, as animals do, can we achieve happiness, or at least live without boredom and dissimulation—a condition that Nietzsche likens to happiness.

Nietzsche also introduces a third category, the "superhistorical," which he describes as follows: "If someone could, in numerous instances, discern and breathe again the unhistorical atmosphere in which every great historical event came to be, then such a one might, as a cognitive being, perhaps elevate himself to a *superhistorical* standpoint" (*ADH* 12). We recognize the superhistorical individual as an observer of the historical process, as a sovereign meditator, perhaps even as an "untimely meditator." That is, the superhistorical seems to result from the study of history, from observing or taking in history, not from action itself. In a sense, then, it is derived from an unusual merger of the unhistorical, the central category of historical action, and the historical. In the sovereign bearing the superhistorical man seems to partake in features of the unhistorical, while at the same time resembling the historical man in his refusal or inability to take part in the historical process. The superhistorical man is thus involved in a paradox, which potentially applied to Nietzsche and Nietzsche's reader as well: "As far as he is a knower this power has now become powerless for him: not yet perhaps so far as he is a living being" (*ADH* 14). History, Nietzsche suggests here, is only productive when it is subordinated to an ahistorical power. Ultimately these superhistorical men are unable to further the goals of "life," but they are at least able to recognize the debilitating effects of the hegemonical historical education. Because Nietzsche prefers the unhistorical, his pedagogical position, like his view on history itself, comes close to a self-cancellation. From the perspective of "life" those perspectives that entail formal education because they are either historical or historically saturated (the superhistorical) are rejected in favor of an unhistorical and therefore extra-pedagogical imperative.

Three Types of Historical Pedagogy

The paradoxes continue when Nietzsche delineates three types of history or three relationships to historical knowledge. Initially Nietzsche distinguishes among three types of historical activity: the monumental, the antiquarian, and the critical. In each case he takes an identical approach: he outlines first the advantages and then the disadvantages of each particular relationship to the past for that enigmatic term "life." Although Nietzsche had stated in his initial remarks that "*the unhistorical and the historical are equally necessary for the health of an individual, a people and a culture*" (*ADH* 10), he appears to shift ground here. The bulk of the treatise does not, in fact, seek to establish the dual contribution of the historical and the unhistorical to life; rather, implicit in his arguments is an opposition between history and life—or at the very least an economy dominated by an inverse relationship between history and life. Life, the least clearly defined term in the essay, is clearly "an unhistorical power" (*ADH* 14), and thus by definition excludes history. If we wish to make sense of the discussions of the individual approaches to history, we must remember that they partake of the general paradox that informs the essay: only where history belies its own nature, i.e., where it becomes unhistorical or contributes to the unhistorical, does it serve life.

Nietzsche appears most fond of the monumental approach to history, since monumentality is intimately related to "great individuals" and their noble activities, both of which, as we have seen, are the ultimate goal of Nietzschean culture. Accordingly, with regard to monumental history, Nietzsche celebrates "the great moments in the struggle of individuals" as "the high points of humanity" (*ADH* 15). The "advantage" in Nietzsche's evaluation of the monumental is a reaffirmation of existence over the flux of historical events. "It is the knowledge that the great which once existed was at least *possible* once and may well again be possible sometime." Here we should note that history is being rescued for life precisely because of a possibility inscribed in it. The value of history is that its effects transcend the historical and extend into the realm of myth. Nietzsche admits this without hesitation; monumental history, he maintains, is always potentially distorted because "aesthetic criteria" may be introduced into the historical record: "There are even ages which are quite incapable of distinguishing between a monumental past and a mythical fiction: for precisely the same incentives can be given by the one world as by the other" (*ADH* 17).

The case against monumental history is fourfold. First, in monumental history the "past itself" suffers damage since it is not honored simply for being the past. Second and more important, Nietzsche reasons that monumental history leads to a celebration of effects without causes and thus to a certain leveling of historical phenomenon, a failure to recognize the uniqueness of historical actions, in short, to an ahistorical view. In a kind of doubly paradoxical gesture, Nietzsche argues here that the very unhistorical aspect that makes monumental history an advantage constitutes its danger or damage. If on the one hand we are inspired by imitation, we are in danger, on the other hand, of being tempted by analogies and similarities. We thus may fail to appreciate the unique greatness of a historical action. Third, Nietzsche maintains that in some cases monumental history can become a weapon in the hands of the weak instead of an inspiration for the strong. It can take desirable characteristics and exaggerate them, thus making them undesirable: "With tempting similarities the courageous are enticed to rashness, the enthusiastic to fanaticism; and if one thinks of this history as being in the hands and heads of talented egoists and enraptured rascals, then empires are destroyed, princes murdered, wars and revolutions instigated and the number of historical 'effects in themselves,' that is, of effects without sufficient causes, is further increased" (*ADH* 17). Finally, monumental history also deceives others who are not blessed with greatness into thinking that they too can be great or significant in the historical process. Nietzsche draws his illustration from the aesthetic realm. The "feebly artistic natures," perhaps encouraged by a reading of monumental history, may strike against what is truly great in art. These iconoclasts make manifest a disadvantage in monumental history because they destroy, rather than imitate greatness. In this way, as Nietzsche writes, they "let the dead bury the living," since what is truly alive is great art. For Nietzsche, this instrumentalization of monumental history by the pseudo-great represents its worst perversion.

One of the abuses of monumental history—the disregard for the integrity of the past—can be corrected by the second approach to historical knowledge: antiquarian history. In antiquarian history we detect a dialectic similar to the one operative in the discussion of monumental history. The beneficial dimension is related to a preservation of origin and of personal, communal, or national histories. Nietzsche writes of antiquarian history as a personal search for roots: "By tending with loving hands what has long survived he [the antiquarian historian] intends to preserve the conditions in which he grew up for those who will come after him—and so he serves life" (*ADH* 19). The antiquarian historian appears to contribute at most a kind of solace or nostalgic sentiment for himself or for his community. The very metaphors that Nietzsche employs to describe the advantages of the antiquarian indicate a passivity or patient evolutionary procedure: "The contentment of a tree with its roots, the happiness of knowing oneself not to be wholly arbitrary and accidental, but rather as growing out of a past as its heir, flower and fruit and so to be exculpated, even justified in one's existence—this is what one now especially likes to call the proper historical sense" (*ADH* 20). Interesting here—and contradictory—is that Nietzsche ascribes some modicum of happiness to historical man, and that he suggests that existence could be justified on the basis of history. It appears that history is called upon to confront the rootlessness of modern life: To combat the vast movements of populations and the "restless cosmopolitan choosing and searching for novelty and ever more novelty," Nietzsche cites the literal and metaphorical rootedness associated with the antiquarian.

The very attitude of patient preservation for which antiquarian history was lauded, however, becomes its most detrimental feature. In the first place the antiquarian can easily leap to the delusion that one's tradition is important when it is not. As a single tree in a large wooded area, the individual or the group can easily become myopic and ignore the forest. When we become too immersed in antiquarian activities, we are thus threatened with the loss of proportion. Everything seems to be of equal significance; consequently we lose sight of what is really important. Closely related to this disadvantage is the leveling of true greatness. If everything is worthy of preservation, then the truly great achievements of the past shrink before trivial accomplishments. Finally, the antiquarian approach to historical knowledge includes the danger of stifling what is new and promising. We may lose sight not only of the significance of past achievements, but also of the promise of future achievements. In this fashion the antiquarian threatens "to undermine further and especially higher life, when the historical sense no longer preserves life but mummifies it" (*ADH* 21). The result is the withering of the tree that had nurtured its roots, since it has not been encouraged to grow and thrive. Nietzsche presents a blanket condemnation of the antiquarian as well. He argues that antiquarian history "merely understands how to *preserve* life, not how to generate it; therefore it always underestimates what is in process of becoming because it has no instinct for discerning significance—unlike monumental history, for example, which has this instinct" (*ADH* 21). Again we are struck by the contradiction; after praising antiquarian history, albeit in a limited fashion, Nietzsche appears to withdraw all "advantage" by his unqualified criticisms.

The final type of history that Nietzsche discusses is the critical, which is defined by a general iconoclasm: Man "must have the strength, and use it from time to time, to shatter and dissolve something to enable him to live: this he achieves by dragging it to the bar of judgment, interrogating it meticulously and finally condemning it" (*ADH* 21). The liberating moment for the present is purchased at the expense of the past. "Life" alone, which Nietzsche here describes as "that dark, driving, insatiably self-desiring power" delivers the unjust, merciless verdict. It is apparent, however, that the critical is less a historical sense or an approach to knowledge of the past than an imperative to reject the past. Nietzsche's misgivings about critical historiography are related to the attendant distortions of our true origins. Nietzsche affirms that we are not only the results of earlier generations, but also "the results of their aberrations, passions and errors, even crimes" (*ADH* 22). And he further reminds us that "it is not possible quite to free oneself from this chain" (*ADH* 22). In employing the critical sense of history *for life,* we simultaneously condemn life—or at least that part of the past that is always a part of the present. It is as if in affirming ourselves, we are compelled to deny ourselves as well. Thus the discussion of the critical perspective ends in paradox as well. While we cannot act without tearing down the past, we cannot tear down the past without injuring ourselves and our ability to act.

Historical Learning and Cultural Criticism

Not only is the discussion of the various historical senses paradoxical in its own right; it is also at odds with Nietzsche's initial and titular demand that history be advantageous for life. The distinctions that Nietzsche draws and the evenhandedness with which he treats each category are uncharacteristic for the essay and for the pedagogical imperative to rescue German culture. The exceptional nature of his treatment of the monumental, the antiquarian, and the critical sense is borne out by the rest of the work, which consists, in large measure, of a harangue against various abuses of history in the recently unified German state. Many of the points that Nietzsche makes relate to problems he perceives in the educational system or in academic circles of his era. For example, Nietzsche argues persuasively against the narrow disciplinary penchant for considering history "science." He believes that the scientific pretensions of the academy establish an artificial yardstick by which to measure research and knowledge in historical studies, and thus deprive history of the yardstick that really matters: its ability to further life. He bemoans, in short, the penchant on the part of educators and educational institutions to promote irrelevant knowledge: "Now life is no longer the sole ruler and master of knowledge of the past: rather all boundary markers are overthrown and everything which once was rushes in upon man" (*ADH* 23). Nietzsche thus condemns the stranglehold of history on education and culture. The motto he associates with the academic historical attitude, *fiat veritas pereat vita* (let there be truth, even if life perish), reverses the proper cultural and educational priority. The conflict between history, science, and truth, on the one side, and life, on the other, must always be decided in favor of the latter term. No matter what its potential for injustice and falsehood, life is to be preferred.

The balanced discussions of the three historical senses are thus superseded in the essay by a wholesale criticism of German culture and the educational system that spawns cultural mediocrity. Behind Nietzsche's remarks are two unspoken assumptions: that Germany, if it is to achieve cultural excellence, should seek to emulate Greece, and that education in the new empire should head in exactly the opposite direction from the one it has taken. In these two ways his message is "untimely." In contrast to his lecture series from 1872, however, Nietzsche is less precise concerning his criticism of contemporary institutions. Only once does he take on squarely the leveling and weakening of education that was so prominent in his earlier lectures: "In how unnatural, artificial, in any case unworthy a condition must the most sincere of all the sciences, the honest naked goddess philosophy, find herself in an age which suffers from general education! In such a world of forced external conformity she remains a learned monologue of the lonely walker, the chance prey of the solitary thinker, a hidden private secret or harmless gossip of academic old men and children" (*ADH* 29). Most of his comments are general and abstract. History and historical consciousness become a cipher in this work for the neglect of genuine *Bildung*. They are a sign of the lack of originality and of the enervated state of German society, a symptom of a system that has heaped up useless knowledge and annihilated instincts.

Nietzsche's alternative is a society consisting of great men, geniuses, exceptional personalities; in short, of an authentic cultural and academic elite. Only these men exhibit the strength necessary to forge a new culture that can rescue Germany from the precipice of the abyss opened by an excess of knowledge, reflection, history, fact, and objectivity. The Nietzschean alternative is evident in the discussion of justice. Modern man believes in the necessity of justice, but this is only a self-deception of the modern age. The true judge is one who has the strength to pass judgment. In contrast to the popular conception of justice, the standards of judgment are not located in history or in abstract rules; nor are they objective. Justice is ordained, not learned; it results from a gift of genius, not a product of erudition and historical training; it is "the terrible calling of the just man" (*ADH* 37). The truly just man must be able to judge the past from the standpoint of the present, and like the critical historian, be able to condemn it if necessary. "Only from the standpoint of the highest strength of the present may you interpret the past" (*ADH* 37). "History is written by the experienced and superior man . . . ; only the builder of the future has a right to judge the past" (*ADH* 38). The refrain from Nietzsche's initial discussion is here reiterated in connection with justice: history and historical education must be overcome, conquered, and subdued by the present, by life.

Nietzsche's cultural critique thus amounts to a condemnation of all those features of modernity that foster weak personalities as well as a leveled notion of *Bildung,* and a simultaneous affirmation of genius and greatness as an antidote to contemporary mediocrity. The goal of connecting history with life and of a Nietzschean pedagogy that strengthens German culture will not be such items as social justice or political strength, but artistic and philosophical greatness. Citing Schopenhauer's notion of a republic of geniuses, Nietzsche embellishes by evoking the image of giants holding "lofty conversations" across "the bleak intervals of the ages," unconcerned by the prattle of the "noisy dwarfs who creep away beneath them" (*ADH* 53). What is important in history is obviously not the progress of the dwarfs, nor even the progress in the thought of the giants, but simply the production of giants who hold conversations with one another: "The task of history is to be the mediator between them [the giants] and so again and again to provide the occasion for and lend strength to the production of greatness. No, the goal of humanity cannot lie at the end but only in its highest specimens" (*ADH* 53). The non-geniuses, the "noisy dwarfs," have only three purposes on earth: (1) they can emulate great men, but, as Nietzsche notes, they would only be "blurred copies . . . produced on bad paper with worn plates"; (2) they can provide some modicum of resistance to the meteoric rise of the genius; in this way the genius stands out as overcoming their pettiness and triviality; and (3) they can serve as "tools of the great," pawns in the great chess match played out by the giants. Unquestionably for Nietzsche the aim of our culture and our educational institutions should be to promote and facilitate the appearance of genius.

In the final pages of his essay on history Nietzsche makes his pedagogical aims more explicit by directing his thoughts to the youth of Germany. He also returns to a call for the unhistorical and the superhistorical, to those forces or mentalities that reject such notions of history as progress, telos, and rational purpose. Only by swallowing the distasteful but ultmately palliative antidote of the un- and superhistorical can the youth be saved from the baneful fetter of historical consciousness. In order to rescue German culture from the hands of the "historico-aesthetic cultural Philistine, the precocious newly wise chatterbox on matters of state, church and art, the sensorium of thousands of sensations, the insatiable stomach which yet does not know what honest hunger and thirst are" (*ADH* 59–60), Germany is called upon to alter its education, to set free the instincts in its youth before they too become the new race of dwarves. Current educational practice is a violation of the very instincts that could save German culture. A fundamental change is necessary "that will guide the eye away from becoming and toward that which gives existence an eternal and stable character, toward *art* and *religion"* (*ADH* 62). The latter part of Nietzsche's *Advantage and Disadvantage* is thus a passionate plea for an educational program of the future aimed at counteracting the effects of an enervating historical pedagogy.

The Paradigm of Anti-Institutional Education

The paradoxical development of Nietzsche's pedagogical thought is perhaps now evident. While he started in the early 1870s with observations on actual educational institutions and suggested ways in which to improve the system by opposing reforms aimed at leveling and widening, by the middle of the decade he had moved toward an anti-institutional stance. According to this position, genuine education is not—or rarely—connected to an actual university or high school because institutions are set up to cater to the needs of the state and of a broad public. The alternative that Nietzsche appears to have envisioned in his early lectures—a school to train elites—has disappeared and been replaced by a demand that the youth be allowed to express their "instincts." Since the expression of instincts is apparently something that schooling hinders, rather than promotes, the pedagogical lesson is that institutional education is antithetical to precisely what "education" should be furthering. For Nietzsche, and in contrast to the enlightenment tradition of pedagogy still very alive in the nineteenth century, the goal of education was not a knowledgeable, well-informed, or well-trained citizenry, but the production of exceptional individuals. Nietzsche thus gradually came to understand education as institutionalized in the Germany of his time as a perversion of the real purpose of knowledge and learning. Just as the highest purpose of history is embodied in the unhistorical, so too the highest pedagogical goal becomes the anti-educational.

Nietzsche's third *Untimely Meditation, Schopenhauer as Educator,* confirms its author's anti-institutional turn. The ostensible subject of the essay, the philosopher Arthur Schopenhauer, himself had a rather precarious relationship with the educational institutions of his time. Having received his doctorate from Jena in 1813 and having composed the first version of *The World as Will and Representation* (1819) from 1814–18, Schopenhauer decided to disseminate his philosophical teaching at the University of Berlin in 1820. Although he held no chair, he nevertheless received permission to hold lectures, but he had the audacity to schedule his course at the same time at which G. W. F. Hegel was accustomed to teach. Hegel's popularity was evidently too much for the newcomer

Schopenhauer. Attendance was so poor that, after one semester, he decided to abandon a career in higher education and devote himself to a life of learning outside the institution. Nietzsche's selection of the word "educator" in his title was thus an obvious irony—and simultaneously a commentary on the educational establishment. In terms of the institutionalized educational system, Schopenhauer hardly qualifies as an educator at all. Having devoted his life to a pursuit of truth outside the confines of establishment pedagogy, however, Schopenhauer became, in Nietzsche's eyes, the paradigmatic educational spirit. Like the philosopher in the frame of Nietzsche's pedagogical lectures, Schopenhauer instructed outside the institution, imparting wisdom for life, rather than historical knowledge for the sake of convention. Phrased in a slightly different manner, we might conceive of Schopenhauer as an educator whose objective is not education in the institutional sense of the word, but rather *Bildung* as the genuine mission of a superior culture.

Nietzsche makes the reader aware of his unusual characterization of Schopenhauer and the paradoxical nature of the educational process that he newly defines. Addressing a young soul, he comments that the "true educators and cultivators" (*Erzieher und Bildner*) impart "the true primeval sense and elementary material of your being, something that is not subject to education or acculturation at all." Nietzsche's conception of education is thus not only anti-institutional, but also anti-educational. He conceives the educator as a personal emancipator, someone who allows disciples to free themselves from the shackles of convention. In a particularly descriptive passage he clarifies his depiction of education as liberation by applying metaphors from gardening: it is the "removal of all weeds, rubble and vermin that want to attack the tender buds of the plant, an outstreaming of light and warmth, the gentle rustling of nocturnal rain" (*SE* 130).

What appears to be even more important for Nietzsche is that the student does not encounter the educator as a member of the teaching profession, but rather seeks him out for his philosophical wisdom. Nietzsche emphasizes that he found Schopenhauer the philosopher and made him his educator. The task that he assigns to Schopenhauer therefore has nothing to do with integration into the social order or training for a profession—this was Ritschl's role in Nietzsche's life. The educator has the much more difficult task of imparting to his pupil how one becomes a human being. In contrast to institutionalized education, where knowledge and scholarship are the primary goals, Nietzsche's educational goal is humanity. Schopenhauer is especially impressive in this regard because he was rejected by his own era as an educator, because he conducted a philosophical existence independent of the state, and because he constantly harangued the most eminent members of the teaching profession. The very characteristics that disqualified him as an actual teacher at a Prussian university make him more suitable for Nietzsche's pedagogical imperative.

Nietzsche's stylization of Schopenhauer into the prototypical non-institutional educator is nowhere more apparent than in his typology of three images of man in contemporary society. The first type is identified with the French philosopher Jean-Jacques Rousseau. This individual advocates hasty revolutions and socialist upheavals under the guise of a return to nature. Nietzsche despises such types and finds that they are repressed creatures who secretly loathe themselves. It is not insignificant that Rousseauean man is viewed so negatively, since Rousseau himself is commonly identified with enlightenment ideals of education. In opposing this type so categorically, Nietzsche once again rejects a naive optimism associated with certain strands in enlightenment thinking.

As a counterbalance to Rousseauean man Nietzsche posits an individual modeled on Goethean principles. Throughout his works Nietzsche displayed a great deal of respect for Goethe, in particular for his literary abilities and aristocratic tastes. Here, however, Goethean man is depicted as a contemplative and quietistic corrective to the rebelliousness of Rousseauean individuals. Two characteristics stand out: First, Goethean man is evolutionary; in contrast to Rousseauean man, he dislikes violence, jumps, and discontinuities. Second, this type of man prefers contemplation to action. The danger Nietzsche sees in Goethean man is that once he ceases to strive in a Faust-like fashion, he can easily become the prototype of a philistine.

The final image of man, the Schopenhauerian, contains the hope for the future. By accepting voluntarily the suffering of earthly existence, Schopenhauerian man can accomplish a complete alteration of his being and thereby reach a higher stage of humanity. Although Schopenhauer's philosophy would seem to qualify him as a model for the contemplative and resigned individual, Nietzsche maintains that his pessimism and negativity lead to a "mighty longing for sanctification and salvation" (*SE* 153). Ultimately Schopehauerian man is seen as a model for a heroic life and for "the great individual," and by following his teaching, by adhering to the ideal man and quasi-Platonic idea in Schopenhauer's philosophy, Nietzsche believes that human beings can achieve the highest goals.

Nietzsche often speaks as if every individual had equal access to a Schopenhauerian education, as if this anti-establishment pedagogy had as its goal a society of great individuals. But as in his *Untimely Meditation* on history, his further reflections indicate clearly that his educational and cultural philosophy is hierarchical. The basic thought of any culture, Nietzsche claims, should be "the production of the philosopher, the artist and the saint within us and without us" (*SE* 160), since the appearance of these three types of exceptional human beings would signify the perfection of nature. It is possible, of course, that all of us could be taken into that sublime order of philosophers, artists, and saints, that everyone could participate in the transition to a higher type of human being. But Nietzsche makes it clear that most of humanity will never attain such a lofty objective, and that the happiness of the "mass of exemplars" is of no consequence in his scheme. He can therefore stage the following hypothetical question-and-answer session for his readers: "How can your life, the individual life, receive the highest value, the deepest significance? How can it be least squandered? Certainly only by your living for the good of the rarest and most valuable exemplars, and not for the good of the majority, that is to say those who, taken individually, are the most worthless exemplars" (*SE* 162). Nietzsche's critique of culture and his praise of Schopenhauer's educational program culminates in the imperative to oppose the training of mediocre civil servants and myopic scholars and to concentrate instead on the production of genius. Nietzsche recognizes the practical limitations on this ideal. His suggestion that all philosophical education be removed from the auspices of the state— since it and its academies are unable to evaluate true philosophy (*SE* 190)—is clearly untenable. But if a Nietzschean pedagogy inspired by a Schopenhauerian vision was going to have any chance of success, it had to depend on an abrupt reversal of the state of affairs at nineteenth-century educational institutions.

This reversal, of course, did not take place. But the absence of any signs of a shift in educational priorities was not the only reason that Nietzsche's interest in educational institutions and pedagogy waned in the late 1870s and 1880s. On a personal level, Nietzsche himself began to grow weary of his own position as professor. In part because of ill health, which kept him from fulfilling the complete range of his duties during the latter part of the decade, and in part because of his gradual loss of enthusiasm for philology and institutionalized instruction, Nietzsche no longer identified with the *Gymnasium*, the university, and their reform. However, Nietzsche's growing disinterest in educational matters can also be attributed to a shift in his philosophical position. We have seen that Nietzsche departed significantly from enlightenment pedagogical principles, but in his early writings he appears to adhere, nonetheless, to the central enlightenment tenet that education could be a vehicle for change. By the early 1880s he appears to have relinquished even this remnant of enlightened thought. In place of a belief in pedagogy as a tool for change, we begin to find with increasing frequency metaphors and thoughts drawn from biology and genetics. In an aphorism from *Beyond Good and Evil,* for example, Nietzsche juxtaposed heredity with education and culture.

> If one knows something about the parents, it is permissible to draw a conclusion about the child: any sort of untoward intemperance, any sort of narrow enviousness, a clumsy obstinate self-assertiveness—these three things together have at all times constituted the characteristics of the plebeian type—qualities of this sort must be transferred to the child as surely as bad blood; and the best education and culture will succeed only in *deceiving* with regard to such an inheritance.—And what else is the objective of education and culture today? In our very democratic, that is to say plebeian age, 'education' and 'culture' *have* to be in essence the art of deceiving—of deceiving with regard to origins, to the inherited plebeian in soul and body. (*BGE* 184)

With the rise of biologism, education declines as an ideal. Reduced to deceiving a population that fails to recognize the Nietzschean alternative, pedagogy cedes to such ominous notions as eugenics and breeding. Nietzsche never renounced completely his hope for a true cultural renaissance, but by the end of the 1870s he appears to have repudiated the role that pedagogy could play in this transformation.

Chapter 4
The Scientific Dilettante

In the nineteenth century the separation between the natural sciences and philosophy was not quite as large as it has become in the twentieth century. In general, it was not inappropriate to believe that a generally educated person, like Nietzsche, would have a good foundation in the latest discoveries and theories in the world of science. However, because we have become accustomed to more rigid disciplinary distinctions, Nietzsche's thought is rarely considered as part of a dialogue with the natural sciences. His classification as a philosopher or as a literary and cultural figure has usually meant that his scientific preoccupations are ignored, even though Nietzsche clearly considered science important for his philosophy. It is true, of course, that his education was somewhat deficient in actual scientific training; Schulpforta concentrated on classical languages, and Nietzsche's early recruitment into philological circles at Bonn and Leipzig reduced his exposure to other fields of knowledge. But Nietzsche himself was keenly aware of this deficiency and spent the rest of his life trying to compensate for this obvious lacuna in his formal education. If Nietzsche had not become a young professor at Basel in 1869, he might have supplemented his knowledge of natural science more systematically. His plan for 1869 was to travel to Paris with a friend and study natural sciences there.[1] The offer of the professorship at Basel obviously persuaded Nietzsche to postpone his plans, but there is considerable evidence that his growing interest in natural science and his own perception that he lacked sufficient knowledge in this area guided his reading during the next two decades. During that period he frequently purchased books that dealt with natural science, or borrowed such books from the library.[2] He appears to have been a particularly avid reader of volumes on physiology and medicine, although at one point or another he also consulted works on almost all manner of scientific endeavor.

The extent to which scientific theories actually affected Nietzsche's philosophy is apt to be a matter of considerable dispute. Philosophical opinion in the twentieth century, with some notable exceptions, has chosen to ignore much of the scientific grounding of Nietzsche's thought, but this neglect may say more about how philosophy has been read in our times than about Nietzsche's own understanding of his thought. What is remarkable is not only that Nietzsche's interest in natural science remained strong throughout his life, but also that almost all the concepts for which he has rightfully become famous were developed and explicated in published texts and unpublished notebooks in dialogue with the natural scientific knowledge of his age. The following discussions will deal with four central areas of Nietzschean conceptuality: the overman, eternal recurrence of the same, perspectivism, and breeding. In each an endeavor is made to comprehend Nietzsche's philosophy qua philosophy, but also within the context that he himself defined. For the "overman" this entails evolutionary biology, which frames Nietzsche's very introduction of the term. When developing the notion of "eternal recurrence" Nietzsche often alluded to the laws of thermodynamics, which would have been understood in his own time as theories of heat and energy transfer. "Perspectivism," a concept that Nietzsche equated with "phenomenalism," is more than an affirmation of relativism; its more important aspect brings it into the proximity of physiology, consciousness as an organ of perception, and nerve stimulation. Finally, breeding is not a metaphor that Nietzsche employed for some method of selecting the very best of our species for distinction, but a program that entered a nineteenth-century discourse of heredity and eugenics. In connection with all these concepts, which are at the heart of Nietzsche's philosophy, natural science played a seminal and, in some cases, determinate role.

The Evolution of the Overman

The word "overman" (*Übermensch*), sometimes translated as "superman," is perhaps the one notion most often associated with Nietzsche's philosophy. Introduced in *Zarathustra,* "overman" resonates not only with the "last man" and the "higher man" to which it is opposed, but also with several other terms that occur more frequently in this text, in particular, "overcoming" (*Überwindung*), with which it is closely associated.[3] If the "overman" is characterized best by the notion of "overcoming," then the question will be: What does he overcome? The answer is "man" as he exists in his present state. Nietzsche's first mention of the "overman" in *Zarathustra* makes it clear that the overman results from an overcoming of man. Descending from his mountain retreat, Zarathustra, the prophetic voice of Nietzsche, declares to the first townspeople assembled in the marketplace: "I teach you the overman. Man is something that shall be overcome. What have you done to overcome him?" Like many of Zarathustra's pronouncements, this one is riddled with ambiguity. The nature of the overcoming, however, especially its biological dimension, comes into clearer focus in Zarathustra's next utterance: "All beings so far have created something beyond themselves; and do you want to be the ebb of this great flood and even go back to the beasts rather than overcome man? What is the ape to man? A laughing-stock or a painful embarrassment. And man shall be just that for the overman: a laughing-stock or a painful embarrassment. You have made your way from worm to man, and much in you is still worm. Once you were apes, and even now, too, man is more ape than any ape" (Z 124).

The evolutionary context is rather plainly articulated. The transition from ape to man, a commonplace assumption for nineteenth-century evolutionists even before the publication of Charles Darwin's *Origin of the Species,* is cited as an analog for the future evolution from man to overman. Furthermore, the entire course of evolution, summarized poetically as the transition from the invertebrate worm to the human being, is presented to a reader who could hardly avoid association with Darwin and Darwinism. Zarathustra's point is that man should not be considered the pinnacle of the development of the species; mankind, like other species, must be surpassed or overcome, and the name that Zarathustra applies to this future and unknown species is overman.

Despite this passage there are two reasons that commentators have shied away from the obvious connection with evolutionary biology. The first is an outgrowth of Nietzsche's own remarks. In *Ecce Homo* he explicitly denied a similarity between the overman and Darwinism when he commented: "Other learned cattle caused me on its [the overman's] account to be suspected of Darwinism" (*EH* 71). What commentators have failed to notice is that Nietzsche distinguished carefully between Darwinism, which he rejected, and evolutionary thought, which he accepted in some form with several reservations. Thus the notion of the overman, while perhaps not derived from or exemplary of Darwinism— or what Nietzsche understood under Darwinsim—nonetheless partakes in the general framework of evolutionary biology of the nineteenth century. Indeed, instead of conceiving it as an influence of Darwinism, we might more accurately view the overman as Nietzsche's answer to the problems raised by Darwin and his European followers.

The second reason for avoiding the connection with evolutionary biology has to do with subsequent discussions of the overman. In most passages in *Zarathustra* the overman is not connected with evolution, but rather characterized by his ties to this world, to material reality, and with a rejection of previous ethical systems and religious ideals. He is called *over*man because he has overcome the values that have hitherto been constitutive of the human species. But these passages do not contradict Nietzsche's understanding of evolution either. In fact, Nietzsche's characterization of man as a tightrope or a bridge reinforces the biologistic associations found in Zarathustra's initial discussion. In this image Zarathustra evokes the transitory nature of the human being. In serving as a transition (*Übergang*) to the overman, the human being simultaneously rushes toward its own demise (*Untergang*). The human species is thus not the final development in evolutionary history, but an intermediate stage that will itself cede to a higher order of being. As in the initial passages, the imagery throughout *Zarathustra* suggests a proximity to evolution, as it was popularly understood in the nineteenth century.

Part of the problem in our identifying Nietzsche's overman as an essentially Darwinian notion is that our knowledge of Darwin's theories is apt to differ significantly from what Nietzsche and his contemporaries understood by the term. There is no question that Nietzsche became acquainted with the name Darwin and the general outlines of evolution at a rather early age, and that he continued to encounter reflections on Darwin's theory in his scientific readings from the 1870s and 1880s. By the time Nietzsche began composing *Zarathustra* in the early 1880s he was conversant with a representative set of issues in evolutionary biology, even if he, like his contemporaries, was not always able to identify correctly the specific source of a particular concept or hypothesis.

Nietzsche's specific remarks about Darwin, in particular his polemical self-understanding as an anti-Darwinian, must therefore not be considered a rejection of evolutionary theory.[4] A more fruitful way to understand his comments on evolutionary topics is as a dialogue with the biology of his time. Two aspects of what Nietzsche understood as Darwinism were particularly problematic for him: the explanation for the mechanisms by which species evolve and separate from one another, and the notion of progress or perfection of forms. With regard to the first of these issues, Nietzsche obviously believed that Darwin had generalized from a limited situation. The notion of a "struggle for existence," the most popular slogan in the popularized German reception of Darwinism, was inadequate to explain the development of a species or the evolution from one species to another.[5] Nietzsche comments critically in *Twilight of the Idols*: "As for the famous 'struggle for existence,' so far it seems to me to be asserted rather than proved. It occurs, but as an exception" (*TI* 522). He attributes the "inconceivably one-sided teaching of the 'struggle for existence'" to a peculiarity in the heritage of natural sciences and to England in particular. Natural scientists, he claims, stem from the commoners; "their ancestors were poor and undistinguished people who knew the difficulties of survival only too well at firsthand." Because of a perceived overpopulation in Britain, English scientists contribute to a false interpretation of evolutionary change by fostering a notion of privation and scarcity: "The whole of English Darwinism breathes something like the musty air of English overpopulation, like the smell of the distress and crowding of small people" (*GS* 292). Although the reader may be tempted to dismiss these explanations as non-serious, from remarks in other works it appears that Nietzsche consistently regarded such items as heritage, climate, and even diet as constitutive for intellectual positions.

Up until 1888 Nietzsche objected less to the limited purview in the notion of "struggle for existence" than to the reliance on external features and milieu to explain natural selection. In harmony with objections voiced by various Darwinian critics of his era, he counters the perception that Darwinism is dominated by an environmental determinism by postulating an inner power that accounts for adaptive changes and ultimately the evolution of the species.[6] In his last year of writing, however, once he comes to regard the "struggle for existence" as the key to Darwinism, he shifts grounds slightly and suggests as an alternative that evolution is based on abundance, on will, and on superfluity, rather than want, deprivation, and scarcity. The struggle for existence does in fact occur, "but as an exception; the total appearance of life is not the extremity, not starvation, but rather riches, profusion, even absurd squandering—and where there is a struggle, it is a struggle for *power*." Nietzsche's counterhypothesis as an explanation for natural selection is the ubiquitous and somewhat vaguely defined "will to power": "The struggle for existence is only an *exception,* a temporary restriction of the will to life. The great and the small struggle always revolves around superiority, around growth and expansion, around power—in accordance with the will to power which is the will of life" (*GS* 292). This explanation involving the "will to power," a term that is best conceived as the elementary life force, appears to have superseded the earlier reliance on internal features. What had originally been conceived as an expression of an inner and individual struggle with the environment becomes a manifestation of a more general, supra-individual power.

Nietzsche's most serious objection to Darwinism involves what he takes to be an implicit claim concerning the progress and perfection of the species. His views are based almost entirely on observations concerning the human species, which, we should note, was mentioned in Darwin's *Origin of the Species* just a single time. According to Nietzsche, if there is a struggle for existence, then it is not the strongest, the most beautiful, and the most genial who prevail, but the most base and common. For this reason the species as a whole is not headed for perfection, but for mediocrity based on the lowest common denominator: "With the struggle for existence one counts on the death of the weakest beings and the survival of the most robust and most gifted; as a consequence one imagines a continuous growth of perfection for the species. We have assured ourselves, in contrast, that in the struggle for life chance benefits the weak as well as it does the strong, that cunning often supplements strength with an advantage, that the fruitfulness of the species stands in a remarkable rapport with the chances for destruction" (*SW* 13: 315).

We can resolve the paradoxical situation that Nietzsche describes, in which the weak prevail over the strong, if we consider that the strong and the genial in Nietzsche's terms are not necessarily the best suited to the exigencies of life, especially modern life. In Nietzsche's view the weak are associated with intelligence and spirit, which enable them to overcome their natural weakness and to survive. The "strongest and happiest are weak" (*SW* 13: 303), especially when these exceptional human beings have to confront the great masses with their herd instincts. Nietzsche's chief difficulty with Darwinism is therefore that it does not account adequately for the very phenomenon that he detects in Germany and Europe of his own time: the decline in greatness, the destruction of genuine culture, the disappearance of exceptional figures that he considers the highest specimens. If the fittest have indeed prevailed, if the struggle for life has resulted in a victory for the masses, in short, if Darwin's theory has accurately predicted the dubious "progress" of Nietzsche's contemporary Europe, then Darwinism must be considered simply a biologistic apology for the decadence of the nineteenth century. Nietzsche's anti-Darwinism is firmly rooted in his conviction that the mediocrity and leveling he witnesses around him are not progress and do not represent the survival of anything but the average and contemptuous, and in his hope that this mediocrity and leveling can be overcome.

The instrument that Nietzsche introduces to embody this overcoming is the overman. It is his evolutionary alternative, his contribution to a biologistic theory of development that would lead to something more noble and more elite than the herd that comprises nineteenth-century reality. His differences with Darwinism are thus not to be understood as a dispute about the possibility of evolution, but about the direction and goal of evolution. His belief is that the "human being as a species is *not* progressing. Higher types are certainly achieved, but they do not survive. The level of the species is *not* raised" (*SW* 13: 316). Simultaneously he holds that the present "domestication" of the human being, the adaptation of the human being to exigencies of his contemporary society, is not a development that cannot be reversed. Beneath the surface of the tame, moral, and religious creatures that populate Europe is the "wild" man, the genuine "return to nature" (*SW* 13: 317). Because the natural course of "evolution" appears to favor leveling and disadvantage geniality, his vision calls for a conscious development, a willed evolution toward a higher type of human being. In a late section in the notebooks entitled "The Overman," Nietzsche clarifies as follows:

> My question is *not* what will supersede man: rather, what kind of man of higher value should be chosen, willed, *bred*. . . . Humankind does not represent a development to something better; or something higher; in the sense in which it is believed today: the European of the 19th century is, in his value, far inferior to the European of the Renaissance; progression in time is simply not with any necessity a raising, an increasing, a strengthening. . . . In another sense there is a continuous success in individual cases in the most different places on earth and from the most various cultures; in these cases a higher type is indeed apparent: something that is an "overman" in relationship to the totality of humanity. Such fortunate cases of great success were always possible and will perhaps always be possible. (*SW* 13: 191)

The overman in Nietzsche's thought is thus the answer to a series of problems presented to him by his study of evolutionary biology and his observation of a decadent society. He represents the overcoming of all that is wrong—in Nietzsche's view—with nineteenth century society and at the same time the realization of a conscious act of will. He is the antithesis of the Judeo-Christian morality and the democratic spirit of the age. He is the answer to Darwin, John Stuart Mill, and Karl Marx, the perfect response to the biological, the philosophical, and the historical tendencies of Nietzsche's times.

Eternal Recurrence and the Conservation of Energy

Along with the overman the second philosophical highlight of
Zarathustra in most Nietzsche interpretations is the teaching of eternal
recurrence, which is explicated most fully in the third book. Nietzsche
presents the hypothesis of the infinite repetition of all things and events
as a revelation of the early 1880s, but there are anticipations of it already
in the second of the *Untimely Meditations* (*ADH* 12–13). In aphorism 341
of the *Gay Science* the notion is presented for the first time in its fully
developed form. Unlike most of the other aphorisms in the volume, this
one is structured as a question followed by a choice of alternative
responses. Under the title "The greatest weight," Nietzsche poses the
following query to his reader:

> What, if some day or night a demon were to steal after you into your
> loneliest loneliness and say to you: "This life as you now live it and have
> lived it, you will have to live once more and innumerable times more; and
> there will be nothing new in it, but every pain and every joy and every
> thought and sigh and everything unutterably small or great in your life
> will have to return to you, all in the same succession and sequence—even
> this spider and this moonlight between the trees, and even this moment
> and I myself. The eternal hourglass of existence is turned upside down
> again and again, and you with it, speck of dust!" (*GS* 273)

Nietzsche gives two alternative responses to the hypothetical question of
this demon. The first is a reaction of extreme despair that would be
accompanied by the gnashing of teeth and the cursing of the bearer of
such ill tidings. The second and obviously preferable response is an affirmation of the divinity of such a thought. In Nietzsche's view the
hypothesis of eternal recurrence—or, more accurately, the acceptance of
this hypothesis—has the power to transform the individual and to place
the heaviest weight on human action. It can potentially lead to a radically different self-understanding, for one would have to be well disposed
toward oneself in order to "*crave nothing more fervently* than this ultimate
eternal confirmation and seal" (*GS* 274). In terms of personal behavior
and action, the stakes that Nietzsche sets are extremely high; eternal
recurrence has ramifications for the core of our very being.

In *Zarathustra* Nietzsche presents "eternal recurrence" less hypotheti-
cally. It is mentioned in the second section of volume three, which bears
the title "On the Vision and the Riddle." At this point in the loose narrative of the book Zarathustra is aboard a ship, and after two day's

silence he deigns to speak to his comrades, relating to them a riddle. He tells of walking upward on a rocky path, when his devil, half dwarf and half mole, dripped lead into his ear. The lead is the statement that what goes up must come down. "O Zarathustra, far indeed have you thrown the stone, but it will fall back on yourself," says the "spirit of gravity" (*Geist der Schwere*). After the dwarf falls silent, and silence reigns for a long time, Zarathustra finally bursts out his reply, more or less a challenge: "Dwarf! It is you or I!" And he continues: "But I am the stronger of us two: you do not know my abysmal thought. *That* you could not bear!" The thought Zarathustra hides within him is the hypothesis of eternal recurrence. He relates it to the dwarf (and hence to the reader) as a parable: "Behold this gateway, dwarf! . . . It has two faces. Two paths meet here; no one has yet followed either to its end. This long lane stretches back for an eternity. And the long lane out there, that is another eternity. They contradict each other, these paths; they offend each other face to face; and it is here at this gateway that they come together. The name of the gateway is inscribed above 'Moment.' But whoever would follow one of them, on and on, farther and farther—do you believe, dwarf, that these paths contradict each other eternally?" The dwarf tries to interpret this parable in a simple fashion, claiming that all truth is crooked and time is circular. But Zarathustra, however, believes that his thoughts are more profound and more momentous:

> "Behold," I continued, "this moment! From this gateway, Moment, a long, eternal lane leads *backward*: behind us lies an eternity. Must not whatever *can* walk have walked on this lane before? Must not whatever *can* happen have happened, have been done, have passed by before? And if everything has been there before—what do you think, dwarf, of this moment? Must not this gateway too have been there before? And are not all things knotted together so firmly that this moment draws after it *all* that is to come? Therefore—itself too? For whatever *can* walk—in this long lane out *there* too, it *must* walk once more.
>
> And this low spider, which crawls in the moonlight, and this moonlight itself, and I and you in the gateway, whispering together, whispering of eternal things—must not all of us have been there before? And return and walk in that other lane, out there, before us, in this long dreadful lane—must we not eternally return?" (*Z* 267–71)

The parable continues with the tale of the black snake in the throat of the young shepherd. But this portion of the text relates less to the doctrine of eternal recurrence than to Zarathustra as the possessor of the doctrine.

No matter how we as readers may evaluate the doctrine of eternal recurrence, it is clear that Nietzsche was fascinated by it, indeed, at times obsessed with it. In *Twilight of the Idols,* for example, he connects eternal recurrence with the Dionysian, declaring himself to be "the last disciple of the philosopher Dionysus, — I, the teacher of eternal recurrence" (*TI* 563). And in his notes from the 1880s we find frequent reference to the doctrine. Usually eternal recurrence has been viewed exclusively as a postulate that has ontological, ethical, or metaphysical dimensions. As we have already seen, Nietzsche's own discussions are suggestive for these aspects, and there is no reason to deny that the belief in such a doctrine would significantly alter our way of understanding ourselves in relationship to the world and to history. At the same time it is relatively certain that at the origin of this controversial hypothesis lies Nietzsche's preoccupation with theories of natural science in the nineteenth century. In particular eternal recurrence is informed by the principles of thermodynamics, or at least by the way in which Nietzsche most likely understood these principles.

We should remember that thermodynamics was "in the air" at the time that Nietzsche was writing. The clear enunciation of the first two principles of thermodynamics was the accomplishment of Rudolf Julius Clausius, a German mathematician and physicist, in 1850, and throughout the century it was a topic that was often discussed. Although Nietzsche never refers to Clausius, he does make reference to Julius Robert Mayer (1814–73), a physicist and physician who was one of the key theorists dealing with the transfer of heat into work. It is not surprising to find that Nietzsche's first mention of Mayer comes in notebooks written from the spring to the autumn of 1881. Eternal recurrence is the great discovery of August 1881. Obviously Mayer is not the "source" of Nietzsche's eternal recurrence; we have already noted that the notion is anticipated in earlier works, and it was certainly a familiar philosophical notion in ancient and modern times. Rather, the theories dealing with the transfer of energy, as they were formulated in the nineteenth century, provide a scientific legitimization for Nietzsche's own endeavors to discover laws that reign in the universe. As with the overman and evolutionary biology, Nietzsche's eternal recurrence participates in an ongoing discourse that encompasses the science of his times.[7]

Especially significant for eternal recurrence are what have become known as the first two laws of thermodynamics, which deal with the relationship of heat to other forms of energy. The first law of thermodynamics, which postulates that energy can be neither created nor destroyed, accords rather well with Nietzsche's doctrine of eternal recurrence. Known popularly as a theory of the conservation of energy, the first law suggested to Nietzsche that at one point or another in time the specific amounts of energy in specific forms would be the same as they were at another point, and that if one waited long enough the same situation would again come about. Indeed, Nietzsche evidently believed that the first law of thermodynamics actually entails his hypothesis: "The proposition of the conservation of energy demands *eternal recurrence*" (*SW* 12: 205). The second law of thermodynamics, however, presented Nietzsche with a philosophical conundrum, since it apparently contradicts eternal recurrence. Commonly conceived as postulating an eventual and inevitable state of equilibrium or stasis, this scientific postulate suggested to Nietzsche that identical states of matter would not occur no matter how long one waited. If a state of equilibrium were in fact reached at some point in time, then it would be wrong to insist on the recurrence of a previous state before equilibrium. The notion of a state of equilibrium thus directly negates Nietzsche's hypothesis of eternal recurrence, and he therefore felt compelled to confront the second law of thermodynamics, as we shall see, in the notes he composed around the time of the writing of *Zarathustra*.

At the very least, however, Nietzsche's reflections during the late summer and autumn of 1881 indicate clearly that he took natural science very seriously when writing his philosophy, and that his postulate of eternal recurrence in *The Gay Science* and in *Zarathustra* is inextricably bound to his scientific readings at the time. The following is a sampling from his reasoning in his notebooks prior to the inclusion of eternal recurrence in published works:

> The total amount of energy [*All-Kraft*] is limited, not "infinite." Let us beware of such conceptual excesses! Consequently, the number of states [*Lagen*], combinations, changes, and evolutions [*Entwicklungen*] of this energy is tremendously great and practically immeasurable, but in any case finite and not infinite. But the time through which this total energy works is infinite. That means that all possible developments must have taken place already. Consequently, the present development is a repetition, and thus also that which gave rise to it, and that which arises from it, and so backward and forward again! Insofar as the totality of states of energy [*die Gesammtlage aller Kräfte*] always recurs, everything has happened innumerable times. (*SW* 9: 523)
>
> . . .
>
> *Infinitely* new alterations and states of a definite energy is a contradiction, no matter how numerous and slight one conceives the alterations,

presupposing that the energy exists in perpetuity. One can conclude from this (1) either energy is active only from a specific time onward and will cease to be active at some point—but the beginning of activity is *absurd*: if it were in equilibrium, it would be eternally in this state. (2) Or there are not infinitely new alterations, but one circle of a definite number of alterations plays itself repeatedly: activity is infinite, the number of products and states of energy is finite. (*SW* 9: 558–59)

. . .

If all possibilities of order and relation of energies are not already exhausted, then infinity would not have occurred. Because this must be, there must be no new possibilities, and everything must have already been, infinite times. (*SW* 9: 500)

Nietzsche proceeds with similar thoughts in quite a few reflections in this section of his notebooks, playing with different possibilities and formulations. While the scientific value of his musings is probably not very high, it is significant that the value of natural science for him was. Most important is that the notion of eternal recurrence is developed in 1881 in conjunction with what Nietzsche views as scientific theory and is corroborated, he believes, by discoveries in natural science.

It is also interesting to note that where Nietzsche's theory of eternal recurrence does not agree with scientific theory, he feels he is equally up to the challenge. A case in point is the second principle of thermodynamics. In 1881 he writes: "If an equilibrium of energy had been reached at any time, then it would still persist: therefore it has not occurred. The current conditions contradict the hypothesis" (*SW* 9: 534). Evidently disturbed by the fact that his doctrine of eternal recurrence is not supported by accepted scientific theory, he returns to this problem in the late 1880s.

I came across this thought (eternal recurrence) in earlier thinkers: every time it was limited by some additional second thoughts (—mostly theological, in favor of a *creator spiritus*). If the world could really reach stasis, dry up, die out, become *nothing,* or if it could reach a state of equilibrium, or if it in general really had some kind of a goal, which would include in itself duration, invariability, the once-and-for-all (in short, metaphysically stated, if becoming *could* flow into being or into nothing), then it should have reached this state already. But it has not reached this state, and it follows from this. . . . This is the only certainty, which we have in our hands, to serve as a corrective against the great mass of possible world-hypotheses. If, for example, mechanics [*der Mechanismus*] cannot escape the consequence of a final state, which Thomson deduced from it [Nietzsche means William

Thomson, better known as Lord Kelvin, the noted Scottish physicist (1824–1907), who was a leading figure in the development of thermodynamics], then mechanics is thereby refuted. (*SW* 13: 375)

The point, again, is not how accurately Nietzsche understood thermodynamics (which he calls here mechanics), or whether his theory was original or derivative, but rather that his "refutation" of the second law of thermodynamics as well as his hypothesis of eternal recurrence were a part of an ongoing discourse that included both philosophy and natural science as partners in the discovery of truth.[8]

A Scientific Perspective on Perspectivism

A third "philosophical" notion that has a definite relationship to the natural sciences is "perspectivism." In its most accessible form perspectivism suggests simply a relativistic manner of observing the world and its phenomena: everyone has his own individual perspective on the world; there is no single and universal objective standard, as the methods adopted by natural sciences maintain. But while there is no doubt that Nietzsche disputed the ability of human beings to grasp the world objectively, and that he therefore undercut some presumptions of a simplistically conceived scientific method, his actual notion of perspectivism was much more complex and, in fact, had a good deal to do with his understanding of the natural world. Indeed, he explicitly criticized the facile understanding of perspectivism as a subjective comprehension of the world: "'Everything is *subjective*,' you say: but even that is an interpretation. The 'subject' is nothing given, rather something added on, something that hides behind. — Is it not ultimately necessary to place the interpreter behind the interpretation? Even that is fiction, hypothesis" (*SW* 12: 315). What is obvious from this passage is that Nietzsche did not believe in perspectival relativism. His particular criticism here is aimed at the notion of an already constituted subject perceiving from a fixed position. If we go along with Nietzsche and consider the subject itself as something that is a result of interpretation, just as the different views of the world are interpretations, then we cannot subscribe so easily to a relativistic hypothesis predicated on individual sovereignty and equality. The central point here is that the non-existence of facts or an objective standard does not imply an equality of interpretations or subject positions.

Indeed, the remainder of this passage makes two seminal points about perspectivism. First, it asserts a clear connection between perspectivism and a general theory of epistemology. Nietzsche's main concern in developing the notion of perspectivism is to correct common theories about how we know the world. Time and again he stresses that there is no eternal sense or meaning behind the world of perceptions. Nietzsche is referring to a long tradition of Western thought that postulates something real or something more real than what we perceive. Plato's realm of ideas, which Nietzsche considers to be the first in a long line of epistemological errors, is exemplary for a tradition that propagates a split between appearance and reality. For Nietzsche, this split is the fundamental principle of all metaphysical thought, and his opposition to it is consistently maintained in his writings of the 1880s. With regard to perspectivism, Nietzsche writes as follows: "To the extent that the word 'knowledge' has any meaning at all, the world is knowable: but it is *interpretable* in different ways; it does not have any meaning behind it, rather countless meanings 'Perspectivism'" (*SW* 12: 315). It would be a mistake to reduce this view to subjective idealism; Nietzsche is not making the existence of the world dependent on the existence of a knowing subject. Rather, he is stating that knowledge is a human way of interacting with the world, and that for this reason there is no sense or meaning hidden from us. The interpretations or perspectives that we have are all that there is.

It is perhaps inaccurate to state that "we have" these perspectives, however, since Nietzsche does not admit that there is a constituted and integral subject, a stable and uniform perspective from which phenomena of the external world are perceived. The relativist interpretation of perspectivism is wrong because it introduces just such a subject. Nietzsche's view is that, first, the very fact that we interpret the world in interacting with it reveals that interpretation is a human need. His reasoning seems to be that the human being, in contrast to other creatures on earth, is the only species that exhibits the quirk of trying to understand the world during its confrontations with it. That there is no necessity to have knowledge, to interact with the world as a knowing being, seems to him proven by the observation of other animal species. For him it is not a subject located somewhere inside the brain or a spirit somewhere outside the body that enters into cognition, but rather a part of the material being. Our cognition is therefore part of the necessity that comes with our humanity: it is "our needs" that interpret the world.

Second, Nietzsche believes there is no single position from which we interact with the world, but rather several competing positions from which we may receive conflicting interpretations. This proposition would follow from the fact that we have various needs and not one unified need with regard to external phenomena. It is "our drives and their pro and con" that determine our interpretation and cognition: "Every drive is a type of thirst for power; every one has its perspective, which it wants to force on the other drives as a norm" (*SW* 12: 315). The human being is comprised of warring factions, not of unanimity. Our knowledge of the world is a product of conflicts and victories that go on within us and without our knowledge. Perspectivism, far from describing a notion of liberal tolerance for all viewpoints, is actually closer to a theory of drives and of the way in which internal struggles are fought out in the process we conceive as cognition.

The single mention of perspectivism in Nietzsche's published works bears out this view. It occurs in *The Gay Science* in one of the lengthiest aphorisms (#354), which bears the title *On the "genius of the species."*[9] The largest part of the discussion revolves around consciousness, its origins, its functions, and its ramifications for the human being. Not surprisingly Nietzsche alludes from the outset to two realms of knowledge that have helped to provide the explanations he finds most useful: physiology and evolution ("the history of the animals"). Physiology and its adjectival forms appear with increasing frequency in Nietzsche's works of the 1880s and designate types of explanations that are tied to vital life forces. Often physiology is placed in juxtaposition to metaphysics, theology, ethics, politics, and economics as a mode of clarifying real interactions rather than their reflexes in the mind. Evolutionary biology, as we have already seen, is a constant source of reference for Nietzsche when passing judgment on human development. Nietzsche believes that the scientific theories of his times verify that consciousness is a secondary organ. All of the functions that are necessary for life can be carried out well—perhaps even better— without recourse to consciousness, which consists of a mirror of these actions in the mind. "We could think, feel, will, and remember, and we could also 'act' in every sense of that word, and yet none of all this would have to 'enter our consciousness' (as one says metaphorically)" (*GS* 297). Indeed, for most of what we do consciousness is superfluous or, as Nietzsche will contend when he dissects moral values, pernicious. Although it is lauded as the "genius of the species," in reality consciousness is extra baggage, something that has no value for those actions that we usually consider most important in our lives.

This reevaluation of the role of consciousness is perhaps the most original and provocative dimension of Nietzsche's philosophy. In previous philosophical systems, and particularly in the German idalists of the nineteenth century, consciousness was conceived as the pinnacle of development and as the most commonly cited feature that distinguishes the human being from the animal world. Nietzsche disagrees. While most philosophers considered consciousness a source of perfection, Nietzsche feels it is a symptom of immaturity; while previous thinkers counted on consciousness to rectify mistakes and to bridle the wayward passions, Nietzsche believes it is the source of errors; and while common wisdom placed thought above drives in their contribution to human behavior, Nietzsche overturns this hierarchy.

> Consciousness is the last and latest development of the organic and hence what is most unfinished and unstrong. Consciousness gives rise to countless errors that lead an animal or man to perish sooner than necessary, "exceeding destiny," as Homer puts it. If the conserving association of the instincts were not so very much more powerful, and if it did not serve on the whole as a regulator, humanity would have to perish of its misjudgments and its fantasies with open eyes, of its lack of thoroughness and its credulity—in short, of its consciousness; rather, without the former, humanity would long have disappeared. (GS 85)

Of note in this passage is that Nietzsche, as always, conceives of the development of consciousness in terms of the paradigm of evolutionary biology and physiology. For him consciousness is one way—and not a very efficient way at that—in which the human being mediates drives and desires with the external world.[10]

Two questions arise from this view of consciousness. The first has to do with the reason that most previous thinkers and traditional wisdom ascribe such a priority to thought. If the situation is really as Nietzsche describes it, then why have we been deceived for so long about the real role of consciousness in our interactions with the world? For Nietzsche the answer to this question is that the hegemony of consciousness—not over our actions, but over our belief concerning what guides our actions—is itself a long process in the evolution of humankind.[11] The second question is why consciousness came into being in the first place. If reason and intellect are so inefficient in dealing with the world, if we are better off relying on our instincts, then why did the species need to develop an organ that reflects on knowledge? Nietzsche's answer to this is that the development of consciousness was ultimately driven by our need to communicate with one another. At first this need arose only between human beings, but later communication also provided a protection for the vulnerable human species in a hostile environment.

Gradually humankind therefore had to receive some kind of understanding of its actions, thoughts, feelings, and movements, and the entrance of these "reflections" into consciousness—and into language—occurs in order to facilitate communication with others. Consciousness develops, in short, so that the human being will "know" him/herself and can pass this "knowledge" along to other members of the species.

The role Nietzsche ascribes to language is thus interesting and often misunderstood. In contrast to twentieth-century theorists who place language at the center of the human universe, linguistic ability represents for Nietzsche a secondary characteristic that is on the same level as consciousness. Language, of course, is not representational in Nietzsche's scheme; it does not reflect the external world. But it is a mirror, however distorted this mirror may be, of *internal* sensations. In his notes for a lecture course on ancient rhetoric, Nietzsche provides a brief sketch of linguistic utterance based on a neurological model:

> The human being creating language does not capture things or events, but *stimuli*: he does not reproduce sensations, but rather reproductions of sensations. The sensation, through which a nerve stimulus is called forth, does not capture the thing itself: this sensation is represented externally by an image. . . . It is not things that enter our consciousness, but the way in which we relate to these things: the *pithanon* [persuasiveness]. The complete essence of things is never captured. Our tonal utterances in no way wait until our perception and experience have helped us to a many-sided, somehow respectable cognition of things: they occur immediately when the stimulus has been felt.[12]

In 1888 the explanation is similar in its scientific assumptions. Nietzsche believes that internal experience enters consciousness after it finds a language that the individual understands, but the entire process is precipitated by the stimulation of nerves: "The whole notion of 'inner experience' rests on the fact that one seeks and imagines a cause for the excitation of nerve centers" (*SW* 13: 459). The secret to language, whose development goes "hand in hand" (*GS* 299) with the appearance of consciousness, is that it is reaction to neurological stimuli.

One of the consequences Nietzsche draws from this "scientifically" informed view of language and consciousness is that both are inaccurate registers of individual sensations. By the time that nerve stimuli have been translated into consciousness and are expressed in language, they have been reduced to a common denominator and robbed of their uniqueness. The social nature of language and consciousness is part of our "herd mentality" and has to be carefully distinguished from our individuality, which is leveled in the process of translation. This is the essence of perspectivism for Nietzsche, a word that he used synonymously with phenomenalism. It refers not to the equal validity of all viewpoints, but rather to the necessary inaccuracy of all contents of consciousness and all expressions of these contents in language. "This is the essence of phenomenalism and perspectivism as *I* understand them: Owing to the nature of *animal consciousness,* the world of which we can become conscious is only a surface- and sign-world, a world that is made common and meaner; whatever becomes conscious *becomes* by the same token shallow, thin, relatively stupid, general, sign, herd signal; all becoming conscious involves a great and thorough corruption, falsification, reduction to superficialities, and generalization" (*GS* 299–300).

References to perspectivism in Nietzsche's work are therefore usually accompanied by disparaging remarks. For example, in an extensive note written in the spring of 1884, Nietzsche observes that in making the "mechanical world order" conscious, we need a "perspective-apparatus," which makes possible "(1) a certain stability [*ein gewisses Stillstehen*], (2) simplification (3) selection and elimination" (*SW* 11: 99). This apparatus creates the impression of constant being instead of allowing us to perceive eternal becoming, and it permits us only a limited and therefore inaccurate perspective on the world. For this reason Nietzsche claims: "This perspectival world, this world for the eye, feeling, and ear is very false, compared even with a much finer sensory apparatus" (*SW* 11: 146). Nietzsche holds out the possibility that we can achieve more sensitive and accurate views of the world as our consciousness develops. He emphasizes that in evolutionary terms consciousness is a recently acquired capability that has perhaps not reached its fullest potential in the species. But for the time being, consciousness, language, reason, and intellect—all those features of the human species that have usually been valued most highly—condemn us to a false and limited perspectivism.

Breeding: The Scientific Solution to Social Ills

Until now we have seen that Nietzsche's reception of natural science is intimately linked with his conceptual, philosophical universe. Most of the central notions in his works were developed in close connection with theories in the physical or biological sciences, and his notes and works make frequent reference to contemporary research and publications. Nietzsche most frequently adopted notions from the natural sciences to explain the world and the human beings that inhabited the world. Like most of his contemporaries, however, Nietzsche also harbored thoughts of applying natural scientific theories to cure social ills. For Nietzsche the problems in nineteenth-century Europe, in particular in Germany, were many and manifest. In the cultural realm, as we have witnessed in chapters 2 and 3, Nietzsche was aware of a severe decline in excellence. Although he had hoped for a renaissance in European societies with the music of Richard Wagner, he was soon disappointed in these hopes, and his outlook became bleaker as time progressed. In the social and political world Nietzsche observed a similar degeneracy. As we shall see in the next chapter, the democratizing tendencies in European countries, which extended suffrage to the working class and encouraged such "leveling" movements as socialism and women's emancipation, were symptoms of a decay in the social fabric and a hindrance to the production of greatness. The widespread adherence to various moral and religion value systems, two enervating manifestations in the evolution of the human species (to be discussed in chapters 6 and 7), demonstrated similarly that modern Europe was headed in the wrong direction.

To remedy the disastrous conditions that prevailed across Europe and to reverse the cultural and intellectual decline on the continent, Nietzsche, like many of his contemporaries, contemplated a biological solution to this situation in turning to eugenics. This biologically based remedy to a perceived social degeneracy had a slightly different meaning in the nineteenth century than it does today. In the aftermath of the rampant racism under National Socialism, as well as various eugenic "experiments" in the United States, we are apt to consider state intervention into reproduction in the private sphere to be a repugnant and fascist solution to social ills. In the late nineteenth and early twentieth century, however, it was a respected, if hotly disputed, theory that could claim reputable adherents among many intellectuals and a good portion of the medical establishment.[13] The word "eugenics," which Nietzsche did not use, was introduced in 1881 by Sir Francis Galton, a cousin of Charles Darwin, to describe a program of breeding that would combat the decay in European civilization.[14] Shortly after Galton articulated his program, it had gained many adherents and attracted much commentary both positive and negative. Not all advocates of eugenics were racists or racial purists; many would have considered themselves progressives trying to deal with complex social problems in the most effective manner.

Nietzsche's views on this issue are complex. In many of his published writings his remarks on breeding tend to be more circumspect.

In some texts, however, the biological trappings of eugenics are rather evident. At the end of the fifth chapter of *Beyond Good and Evil,* for example, Nietzsche writes despairingly about the degenerate forms of political organizations he finds around him—he refers specifically to the "democratic movement"—and seeks hope in new philosophers and new leaders.

> To teach man the future of man as his *will,* as dependence on a human will, and to prepare for great enterprises and collective experiments in discipline and breeding (*Zucht und Züchtung*), so as to make an end to the gruesome domination of chance and nonsense that has hitherto been called 'history'—the nonsense of the 'greatest number' is only its latest form—for that a new kind of philosopher and commander will some time be needed, in face of whom whatever has existed on earth of hidden, dreadful and benevolent spirits may well look pale and dwarfed. It is the image of such leaders which hovers before *our* eyes. (*BGE* 108)

Nietzsche is here responding to the perceived problem of social degeneracy. His solution is somewhat vague, but it involves a reversal of the decline in the social order by refusing to leave procreation to chance; the new philosophers and leaders will have the task of introducing experimentation in genetic engineering—the rendition of *Zucht und Züchtung* as "discipline and breeding" contains far too little nature and far too much nurture. At one point Nietzsche voices his fear that such leaders will "not appear or might fail or might degenerate," thus reinforcing the biological foundation of his vision (*BGE* 108). The "collective degeneration of man" can be countered, Nietzsche indicates, by the controlled production of a species according to "a transvaluation of values" (*BGE* 109).

In the final chapter of *Beyond Good and Evil* the specific evolutionary character of Nietzsche's reflections on a higher type of human being becomes apparent. Aphorism 262 begins with general observations on the development of species: "A *species* arises, a type becomes fixed and strong, through protracted struggle against essentially constant *unfavourable* conditions" (*BGE* 180). Nietzsche then cites the experience of "breeders" (*Züchter*), according to which superfluity in nourishment leads to the production of prodigious as well as monstrous variations. In human societies Nietzsche sees an analogous case in aristocratic communities. In the Greek city states or in Venice the population was subjected to voluntary or involuntary principles of breeding in order to preserve the species. The difficulty in these societies was that a superabundance did not exist and that they were constantly threatened by neighbors. To maintain and propagate excellence, therefore, a strict morality had to be developed. "Every aristocratic morality is intolerant, in the education of the young, in the measures it takes with respect to women, in marriage customs, in the relations between young and old, in the penal laws (which are directed only at deviants): it counts intolerance itself among the virtues under the name of 'justice'" (*BGE* 181).

Important here is that Nietzsche conceives of certain practical measures regarding procreation—marriage and the dispensation over women—as acceptable, as well as historical, means for protecting societies against degeneration. It is evident that Nietzsche's notion of breeding (*Züchtung*) in this aphorism goes beyond the simple biological since he conceives of ethics and law as part of social "breeding" mechanisms. At the same time, it is also evident that procreation is included as part of breeding, and that Nietzsche expresses approval of such control over procreation, especially when compared to the "chance" factors that predominate in modern societies. What separates Nietzsche's notion of breeding from eugenics, therefore, is not that he did not subscribe to evolutionary and biological principles, but rather that he conceives of even social and juridical values as part of the evolutionary process.

One of the reasons that it is so difficult to separate neatly the social from the biological in Nietzsche's notion of breeding is that he appears to have accepted the inheritance of acquired physical and mental characteristics. This "Lamarckian" dimension to his thought appears often in notes he composed during the 1880s.[15] At one point he observes that "what the father bequeaths to the son are the *most practiced* habits (*not* the most valued!). The son *betrays* the father. The diligence of a scholar corresponds to the activity of his father; for example, when he sat in the office or when he 'worked' only as country parish" (*SW* 9: 506). Quite obviously Nietzsche is thinking here about his own abilities as a scholar and researcher, and how he inherited these dispositions from his own father. In another passage Nietzsche indicates that he, like his contemporaries, was not quite clear about the mechanisms by which these inherited characteristics could affect the son. If habits develop in the father at a later time, after the birth of the son, or after his conception, then it is difficult to see how this genetic material could be transferred to his offspring. Nietzsche suggests a theory that would have these characteristics present in a latent state, so that they can develop in both the father—at a time after the birth—and in the children—because the disposition is what is really inherited. "Our parents still grow in us; their characteristics, which are acquired later and are also present in the embryo, need time. We become acquainted with the characteristics of the father when he was a man only when we become a man" (*SW* 9: 538). From such passages we can conclude at the very least that heredity, as conceived by thinkers such as Galton, was very much a part of Nietzsche's worldview.

In his notes we can also confirm without much effort that Nietzsche did not shy away from even the most abhorrent consequences of eugenics. He was fully conscious of the fact that the type of breeding that he advocated could not be a general phenomenon. As in past "aristocratic" societies, the masses would be sacrificed for the sake of a select portion of the species. His notion of breeding was thus in consonance with his cultural theory from the early 1870s, which also advocated the sacrifice of the masses for the sake of higher specimens of humanity. As early as 1881, he wrote that the "new problem" is "whether one part of humanity can be educated at the cost of the other to a higher race. Breeding—" (*SW* 9: 577). Repeatedly he regrets the failure or the ponderousness with which the "natural process of breeding" proceeds, proposing instead that "*whole parts* of the earth" be devoted to "*conscious experiments*": "why shouldn't we be able to accomplish with human beings what the Chinese have learned to do with trees—that it carries roses on one side and pears on the other?" (*SW* 9: 547–48).

The notion that one part of the human species would be devoted to "fruitful" activities for the benefit of a "rosier" and privileged few is usually expressed by Nietzsche less symbolically and occasionally even with a shocking crassness. After advocating "*selection,*" he comments that "the tendency" should be the "extermination of all the pitiful, disfigured, degenerate! Not preservation at any price!" (*SW* 9: 250). In another instance, he wrote with a callousness uncommon for even his works: "— to acquire that tremendous energy of greatness, in order to form the future human being through breeding and, on the other hand, through the annihilation of millions of deformed failures, and *not to perish* because of the suffering that one *creates,* whose equal was never known!—" (*SW* 11: 98). Throughout his notes from the 1880s we find similar passages in which Nietzsche affirms genetic experimentation as a means to improve the species and to reinstitute greatness and geniality in human endeavor.

Nietzsche must have recognized that the eugenically perfected species of which he dreamed would not be attainable without strict regulations, and his pronouncements about breeding are therefore often accompanied by references to specific social mechanisms to accomplish his goals. Above all his reflections focus on marriage, sexual desire, and procreation. Nietzsche recognized that sexual pleasure could not be legislated or regulated out of existence. At the same time and in accord with the aim of "ennobling" the species, he believed that marriage should not be left to chance, and that greatness could only be achieved with the restriction of procreation to those who would produce appropriate offspring. The following remarks penned in 1881 provide us with the full scope of his concerns.

> The satisfaction of sexual desire [*des Triebes*] should not lead to a practice by which the race suffers, that is, where there is no selection any more and everyone can pair off with everyone else and produce children. The extinction of many kinds of people is just as desirable as their reproduction. . . . Only marriages 1) for the purpose of higher evolution 2) in order to leave behind the fruits of such humanity.—For all others concubinage suffices, with the prevention of conception.—We must make an end to this silly frivolity. These silly women [*Gänse*] should not marry. Marriage should become more infrequent. Just walk though the big cities and ask yourself whether these people should procreate. Let them go to their whores. (*SW* 9:189)

Comments about the benefits of prostitution, especially for the working class so that their sexual desires could be satisfied outside of wedlock (*SW* 9: 597 and 472); about permission for marriages, which should not be a right, but something granted by higher authority; and about qualifications for parents (*SW* 9: 508–9) recur frequently in his notes during the next eight years. In some instances Nietzsche considered these matters in the most concrete terms, when he writes on measures of taxation, medical documentation, and legal prohibition for marriage and procreation.[16] It remains unclear who would be responsible for developing and enforcing such bureaucratic regulations since the state, in Nietzsche's view, had no interest in the "breeding of human beings" for "better quality," but only for "masses" (*SW* 9: 508). What is more evident is that Nietzsche, like many of his contemporaries, including a man such as Francis Galton, conceived of social mechanisms as an indispensable aid to solving a problem of degeneracy regarded as fundamentally biological.

The notes in which Nietzsche discusses breeding and social control in his posthumous writings are among the most unfortunate and embarrassing texts in his works. Although the most repugnant comments appear in his unpublished works, the statements in published volumes are only less abrasive and more ambiguous versions of his posthumous notebooks. In both cases they show us a man deeply troubled by perceptions of rampant decay and widespread triviality, by a perceived decline in greatness and creativity, and by the expansion of participatory government to those he felt unworthy of enfranchisement. But they also demonstrate the extent to which Nietzsche was involved with issues stemming from contemporary discussions of natural science. His references to the inheritance of acquired characteristics indicates he was informed about controversies in evolutionary biology, and his frequent allusions to breeding as a way to remedy the greatest challenges of his age exhibit a similarity to other, more properly "scientific" researchers in the nineteenth century. It remains unclear, of course, how much natural science Nietzsche really knew at firsthand, and how deeply versed he was in the details of the theories on which he appears to depend. There is nothing in his works that indicates he had anything more than a rudimentary comprehension of the "hard sciences" that informed theoretical developments in biology, chemistry, or physics. More important, however, is that, even in their "popular" dissemination, the natural sciences were for him fields of knowledge from which his philosophy drew and to which it responded. Although Nietzsche frequently expressed skepticism about the ultimate value and methods of the natural sciences, he, like many other nineteenth-century thinkers, was both fascinated and profoundly influenced by the "scientific" perspective of his age.

Chapter 5
The Social Observer

Nietzsche's direct exposure to issues of contemporary politics and society was extremely limited. In contrast to his preoccupation with the natural sciences, we find little evidence that he focused on the world of nineteenth-century Germany or Europe. He often expressed his intense dislike for newspapers and journalism and consequently avoided the very books and magazines that would have shed light on contemporary social and political affairs. Moreover, his life did not lend itself to extended contact with politics or with diverse social spheres. Although the majority of his social and political comments concern German affairs, he spent most of his mature and sane years in Switzerland, Italy, or France, and there is no evidence that he took a particular interest in current events in the "fatherland." His teaching kept him in academic circles; his enthusiasm for Wagner led him into a clique that was unrepresentative of most of German society; and in his later years illness confined him much of the time to his room or bed. That he was more familiar with—and influenced by—European events than most "philosophical" accounts admit is certainly true, but, at the same time, his reflections on current issues in European politics and society appear to be less the result of concerted study than of general, ingrained attitudes that were relatively uninformed by specifics.

We should therefore not expect to find in Nietzsche's works any detailed analysis of the social restructuring that was taking place in Germany and across Europe as part of the general process of industrialization and modernization. What we encounter most frequently are observations, usually in the form of aphorisms, small pieces of "wisdom" about politics and society. Since Nietzsche treated a great variety of topics in this off-hand fashion, the following discussions will concentrate on four areas in which his views have become most controversial and about which he has commented frequently: (1) The German Question, in particular his relationship to the German state and to German nationalism; (2) The Social Question, which includes his views on social stratification, but in particular issues surrounding workers and the working class; (3) The Women's Question, a topic that entails his attitude toward women, the women's movement of his times, and "feminism"; (4) The Jewish Question, encompassing his attitude toward Jews, anti-Semitism, and emancipation/integration. In all these areas Nietzsche drew on limited personal experience as well as literature of his era, sometimes adopting positions that are reprehensible to us today, while at other times disagreeing with the dominant tendencies in the European discussion. Although these four discussions will hardly exhaust Nietzsche's thought on politics and society, they will account for his views on perhaps the most important "questions" of his times.

The German Question

Like most young men growing up in the 1850s and 1860s, Nietzsche was initially attracted to the romantic nationalism prevalent in post-1848 Germany society. In his early life signs of nationalism abound. As a teenager Nietzsche formed a club intended to foster artistic creativity, but it was not coincidental that it was called "Germania." In Bonn, he joined one of the many nationalist fraternity clubs. And in correspondence with friends he wrote favorably of the Prussian army and its pan-German cause, celebrating the Prussian victory over Austria (SB 2: 142–43). Indeed, in Leipzig Nietzsche even engaged himself in an actual political campaign on the side of a nationalist candidate who was opposed to regional particularism. By the time the Franco-Prussian war broke out in 1870, Nietzsche felt it was his duty to participate on the German side, and his voluntary service indicates that he still believed in the German cause, although he had recently renounced his Prussian citizenship. However, even at this time, Nietzsche's nationalism was more focused on cultural revival than political supremacy. Unlike the Wagners, for example, who held a grudge against France and apparently beat the Prussian drums as much out of revenge as out of patriotism, Nietzsche was rather restrained in his pro-German and anti-French sentiments, concentrating instead on the task of preserving and promoting cultural excellence.[1] His relationship to the "German Question," even at this early stage in his career, was a matter of *Bildung* rather than political power.

Nietzsche's relatively reserved attitude toward German nationalism at the height of nationalist sentiment and his hopes for a rebirth of Greece on German soil help to explain his subsequent remarks about Germany and the Germans. To a large extent his disparaging comments on his countrymen and fatherland emanate from his bitter disappointment that

Germany had failed to carry out the cultural mission he had appointed to it. Although we encounter criticism of Germans and Germany in most of Nietzsche's works after 1872, his anti-German sentiments reach a climax in *Ecce Homo,* where "the German" comes to embody all the pernicious qualities associated with modern civilization.

> It is even part of my ambition to count as the despiser of the German *par excellence.* I expressed my *mistrust* of the German character already at the age of twenty-six (third untimely essay)—the Germans are impossible for me. Whenever I picture to myself a type of man that goes against all my instincts it always turns into a German. . . . The Germans are *canaille* [rabble, scum]. . . . One lowers oneself by commerce with Germans. . . . If I subtract my commerce with a few artists, above all with Richard Wagner, I have experienced not a single good hour with Germans. . . . Supposing the profoundest spirit of all the millennia appeared among the Germans, some goose of the Capitol would opine that its very unbeautiful soul came at least equally into consideration. (*EH* 123)

Even if we discount a large part of this vituperation as the ravings of a half-insane man, it seems evident that Nietzsche had a good deal of pent-up anger and malice against "the German" in him. We must suspect, therefore, that more than the dashing of a cultural dream was at stake for Nietzsche. Such emotional outbursts indicate not only disappointment and a resulting antipathy, but also the violation of a strong and powerful psychological bond. In Nietzsche's case he was probably separating himself emotionally from his Protestant upbringing and his family, from the German critics and readers who had not given him his due, and from the Wagnerians, who had succeeded where he failed in capturing public attention. The German Question in Nietzsche's writings is connected with a host of personal factors that structured Nietzsche's life, his aspirations, and his disappointments.

Nietzsche also had non-personal reasons for his attitude toward Germany. Chief among these was his opinion about the modern state, of which Germany was for him a prime example. Since at least the mid-1870s, Nietzsche portrays the contemporary European state as a promoter of decline and decadence. Arguing that it is the protector of the rights of the masses and the sign of a creeping democracy, he places the state in strict opposition to the hallowed notion of culture. As we have seen, the state is partially responsible for the decline in the educational institutions and the confounding of *Bildung* with training for the civil service. Nietzsche is not oblivious to the function of the state in protecting its population; particularly in his more mellow, middle peri-od, he recognizes some benefits that have accrued to the citizenry. But the advantages threaten to turn into disadvantages when the state becomes too expansive: "The state is a prudent institution for the pro-tection of individuals against one another: if it is completed and perfect-ed too far it will in the end enfeeble the individual and, indeed, dissolve him—that is to say, thwart the original purpose of the state in the most thorough way possible" (*HA* 113).

In his later works, however, Nietzsche becomes less differentiated in his views. By the appearance of *Twilight of the Idols* he had begun to reject all modern forms of government: "All our political theories and constitu-tions—and the 'German *Reich*' is by no means an exception—are conse-quences, necessary consequences, of decline; the unconscious effect of decadence has assumed mastery even over the ideals of some of the sci-ences" (*TI* 540–41). Although we today probably identify Bismarck's Germany with an autocratic régime in which the military and the aris-tocracy exercised an undemocratic hegemony under pseudo-parliamen-tary rule, Nietzsche's view is that the "Second *Reich*" is the symptom of a baneful democratizing movement that threatened to drag all of Europe into mediocrity. As a typical "modern" state, Germany, in Nietzsche's worldview, merits only abuse and disgust.

One of the chief reasons for Nietzsche's dismissive attitude toward the modern state has to do with its protection of a system of political parties. Nietzsche's early involvement with electoral politics evidently soured him to the parliamentary system in general, and his hostility became increasingly apparent in his writings. Throughout the 1870s and 1880s he remained a staunch opponent of politics as such. This does not mean that his writings have no political implications or that he desired no political effects—in the broader sense of the word "political"—but only that he disdained day-to-day political activity. Indeed, Nietzsche's cele-brated claim that he was "the last *anti-political* German" (*EH* 136) refers specifically to his antagonistic attitude to parliamentary politics and to the hegemony of politics over more important areas, such as cultural affairs.[2] Again Nietzsche's views are partially attributable to an antipa-thy toward what he perceived as a democratizing tendency in gover-nance. In *The Gay Science* he points out that at one time politics, like the military, was the domain of the nobility, and that Europe has gradually seen a shift away from aristocratic control. He continues: "And it is quite possible that some day one may find it [politics] so common and vulgar that, along with all party literature and journalism, one would classify it as 'prostitution of the spirit'" (*GS* 103).

His larger, "philosophical" objections have to do with what we might call the necessity to compromise and to reach consensus. Political parties, because they are organizations of many individuals, are based on falsehood and self-deception; they are an affirmation of another pernicious collective phenomenon, slave morality, and as such, they perpetrate (self-)deceit and decadence. In *The Antichrist* Nietzsche contends that lying to oneself is the precondition for any party: "of necessity, the party man becomes a liar" (*AC* 640). And in his initial remarks in the section on the state in *Human, All Too Human* he suggests that it is the necessity to pander to the populace that compels parties into simplistic propaganda: "The demagogic character and the intention to appeal to the masses is at present common to all political parties: on account of this intention they are all compelled to transform their principles into great *al fresco* stupidities and thus to paint them on the wall" (*HA* 161). Nietzsche's objection to parties is thus intimately related to his rejection of the new German state: instead of promoting greatness and genius, they cater to the rabble and destroy the hierarchy that is so essential for cultural achievement.

Nietzsche's politics are often identified with two terms that he mentions consistently in a positive light: the "good European" and "great politics." We should be careful, however, not to judge these notions uncritically. While there is little doubt that his "Europeanism" is meant to contrast with a narrow German nationalism, and that "great politics" are juxtaposed to the petty parliamentary maneuvers and election campaigns of the Second Reich, the ideological implications of these terms violate twentieth-century sensibilities. We should recall that at about the time Nietzsche was writing, the first discussions of German colonies were in progress. During the middle of the 1880s Germany, a late-comer to colonialism, obtained its first foreign acquisitions. Nietzsche, who had not previously commented on colonialism, but who was obviously sensitive to current events, wrote in his notebooks in the spring of 1884: "The way the Europeans found colonies proves their predatory nature" (*SW* 11: 56). Although this statement would appear to condemn European colonialism, the German term Nietzsche employs—*Raubtier-Natur* (nature of a beast of prey)—is often found in other contexts without any pejorative sense. In most writings from the 1880s the beast of prey (*Raubtier*) is contrasted with the despised herd, the domesticated animal that human beings have become under the leveling influences of Christianity and democracy.

Other texts from the 1880s indicate that these imperialist Europeans are the forerunners of the "good Europeans." In *Human, All Too Human,* for example, the "free spirits" and the "good Europeans" are equated and assigned the task of "the direction and supervision of the earth" (*HA* 332). And in *The Gay Science,* under the general heading "Our faith that Europe will become more virile," Nietzsche praises Napoleon as the destroyer of nationalism and a propagator of a European unity accomplished by force (*GS* 362). The *locus classicus* for "great politics," which is the outgrowth of good Europeanism, occurs in *Beyond Good and Evil.* Observing a "paralysis of will" spread unevenly across Europe, Nietzsche first catalogues the relative health and sickness of individual nations before he turns to his hope that Russia will become such a danger that the European nations will be compelled to band together and carry out their appointed task: *"to acquire a single will* by means of a new caste dominating all Europe, a protracted terrible will of its own which could set its objectives thousands of years ahead—so that the long-drawn-out comedy of its petty states and the divided will of its dynasties and democracies should finally come to an end. The time for petty politics is past: the very next century will bring with it the struggle for world dominion—the *compulsion* to great politics" (*BGE* 119). Nietzsche's vision for the European future negates the nationalism and party politics associated with Germany and thus solves the German Question; but it does so only at the cost of democracy and in the name of European imperialism. Consistent with the "beast-of-prey" morality that Nietzsche affirms in his ethical writings, the "good European," practicing "great politics," will have the task of subjugating the entire earth.

What role does Nietzsche ascribe to Germany in this "new world order" of European hegemony?[3] Despite his deprecation of German nationalism and his disappointment at Germany's political and cultural direction under Bismarck, Nietzsche occasionally harbors hope for a significant German contribution to the new united Europe. A feature that Nietzsche frequently associates with the Germans is their diversity. Composed of a great mixture of races, this "people of the middle" has multiple identities and a multivalent personality. The reason for this is that German nature is still in the process of becoming. As a not-yet-finished people, it loves everything that is obscure and uncertain, but it has the possibility to evolve into something great and dominant: "'Development' is thus the truly German discovery and lucky shot in the great domain of philosophical formulas—a ruling concept which, in concert with German beer and German music, is at work at the Germanization of all Europe" (*BGE* 156). Nietzsche's thoughts here are tongue-in-cheek, yet there remains a serious residue to his favoring of Germans, as we see evidenced in other passages.

Wagner, for example, could never have been possible without "*supra-German*" sources, but his "German nature" allowed him to create "stronger, more daring, more severe and more elevated things than a nineteenth-century Frenchman could have done" (*BGE* 171). Nietzsche takes pride in the fact that "we Germans are still closer to barbarism than the French," a statement whose significance lies not only in the affirmation of a "barbaric," i.e., anti-religious and amoral dimension of cultural achievement, but also in the identification signaled by the first-person plural pronoun. Indeed, in some of his more generous moments, Nietzsche fantasizes about the Germans breeding "a ruling caste" (*SW* 11: 457) or expresses the faint hope that with much effort the Germans can throw off their multiple features and become something great (*SW* 11: 572). The sheer amount of ink Nietzsche devotes to the Germans and Germany indicates that the German Question was not a settled matter in his mind. That the Germans had not realized their potential and that the jingoism of the Second Reich is contemptible are propositions that Nietzsche propounds for the last decade-and-a-half of his conscious life. But there are also faint hints that he believed Germany could overcome its nationalism, its parliamentary imbecility, its journalistic culture, and its philistinism and become a leader in a new European order.

The Social Question

Germany's late political unity—in comparison to England and France—contributed to a tardiness in industrial development. In the early 1870s, Germany entered into a process of modernization that, by the dawn of the twentieth century, made it one of the most powerful nations on earth, both militarily and economically. Spurred on by unification, Germany experienced an unprecedented prosperity in a period that came to be known as the "Founding Age" (*Gründerzeit*). The process of modernization in Germany, like elsewhere in Europe, produced severe and lasting social problems. In the Germany of Nietzsche's time, however, when one referred to "the social question," it was understood to mean quite specifically the question or series of issues surrounding the working class. There was good reason for this. In the first place the size of the industrial proletariat had multiplied dramatically during Nietzsche's lifetime. When he was born in 1844 there were about one million workers in Germany, but by the time he began writing the first volume of *Zarathustra* this figure had increased over seventeen-fold. Accompanying this proliferation of workers was a restructuring of the German social order, one of whose ramifications was that the proletariat gradually became a political and economic power. Labor unions and unionized workers became increasingly frequent. In the political realm the formation of the General German Workers Union in 1863 under the leadership of Ferdinand Lasalle and, in the same year, the rival Union of German Workers Organizations, headed by August Bebel and Wilhelm Liebknecht, thrust the working class into the political arena more strongly than ever before. And when Lasalle was killed in a duel in 1864, it took only five years before the two workers' organizations merged and were renamed the Social Democratic Workers' Party.

Although Nietzsche had very little contact with the working class or Social Democrats, he frequently expressed opinions on both. In general, Nietzsche remained singularly unsympathetic to the plight of actual workers, although, as the following citation demonstrates, he was hardly flattering toward the employers either:

> What the worker sees in the employer is usually only a cunning, blood-sucking dog of a man who speculates on all misery; and the employer's name, shape, manner, and reputation are a matter of complete indifference to them. The manufacturers and entrepreneurs of business probably have been too deficient so far in all those forms and signs of a *higher race* that alone make a *person* interesting. If the nobility of birth showed in their eyes and gestures, there might not be any socialism of the masses. For at bottom the masses are willing to submit to slavery of any kind, if only the higher-ups constantly legitimize themselves as higher, as *born* to command—by having noble manners. The most common man feels that nobility cannot be improvised and that one has to honor in it the fruit of long periods of time. But the lack of higher manners and the notorious vulgarity of manufacturers with their ruddy, fat hands give him the idea that it is only accident and luck that have elevated one person above another. (*GS* 108)

Nietzsche's unbecoming depiction of capitalists shows that he did not approve of the character of the new ruling class. But his view of the workers, and of the relationship between capitalists and workers, indicates just as clearly that his esteem for the working class was even lower. Workers are justified in hating their bosses only because they do not embody values worthy of those who command other human beings. With this notion Nietzsche placed his solution to the worker's question in the realm of hierarchical relationships based on a military model. He began his reflections with the contention that "soldiers and leaders still have far better relationships with each other than workers and employers." Nietzsche was thus aware of class struggle as a nineteenth-century reality, but was not a partisan for either side. His perspective on worker-employer relations depended on a model that combined workers' discipline and obedience along with charisma and nobility on the part of the capitalist. The proletariat was for him a potentially pliable and exploitable tool for appropriately superior leaders.

Nietzsche's militaristic views on the class struggle hearken back to a time when relations of dominance were unquestioned and based on "natural" hierarchies. Unlike his contemporaries in the political arena who had to deal with the realities of growing union organization and an active and popular working-class party, Nietzsche could simply rail against the very existence of a "social question" and find fault with the weakness of the ruling classes in allowing the proletariat to become a part of the political landscape.

> *The workers' question.* The stupidity—at bottom, the degeneration of instinct, which is today the cause of *all* stupidities—is that there is a workers' question at all. Certain things one does not question: that is the first imperative of instinct. I simply cannot see what one proposes to do with the European worker now that one has made a question of him. He is far too well off not to ask for more and more, not to ask more immodestly. In the end, he has numbers on his side. The hope is gone forever that a modest and self-satisfied kind of man, a Chinese type, might here develop as a class: and there would have been reason in that, it would have been a necessity. . . . The worker was qualified for military service, granted the right to organize and to vote: is it any wonder that the worker today experiences his own existence as distressing—morally speaking, as an injustice? But what is *wanted?* I ask once more. If one wants an end, one must also want the means: if one wants slaves, then one is a fool if one educates them to be masters. (*TI* 545)

The brunt of the criticism for the existence of a workers' question must be borne in Nietzsche's view by those who have allowed the workers to have rights, to make demands, to develop into more than simply a slave caste. That the workers could be agents or that they could have contributed to their relative rise in the social hierarchy are thoughts that Nietzsche cannot entertain. Nor can he admit the possibility that there exist certain political and social rights to which workers—or all citizens—are entitled. Nietzsche's views thus oppose the dominant tendency in European societies toward civil rights and universal suffrage.

In the passage cited above Nietzsche expresses regret that unnamed individuals or groups did not act to prevent working-class organizations and rights. He also indicates that the opportunity to create a servile caste, once lost, will not recur. Despite this pessimism with regard to the institution (or reinstitution) of a class society without rancor and ill-will, occasionally, in other passages, Nietzsche indicates that such a restructuring of society could, indeed, be achieved. Speaking in the name of good Europeans, Nietzsche adopts his prophetic voice and predicts ominous transformations for the future. The ice on which people are skating has become very thin; the winds of change are blowing; and the Europeans "constitute a force that breaks open ice and other all too thin 'realities.'" Adopting the first-person plural to indicate his membership in a wide movement—which at that point was a complete fantasy—he then explicates a vague and dystopian vision of a "more desirable" social order:

> We "conserve" nothing; neither do we want to return to any past periods; we are not by any means "liberal"; we do not work for "progress"; we do not need to plug up our ears against the sirens who in the market place sing of the future: their song about "equal rights," "a free society," "no more masters and no servants" has no allure for us. We simply do not consider it desirable that a realm of justice and concord should be established on earth (because it would certainly be the realm of the deepest leveling and *chinoiserie*); we are delighted with all who love, as we do, danger, war, and adventure, who refuse to compromise, to be captured, reconciled, and castrated; we count ourselves among conquerors; we think about the necessity for new orders, also for a new slavery—for every strengthening and enhancement of the human type also involves a new kind of enslavement. (*GS* 338)

It is, of course, possible to read Nietzsche's "new slavery" as an "existential" imperative, as a call for a new self-discipline, an enslaving of certain passions and desires in an effort to become healthy and strong. But from Nietzsche's remarks about workers, about the masses, about slavery in Greece, and about the necessity of hierarchies and castes, it is not improbable that he envisioned a social order in which some large group of people would serve a select few—either by compulsion or voluntarily.[4] Although his response to the working class here resembles the most cynical and aggressive position of the extreme right-wing parties of his time, we should recall that his ideological position is not predicated on profits or industry, but rather, ultimately, on the production of cultural greatness. The working class—and its oppression—was important for him only insofar as its sacrifice could be translated into a cultural renaissance.

That Nietzsche was disinclined toward the working-class movement of socialism should be evident. It came to embody in his thought a complex unity of tendencies that he considered deleterious to European society. Despite the endeavors of other parties to discredit the Social Democrats, he viewed socialism as the most typical political party. Because of the introduction of participatory democracy, all parties will have to appeal to the masses; the socialists have merely initiated a process that all other political groups would have to emulate (*HA* 383). Nietzsche also associated socialism with the state and with state power, an unlikely association considering the existence of the Socialist Laws from 1878–90, which outlawed most party activity and publications. His reasoning, however, was that both the state and the socialists seek to protect unworthy and non-genial persons by placing all individuals on the same level. Socialism is thus the natural outcome of the modern European state and its party system, and for this reason Nietzsche could mention "socialists and state idolaters" in one breath (*GS* 99). Nietzsche even points out that the *nouveaux riches* and the Liberals, who in Germany represented the middle-class and were theoretically the opponents of socialists, are really the furtive allies of socialism. After advising the wealthy to live modestly and to tax their own luxury items in order to strike at socialism, he comments: "Do you feel disinclined to employ this weapon? In that case, you wealthy bourgeois who call yourselves 'liberal,' admit to yourselves that it is the desires of your own heart that you find so fearful and threatening in the socialists, though in yourselves you consider them inevitable, as though there they were something quite different" (*HA* 282). In a sense, then, Nietzsche was more of a determinist with regard to socialism than Karl Marx. While Marx contended that communism was the inevitable outcome of world history, he also indicated that it would not be achieved without a bitter revolutionary struggle. Nietzsche, whose evaluation of the desirability of socialism was antithetical to Marx's, believed that socialism is the ineluctable and logical consequence of all the tendencies of his time.

Nietzsche's comments on socialism, as unflattering as they may be, must be seen in part as a product of his irrational fears about the destruction of culture and his thoughts on the inevitability of the democratizing processes in Europe. Within his larger speculative framework, however, Nietzsche's critique of socialism has a powerful ethical and philosophical dimension as well. Rightly or wrongly Nietzsche took equality as the most fundamental principle of socialist doctrine. His objections to equality are not based on political or economic motives, but on the observation that similarities of any sort are a contrived and human invention. That socialists insist on equality is thus the continuance of an unnatural prejudice that expresses itself as a moral postulate and then as a political tenet. Nietzsche's condemnation is explicit. In *Zarathustra* he depicts socialists as tarantulas whose teaching of equality is a subterfuge for a venomous and rancorous psyche. They are thus arch-negators of instincts and life. "Although they are sitting in their holes, these poisonous spiders, with their backs turned on life, they speak in favor of life, but only because they wish to hurt." Their psychology is dominated by envy; their intellectual lineage is Christian. "They wish to hurt those who now have power, for among these the preaching of death is still most at home. If it were otherwise, the tarantulas would teach otherwise; they themselves were once the foremost slanderers of this world and burners of heretics" (Z 213). Because they encompass the worst aspects of his times, the half-crazed Nietzsche, in his final works, selected socialists as his most despised enemy. "Whom do I hate most among the rabble of today? The socialist rabble, the chandala apostles, who undermine the instinct, the pleasure, the worker's sense of satisfaction with his small existence—who make him envious, who teach him revenge. The source of wrong is never unequal rights but the claim of 'equal' rights" (AC 647. The party of the working class and its doctrine come to occupy a central position in Nietzsche's rogues' gallery of modernity. In Nietzsche's thought socialism does not represent the solution to the "social question," but its most pernicious continuation.

The Women's Question

Nietzsche's views on women have become infamous because of the following remark found in *Zarathustra*: "You are going to women? Do not forget the whip!" (Z 179). At first glance this statement seems to be extremely unflattering toward women, suggesting physical abuse or servitude. Even if we interpret the "whip" in a metaphorical sense, the citation still advocates putting women in line by force. Complicating this most obvious interpretation, however, is the fact that this outburst does not belong to Zarathustra, Nietzsche's mouthpiece in this work, but to a little old woman whom he meets. This is the "little truth" that she gives to Zarathustra about her own sex. Zarathustra's own comments on women are far from complimentary, of course. In the section "On Little Old and Young Woman," from which the citation about the whip is taken, he asserts that "everything about woman is a riddle, and everything about woman has one solution: that is pregnancy," thus casting women into their traditional role as bearers of children. He continues by maintaining that "man should be educated for war, and woman for the recreation of the warrior; all else is folly." (*Z* 178). And a further comment leaves little doubt that for Zarathustra women are clearly subordinate to men: "The happiness of man is: I will. The happiness of woman is: he wills" (*Z* 178–79). Such statements have been offensive not only to the feminists of the twentieth century, but also to the liberal sentiments of the nineteenth century, including the not inconsiderable women's movement of Nietzsche's own day. But the most reprehensible and infamous statement about women belongs not to the teachings of Zarathustra, but to his interlocutor. The citation also contains a further complication if we consider a photograph taken in May of 1882, shortly before the composition of *Zarathustra*. In it we find Paul Rée and Nietzsche harnessed to a cart in which Lou Salomé is sitting; she is holding a whip in a raised right arm, as if she were about to strike the two men. The idea for this strange grouping was evidently Nietzsche's.

It should not surprise us that Nietzsche's views on the Women's Question, like his views on the Social Question, stem almost exclusively from secondhand sources. Although the last three decades of the nineteenth century saw the growth of a large and vocal women's movement in Germany, there is no evidence that Nietzsche—or most male intellectuals for that matter—took more than passing notice of its existence. In his personal life Nietzsche's relationships with women were usually conflict-laden and indicate a paradoxical and sometimes schizophrenic attitude toward those closest to him. His relationship to his sister and his mother was highly charged emotionally: while Nietzsche tried to break away from everything that the small-town morality of Naumburg represented, he was never quite able to escape the shadow of the petit-bourgeoisie. The two women pampered him throughout much of his early life; from the correspondence we possess it is obvious that Nietzsche's career was the focal point for both women, and that they were willing to sacrifice their own comfort for his success. Nietzsche appears to have considered this attitude as normal as they did. But along with their devotion came an oppressive bondage, the resentment of which only occasionally broke through to the surface.

Although Nietzsche usually expressed loving feelings and concern for both women in his letters and continued to correspond with them until his mental breakdown—after which they cared for him until his death—the following remarks from *Ecce Homo* evidence a considerable amount of pent-up hostility: "When I look for my profoundest opposite, the incalculable pettiness of the instincts, I always find my mother and my sister—to be related to such *canaille* would be a blasphemy against my divinity. The treatment I have received from my mother and my sister, up to the present moment, fills me with inexpressible horror. . . . I confess that the deepest objection to the 'Eternal Recurrence,' my real idea from the abyss, is always my mother and sister" (*EH* 41–42). These mixed emotions toward the women closest to him obviously colored his relationship to other women and his thoughts about the role of women in his and any future social order. Indeed, if we believe Nietzsche's own writings, the image of a man's mother determines "whether, in his dealings with women, he respects or despises them or is in general indifferent to them" (*HA* 150). Although we should refrain from dilettantish psychologizing, it is difficult to believe that Nietzsche's attitude toward women can be fully understood without accounting for his feelings toward his immediate family.

Probably the largest influence on Nietzsche's published comments on women was Lou Salomé. Her break with him in 1882 marked an abrupt turning point in the tenor and content of his reflections on the opposite sex. Throughout much of his middle period, his remarks about women fall under the rubric of "life wisdom," i.e., comments that are more observations on current social mores than ontological distinctions between the sexes. In *Human, All Too Human,* for example, Nietzsche included the heading "Wife and Child" as one of several sections devoted to human interactions. Many aphorisms in this section are simply *bons mots* designed more for humor and wit than for philosophical reflection. Under the title "Diverse Sighs" Nietzsche writes: "Some men have sighed over the abduction of their wives, most however over the fact that no one wanted to abduct them" (*HA* 151). In "Unity of Place and Action," an intentionally misplaced allusion to tragic theory, we read: "If married couples did not live together good marriages would be more common" (*HA* 151).

Other aphorisms may strike us as good advice and be completely non-offensive: "*Marriage as a long conversation.*—When entering into a marriage one ought to ask oneself: do you believe you are going to enjoy talking with this woman up into your old age? Everything else in marriage is transitory, but most of the time you are together will be devoted to conversation" (*HA* 152). Still other aphorisms distinguish men from women, but credit the latter with qualities that are unexpected from a traditional misogynist perspective. With regard to "female intellect" Nietzsche maintains that women exhibit a "complete control and presence of mind and the utilization of every advantage." They possess more reason than men, who are characterized rather by temperament and passion. That in marriage men seek a woman of temperament, while women search for a man of superior reason, demonstrates only, according to Nietzsche, that they are both pursuing a partner that is the ideal of their own sex. Although Nietzsche retains the stereotype of the woman being more attached to persons than to things, thus explaining why women have a distorted relationship to politics and science, he adds in this rather conciliatory set of aphorisms: "Perhaps all this may change, but for the present that is how things are" (*HA* 155). Nietzsche believes that the free spirits to which *Human, All Too Human* is dedicated would probably live without women (*HA* 158), but his remarks here are devoid of the wholesale denigration of a Schopenhauer and of later comments in Nietzsche's own writings.

Nietzsche's relatively favorable remarks on women at the time of *Human, All Too Human,* in particular his fairly conciliatory comments on marriage, may have been related to his own hopes at the time to find a wife. After his break with Lou Salomé and his estrangement from his sister after her marriage to the anti-Semite Bernhard Förster, we find that Nietzsche altered his tone and attitude considerably. From the early 1880s onward Nietzsche begins to propagate the worst clichés from the sexist cultural tradition of Europe. *Beyond Good and Evil* sets the dominant tone for much of the later work. Although women are likened to truth in the preface, they are dissociated from it in the body of the text: "But she [woman] does not *want* truth: what is truth to a woman! From the very first nothing has been more alien, repugnant, inimical to woman than truth—her great art is the lie, her supreme concern is appearance and beauty" (*BGE* 145). Here the influence of Schopenhauer, whose misogynist views were familiar to Nietzsche, is evident: both Nietzsche and Schopenhauer categorize women repeatedly as deceivers and as shallow intellects. Unlike Schopenhauer, however,

Nietzsche was also responding to the women's movement of his time. The beginning of this aphorism makes it clear that Nietzsche was aware of recent struggles for women's rights and equality: "Woman wants to be independent: and to that end she is beginning to enlighten men about 'woman as such'—*this* is one of the worst developments in the general *uglification* of Europe." In Nietzsche's view, if women really established a "female scientificality," it would reveal only shameful qualities: "pedanticism, superficiality, schoolmarmishness, petty presumption, petty unbridledness and petty immodesty" (*BGE* 144). Enlightenment, even as it pertains to women, Nietzsche concludes, is a task for men.

The model role for women that Nietzsche prefers is one in which they depend on their "natural" cunning and sensuality to secure social influence. As Zarathustra had stated, women should be a plaything for men (*Z* 178); in *Human, All Too Human* Nietzsche had remarked that the "shrewdness of women" is demonstrated by the fact that "everywhere they have known how to get themselves fed, like drones in the beehive" (*HA* 154); and in *Beyond Good and Evil* we read that they have learned how to get men to keep, protect, and indulge them "like a delicate, strangely wild and often agreeable domestic animal" (*BGE* 149). In this relationship to men, which they are now, out of ignorance and deception, wanting to sacrifice for equal rights, they were not only better served, but potentially more powerful. Nietzsche is here propagating an image of aristocratic culture in which women exerted influence through their husbands; if the man was particularly weak and his wife particularly willful, then she could attain a commanding position in the social order. As in his general reflections, he is not concerned with the overall welfare of women as a group, but only with the ability of a select few, the highest specimens, to achieve greatness through apposite, gender-specific means. The worsening condition of women that Nietzsche detects in his age is thus really a worsening for only those "higher types" of women—the "sensible," "well-reared" women—who knew how to use their wiles to their own advantage.

Nietzsche adds very little to his views on women and women's emancipation after *Beyond Good and Evil*—except perhaps for nuances and rhetoric. His final and most alarming words about the Women's Question are found in *Ecce Homo*. Declaring himself the "first psychologist of the Eternal Feminine" and the love-object of all women, Nietzsche takes his parting shots at the women's movement.[5] Those who do not love him are "the *abortive* women, the 'emancipated' who lack the stuff for children" (*EH* 75). Here Nietzsche employs the stereotypical defamation for women who resist men and demand equal rights: they are abnormal, not feminine, and unable to procreate. At the same time that he claims all women love him, he simultaneously demonstrates a deep contempt: a woman is a "dangerous, creeping, subterranean little beast of prey"; they are more wicked than men; those who are good are aberrant; "goodness in a woman is already a form of *degeneration*" (*EH* 76). True to the biologism of his later years, Nietzsche attributes to the "beautiful soul," a Goethean ideal of woman, a physiological disadvantage and categorizes the struggle for equal rights as a "symptom of sickness." He reserves his most venomous remarks, however, for the notion of "emancipation of women." For Nietzsche this ill-advised slogan

> is the instinctive hatred of the woman who has *turned out ill,* that is to say is incapable of bearing, for her who has turned out well—the struggle against "man" is always only means, subterfuge, tactic. When they elevate *themselves* as "woman in herself," as "higher woman," as "idealist" woman, they want to *lower* the general level of rank of woman; no surer means for achieving that than high school education [*Gymnasial-Bildung*], trousers and the political rights of voting cattle. At bottom the emancipated are the *anarchists* in the world of the Eternal Feminine, the underprivileged whose deepest instinct is revenge. (*EH* 76)

Amid this semi-insane raving of the near-mad philosopher, we can still glimpse the central motifs of his position on the Women's Question: the rejection of equality in politics and education, the destruction of hierarchy in the leveling of women, the natural biological superiority of men, and therefore the futility of social emancipation. Nietzsche's solution to the Women's Question, like his solution to the Social Question, lies in an imagined hierarchy of the past projected into a future order. The women's movement, another sign of degeneration in contemporary Europe, reaps only derision and disdain from Nietzsche's pen.

The Jewish Question

It would have been difficult for Nietzsche to avoid the Jewish Question. Although during his life he had little sustained contact with actual Jews—with the notable exception of Paul Rée—various discourses about Jews and Judaism were so prevalent in the intellectual and popular circles Nietzsche frequented that he was almost compelled to enter into dialogue with them. As a boy growing up in Naumburg it is not unlikely that he imbibed a cultural anti-Jewish feeling that thrived in this nar-

row-minded, petit-bourgeois atmosphere. In Nietzsche's earliest notebooks, it is therefore not surprising to find him copying down the words
to a popular song that contained the lyrics "Throw out Itzig the Jew,
Out of the Temple," and we can assume that he was exposed to similar,
culturally conditioned anti-Jewish songs and sentiments throughout his
early years.[6] His studies at Bonn and Leipzig brought an increase in neither tolerance nor openness. Although he was not attracted to rabid
racists, from his correspondence we can detect in his friends a commonplace anti-Jewish feeling based less on principles than on cultural clichés.

In Wagner and his circle, however, Nietzsche must have encountered
much more vociferous discussions of Jews. Irritated by what he perceived
to be an excessive Jewish influence on the musical world, Wagner had
already composed a notorious anti-Jewish essay, "Judaism and Music," in
1850. Although in the early 1870s Wagner had not yet become infatuated by the racial theories of Count Joseph Arthur Gobineau and
Houston Stuart Chamberlain (his later son-in-law), the Wagner household was openly ill disposed toward Jews at the time of Nietzsche's frequent visits and actively embroiled in controversies about Wagner's
anti-Jewish sentiments. The 1869 reprint of "Judaism and Music" as a
brochure provoked 170 published responses from both Jews and non-
Jews. That the young Nietzsche, who considered himself to be in the
vanguard of the Wagnerian cultural mission in the late 1860s and early
1870s, would not have been exposed to anti-Jewish convictions is quite
unlikely.[7] When we consider that Nietzsche's publisher Ernst
Schmeitzner and his brother-in-law Bernhard Förster were two of the
central figures in the anti-Semitic movement, then we can understand
why Nietzsche could not avoid forming opinions on the Jewish
Question.

Although Nietzsche was in close association with a great deal of anti-
Jewish sentiment throughout his life, he appears to have been relatively
unfazed by overt religious or racial prejudice. Unlike Wagner or various
Wagner associates, he remained for the most part unconcerned about
Jewish influence on his own work or in the cultural sphere in general.
For quite a few years during the late 1870s his closest friend was Paul
Rée, a Jewish scholar who anticipated Nietzsche's interest in questions of
psychology and ethics with the publication of *Psychological Observations* in
1874 and *The Origin of Moral Sensations* in 1877. Rée was perhaps a pro-
totypical "self-hating Jew," as various commentators have observed, but
he was a Jew nonetheless, and it is likely that his friendship with
Nietzsche contributed to Nietzsche's alienation from the Wagner circle.

Rée was held responsible for Nietzsche's turn from his Wagnerian proclivities to the "analytic" method of *Human, All Too Human*; some of
Nietzsche's friends evidently even believed that Rée was the author of
this collection of aphorisms. Cosima Wagner's remarks probably express
feelings that were common among Wagnerians in the late 1870s.
Discussing Nietzsche's turn from the Wagnerian cause, Cosima attributes his waywardness to the intervention of Israel "in the form of a Dr.
Rée, very sleek, very cool, at the same time as being wrapped up in
Nietzsche and dominated by him, though actually outwitting him—the
relationship between Judaea and Germany in miniature."[8] There is no
evidence that Rée's Judaism troubled Nietzsche, and although he must
have known that the Wagner circle, which had been his main social out-
let in the early 1870s, would be unfavorably disposed toward Rée, their
friendship remained constant until 1882, when the incident with Lou
Salomé, and not Rée's religious heritage, destroyed their relationship.

Nietzsche's relative freedom from anti-Jewish bias does not mean that
he did not partake in the general atmosphere of anti-Jewish feeling of his
time. Throughout his correspondence we repeatedly encounter unflattering references to Jews, in particular in his letters to his family. This "cultural anti-Jewish attitude" was supplemented in the early 1870s when,
probably under the influence of Wagner and his entourage, it is possible
to detect a slight extension into the arena of culture. There is a hint that
Nietzsche began to associate Jews with a complex of contradictory items
that included National Liberalism in politics, journalism as a form of
writing, the newly established German Reich, French influence, and
pseudo-cultural aspirations of a philistine class. Nietzsche's opinion of
the Jews after his break with Wagner is more complex and is characterized by a deep ambiguity. On the one hand, he carries with him many of
the stereotypes that he had picked up from his youth and early career. In
general, however, his comments on Jews become much more positive
after he had escaped the orbit of Wagner's circle.

In August of 1877 he asks Siegfried Lipiner whether he has connections
to the Jews because from recent experience he has reason to harbor "very
great expectations from youths of this ancestry in particular" (*SB* 5: 274).
And as the years go by he seems to take pleasure in praising the Jews in
letters to his sister, who had succumbed entirely to anti-Jewish and anti-
Semitic thought. The ambivalence that inhabits Nietzsche concerning the
Jews is evidenced best perhaps in one of his final notes in which he writes:
"I find it of value that I have the officers and the Jewish bankers on my
side:—Both together represent the *Will to Power*" (13: 642). Composed in

a state of semi-sanity, this sentence combines both the stereotype of the Jew as banker, which fed the anti-Semitic movement, as well as a positive evaluation of the Jews as a representative of one of Nietzsche's beloved notions. Typical for Nietzsche's personal view of the Jews was therefore an evaluation of them in terms of social clichés, from which he was unable to free himself, and a simultaneous willingness to find a positive value in these clichés, which separates him from many of his contemporaries.

Nietzsche's views on Jews do not tell us everything we need to know about his opinions on anti-Semitism. The two are obviously connected, but in his evaluation of anti-Semitism additional factors come into play. The reason for this is that anti-Semitism is a somewhat ambiguous term; in Nietzsche's time it had both a general and a specific referent, and we must be careful to distinguish the two. Used frequently since the late nineteenth century to refer to any anti-Jewish sentiments, rather than biases or hatred for Semitic peoples as a whole, anti-Semitism arose in Germany as the designation for a specific political movement in late 1879. Until that time the word "Semitic" and the less commonly found antithesis "anti-Semitic" were not restricted to the Jewish people. "Semitic" had became popular in the early nineteenth century as a category to classify specific groups of languages and only gradually in the course of the century did it become a description for a race of people. Important for this shift from historical linguistics to racist anthropology was Count Joseph Gobineau, whose *Essai sur l'inégalité des races humaines* (Essay on the Inequality of the Human Races) provided "scientific" legitimation for both the notion of "race" and the hypothesis that the "Aryan" race was opposed to and potentially corrupted by a "Semitic" race. According to such linguistic and race theories, then, not only the Jews, but also the Arabs were included under the category of the Semitic, and anti-Semitism encompassed an opposition to or prejudice against anyone belonging to the "Semitic" race. Because of its pseudo-scientific origin and its precise meaning, anti-Semitism has sometimes been rejected as a term referring specifically to Jews. Even the National Socialists, seeking to distinguish between the Jews and the Arab nations, rejected the use of "anti-Semitism" as a false label, "since this movement directs itself against Jewry, the corrupters of all peoples, but not against the other peoples speaking Semitic languages, who have likewise been anti-Jewish since ancient times." [9] Nietzsche, like any good philologist, was apparently also uncomfortable with the equation of anti-Semitic and anti-Jewish. Even after the emergence of the political movement that went by this name, he employs the neologism "Misojuden" (literally, "Jewish haters," from the Greek *misos,* hatred) to designate people he would later call "anti-Semitic."[10]

Nietzsche's relationship to anti-Semitism, to which he was unequivocally opposed, in contrast to his sentiments toward the Jews, is thus complicated by the fact that anti-Semitism had a specific referent in political agitation, especially in Germany, during the early 1880s. What made matters worse for him was his sister's engagement and marriage to one of the leaders of the anti-Semitic movement, Bernhard Förster. A former high school teacher who was removed from the profession after involvement in anti-Semitic roughhousing, Förster married Nietzsche's sister Elisabeth in 1885 and founded a colony in Paraguay, Nueva Germania, so that Germans could thrive in purity away from the corrupting influence of European Jewry. Nietzsche's dislike for anti-Semitism thus had a significant personal dimension. Nietzsche was quite close to his sister, especially during the 1870s. Although their relationship cooled somewhat in the next decade, due in part to Nietzsche's association with Lou Salomé, it is obvious that he harbored strong feelings for Elisabeth throughout his life. Part of his reaction against anti-Semitism may be explained by the role he attributed to Förster, who took his "beloved llama" away from him.

Nietzsche may have also harbored a personal animus against anti-Semitism because it seemed to emanate—at least ideologically—from the Wagner circle. Förster had been associated for a time with the extended Wagnerian cult, and Wagner's championing of racist anthropologists like Gobineau and Chamberlain underscored and supported the pseudo-scientific pretensions of anti-Judaism. Finally, Nietzsche's aversion to anti-Semitism must have been augmented by the preference his publisher Schmeitzner showed for the movement. In a letter from 1883 he complains with irony to Overbeck that Schmeitzner had put off production of *Zarathustra* because he was attending to anti-Semitic affairs: "Bravo! But who will relieve me from a publisher who finds anti-semitic agitation more important than the distribution of *my* thoughts?" (*SB* 6: 393). None of these personal motives may have been enough to determine Nietzsche's views; but they certainly show that he had many reasons to be ill-disposed toward political anti-Semitism besides principled differences of views.

Of course, Nietzsche had more general, ideological objections to anti-Semitism as well. Although we today commonly consider anti-Semitism, like other racist sentiments, to be part of a right-wing ideology, we find

Nietzsche consistently associating it with the democratizing tendencies that he felt were leveling necessary hierarchies across Europe. Since these democratizing tendencies assume so many forms, the associations are various. In *Ecce Homo,* referring to the Wagner circle in Bayreuth, he notes that anti-Semitism flourished in an atmosphere of narrow German virtues (*EH* 90–91). In *The Genealogy of Morals* Nietzsche observes that one can study rancor up close since it is a dominant trait in both anti-Semites and anarchists (*GM* 205). Later in this work he reinforces this image when he calls Eugen Dühring, a socialist of sorts, an "apostle of vindictiveness" and the "biggest moral-loudmouth that exists, even under his own kind, the anti-Semites" (*GM* 260). And near the close of *The Genealogy* he writes: "I am equally out of patience with those newest speculators in idealism called anti-Semites, who parade as Christian-Aryan worthies and endeavor to stir up all the asinine elements of the nation by that cheapest of propaganda tricks, a moral attitude" (*GM* 294). What emerges from these passages is that Nietzsche opposed anti-Semitism not out of a belief in tolerance or out of a particular respect for the Jews, the Jewish religion, or Jewish culture, but because he saw this movement as a further manifestation of an unhealthy moralism. Connected with anti-Semitism in Nietzsche's mind was a quasi-socialist need to redeem the world through a political movement. Nietzsche's response to and rejection of anti-Semitism, viewed from the perspective of the 1880s, is part and parcel of his assault on Christian ethics, narrow-minded nationalism, and redemptive socialism.

We should thus not confuse Nietzsche's pronouncements opposing anti-Semitism and the decline in a prejudicial attitude toward the Jews in private remarks with anything resembling liberal attitudes, toleration of differences, or compassion for the persecuted. When considering Nietzsche's perspective on the Jewish Question—as well as the other questions considered in this chapter—we must recall that he was responding primarily to movements, literature, and attitudes of the late nineteenth century. Because he was involved in several different discourses about the Jews, and because his evaluation of the Jews inside of these discourses was hardly monolithic, we encounter a wide range of statements and apparently contradictory opinions. Nietzsche held different and sometimes inconsistent views about Jews he met socially or casually, about anti-Semitism as a political movement, about Jews as a cultural and religious group in nineteenth-century German and European society, and about the ancient Jews as the founders of a religious tradition. There is no single image of the Jews in his writings, and if we try to harmonize his remarks without considering textual and historical context, then we will perforce draw even more confusing conclusions. Only by examining Nietzsche's remarks on Jews and the Jewish Question from the perspective of the 1880s can we understand their complexity. As in the case of the other social questions we have examined in this chapter—concerning the nation, workers, and women—Nietzsche's private and public utterances partake in an intricate web of social, political, and scholarly discourses that were peculiar to his era.

Chapter 6
The Genealogist of Morals

Although Nietzsche had been concerned with problems of ethics and values from his earliest writings, these topics became central for his works only in the 1880s. In *Ecce Homo* Nietzsche dated his "campaign against *morality*" (*EH* 95) from the publication of *Daybreak* in 1881, but it is not difficult to find evidence of reflection on morality and ethics even earlier. His classical studies again provided an impetus for this later concern. The literature and philosophy of the Greeks, with which he was preoccupied during most of his student years and his initial university career, are filled with notions of virtues and vices. It would have been impossible for Nietzsche to have read Plato without reflecting on his discussions of the good life and the various directives for proper conduct. Indeed, if we consider morality to be related to the customs or mores of a given society, then Nietzsche's earliest preoccupations with pedagogy and acculturation were moral concerns as well. Much of the early aphoristic work from the mid-1870s onward consists similarly of comments related to social, educational, or artistic value, and we should not forget that the aphoristic style itself was largely derived from French moral philosophers from the seventeenth and eighteenth centuries. Moreover, Nietzsche's remarks on social issues were heavily influenced by his notion of morality; the weight given to hierarchy as opposed to equality is ultimately a result of values to which Nietzsche subscribed. Even his penchant for natural science is not separable from ethics, since Nietzsche, as we shall see, considered the development and perpetuation of value systems to be a manifestation of certain evolutionary and physiological principles. Nietzsche's early works are thus infused with reflections on morality, even where this reflection is not the primary impetus for writing.

Moral Sensations and Moral Relativism

Perhaps the most convincing indication of an early concern with ethical issues comes from the second book of *Human, All Too Human,* which is entitled "On the History of Moral Sensations." Nietzsche's extensive consideration of morality in this first aphoristic work anticipates many of his later insights, but his tone is less abrasive and his comments are more differentiated. Initially he seeks to establish a connection between psychology and morality. For Nietzsche in the mid-1870s the development of abstract moral schemas is an expedient to steer us away from the more fruitful and more arduous task of precise psychological observation. Ethical values merely codify principles that are derived from our "human, all too human" constitution. Morals themselves are just the pretexts we use to validate our passions and the actions resulting from following our passions. In these judgments Nietzsche was concurring not only with the French aphorist La Rouchefoucauld, whom he cites directly, but also with his closest friend at the time, Paul Rée, whose book on *Psychological Observations* from 1875 had contained a similar line of argument. Moreover, Nietzsche's concerns in the second book of *Human, All Too Human* parallel Rée's next book, *On the Origin of the Moral Sensations* from 1877, which Rée wrote in a house in Sorrento, Italy, at the same time that Nietzsche was composing his first collection of aphorisms. At that point both writers were searching for a more psychologically realistic foundation for the origins of morals than had been supplied by previous philosophical schools, and in essence, Nietzsche's reflections on moral values in the 1880s are more intense investigations of the same issues that he and Rée discussed in such intimate surroundings in the previous decade.

In a sense, Nietzsche is not a philosopher of ethics at all since he does not endeavor to write an ethical treatise or to propagate an ethical system. He is more of an historian or genealogist of ethics, since his writings focus on the origin and function of moral value in human history. In *Human, All Too Human* we do find frequent reflection on moral categories as well as brief and witty explanations of behavior and emotions. But these aphorisms, which are written in the tradition of the French moralists, are not as important or original as Nietzsche's exploration of the psychological mechanisms of moral history. In essence Nietzsche claims that our current views of what is moral are the result of distinct historical stages. In one aphorism, "The three phases of morality hitherto" (*HA* 94), he lists three discrete levels of morality. In the first the human being has developed to the point where the procurement of momentary satisfaction is superseded by the procurement of long-term well-being. This stage corresponds with the "free domination of reason." At a higher stage of development individuals are no longer concerned solely with their own short-term or long-term satisfaction, but with receiving recognition from the community. While in the first stage individuals operate under the aegis of "utility" and "purpose," in this second stage they act in accordance with the principle of "honor." In this orientation toward the community, the individual "submits to common sensibilities" and "conceives utility as being dependent on what he thinks of others and what others think of him." In the final stage individuals liberate themselves from the hegemony of communal morality and subscribe to their own standards. At this point the individual is autonomous in the etymological sense of the word, since the individual himself (*auto*) determines moral laws (*nomos*). The individual does not thereby break away from the community, but instead acts in harmony with a higher and less personal notion of utility and honor. The individual "lives and acts as a collective-individual" (*HA* 50).

In this passage Nietzsche appears to be validating Kant's "categorical imperative" as the most highly developed moral precept. In acting as if the maxim of one's action were to become a universal natural law, the individual fulfills both an individual desire and a collective function. It is important to remember, however, that Nietzsche's description of stages of morality does not entail an affirmation of those stages or a belief that any particular stage can be justified in its own terms. Kant, for example, argued that his categorical imperative was formulated in accordance with rationality, but Nietzsche contends only that it represents the most recent and highest stage of morality. Nietzsche consistently maintains, even in these early writings, that there is no rational basis for morality, and that moral precepts are codifications of habits and customs unconnected with truth and reason. In short, he is a moral relativist who believes that ethical values are historical phenomena that serve particular functions at specific times.

Nietzsche's relativism is manifested most clearly in his analysis of the "principle stages in the history of the sensations of virtue." At issue in this aphorism (*HA* 39) is the claim that virtue and vice must exist because we have feelings of pleasure and displeasure after performing virtuous or vicious acts. Not only does Nietzsche argue that virtue is a relative notion that changes as human societies change; he also claims that even the site of virtue alters with time. The reason for ascribing virtue to an individual as well as the entity to which virtue is assigned are not constants in the course of human history. Nietzsche explains as follows:

> First of all, one calls individual actions good or bad quite irrespective of
> their motives but solely on account of their useful or harmful conse-

quences. Soon, however, one forgets the origin of these designations and believes that the quality "good" and "evil" is inherent in the actions themselves, irrespective of their consequences. . . . Then one consigns the being good or being evil to the motives and regards the deeds in themselves as morally ambiguous. One goes further and accords the predicate good and evil no longer to the individual motive but to the whole nature of the man out of whom the motive grows as the plant does from the soil. Thus one successively makes men accountable for the effects they produce, then for their actions, then for their motives, and finally for their nature. (*HA* 34)

This historical chain of ascriptions demonstrates, according to Nietzsche, a fundamental confusion about moral virtue. In the switch from the results of actions, to actions themselves, to motives, and to human nature, morality is not explained, but simply defined differently. In the final step of this succession we discover, Nietzsche continues, that the notion of accountability becomes incoherent. Since the nature of an individual is itself the consequence of innumerable elements and influences, "man can be made accountable for nothing, not for his nature, nor for his motives, nor for his actions, nor for the effects he produces" (*HA* 34). Moral sensations, such as pangs of conscience or feelings of displeasure when doing wrong, are just so many fictions; and the history of moral sensations is tantamount to "the history of an error," a confusion between cause and effect. In his most radical formulation in the early works Nietzsche here claims that morality itself, which in the philosophical tradition had been founded on freedom of volition, consists of a series of erroneous labels for what is in reality a necessity. Morality separates us from the animal world; it makes us the "over-animal" (*Ueber-Thier*). But what really distinguishes us from the rest of the animal kingdom is in reality that we "want to be lied to." Ultimately morality is no more "than an official lie told so that" the beast in us "will not tear us to pieces. Without the errors that repose in the assumptions of morality man would have remained animal" (*HA* 35).

Nietzsche thus counters traditional views of morality with two propositions. First he claims that pleasure, far from being a sensation resulting from moral actions, is in fact at the basis of all actions, whether these actions are judged as moral or immoral. Anticipating Sigmund Freud's psychoanalytic hypotheses, Nietzsche contends that the fundamental motivation for human behavior is the enhancement of pleasure and the avoidance of displeasure. Although these claims occur prior to his intensive reliance on biological and evolutionary theory,

Nietzsche consistently identifies the "pleasure principle" with self-preservation. To a certain extent such a theory eliminates the distinction between good and evil, since all actions are ultimately derived from individuals' desires to defend themselves in an often hostile environment. The difference between good and evil is semantic and conventional. There is really a continuum between good and evil acts, the latter being simply a manifestation of cruder and socially less acceptable behavior that stems, however, from the identical foundation as "good" behavior. Using pleasure as a basis, Nietzsche is also able to explain the perseverance of customs and the social nature of human life. Custom, he speculates, derives from habitual acts that have proved salutary. Because the performance of habitual acts is easier and preferable, it enhances pleasure. Customs combine the pleasurable with the useful for the good of the community. Moreover, Nietzsche maintains that social relations themselves are designed to amplify individual pleasure: "To feel sensations of pleasure on the basis of human relations on the whole makes men better; joy, pleasure, is enhanced when it is enjoyed together with others, it gives the individual security, makes him good-natured, banishes distrust and envy" (HA 52). Nietzsche's point here is that we should reverse the cause-and-effect relationship between morality and pleasure: the original factor is not the good deed; rather, the good deed is the consequence (at times) of our pursuit of pleasure.

Nietzsche's more devastating argument against traditional morality involves the notion of free will. In several aphorisms, including the one cited above, Nietzsche rejects universal ethics by undercutting its foundation in autonomous subjectivity. If we are not at liberty to perform one action rather than another, if we are compelled to behave in predetermined ways, then there can be no individual decisions, hence no moral value, and no meaningful distinction between good and evil. To underscore the absence of free will, Nietzsche often resorts to comparisons between natural occurrences and human behavior. "We do not accuse nature of immorality when it sends us a thunderstorm and makes us wet: why do we call the harmful man immoral? Because in the latter case we assume a voluntarily commanding free will, in the former necessity" (HA 55). Human actions, which in classical ethical formulations escaped the necessities associated with natural laws, are here claimed as yet another natural phenomenon. In a later aphorism (HA 106) Nietzsche proceeds along the same lines, likening human activity to the apparent capriciousness of a waterfall. Just as every motion in a cascade is "mathematically calculable," so too "every advance in knowledge, every error, every piece of wickedness" could be calculated if one were omniscient. "If for one moment the wheel of the world were to stand still, and there were an all-knowing, calculating intelligence there to make use of this pause, it could narrate the future of every creature to the remotest ages and describe every track along which this wheel had yet to roll" (*HA* 57).

The only difference between natural occurrences and human action is that human beings harbor the illusion of free will. Indeed, to be consistent Nietzsche argues that this assumption of free will is itself part of the calculable plan, and that even his discovery of the absence of free will is a necessary moment (*HA* 58). At times, of course, Nietzsche's stark determinism appears to stand in contradiction to other precepts he avows. For example, it is difficult to reconcile his claim that the pursuit of pleasure is at the root of all behavior with a total absence of free will unless pleasure itself were added to the deterministic equation. Similarly it is puzzling to find Nietzsche arguing that punishment and reward are "the strongest motives for performing certain acts and not performing certain acts" and that "mankind's utility requires their continuance" (*HA* 57). The admission of motives appears to grant precisely the choice among actions that Nietzsche otherwise denies—unless, again, we consider motive to be only our way of explaining to ourselves why we make certain choices. Although Nietzsche does not appear to have thought these propositions through to their logical conclusion, his strongest argument against morality is the hypothesis that human behavior is pre-programmed, unfree, and, like natural phenomena, always necessary.

Nietzsche's early reflections on morality are informed strongly by three tendencies. The first is an obvious reliance on the natural sciences. In this period of his writing Nietzsche displays the penchant for conceiving human action in terms of natural laws. This penchant would culminate in the hypothesis of eternal recurrence, which, as we have already seen, represents a philosophical appropriation of "mechanics." Nietzsche's observations on morality in *Human, All Too Human* are also infused with a hierarchy based on a positive evaluation of *Bildung*. Moral and immoral actions are not opposites, but reflections of divergent stages of human development. "'Immoral' . . . means that one is not yet, or not yet sufficiently sensible of the higher, more refined, more spiritual motives which a new culture has introduced: it designates one who is retarded, has remained behind, though always it is only a matter of degree" (*HA* 36). For this reason Nietzsche finds that there is a correlation between intellect and morality. The higher the degree and quality of intellect, the more likely that actions of an individual will be judged good (*HA* 56). Many actions called evil, Nietzsche claims, are in reality just stupid (*HA* 58). Of particular note is that Nietzsche at this stage of his philosophical ruminations apparently validates those actions that are of a higher intellectual order. In contrast to his later writings, in the 1870s morality is obviously a sign of progress of which he approves. Finally, despite the relativity of values and the knowledge that free will is an illusion—or perhaps because of these—Nietzsche remains optimistic about the future:

> It is true that everything in the domain of morality has become and is changeable, unsteady, everything is in flux: but *everything is also flooding forward,* and towards *one* goal. Even if the inherited habit of erroneous evaluation, loving, hating does continue to rule in us, under the influence of increasing knowledge it will grow weaker: a new habit, that of comprehending, not-loving, not-hating, surveying is gradually implanting itself in us on the same soil and will in thousands of years' time perhaps be strong enough to bestow on mankind the power of bringing forth the wise, innocent (conscious of innocence) man as regularly as it now brings forth—*not his antithesis but necessary preliminary*—the unwise, unjust, guilt-conscious man. (*HA* 58–59)

This confidence in the future would wane steadily as Nietzsche moved into the 1880s. In *Zarathustra* the vision of a better future is couched in prophecy. By the time we reach the mature moral writings, the steady progress that Nietzsche had noted in his earlier works appears to be as illusory as morality itself.

Good and Bad/Good and Evil

The most convenient place to turn for a view of Nietzsche's later thought on morality is the book *The Genealogy of Morals: A Polemic,* published in 1887. This work, along with *Beyond Good and Evil,* which appeared in the previous year, represents the largest sustained consideration of morality in Nietzsche's oeuvre. *Beyond Good and Evil,* however, is a bit more difficult to discuss as a coherent set of ideas. Like the writings of his middle period, it consists of aphorisms on a variety of topics, from morality to religion to life wisdom. The *Genealogy,* by contrast, is comprised of three essays and was composed specifically to clarify issues Nietzsche believed were misunderstood in the earlier volume. Moreover, it proposes by its very title to return to the same issues that were thematized in the second book of *Human, All Too Human*. The most obvious overt difference is the introduction of the word "genealogy," which has led many critics to believe that Nietzsche departed from the historical approach of his early works, or that he discovered a new way to assess historical phenomena. In fact, however, Nietzsche's use of the word genealogy is probably rather innocent of the wholesale revision of methodology often ascribed to it. Its inclusion in the title of Nietzsche's 1887 "polemic"—this is the subtitle to the *Genealogy*—is attributable to more mundane reasons. In the first place the notion of genealogy was familiar to Nietzsche as a philologist, where it was commonly employed to discuss the history of ancient texts and their corruptions. It was also a notion that related to current discussions in biology, which had made a considerable impression on Nietzsche. Finally, the term "genealogy" added a flair that would have been missing with the term "history"; Nietzsche, a consummate stylist, was keenly aware of the importance of titles and catch phrases in his writings. His notebooks are replete with tentative titles and tables of contents. Genealogy as a method is actually very similar to what Nietzsche did a decade before. It requires, as he notes in 1887, "historical and philological training, together with a native fastidiousness in matters of psychology" (*GM* 151). These are precisely the tools that produced his reflections in *Human, All Too Human*.

Although the genealogical turn is neither primarily methodological, nor substantive, there are significant changes that occurred in Nietzsche's consideration of morality over the decade that separates the *Genealogy* from his first volume of aphorisms. But these differences can be regarded more accurately as shifts in emphasis and in perspective rather than a difference in approach or worldview. One of the most obvious of these shifts involves the more rigorous concern with origins and descent, rather than with the compilation or the chronicling of changes in moral values, and this concern is announced at the beginning of the initial essay entitled "'Good and Evil' 'Good and Bad.'" Here Nietzsche discusses the views of an unidentified group of English psychologists— he probably means writers like John Stuart Mill and Herbert Spencer— who speculated on the origins of our morality. Their reasoning—at least as it is reproduced by Nietzsche—is as follows: at some point in human history altruistic actions were praised by those who were treated in an altruistic fashion: that is, they were found to be useful to those who were less advantaged. At a later point in human development the reason for the original praise was forgotten; although we no longer knew why these certain actions were praised, force of habit caused them to be praised even after the reason for their praiseworthiness had been lost.

Nietzsche has nothing but contempt for this explanation. In the first place he believes it violated the spirit of history. The English psychologists, Nietzsche contends, thought unhistorically and in an amateurish fashion. About the only thing that is interesting in these explanations is the motivation of the psychologists themselves in positing such an absurd notion of the origins of our moral evaluation of the good. Nietzsche comments as follows: "What drives these psychologists forever in the same direction? A secret, malicious desire to belittle humanity, which they do not acknowledge even to themselves? A pessimistic distrust, the suspiciousness of the soured idealist? Some petty resentment of Christianity (and Plato) which does not rise above the threshold of consciousness? Or could it be a prurient taste for whatver is embarrassing, painfully paradoxical, dubious and absurd in existence? Or is it, perhaps, a kind of stew—a little meanness, a little bitterness, a bit of anti-Christianity, a touch of prurience and desire for condiments?" (*GM* 158). The only interesting feature of the "English psychologists" is their own psychology and what it reveals about contemporary reflections on morality. They are themselves examples of a certain type of morality, and as such unable to fathom the very subject that they treat. Nietzsche's initial essay is devoted to clarifying the very issues that the "English psychologists" muddle.

Nietzsche's contrary theory concerning the origin of the designation "good" is that it was a judgment of those who were active, not those who benefited by receiving passively some altruistic act. Those who coined this term were at the top of the social hierarchy; Nietzsche's morality is thus inextricably intertwined with his social and political thought: "It was the 'good' themselves, that is to say the noble, mighty, highly placed, and high-minded who decreed themselves and their actions to be good, i.e., belonging to the highest rank, in contradistinction to all that was base, low-minded and plebeian." The nobility of former times, distanced from the lower classes of society—Nietzsche refers repeatedly to the "pathos of distance"—is the creative source for a certain type of original morality. These noble souls are credited with the ability to name, to designate, to label, and it is they who then refer to their own actions in terms that later are understood "morally." The label "bad" then is placed on the actions of those who stand outside of their circles, those who are subjected to them, their vassals or slaves or serfs. Thus Nietzsche clearly locates the origins of a certain type of morality in a specific social situation: "The origin of the opposites *good* and *bad* is to be found in the pathos of nobility and distance, representing the dominant temper of a higher, ruling class in relation to a lower dependent class." This type of morality, which Nietzsche conceives to be more original than the variety of morality described by the English psychologists, posits "aristocratic values." Only after they decline—and the *Genealogy* is chiefly about the decline of aristocratic values—only after the "herd instinct" has conquered the minds of humankind do we find the illicit and prejudicial equation of the terms *"moral, altruistic,* and *disinterested"* (*GM* 160) that is propagated as a historical truth. In Nietzsche's view the notions of atruism and utility have neither a psychological nor a historical link with the original designation of actions as "good."

History and psychology are not the only tools that Nietzsche employs to drive home his point. He also brings into play another area of endeavor familiar to him—classical philology, in particular etymologies—to show that his notion of the origin of the good is superior to those of his philosophical adversaries. Nietzsche's most general claim is unobjectionable since it is merely the assertion that certain social realities become encoded in language. From this general premise he observes that "good" in all languages is related to the concept of "noble" (German *vornehm*), and that "bad" is always related to "common," "plebeian," or "base." His conclusion from these linguistic observations is that morality, at least at some point in the distant past, was related to social position or social status. The reason that this genealogy is no longer obvious to us today, Nietzsche claims, is "due to the retarding influence which democratic prejudice has had upon all investigation of origins" (*GM* 162). Nietzsche's chief illustrations of social and etymological overlap come, as we might expect, from ancient Greece. Citing the views of the Megarian poet Theognis, on whom he had written in his youth, he examines the intimate relationship between ethical value and its reflection in language. The Greek nobility

> speak of themselves as "the truthful"; most resolute in doing this were members of the Greek aristocracy, whose mouthpiece is the Megarian poet Theognis. The word they used was *esthlos,* meaning one who *is,* who has true reality, who is true. By a subjective turn the *true* later became the *truthful.* During this phase the word provided the shibboleth of the nobility, describing the aristocrat, as Theognis saw and portrayed him, in distinction from the lying plebeian, until finally, after the decline of the aristocracy, the word came to stand for spiritual nobility, and ripened and sweetened. (*GM* 163)

The vestiges of another, older system of values is thus contained in scattered linguistic clues, giving us insight into the original meaning of good and bad as social distinctions.

Such hypotheses on language and social stratification in the ancient world are plausible, even if they are highly speculative. It is likely that certain designations arose in and relate to specific social contexts, and as long as we do not validate these labels, as long as we understand them as a product of domination, such conjecture is relatively inoffensive. Nietzsche, however, appears to be interested in more than the mere description of origins; the weight of his rhetoric is clearly and consistently on the side of the "nobles" against the "plebeians." Nietzsche's partisanship is also evident when he expands his speculation into another, more dubious realm in his discussion of inherent racial characteristics. Nietzsche claims that "good" and "bad" reflect not only class distinctions, but racial ones as well. The derivation of the Latin *malus* is his primary illustration: besides meaning the common man, it could also refer to someone with darker skin, "especially black-haired . . . as the pre-Aryan settler of the Italian soil, notably distinguished from the new blond conqueror race by his color." In general, Nietzsche, like many of his contemporaries, was extremely race conscious with regard to European tribes. He remarked that the Celts were a fair-haired race, observed and at times regreted the decline of the pure Aryan population of Germany, and looked with some dismay at the prevalence of the "subject races," recognizable by their "color, shortness of skull, perhaps also in their intellectual and social instincts" (*GM* 164).

It is in this context that Nietzsche, obviously still very much affected by the events following the Franco-Prussian war, denigrates not only "democracy," but also "the even more fashionable anarchism, and especially that preference for the *commune*, the most primitive of all social forms, which is now shared by all European socialists." The Paris commune of 1871, when for a short period of time the common people of Paris assumed control of their city government, is viewed as a struggle between the inferior "subject races" and "the Aryan race of conquerors" (*GM* 164). In Nietzsche's hands philology is thus a powerful and perilous tool. Through the narrow focus on etymology, Nietzsche manages to expound a political preference (a society based on hierarchy and hegemony rather than socialism and democracy), a theory of race (the Aryans are clearly superior to the races that they conquered, just as the Aryan myth was superior to the Semitic in the *Birth of Tragedy*), as well as a view of historical decline (the victorious fair-haired Europeans who named themselves *agathos, bonus, gut* are gradually succumbing to inferior races, destroying an older and more noble system of values that Nietzsche apparently condones).

After defining an original moral system in terms of a non-antagonistic set of concepts "good" and "bad," Nietzsche turns to the important task of explaining how this "noble," "Aryan" system of values waned. In Nietzsche's view the demise grew organically from a further differentiation among those who were "good." To provide an explanation Nietzsche introduces a new pair of terms for consideration—the pure and the impure—and a new character on the historical stage: the priest. Originally the priest adheres to a doctrine of purity understood in a strictly literal sense: "The pure man was originally one who washed himself, who refused to eat certain foods that produce skin diseases, who did not sleep with the unwashed plebeian women, who held blood in abomination" (*GM* 165). These priestly aristocrats form a caste alongside but separate from the noble warriors; and in contrast to their aristocratic brethren, they advocate an "anti-sensual metaphysics," a denial of pleasure and life that would seem to oppose the class out of which they arose. Nietzsche is not totally without admiration for this caste; it would be wrong to say that he is a complete partisan of the earlier and more original "good" nobles. As a "priest" himself, or as a product of "priestly" culture, and as someone who appreciated the hegemonic role that the priestly caste has exercised throughout much of human history, Nietzsche is clearly ambivalent toward the appearance of power in this new form: "Among the priests everything becomes more dangerous, not cures and specifics alone but also arrogance, vindictiveness, acumen, profligacy, love, the desire for power, disease. In all fairness it should be added, however, that only on this soil, the precarious soil of priestly existence, has man been able to develop into an interesting creature; that only here has the human mind grown both profound and evil; and it is in these two respects, after all, that man has proved his superiority over the rest of creation" (*GM* 166). Nothing sums up the ambivalence of Nietzsche's views of the priests and of priestly morality better than this passage.

Three items are particularly worth noting: (1) There is a relationship between the appearance of the priestly caste in Nietzsche's historical narrative and the features that previous thinkers associate with the definition of the historical human being. Nietzsche states that only with the priests does humankind prove its "superiority over the rest of creation." It is as if the priests were the first humans to exhibit what many philosophers had

called consciousness, as well as conscience. The priests are the first individuals to rely on reflection, on thought; they are separated from their
noble counterparts by their rejection of non-reflective, instinctual behavior. They establish laws and rites; they rule by intellect and not physical
power. (2) For this reason the priests are "interesting." As masters of the
intellect, as manipulators of human nature, the priests are associated
with the non-preferred terms that we found in Nietzsche's early writings: with the Socratic, with Euripides, with realism, with rationality,
with historical consciousness. In contrast to his discussion of morality in
Human, All Too Human, however, Nietzsche is here ambivalent toward
progress and toward a morality that is associated with intellect. (3) In his
discussions Nietzsche does not refer specifically to any historical epoch.
The priests to whom he refers are not identifiable in terms of time or
place; they are not derived from anthropological studies. All of the
agents involved with early moral values are psychologically defined types
rather than empirical beings. His explanation for the origin of morality
is thus heavily dependent on a cast of characters drawn from what we
might call a historical mythology.

Gradually the value system characterized by the non-opposition of
"good" and "bad" is superseded by a morality of "good" and "evil."
Nietzsche associates the new value system with types that are drawn from
religious or racial groups. Nobles exist in all societies, but in Europe they
are identified primarily with the fair-haired, the Aryans, and the
Germanic peoples. The priests, the caste that brought about the downfall
of the noble value system, appeared to be originally a subgroup of the
nobles themselves. But at some point Nietzsche shifts ground and attributes "the priestly system of valuations" to a different group of people.
"How readily," Nietzsche notes, "the priestly system of valuations can
branch off from the aristocratic and develop into its opposite" (*GM*
166–67). The true aristocrats are characterized by "a strong physique,
blooming, even exuberant health, together with all the conditions that
guarantee its preservation: combat, adventure, the chase, the dance, war
games etc." The priests, by contrast, evolve into or emanate from an
opposing type, defined at first by a single word—impotence—and by a
single religious/cultural group: the Jews. Again we note a true ambivalence: although the priests are the greatest haters in history—because
they are physically impotent—Nietzsche is compelled to concede that
"human history would be a dull and stupid thing without the intelligence
furnished by its impotents" (*GM* 167). The way that the Jews/priests
attack the aristocrats is to invert the value system that the latter has

established. Instead of the valorization of the "good/noble/powerful/beautiful/happy/favored-of-the-gods," the Jews prefer the poor, the sick, the downtrodden, the suffering, the ugly. The profound hatred of the Jews for the aristocrats also manifests itself in its opposite: in love, in particular in the love proclaimed by Jesus Christ and the Christian religion.

As we shall see in the next chapter, Nietzsche views the Judeo-Christian tradition as a totality, and although the Jews are more original and thus more responsible for overturning aristocratic values, the Christians are part of, a continuation of, that original Jewish/priestly impulse. We should note that in the *Genealogy* the Jews are accorded a much more central role in human—or at least Western—history than are the Christians, who are a mere strategy of a Jewish drive for hegemony. But we should also note the unfortunate coincidence that the opposing forces in European civilization, as described by Nietzsche in this work, are the Aryans, typified by the German warrior caste, and the Jews, who have "triumphed over all other, nobler values" (*GM* 169). Nietzsche could not know, of course, that this sort of opposition would have such implications for the course of history during the third and fourth decades of the twentieth century, and we can hardly hold him responsible for what occurred during the Third Reich, even if the National Socialists, as we shall see in chapter 8, often alluded to his writings and acted in what many assumed was his spirit. Nietzsche's blame of the Jews is certainly different from the traditional Christian rebuke of blood sacrifice, or from the cultural racist's contention that the Jews controlled too much of the social and cultural realm, or the biological racist's drivel about superiority based on pure ancestry. But we should not forget either that Nietzsche, despite significant differences, adheres here and throughout his writings to a number of racist, classist, and nationalist discourses that were most often part of a conservative or reactionary heritage even in the Europe of his own time.

The priests, originally a part of the noble order, then separated from that order and associated with Jews, are further transformed in Nietzsche's historical mythology into slaves. The genuine opposition in the first essay of the *Genealogy* thus can be summarized in its most concise form as: slave morality versus noble morality. Slave morality "begins by rancor turning creative and giving birth to values," "begins by saying *no* to an 'outside,' an 'other,' a non-self, and that *no* is its creative act." Noble morality, by contrast, appears to be more basic, more primitive, or at least more original; it "grows out of triumphant self affirmation" (*GM* 170). Although both of these moral systems are apparently founded on two terms with opposing valences, we should take care to distinguish the way in which their positive and negative evaluations relate to each other. Slave ethics, an ethical system that we can more readily recognize because it is our own ethical system, is founded on opposition. Indeed, it comes into being by positing itself against aristocratic values. Thus it creates an enemy, who is accorded the label of "evil." The valuation "good" is conceived "as a pendant" (*GM* 173) and is assigned almost by default to the Jew/priest making the negative assessment. In aristocratic valuation the pair "good" and "bad" are related in a much different manner. These values are spontaneous; they do not set up antagonisms. The aristocrats seek "out their contraries only in order to affirm themselves even more gratefully and delightedly" (*GM* 171). Thus the "evil" of the slave morality and the "bad" of the noble morality are "ill-matched." "Bad" is a "by-product, a complementary color, almost an afterthought"; "evil" is "the beginning, the original creative act of slave ethics," which thrives on opposition rather than affirmation (*GM* 174). "Good" and "bad" co-exist in non-antagonism until something arises that opposes the "good." The result again is a new system of evaluation that is based on opposition, that begins by saying no and then evaluates itself as a yes.

Since our own moral systems, whether derived from religious beliefs or not, are derivate from slave ethics, we should have no difficulty grasping a system of values based on "good" and "evil." Noble morality, since it is foreign to us, is more elusive, and perhaps for this reason Nietzsche feels compelled to provide his reader with vivid descriptions. The men who adhere to noble morality, he claims, are "strictly constrained by custom, worship, ritual, gratitude, and by mutual surveillance and jealousy" when they are among themselves. In their internal circles they are also marked by "consideration, tenderness, loyalty, pride and friendship." But once they step outside their exclusive circles and enter into a relationship with those who are the common, the lowly, the bad, they appear as "uncaged beasts of prey," "wild animals," or "blond Teutonic beasts." To the "slaves" their actions are rather horrific: "we can imagine them returning from an orgy of murder, arson, rape, and torture, jubilant and at peace with themselves as though they had committed a fraternity prank." These noble races—Nietzsche seems to waver between seeing these nobles as part of a people or as a race unto themselves—are "bent on spoil and conquest" (*GM* 174). Although we have been introduced to the nobles as Aryans, Nietzsche writes that such races are to be found throughout humankind, and he mentions specifically the Romans, the Arabians, the Germans, the Japanese, the Homeric heroes, and the

Scandinavian Vikings. How closely he identifies this noble race with something German and Aryan, however, is evidenced in his remark about the Europe of his day. "The profound and icy suspicion which the German arouses as soon as he assumes power (we see it happening today) harks back to the persistent horror with which Europe for many centuries witnesses the raging of the blond Teutonic beast (although all racial connection between the old Teutonic tribes and ourselves has been lost)" (*GM* 175). No matter how repulsive the actions of the nobles may seem to us, Nietzsche leaves no doubt that he prefers them and their values to the alternative. Although he postulates that "the real meaning of culture resides in its power to domesticate man's savage instincts" (*GM* 176)—thus anticipating the central thesis in Freud's *Civilization and Its Discontents*—he is filled with contempt for the putative slaves: "These carriers of the leveling and retributive instincts, these descendants of every European and extra-European slavedom, and especially of the pre-Aryan populations, represent human retrogression most flagrantly. Such 'instruments of culture' are a disgrace to man and might make one suspicious of culture altogether." And he poses the rhetorical questions: "Who would not a thousand times prefer fear when it is accompanied with admiration to security accompanied by the loathsome sight of perversion, dwarfishness, degeneracy?" (*GM* 176). Although some commentators have wanted to view Nietzsche as a neutral observer of these two systems of values, as a perspectival outsider without preferences, it is difficult not to conclude from the tenor of his descriptions and the rhetoric that accompanies them that he much preferred the blond beasts, despite their violent ways, to the domesticated, cultured Europeans descendants of "Jewish" and "priestly" morals.

Punishment and the Origin of Guilt

The subjects Nietzsche tackles in his second essay are somewhat different. He is less interested in distinguishing two separate systems of values than in explaining the evolution of our feeling of guilt. In some ways the problem that he attacks here is not far removed from topics that preoccupied him in *On the Advantage and Disadvantage of History for Life*. At issue is the creation of a human animal that has memory, that can therefore make promises, that feels responsible, and that therefore has the potential for guilt. Nietzsche first approaches this topic by asking what it takes "to breed an animal with the right to make promises?" (*GM* 189). From this sort of statement we can again see that Nietzsche is working within the familiar dichotomy that operates in much of his thought: an original animal state of happiness, danger, and vitality is compared to a human(e) condition of history, memory, and misery. Here the dichotomy set into play entails memory and oblivion. The latter term is something necessary for the human being; active oblivion, as we saw in chapter 3, is the precondition for action. It functions as a concierge "to shut temporarily the doors and windows of consciousness; to protect us from the noise and agitation with which our lower organs work for or against one another; to introduce a little quiet into our consciousness so as to make room for the nobler functions and functionaries of our organism which do the governing and planning." In short, oblivion clears away the barriers to action: "there can be no happiness, no serenity, no hope, no pride, no *present,* without oblivion" (*GM* 189).

Opposed to this notion of oblivion are remembering, memory, and consciousness of the past. The civilized human being must learn to think causally, to see events as part of a continuity, "to separate necessary from accidental acts." Such a human being is not only capable of calculation and reflection, but has himself become "calculable, regular, necessary even to his own perception" (*GM* 190). The question posed in this second essay is thus the following: How is the human being—according to Nietzsche, a naturally forgetful animal without responsibility or guilt, without regard for promises or obligations—transformed into one who remembers, who is responsible, and who feels remorse, pity, and compassion, one who has a conscience? The answer to this question, which involves exploring the origin or genesis of responsibility, is that the instilling of a conscience was a long process that was etched into him by punishment. The process by which the human being acquires a memory and a conscience is anything but pretty: Nietzsche contends that "there is perhaps nothing more terrible in man's earliest history than his mnemotechnics" (*GM* 192). The main ingredients of conscience were repetition and pain; only those things that hurt will be remembered. Thus, "whenever man has thought it necessary to create a memory for himself, his effort has been attended with torture, blood sacrifice" (*GM* 192–93).

That these statements are not metaphorical is apparent from the evidence that Nietzsche supplies. Referring to primitive penal codes as proof for the difficulty of overcoming forgetfulness and for the necessity to drum "into these slaves of momentary whims and desires a few basic requirements of communal living," he cites techniques that are anything but figures of speech: "stoning, breaking on the wheel, piercing with stakes, drawing and quartering, trampling to death with horses, boiling in oil or wine, the popular flaying alive, cutting out of flesh from the chest, smearing the victim with honey and leaving him in the sun, a prey to flies" (*GM* 193–94). These various practices, Nietzsche suggests, are the basis of our civilization. In this assertion Nietzsche is not really very different from other writers in the German tradition. Like Karl Marx, Sigmund Freud, and Walter Benjamin—to name but a few—he appreciates that civilization is in part a façade for barbarism, and he too contends that the barbarity at the origins of civilization is now concealed or under the surface: "wherever on earth one still finds solemnity, gravity, secrecy, somber hues in the life of an individual or a nation, one also senses a residuum of that terror with which men must formerly have promised, pledged, vouched" (*GM* 192). Where Nietzsche differs from most others writers is in viewing the introduction of reason and consciousness as part of the "civilizing" barbarity. After listing the various methods of torture used to create conscience, Nietzsche concludes: "By such methods the individual was finally taught to remember five or six 'I won'ts' which entitled him to participate in the benefits of society; and indeed, with the aid of this sort of memory, people eventually 'came to their senses'" [literally, "came to reason"] (*GM* 194). For most philosophers reason, or at least consciousness, is still a tool that can assist us in ridding ourselves of barbarity; for Nietzsche reason, consciousness, and conscience are the very tokens of our barbarous condition. Because of this Nietzsche harbors a different evaluation of the primitive state. While most writers believed that we had to overcome our primitive state in order to reach maturity as human beings, Nietzsche appears to mourn its demise. Nietzsche is intrigued by humankind when it becomes "interesting," but his sympathies lie always with an epoch that antedates guilt, bad conscience, historical man, and reason.

As in his first essay, Nietzsche bases his views on the origins of morality in part on linguistic evidence. He believes that compensation lies at the basis of ethical notions, and he cites the proximity of the German words *Schuld* (guilt) and *schulden* (to be indebted) as evidence for this view. Punishment, according to Nietzsche, is the result of a compensation for damages done. It originally resembles the contractual relationship between a creditor and a debtor, and at this stage has nothing to do with guilt or remorse. The question is how can damage incurred by theft or non-payment be balanced out with punishment? How can we establish an equivalence between loss of material goods and the infliction of suffering on someone? Nietzsche's answer to these questions presumes that the infliction of punishment or even the witnessing of punishment is a pleasure for the human being. "An equivalence is provided by the creditor's receiving, in place of material compensation such as money, land, or other possessions, a kind of *pleasure*. That pleasure is induced by his being able to exercise his power freely upon one who is powerless by the pleasure of *faire le mal pour le plaisir de le faire*, the pleasure of rape" (*GM* 196). The pleasure resulting from exercising power over another human being, from having another human being at one's disposal— these primitive legal and contractual obligations are the originative moments in moral conscience. The lower the creditor was in the social order, the more pleasure he derived from this unbridled exercise of power. Nietzsche's support for his hypothesis again comes from historical anecdotes. He notes that celebrations in the past were often accompanied by executions, or that hangings and burnings were moments of communal festivity. Only today, now that we have become "domestic animals" do we shrink from that old, powerful, human, all-too-human sentiment: "To behold suffering gives pleasure, but to cause another to suffer affords an even greater pleasure" (*GM* 198).

Once again we should not be deceived into thinking that the advent of more civilized ways of dealing with punishment and compensation has been beneficial to the human race. In the contemporary world, Nietzsche suggests, we merely sublimate the attendant horror of existence, because we are unable to face what punishment really is and what our original nature continues to desire. "It should be clearly understood," Nietzsche writes, "that in the days when people were unashamed of their cruelty life was a great deal more enjoyable than it is now in the heyday of pessimism." Nietzsche thus conceives of the course of civilization as an alienation from what we originally were. He speaks of "the bog of morbid finickiness and moralistic drivel which has made man ashamed of his natural instincts" (*GM* 199). With the progress of civilization, the elimination of various primitive customs, and the suppression of natural drives, we have distanced ourselves from our nature or from our natural instincts. The cipher for this distancing is not only conscience and morality, but also certain psychological alterations. For one thing, Nietzsche claims that pain is not the same phenomenon today that it was in former times. Regarding black Africans as human beings at a more primitive stage of development, Nietzsche claims that they are able to withstand greater pain than even the most stoic European.[1] Not only has our ability to withstand pain changed, but our enjoyment of pleasure has altered as well. It has been sublimated and "subtilized," so that we no longer take obvious pleasure in cruelty and inflicting punishment as we did in the past. These are further signs for Nietzsche of the destruction of instincts by civilization.

Punishment thus originates, according to Nietzsche, in the nexus of buyer and seller, creditor and debtor, "purchase and sale, together with their psychological trappings" (*GM* 202). In its essence, punishment consists of two parts. Certain permanent and formal features—"custom, the act, the *drama,* a certain strict sequence of procedures" (*GM* 211)— are common to all punishment, while its meaning, its purpose, the expectations attending on the execution of such procedures—in short, the content of and rationale for punishment vary considerably with time and place. The error that is most frequently made in considering punishment, however, is that it is the source of guilt and of bad conscience. Although Nietzsche recognizes the variability of punishment, he emphatically denies that it can instill guilt. He claims, in fact, that punishment actually retards the development of conscience in human beings. Empirically and psychologically, punishment does not introduce a moral feeling or a moral pang; it is experienced as a part of one's fate. The result of punishment is therefore not remorse and guilt, but "a sharpening of man's wits, an extension of his memory, a determination to proceed henceforth more prudently, suspiciously, secretly, a realization that the individual is simply too weak to accomplish certain things; in brief, an increase in self-knowledge" (*GM* 216). Punishment is able to control our instincts and to tame us, but is not able to make us moral.

The source of guilt and bad conscience is quite different. Nietzsche speculates that they originate in an internalization or interiorization of instincts. This interiorization marks simultaneously the transition from "semi-animals, happily adapted to the wilderness, to war, free roaming, and adventure," from "a pack of savages, a race of conquerors, themselves organized for war and able to organize others, fiercely dominating a population perhaps vastly superior in numbers yet amorphous and nomadic," to the human being as a "sociable and pacific creature" (*GM* 217). Unlike punishment, which sharpens our wits for combat, this war against the instincts forces the happy animal, man, to "think, deduce, calculate, weigh cause and effect," reducing us "to our most fallible organ, consciousness" (*GM* 217); our instinct of freedom is forced "to become latent, driven underground, and forced to vent its energy upon itself" (*GM* 220). Punishment produces cunning adaptability, but it does not compel interiorization and self-repression. It does not entail a fundamental break with our animal past. Guilt and bad conscience, however, presuppose a transition to a different type of human being. This transition, like the shift from noble to slave morality, is conceived as a "violent severance" from the animal past, as a leap and a fall at the same time, "an abrupt break," "a thing compelled, an ineluctable disaster" (*GM* 218–19). Similar to his discussion of priestly virtues, Nietzsche admits here too that he holds a certain fascination with this transformation of the human species: it was "so novel, profound, mysterious, contradictory, and pregnant with possibility, that the whole complexion of the universe was changed thereby" (*GM* 218). And later he writes that "bad conscience" has given "birth to a wealth of strange beauty and affirmation" and suggests that it may have "given birth to beauty itself" (*GM* 221). But again from his rhetoric it is apparent that Nietzsche regarded the transformation from rapacious, non-guilty creatures to domesticated human beings to be a misfortune.

Ascetic Ideals

Nietzsche's reflections on ethics and values thus conclude that the human being has undergone a lamentable change with the introduction of evil, guilt, and bad conscience. The negation and interiorization of instinct, however, must have some function, since otherwise there would be no impetus for us to have altered our original and happier mode of existence. Ultimately Nietzsche understands ethics as a branch of human biology. Species change and adapt—in both physical manifestations and intellectual abilities—in order to prosper in a hostile environment. The introduction of a new system of values must therefore preserve or further the species in some fashion, and the last essay in the *Genealogy* is accordingly devoted to answering the question: What is the function of precisely the kind of "ascetic values" that have arisen from repressive and internalized morality? In contrast to the first two essays, Nietzsche's final thoughts abandon the contrast between value systems—good and bad versus good and evil, and punishment versus guilt and bad conscience—and focus the reader's attention instead inside the framework of slave morality. The question Nietzsche articulates at the outset—"What do ascetic ideals betoken?" (*GM* 231)—guides his discussion throughout.[2] His initial answer, that they mean many things, is too vague, however, and the remainder of his analysis consists of his developing a more precise economy of the rancorous sentiments he assigns to modern moral systems.

Nietzsche begins by citing two special cases: artists and philosophers. For the artist, ascetic ideals are indeterminate: they mean either "nothing at all" or such a variety of things "that the result is the same" (*GM* 236). The reason for this is that the artist, in Nietzsche's conception, is a ventriloquist, someone who does not speak with a genuine voice. This is not just a contingency of artistry; it is its very essence. "The truth of the matter is that if he [the artist] *were* the thing, he would be unable to imagine or express it: Homer would not have created Achilles, nor Goethe Faust, if Homer had been an Achilles or Goethe a Faust. An artist worth his salt is permanently separated from ordinary reality" (*GM* 235). Nietzsche suggests that artists, because they are quintessentially derivative and secondary, may become "mouthpieces of the absolute"; they may set up a "telephone line of Transcendence," and wind up, like Richard Wagner in his opera *Parsifal,* spouting ascetic ideals.[3] The philosopher is more directly involved with ascetic ideals. For Nietzsche the philosopher is an individual operating within the confines of post-Socratic thought, whose goal is to maximize his own powers. Ascetic ideals assist him in this endeavor. Proof of the adherence to asceticism and the drive to maximize power comes anecdotally from the biographies of philosophers, in particular from the fact that "the pilosopher abhors marriage and all that would persuade him to marriage, for he sees the married state as an obstacle to fulfillment" (*GM* 242). A married philosopher belongs in a comedy, Nietzsche contends, and to explain the fact that Socrates got married, he attributes it to his great talent for irony.

Behind these half-serious remarks on marriage and philosophers, of course, there is a serious point: Philosophers, Nietzsche is claiming, ruthlessly pursue their own power, and the most effective way to accomplish this is to adopt ascetic ideals. Poverty, humility, and chastity, the three slogans of asceticism, should not be conceived as virtues, but as conditions for the strongest philosophical productivity. Philosophers withdraw from the world, place themselves in the desert or the mountains, travel alone, abuse their bodies, negate their spirits, shun, above all, "three shiny, loud things—fame, princes, and women," and finally, place their animal and sexual instincts in the service of their philosophy (as the artist does in the service of his art) (*GM* 245). The "fondness" that philosophers have evidenced for ascetic values is really part of their strategy to extend their power (*GM* 248). By thus assisting us in our self-violation, they propagate the image of human beings as "nutcrackers" of their own souls; in short, they help affirm the value system that Nietzsche has designated previously and often as slave morality.

The situation Nietzsche has sketched for us is thus somewhat paradoxical. We have, on the one hand, the increasing power and almost infinite adaptability of ascetic values, propagated by the ubiquitous breed of artists and philosophers. Nietzsche's description of the origins of philosophy leaves no doubt that the original philosophers are related to the priests we met in the first essay: "Self-inflicted cruelty, ingenious self-castigation, was the principal instrument of these power-hungry anchorites and innovators, who had first of all to subdue tradition and the gods in themselves in order to be able to *believe* in their new departure." And in its basic character, philosophy has not altered much over the centuries, even if the necessity for its original posture seems to have been eliminated: "The peculiarly withdrawn, anti-sensual, austere attitude of philosophers, which has persisted to this day and has actually come to be seen as the philosophical attitude *par excellence,* is really the product of the emergency in which philosophy found itself at its inception. That is to say, for an unconscionably long time philosophy would not have been possible without an ascetic disguise, an ascetic misinterpretation of motive" (*GM* 251). Nietzsche also affirms the ubiquity of asceticism in the mythological guise of the ascetic priest: "This type is not confined to a single race: he thrives everywhere; all classes of society produce him." On the other hand, however, Nietzsche wants to account for the fact that humankind appears to thrive on the denial and abnegation propagated by ascetic artists and philosophers. Why is it that we continue to live ascetically, why has earth become "strictly an ascetic star, the habitation of disgruntled, proud, repulsive creatures, unable to rid themselves of self-loathing, hatred of the earth and of all living things, who inflict as much pain as possible on themselves, solely out of pleasure in giving pain—perhaps the only kind of pleasure they know"? Or, to frame the question somewhat differently, how is it possible that we have produced in the ascetic priest an "anti-biological species" (*GM* 253), a type of person apparently contrary to life itself? Or, framed in yet another version, Nietzsche can now restate his original question again so that his readers understand its paradoxical content: What do ascetic ideals mean?

The short answer to this question is that ascetic ideals must contribute in some indirect fashion to the survival of the species. If ascetic priests continue to thrive, if asceticism prospers, if we continue to be creatures of self-denial, then it must serve the interests of humankind. We observe here that Nietzsche never abandons his biological assumptions about the human being. Ascetic ideals cannot be completely destructive or else they would not have arisen in the first place. Nietzsche's initial attempt to unravel this riddle reads as follows: "The ascetic ideal arises from the protection and curative instinct of a life that is degenerating and yet fighting tooth and nail for its preservation. It points to a partial physiological blocking and exhaustion, against which the deepest vital instincts, still intact, are battling doggedly and resourcefully. The ascetic ideal is one of their weapons. The situation, then, is exactly the opposite from what the worshipers of that ideal believe it to be. Life employs asceticism in its desperate struggle against death; the ascetic ideal is a dodge for the preservation of life" (*GM* 256). This is indeed a paradoxical situation. According to Nietzsche the ideal that apparently negates life, or at least life-affirming instincts, is secretly employed to foster life. Rather than conceiving of the ascetic ideal as a negative, destructive force, it becomes "one of the major conserving and affirmative forces" (*GM* 257).

The paradox of Nietzsche's argument can be unraveled a bit further if we follow him into the realm of sociology and consider what he has to say about the differential function of ascetic ideals for various social groups. Originally Nietzsche leaves the term "life" undifferentiated, but it becomes obvious that life for him—or at least its justification—lies in the highest specimens, or, as they are called at one point, the "windfalls" (*Glücksfälle*). The function that the ascetic ideal performs in terms of the social order is one of segregation. Since "it is the sick who are the greatest threat to the healthy," since "it is the weaklings, and not their own peers, who visit disaster upon the strong," since "it is the diseased who imperil mankind, and not the 'beasts of prey,'" the ascetic ideal acts to keep the less fortunate away from those who are constitutionally or otherwise blessed with health, strength, and vitality. "Life" obviously refers to something other than the life of every individual human being. What is important in the notion of life for Nietzsche is, as in his essay on history, the survival and perpetuation of the great, the strong, the "windfalls" of humanity (*GM* 258). Nietzsche has little sympathy for those less fortunate in body and mind: "It is the predestined failures and victims who undermine the social structure, who poison our faith in life and our fellow men. Is there anyone who has not encountered the veiled, shuttered gaze of the born misfit, that introverted gaze which saddens us and makes us imagine how such a man must speak to himself?" Nietzsche even speculates about "the conspiracy of the sufferers against the happy and successful" (*GM* 259), and includes in this grouping "sick females, who have unrivaled resources for dominating, oppressing, tyrannizing. The sick woman spares nothing dead or alive; she digs up the longest-buried things" (*GM* 260). The consequence of this venom on the part of rancorous humans is that the strong must be "isolated from the sick, be spared even the sight of the sick, lest they mistake that foreign sickness for their own" (*GM* 261). Life in its highest form must be protected, and it becomes the function of the ascetic ideal, dispensed from the pharmacy of the ascetic priest, to assist in keeping the infirm slaves in line and out of sight.

The ascetic priest is thus thrust into the limelight of Nietzsche's historical mythology again. His function—and the function of ascetic ideals—is to protect life and everything that is worthwhile by caring for the sick, the downtrodden, the poor, the less fortunate. We could conceive of him as a moral welfare system, appearing in various guises throughout history. In his opposition to the beasts of prey, he might be transformed into a new animal, part polar bear, part tiger, part fox. At other moments he becomes a magician or animal tamer (*GM* 262–63). Above all he is a munitions expert, who makes certain that the explosives he handles cause a minimum of damage: "His essential task is to set off the dynamite in such a way that the blast will injure neither himself nor the herd." Translated into less metaphorical language this means that "it is up to the priest to redirect resentment toward a new object," that is, away from the strong and privileged (*GM* 263). And the most cunning way in which the ascetic priest does this is to direct the fault for sickness and weakness back onto those who suffer, to deflect attention from the more fortunate and to make the target of resentment and rancor the weak themselves. Thus the ascetic priest controls the dispensary of "*guilt, sin* or *sinfulness, perdition, damnation.*" His goal is "to render the sick, up to a certain point, harmless, to make the incurable destroy themselves and to introvert the resentment of the less severely afflicted. In other words, his goal is to utilize the evil instincts of all sufferers for the purposes of self-discipline, self-surveillance, self-conquest" (*GM* 265).

The discussion of ascetic values in the *Genealogy* shows most clearly the shift in Nietzsche's ethical thought. In contrast to the 1870s, Nietzsche appears less optimistic about the course of human history. Although the ascetic priests struggle to segregate the weak from the strong, society increasingly accords more room and validity to those who are less "vital." In the *Genealogy* we find a heavy reliance on the natural sciences, as we did in *Human, All Too Human,* but in the later period the only branch of science that is important is biology. Although Nietzsche retains the mechanistic determinism of his earlier years, he is less concerned with the calculability of human actions than he is with the role ethics had played in the evolution of the human species. Finally, the affirmation of progress, of intellect, and of civilization that marked Nietzsche's early position are absent in his later reflections. Older morality is no longer considered crude or retarded, but rather less repressive and more conducive to happiness. The progression of ethical systems and shifts becomes less important than a dichotomized view of human history in which an original, instinctual, and happy animal called man "falls from grace" and becomes the enervated, domesticated, and miserable creatures known as modern moral man. Alongside the vast majority with their ascetic values and priests, Nietzsche detects a breed that combines "sound physical organization with intellectual authority" (*GM* 258). But as the decade of the 1880s proceeds, he appears to believe that in terms of ethics most individuals have reached a nadir in which self-denial and self-afflicted psychological wounds cripple all behavior. The verdict he pronounces on his own era is one of nihilism and decadence. Nietzsche's moral philosophy, which propagates the overcoming of morality, is powerless to do anything but analyze and record this deplorable state of affairs.

Chapter 7
The Anti-Theologian

The second issue that emerges in Nietzsche's later writings is religion. Again we are dealing with matters that had preoccupied Nietzsche for many years. Raised in strict Lutheran surroundings and originally destined for the study of theology, Nietzsche was familiar at firsthand with what religion had become in nineteenth-century Europe. Much to the dismay of his mother, however, he turned away from theology, forsaking the career his father had pursued. Perhaps more important is that from very early on he abandoned a belief in God. His remarks on religion are therefore not criticism from inside the religious community, but an assault on religion from someone standing outside the church. To a certain extent his comments are colored by his rejection of the environment in which he was reared and schooled, that is, by an attempt on Nietzsche's part to separate himself from his roots. The increasing harshness in his anti-religious rhetoric probably has the same source as his increasing estrangement from German nationalism. Indeed, perhaps more than any other element of his work, Nietzsche's critique of religion, especially in the first few decades after his death, accounts for the attractiveness of his views among youthful followers and the vehemence with which he was disdained by more traditional sectors of European society. Criticism of religion and even the avowal of atheism were, of course, hardly novel in the nineteenth century. But seldom in previous writers had the critique been accomplished with such a brilliant style, and never before had large sectors of the population been willing to listen to such harsh pronouncements about matters formerly considered sacrosanct. Nietzsche the anti-theologian continued a long line of German philosophical speculation on religion, but only in the modern era, when belief in orthodox religious notions was on the wane, could his message have achieved such immense popularity.

Religion, Science, and the Christian Psyche

Like his critique of morality, Nietzsche's anti-theology appeared in preliminary form in the 1870s. The first sustained discussion of religious issues is again found in *Human, All Too Human* in a section entitled "The Religious Life." Religion is initially characterized as a systematic attempt to reinterpret our experiences. When we meet with misfortune, Nietzsche claims, we evoke religion because it functions as a palliative and as a hope for some future good. In this regard religion is similar to art since both "endeavour to bring about a change of sensibility, partly through changing our judgement as to the nature of our experience" (*HA* 60). Implicit in this view is the notion common to the nineteenth century that organized religion has the function of obfuscating reality and steering us away from what the actual causes of our afflictions are. Karl Marx's famous dictum that religion is "the opium of the people"[1] comes to mind when Nietzsche remarks that religion is a "momentary amelioration and narcoticizing" (*HA* 60).

Indeed, in keeping with the optimism of his "middle period" and the general faith in science throughout the nineteenth century, Nietzsche notes with approval the demise of belief among his contemporaries and the concomitant rise of more realistic ways of comprehending the world: "The more the domination of religions and all the arts of narcosis declines, the stricter attention men pay to the actual abolition of the ill." Religion is incompatible with knowledge: "one cannot *believe* these dogmas of religion and metaphysics if one has in one's heart and head the rigorous methods of acquiring truth" (*HA* 60). Nietzsche even rejects the hypothesis that would regard belief as an anticipatory form or allegorical form of knowledge. This notion, found in the writings of Schopenhauer, is false because "every religion was born out of fear and need, it has crept into existence along paths of aberrations of reason." For this reason there is an absolute gulf between religious belief and genuine knowledge: "there exists between religion and true science neither affinity, nor friendship, nor even enmity: they dwell on different stars" (*HA* 62). In this period Nietzsche is quite obviously writing in the tradition of the Enlightenment, which juxtaposed religion as narcotic, deception, and superstition to science, truth, and knowledge.

Further evidence of Nietzsche's debt to the Enlightenment is found in his remarks on religion and nature. Once again he sets up two opposing and incompatible ways of comprehending natural forces. At some early phase in human development natural laws are unknown, and humankind conceives of nature magically. Natural occurrences are considered the result of arbitrary actions of divinities that control the world. The introduction of chance and fate as explanations is due to the capriciousness of the gods who act on and in our sphere. "The whole of nature is in the conception of religious men a sum of actions by conscious and volitional beings, a tremendous complex of *arbitrariness.*" In contrast to modern thought, "rude, religiously productive primitive cultures" considered nature to be uncertain and irregular, while human beings were a more or less constant measure. By contrast, in today's society, Nietzsche notes, relying on the writer Johann Wolfgang Goethe, "the more polyphonic human" subjectivity is, the more powerfully is the individual "impressed by the uniformity of nature" (*HA* 63).

These two distinct ways of relating to nature result in radically different practices. Religious men depend on ceremonies and rituals that are intended to control nature, but since nature is considered arbitrary and willful, that control takes the form of imposing regulation on something that is without order or cause: "the meaning of the religious cult is to determine and constrain nature for the benefit of mankind, that is to say *to impress upon it a regularity and rule of law which it does not at first possess*" (*HA* 65). In modern, enlightened thought we endeavor to comprehend the workings of natural forces so that we can better accommodate ourselves to those forces. Perhaps because of his philological training and his continued admiration for the Greeks, Nietzsche, even at his most "enlightened" and "scientific," did not completely reject "primitive" man. He believed that the religious cult is also an expression of "nobler ideas," such as "sympathy between man and man, the existence of goodwill, gratitude, the hearing of petitions, treaties between enemies, the bestowal of pledges, the claim to protection of property" (*HA* 65). Significantly, however, all the advantages of the religious cult appear to be located in social relations between human beings rather than in the relationship between the human being and nature. With regard to the understanding of nature, Nietzsche is clearly a child of the Enlightenment heritage.[2]

Nietzsche's initial discussion of the religious life fails to distinguish among ancient religions, but in subsequent passages he contrasts Hellenic practices with Christian, not surprisingly favoring the former quite heavily over the latter. Christianity is cast as a gruesome belief based on unfounded assertions. When the church bells toll, Nietzsche asserts, it was "because of a Jew crucified 2000 years ago who said he was the son of God. The proof of such an assertion is lacking." The entire mythological configuration of Christianity smacks of magic and superstition; the religion itself is an anachronistic piece of antiquity that fits uncomfortably in the modern era.

> A god who begets children on a mortal woman; a sage who calls upon us
> no longer to work, no longer to sit in judgement, but to heed the signs of
> the imminent end of the world; a justice which accepts an innocent man
> as a substitute sacrifice; someone who bids his disciples drink his blood;
> prayers for miraculous interventions; sin perpetrated against a god atoned
> for by a god; fear of a Beyond to which death is the gateway; the figure
> of the Cross as a symbol of an age which no longer knows the meaning
> and shame of the Cross — how gruesomely all this is wafted to us, as if
> out of the grave of a primeval past! Can one believe that things of this
> sort are still believed in? (*HA* 66)

The most debilitating aspect of the Judeo-Christian heritage, however, is
the relationship between humankind and the godhead, in which humanity is clearly inferior and in servitude to an all-powerful being. By contrast, the Greeks, Nietzsche claims, conceived their gods as reflections of
themselves, as the most "perfect exemplars of their own caste," as an
ideal, rather than an antithesis. In these passages we begin to discern
that the real target of Nietzsche's anti-theological stance is not religion
per se, but Christianity and the Christian heritage. In Greece, individuals could still think of themselves as noble. By contrast, Christianity
"crushed and shattered man completely and buried him as though in
mud: into a total depravity it then suddenly shone a beam of divine
mercy, so that, surprised and stupefied by this act of grace, man gave
vent to a cry of rapture and for a moment believed he bore all heaven
within him" (*HA* 66). The most profound changes in the human being
in terms of psychology and morality are connected with Christianity,
which is actually antithetical to Hellenic beliefs: "it desires to destroy,
shatter, stupefy, intoxicate, the one thing it does not desire is *measure*:
and that is why it is in the profoundest sense barbaric, Asiatic, ignoble,
un-Hellenic" (*HA* 66).

Nietzsche's reflections on the religious life gradually shifted away
from a wholesale anthropological critique of religion, where he was faithful to an Enlightenment lineage, into a criticism of specifically Christian
states of mind, where he made more of an original contribution. Indeed,
the latter part of Nietzsche's discussion of religion in *Human, All Too
Human* could be aptly labeled "the Christian psyche," since in these
aphorisms he explored the psychological constitution of various types of
Christian beliefs. One of these is the prophet or saint. While Christians
have tended to ascribe visionary powers to such a figure, Nietzsche saw
in these individuals "familiar pathological conditions." Ultimately there

are material, physiological sources for the "visions, terrors, states of exhaustion and rapture" of individuals that the church has regarded as holy, but it interprets the malady that they suffer not as an illness, but as a religious experience. Nietzsche uses Socrates to clarify how this attribution functions. "The daemon of Socrates too was perhaps an ear-infection which, in accordance with the moralizing manner of thinking that dominated him he only *interpreted* differently from how it would be interpreted now" (*HA* 68). Analogously the "madness and ravings" of religious figures should be understood as a physical affliction that receives a favorable interpretive overlay. "It is always the degree of knowledge, imagination, exertion, morality in the head and heart of the *interpreters* that has *made* so much of them. For those men called geniuses and saints to produce their greatest effect they have to have constrained to their side interpreters who for the good of mankind *misunderstand* them" (*HA* 69). Religious truths are not simply obfuscations, they are physical duress (mis)understood as a state of revelation.

Nietzsche undertook a similar analysis of the Christian need for redemption. It arises from a certain set of circumstances connected with the human condition after certain religious and moral standards have been inculcated into the individual. Human beings, according to Nietzsche, recognize that there are definite activities that rank low "in the customary order of rank of actions," but that they want nonetheless to perform and do indeed perform (*HA* 70). Individuals also recognize another species of action—altruistic and non-egotistical behaviors— which they get no further than desiring to perform. The result of this inability on the part of the individual to refrain from performing egotistical actions and to perform altruistic actions is depression. This psychological state is exacerbated by religion—and here Nietzsche again seems to refer to the Judeo-Christian heritage—since individuals are compelled to compare their actions not only to those of other men, who are similarly inclined, but to those of God, who is able to perform only selfless acts. At the same time that individuals envy God, they also become fearful of him, imagining that God is punishing them for their inability to emulate his acts. It matters little that this entire scenario is "a succession of errors of reason" that distorts human nature and measures the individual against a false and fantastic standard (*HA* 71). What is important is that Christians actually experience these feelings of self-contempt. At the same time, however, they will also experience momentary respites from their pangs of conscience in occasional feelings of pleasure and contentment. They then reason that these undeserved feelings of pleasure are

the benevolent gifts of the godhead. Just as they had formerly interpreted all unfortunate experiences as a token of divine wrath, now they
believe divine goodness to be the cause of their pleasurable sensations.
"He [the Christian] conceives his mood of consolation as the effect upon
him of an external power, the love with which fundamentally he loves
himself appears as divine love; that which he calls mercy and the prelude
to redemption is in truth self-pardon, self-redemption" (*HA* 73). Thus
through an aberration of reason, fantastic assumptions, and misinterpre-
tations, the Christian psyche invents the need for redemption.

Nietzsche's final psychological observations on religion in *Human, All
Too Human* involve Christian asceticism and holiness. We have already
seen the social and species-specific function attributed to ascetic ideals in
the *Genealogy*. In this earlier work, by contrast, Nietzsche is more interested in the psychology of individuals who themselves practice asceticism
and aspire to saintliness. Nietzsche begins with the observation that by
attempting a rational, psychological explanation, he is violating the
alleged miraculousness and inexplicability of the phenomenon. He then
proceeds to a dissection of the soul of the ascetic, endeavoring to separate
out the complex individual drives that operate within such a person. In
Nietzsche's analysis self-denial is not what it appears to be. Apparently a
self-sacrificing and non-egotistical action, in reality it is a resolution to
an extraordinary state of tension, and thus self-serving. Sacrifice of
another, or revenge, and sacrifice of oneself, or self-denial, both have the
identical function of relieving an intolerable situation. Indeed, Nietzsche
hypothesizes that self-denial, whether it is subordination to an other or
to an abstract set of principles, is often easier than the more hostile alternative, which would call for struggle and conflict. "The saint . . . makes
his life easier through this complete surrender of his personality, and one
deceives oneself if one admires in this phenomenon the supreme heroic
feat of morality" (*HA* 75). With regard to the self-tortures that the saint
or the ascetic often inflicts, Nietzsche comments that these should be
understood as "a means by which these natures combat the general ener-
vation of their will to live." Self-flagellation is a painful stimulant to
counteract the boredom and "great spiritual indolence" associated with
the total subordination of the will to an other or to abstract principles of
morality (*HA* 75).

Finally, Nietzsche considers the "most unusual means the ascetic and
saint employs to make his life nonetheless endurable and enjoyable." The
psychological mechanism to which he refers consists of the internal
enemy that this person sets up within himself. "He exploits especially his

tendency to vanity, to a thirst for honours and domination, then his sensual desires, in an attempt to see his life as a continual battle and himself as a battlefield upon which good and evil spirits wrestle with alternating success" (*HA* 75–76). What Nietzsche is claiming is that the saintly person creates temptation in order to appear as a saint when he overcomes it. Often this temptation takes the form of sexual desire, but what is most important about the temptation is that it be "universally recognized" as an "enemy within" whose combating and overcoming could repeatedly allow the saint to "appear to the non-saints as half incomprehensible, supernatural beings" (*HA* 76). Christianity is the paradigmatic religion of sainthood because it has established a code of values that establishes a vast array of sinfulness. Nietzsche's brilliant insight into this code is that it was not established so that it could be followed, which is humanly impossible, but so that the individual would feel as sinful as possible. This feeling of sinfulness functions as a stimulus to keep us "excited, animated, enlivened in general." At our late stage of development the saint saves us not through his exemplary behavior or his self-denial, but through his creation of new values that relieve us of boredom. "The circle of all natural sensations had been run through a hundred times, the soul had grown tired of them: thereupon the saint and the ascetic invented a new species of stimulant" (*HA* 77). Hitherto the saint as a world-historic figure has been misunderstood and regarded as a proof for the existence of God or the miraculous. Nietzsche's view, however, is that the saint is in reality not a religious phenomenon, but a psychologically extreme specimen in the "perverse and pathological" development of the human species.

The Death of God

In addition to his analysis of religion as an anthropological and a psychological phenomenon, the writings from Nietzsche's middle period also contain perhaps his most celebrated anti-theological claim: the death of God. Formulated partly as a hypothesis about the nature of religion, partly as an observation on the growth of disbelief with regard to the supernatural in the nineteenth century, and partly as a confirmation of the decline of any ethical, epistemological, or metaphysical center for our human endeavors, the death of God was not a novel notion in Nietzsche's era. Heinrich Heine, a German writer from an earlier part of the century, whom Nietzsche admired greatly, had alluded several times to the death of God, most extensively at the close of the second book of

History of Religion and Philosophy in Germany. Heine believed that Kant's *Critique of Pure Reason* was tantamount to the death of God since it shifts epistemological questions from a theocentric to an anthropocentric frame of reference. His poetic description of God's demise obviously stimulated Nietzsche's later formulations:

> Our heart is filled with shuddering compassion—it is ancient Jehovah himself who is preparing for death. We knew him so well, from his cradle in Egypt, where he was reared among divine calves and crocodiles, sacred onions, ibis, and cats. . . . We saw him emigrate to Rome, the capital, where he renounced all national prejudices and proclaimed the divine equality of all nations, and with such fine phrases established an opposition to old Jupiter, and intrigued until he gained supreme authority and from the Capitol ruled the city and the world *urbem et orbem.* We saw how he became even more spiritual, how he whimpered in bland bliss, becoming a loving father, a universal friend of man, a world benefactor, a philanthropist—but all this could avail him nothing—
> Do you hear the little bell ringing? Kneel down. They are bringing the sacraments to a dying god.[3]

Nietzsche could have also drawn on a wealth of other atheistic trends in philosophy. The left Hegelians, for example, initiated a radical criticism of religion by anthropomorphizing the divinity and making him a projection of human thought, while the radical socialists of the pre-1848 period, among them Karl Marx, openly embraced atheism.

Nietzsche's declaration of the death of God, while hardly innovative, is slightly different from those of his predecessors. The first time it occurs in his writings it is formulated as a parable. In the second book of *Human, All Too Human* Nietzsche presents the tale of prisoners who enter a workyard one morning only to discover that their warder has disappeared. Many of these prisoners, however, because of habit, continue to perform their accustomed duties; others remain idle. Suddenly one of the prisoners, who believes he has recognized what the warder's absence means, calls out to his fellow inmates: "Work as much as you like, or do nothing: it is all one. Your secret designs have come to light, the prison warder has been eavesdropping on you and in the next few days intends to pass a fearful judgement upon you. You know him, he is harsh and vindictive." Quite obviously the prisoners here represent humankind, and the absent warder is the Jewish God Jehovah. The first prisoner soon reveals himself to be Jesus Christ: "But pay heed: you have hitherto mistaken me: I am not what I seem but much more. I am the son of the prison warder and I mean everything to him. I can save you, I will save you: but note well, only those of you who *believe* me that I am the son of the prison warder; the rest may enjoy the fruit of their unbelief." After a brief silence various prisoners respond: one says he should put in a good word for the prisoners anyway and leave the matter of belief aside. Another does not believe him at all. A third replies that the prison warder no longer knows anything, because he "has just suddenly died." The first prisoner tries to regain their confidence by promising to set them all free "as surely as my father still lives," but the other prisoners "shrugged their shoulders and left him standing" (*HA* 331). In this parable the death of God as omniscient prison warder has no implications for humankind; the prisoners are neither liberated from their prison, nor relieved psychologically. They simply forfeit their belief in a supreme and omnipotent entity.

Perhaps the most famous passage concerning the death of God occurs in the third book of *The Gay Science*. But in this work, too, the discussion appears in an unusual form. Up to this point most of Nietzsche's aphorisms in this book contained declarative, apodictic statements interspersed with exclamations, occasional questions, and sporadic forms of direct address, but the aphorism that deals with the death of God (#125) is framed as a narrative, similar to the parable in *Human, All Too Human*. It is thus not quite as simple as most commentators have taken it to be, and it certainly is not a simple and unequivocal affirmation of atheism. Significant for this aphorism and for its purported atheistic message is that the main character is mad, and Nietzsche does very little to try to convince us that he is playing with the old trope of madness as a sign of prophesy. The first lines make the incongruence of the madman's actions evident: he brings a lit lantern into the marketplace in the middle of the morning.

Is the implication that his illumination is wasted, or that he is unable to distinguish between dark and light, between Enlightenment and the darkness of superstition? His first words are unusual for an aphorism that would become famous for its atheistic content. The madman cries: "I seek God," and since he has encountered a crowd of non-believers, they mock his apparent faith in a supreme being. Unfazed by this ridicule, the madman changes his tune slightly; instead of seeking God, he turns on the mocking crowd and explains to them where God has gone. God has been the victim of murder, and we, as human beings, are the murderers. The enormity of this crime is emphasized by the images that the madman employs, but these images also suggest what God has meant for humankind: God has been the horizon for our world, the sun to which our earth is chained. Without God, we are set adrift in a universe without mooring, without direction, without orientation, without light, without warmth. Suddenly the image that started the aphorism makes more sense, as the madman asks whether, because of the murder of God, it is not necessary to light lanterns at midday. The madman turns again to the enormity of the deed by stating how difficult it is to atone for such an act. Paradoxically, of course, he frames his discourse about atonement in quasi-religious terms. Finally the madman falls silent, and the drama of the scene continues when he throws down his lantern, which bursts among the onlookers. He continues then in a somewhat different vein, claiming that he has come too early, that the deed of which he speaks occurs slowly, or at least that the news of it travels slowly. The very men who are atheists are still far away from recognizing the import of their own deed. The aphorism ends with a report that the madman has sung the requiem for God in churches and was asked to account for his actions. He did so by calling the churches the tombs and sepulchers of God (*GS* 179–80).

Nietzsche's distance from many other nineteenth-century atheists is signaled by the fact that the death of God is preached to an audience of non-believers by a madman who first announces he is seeking God, before claiming that humankind has murdered him. Nietzsche obviously wanted to distinguish, therefore, between the ordinary non-believers, who may be associated with the Philistine population of Germany and Europe in his times, and a non-believer who, even in his semi-sane state of mind, has a premonition of the enormous significance of the death of God. This aphorism does not discuss the significance, but a passage from *Daybreak* gives us an indication of what Nietzsche may have been thinking. In an aphorism entitled "Egoism against Egoism" he contrasts the common wisdom about religion with his own insights. "How many there are who still conclude: 'life could not be endured if there were no God!' (or, as it is put among the idealists: 'life could not be endured if its foundation lacked an ethical significance')—therefore there *must* be a God (or existence *must* have an ethical significance)!" (*D* 52). Here the existence of God is firmly connected to certain ethical postulates. God is the entity that provides ethical substance for one's action, and that supplies meaning and purpose for life. Nietzsche, of course, disagreed with this theological and idealist postulate, feeling that only those who have become accustomed to this notion would not want to live without believing it. He much preferred to decree the opposite: that life would not be worth living if one had to live under the hegemony of God and ethical imperatives. The key to the madman parable in *The Gay Science* and to Nietzsche's death of God is not simply an affirmation of atheism, but a liberation from the moral constraints that accompany the belief in an omniscient and omnipotent creator.

There are a few other aspects of Nietzsche's assertion of the death of God that merit our attention. The first is articulated most precisely in the final book of *Zarathustra,* when the main character proclaims: "God died: now *we* want the overman to live" (*Z* 399). Evidently Nietzsche connected the death of God and the collapse of "our European morality" (*GS* 279) with the rise of a new type of human being, referred to prominently in *Zarathustra* as the overman. In *The Gay Science* Nietzsche cautions that we are still too much under the initial impression of God's demise to recognize fully the consequences of that event. But the consequences of this death are certainly not sadness and gloom; there is no funeral atmosphere at this wake for the divinity. Rather Nietzsche discerns "a new and scarcely describable kind of light, happiness, relief, exhilaration, encouragement, dawn" (*GS* 280). In characteristic fashion the declaration of a liberation and the general atmosphere of elation do not give us any indication of what the precise ramifications of God's death are. We encounter frequent references to "a new dawn," a free horizon, or an open sea, but we never learn what, besides the absence of Christian morality, has really changed. Another passage may give us a clue to the profundity of this event, however. In *Twilight of the Idols* Nietzsche writes about the role of language in shaping our way of conceiving actions. Essentially Nietzsche assigns language the responsibility for deceiving us about reason, causality, the will as cause, and the autonomy of the ego. His final comments are: "'Reason' in language—oh, what an old deceptive female she is! I am afraid we are not rid of God because we still have faith in grammar." The implications of this statement are far-reaching since they connect God not just with theology and morality, but with epistemology and ontology as well. Thus, although the consequences of the death of God in Nietzsche's work are primarily moral, at times he indicates that this event has the potential to overthrow all conventions of thought and action in Western civilization.

Origin and Function of Christianity

One of the more interesting problems that preoccupied Nietzsche during his final period is the origin of religion. When Nietzsche wrote about this topic he did not mean the historical origin, but rather the psychological origin of, and necessity for, the rise of religious observance and a religious way of life. In a parable devoted to this topic in *The Gay Science* Nietzsche remarks that founders of religions inevitably posit a definitive style of life, a series of customs and regulations that have three characteristics: (1) they discipline the will; (2) they rid the human being of boredom by the mechanisms we have already examined in Nietzsche's analysis of the saint; and (3) they "bestow on this life style an *interpretation* that makes it appear to be illuminated by the highest value so that this life style becomes something for which one fights and under circumstances sacrifices one's life" (*GS* 296). Significant here is the intimate connection between religion and both social customs or the mores of a people and a human psychology that needs to validate existence by reference to a power beyond itself. Among the most insightful and progressive moments in Nietzsche's later writings are those in which he analyzes customs as products of "religious" discipline and admonishes individuals for enslaving themselves to ideal entities, such as God, rather than relying on themselves. Nietzsche speculates that the founders of Christianity met with success because they appealed to the populace in the Roman provinces and their actual way of life. Early Christian evangelists were able to provide an exegesis for life that supplied it with the highest meaning. In a similar vein Buddha appealed to people who were "good and good-natured from inertia," who "lived abstinently, almost without needs" (*GS* 296–97). Founders of religion are genial in that they understand how to create values that clarify existence, how to codify behaviors already performed, and how to collect otherwise dispersed persons into a communty of believers.

Nietzsche's interest in the origin of religions is ultimately related to his critique of the Judeo-Christian heritage. What is significant about this heritage is that it represents the most drastic and consequential overturning of natural values, of instincts, and of aristocratic ethics. In *The Antichrist,* where Nietzsche articulates his most sustained assessment of the Christian tradition, he notes that Judaism initially promulgated the "correct" and "natural" relationship to things. "Yahweh was the expression of a consciousness of power, of joy in oneself, of hope for one-self: through him victory and welfare were expected; through him nature was trusted to give what the people needed—above all, rain" (*AC* 594). The Jewish religion was thus originally a natural religion in which God assumed the role of an all-powerful and vengeful monarch. At some point, however, the essence of the Hebrew God changed. Yahweh ceased being the God who dispensed justice to a given people; he became "denatured" and abstract, "a god only under certain conditions." The essential change occurs with the introduction of the notions of sin and blessing, and with a morality based on punishment for bad deeds and on rewards for good deeds. According to Nietzsche, this moral system represents an anti-natural substitution for a morality that was formerly natural: "Morality—no longer the expression of the conditions for the life and growth of a people, no longer its most basic instinct of life, but become abstract, become the antithesis of life—morality as the systematic degradation of the imagination, as the 'evil eye' for all things" (*AC* 595). This turn to a supreme being who makes ethical demands on a people, who is conceived in terms of conscience and abstract morality, is the most fateful turn in the history of European civilization.

The chief responsibility for inculcating this new religious doctrine into the Jewish people fell to the priests. We will recall that the priests to whom Nietzsche refers in the *Genealogy of Morals* were part of a historical mythology and not readily locatable in time. In *The Antichrist* they emerge as historical agents connected with a specific phase in the history of Judaism. Their masterful plan involved a massive falsification of history, according to which they translated past words and deeds into the religious terminology of salvation, guilt, and piety. The Bible is the record of that falsification. Because of thousands of years of indoctrination, we no longer conceive of the "moral world order" as something false and unnatural. We have become used to the ecclesiastical interpretation of history, which consists of the following premises: "That there is a will of God, once and for all, as to what man is to do and what he is not to do; that the value of a people, of an individual, is to be measured according to how much or how little the will of God is obeyed; that the will of God manifests itself in the destinies of a people, of an individual, as a ruling factor, that is to say, as punishing and rewarding according to the degree of obedience" (*AC* 596). These tenets with which the Judeo-Christian tradition has operated for millennia deflect attention from the real beneficiaries of religious morality: the priests themselves. The priest represents "a parasitical type of man, thriving only at the expense of all healthy forms of life"; he "uses the name of God in vain; he calls a state of affairs in which the priest determines the value of things 'the Kingdom of God'" (*AC* 596). The hegemony of the priest means that all natural behavior, everything that formerly emanated from the instincts and contained value in itself, is ritualized and conferred with a new value, an anti-value resulting from a desecration of natural existence.

Christianity represents an extension and continuation of the regime of the Jewish priesthood. The difference between Christianity and Judaism is that the former negates the remnants of the older Jewish religion and thus turns religion into a unremitting advocate of self-abnegation. It does this by negating the notion of the Jewish people as a chosen people. The Christian God claims domination over the entire globe and demands obedience from everyone, not just a single tribe. As a divinity he therefore becomes more abstract and more unreal. In thus negating the specifically Jewish church, Christianity also rebels against the hierarchy that still existed in the Jewish social order, that last remnant of a more noble Judaism prior to its infiltration by the priesthood. In Nietzsche's interpretation Christ was not opposing the corruption of Jewish leaders, as the Gospels lead us to believe, but "caste, privilege, order, and formula as such," in short, the "hard-won *last* chance of survival, the residue of its [the Jewish people's] independent political existence" (*AC* 599). In the origins of Christianity Nietzsche locates the same political tendency that he finds so pernicious in his own era.[4] As the codification of Christ's morality—whether distorted or not—the Christian religion amounts to the most consequential reversal and perversion of natural hierarchy.[5] Christ is the original anarchist; his death on the cross is not for our moral guilt, but for his own *political* guilt in attempting to overturn an established order. In Nietzsche's worldview the Christian religion originates in a revaluation of values that is antiinstinctual, democratic, and antithetical to natural hierarchies.

Nietzsche's reflections on the origin and function of religious beliefs are also framed at times in terms of the notions of debtor and creditor. In sections of *The Genealogy of Morals,* for example, Nietzsche speculates that humankind's notion of the divinity arises from the relationship between creditor and debtor as it manifests itself in the relationship between the living and their deceased ancestors. From respect for their ancestors and sacrifices made to them, the attitude of humankind gradually developed into a veneration of the divine. As the power of a particular tribe increases, the debt grows until "we arrive at a situation in which the ancestors of the most powerful tribes have become so fearful to the imagination that they have receded at last into a numinous shadow: the ancestor becomes a god" (*GM* 222). Divinities arise, like punishment, from an endeavor to pay off a debt; the emotion connected with the rise of divinities is fear. Although Nietzsche is referring to tribal worship here, it is obvious that the same pattern applies to monotheistic religions as well. From this logic of origin, however, it would seem to follow that the decline in religious belief and the concomitant rise of atheism would lessen the guilty conscience. If there is no god, then there is no creditor, and if there is no creditor, then there is no debt or guilt (again the German word *Schuld* means both "debt" and "guilt"). Christianity is fascinating in this regard because it presents us with a situation in which God sacrifices himself for humankind. Christ, Nietzsche explains, pays our debt to God the father, but in so doing, he places us only further in his debt. The paradoxical situation of a creditor paying a debt for a debtor out of love is one that arouses disbelief in Nietzsche, and his analysis is meant to show us what is happening "behind all these façades" (*GM* 225). The real story for Nietzsche has little to do with the biblical myth. Rather it is a macabre tale of the human psyche in which we long for self-torture, embracing the guilt and bad conscience that arose when we were converted from our semi-animal state into domesticated house pets:

> The thought of being in God's debt became his new instrument of torture. He [man] focused in God the last of the opposites he could find to his true and inveterate animal instincts, making these a sin against God. . . . He stretched himself upon the contradiction "God" and "Devil" as on a rack. He projected all his denials of self, nature, naturalness out of himself as affirmations, as true being, embodiment, reality, as God (the divine Judge and Executioner) as transcendence, as eternity, as endless torture, as hell, as the infinitude of guilt and punishment. In such psychological cruelty we see an insanity of the *will* that is without parallel: man's will to find himself guilty, and unredeemably so; his will to believe that he might be punished to all eternity without ever expunging his guilt; his will to poison the very foundation of things with the problem of guilt and punishment and thus to cut off once and for all his escape from this labyrinth of obsession; his will to erect an ideal (God's holiness) in order to assure himself of his own absolute unworthiness. What a mad, unhappy animal is man! (*GM* 226)

Nietzsche's analysis of the Christian divinity is that he serves as a focal point to heighten and exacerbate our bad conscience. We preserve and increase our guilt by a process of self-denial, and intensify our guilt by pro-jecting a perfect creditor, one who even sacrifices himself for us his debtors, and in whose debt we will be eternally. Christianity thus comes into being and functions as an aid in our self-tortuous process of domestication.

There are two moments in the Western world that counterbalance the self-abnegation of the Christian tradition.[6] The first is located in Greece, where a different relationship to the divinities prevailed. In Nietzsche's view the Greek gods are no more real than their tribal counterparts, but unlike these, they represent "nobler ways of creating divine figments." Indeed, Greek gods, according to Nietzsche, function in a manner that is directly antagonistic to the function of tribal gods and the Christian trinity. Nietzsche explains this function as follows: "For a very long time the Greeks used their gods precisely to keep bad conscience at a dis-tance, in order to enjoy their inner freedom undisturbed." Sin is a notion that is foreign to Nietzsche's conception of the Greek world; when a god criticizes a human action, it is not placed in a framework of evil or sin, but "foolishness, lack of discretion, slight mental aberration." The gods served as the source of evil and misfortune; they "were not agents of punishment," Nietzsche maintains, "but, what is nobler, repositories of guilt" (*GM* 228).

The other moment of nobler sentiments lies in Nietzsche's vision of a world in which the Christian worldview has run its course. Nietzsche longs for a time when the "millennial heritage of conscience-vivisection and cruelty to the animals in ourselves" will be overcome, and a "con-verse effort" will be born. His rhetoric about the change from the Judeo-Christian regime of guilt and bad conscience to a validation of the instincts is ominous and vague: "To accomplish that aim, different minds are needed than are likely to appear in this age of ours: minds strength-ened by struggles and victories, for whom conquest, adventure, danger, even pain, have become second nature. Minds accustomed to the keen atmosphere of high altitudes, to wintry walks, to ice and mountains in every sense. Minds possessed of a sublime kind of malice, of that self-assured recklessness which is a sign of strong health" (*GM* 229). He calls for a "true Redeemer of great love," a creative spirit, a person of the future, a "great and decisive stroke of midday," an antichrist and antini-hilist, "a conqueror of God and nothingness" (*GM* 230). Unlike Christ, this redeemer will deliver us from guilt, from bad conscience, from the will to nothingness; he will liberate our will from its present tyranny and restore our hope. Who can doubt that Nietzsche's Zarathustra is the mythological figure embodying just such a positive redemptive spirit?

Religion and Social Hierarchy

Perhaps because of his antipathy to the Judeo-Christian tradition, Nietzsche also comments frequently that Eastern religions are an alternative to the nihilistic reign of Christianity. Essentially Nietzsche finds these religions to be more honest and appropriate responses to life. Islam, for example, is extolled for appealing to "noble, to *male* instincts" and for saying "Yes to life." Indeed, Nietzsche views Moorish culture in Spain as even "more congenial to our senses and tastes than Rome and Greece"; the demise of Islamic influence in Europe is a sign of a pernicious moral depravity (*AC* 652). Similarly he evaluates Buddhism as "a hundred times more realistic than Christianity." Although, like Christianity, it is a nihilistic religion that relies on internalization and denial, Nietzsche believes that it has overcome the ethical constraints that mark Christian denominations. Buddhism has already disposed of both the concept of God and the necessity to struggle against sin; it is "beyond good and evil." What Nietzsche seems to admire in Buddhism is that it takes into account two physiological and evolutionary realities: our increased susceptibility to pain and an overspiritualization of our beings that has resulted in a subordination of personality to abstractions. In proscribing "hygienic measures" to counter our real situation, Buddha took into account our actual condition and sought to soothe and comfort. In comparison to Christianity, Buddhism proscribes no prayer and no ascetic measures; it promotes life in the open air, moderation in eating, avoidance of intoxicants. Most important of all, however, it needs no enemy. Rancor and *ressentiment* are absent; individuals are compelled to concentrate on themselves in a positive fashion. "In the Buddha's doctrine, egoism becomes a duty." Contributing further to Nietzsche's admiration of Buddhism is his belief that it is a religion of the elite: "the movement had to originate among the higher, and even the scholarly, classes." In general, Islam and Buddhism—at least as Nietzsche portrays them in *The Antichrist*—are the result of ethical responses antithetical to Christianity. They therefore qualify as religions of affirmation and positive spirituality.

Nietzsche reserves his most fervent praise, however, for the Hindu religion, especially as it is represented in a particular tract of behavioral codes: "The Law of Manu." Discovered by Nietzsche in May of 1888 in a French translation[7] and mentioned frequently in notes and works of his last year of sanity, the "Law of Manu," more literally translated as "Tradition of Manu," is a Sanskrit text (the *Manu-Smrti* or, more officially, *Manava-Dharmasastra*) that is one of the most authoritative of the books of the Hindu code (*Dharmasastra*). Although the work that comes down to us was probably written between the first century B.C. and the first century A.D., the original texts on which it is based probably date back to the fifth or sixth century B.C. The text is actually less a lawbook in the strict sense of the word than a tract that talks about customs, traditions, or behavior, which is the approximate meaning of *dharma*. In short, it is a book of what we might call practical morality. The "Tradition of Manu" prescribes to the Hindu believer his *dharma,* or set of obligations as a member of a certain caste (*varna*) and at a certain stage of life (*asramas*). Composed in verse form and consisting of 12 chapters with 2,694 stanzas, the work ranges over a wide variety of subjects, not distinguishing between what we would classify as secular and religious spheres. Among the topics it discusses are dietary restrictions, marriage, donations, rites, the soul, and hell. Its actual author is unknown, but authorship is attributed to the mythological figure Manu, who is an amalgamation of both Adam and Noah in the Indian tradition. Obviously this attribution of authorship gives the work an authority that is immense, and this accounts for the extreme importance of this document in the Hindu tradition.

Nietzsche's interest in this important religious text focuses almost exclusively on the descriptions of social structure, which he associates with a morality of breeding. He is fascinated in particular by the description of four castes, which he takes to be different "races" that are to be bred at the same time: the priest (*Brahmana*), the warrior (*Ksatriya*), the farmer and merchant (*Vaisya*), and the servant (*Sudra*). In *Twilight of the Idols* Nietzsche expresses admiration for the attempt to distinguish classes of people by social function: "Obviously, we are here no longer among animal tamers: a kind of man that is a hundred times milder and more reasonable is the condition for even conceiving such a plan of breeding. One heaves a sigh of relief at leaving the Christian atmosphere of disease and dungeons for this healthier, higher, and *wider* world. How wretched is the New Testament compared to Manu, how foul it smells!" (*TI* 503). In *The Antichrist* Nietzsche returns to Manu (*AC* 642–47), again comparing it favorably with the Bible of the Judeo-Christian heritage. In the Christian tradition he finds only "*bad* ends": "poisoning, slandering, negation of life, contempt for the body, the degradation and self-violation of man through the concept of sin." The Hindu tradition brings a welcome antidote for him. "It is with an opposite feeling that I read the law of Manu, an incomparably spiritual and superior work: even to mention it in the same breath with the Bible would be a sin against the spirit." In Manu he finds a real philosophy, in contrast to the "foul-smelling Judaine of rabbinism and superstition." Again what seems to attract Nietzsche is the strict social differentiation: "Not to forget the main point, the basic difference from every kind of Bible: here the *noble* classes, the philosophers and the warriors, stand above the mass; noble values everywhere, a feeling of perfection, an affirmation of life, a triumphant delight in oneself and in life." If we consider Nietzsche's repeated and incessant polemic against democratizing and leveling tendencies in the nineteenth century, we can understand better the appeal that Manu had for him. Within the framework of his social philosophy, Manu confirmed for him the existence of religions based on a "natural" and orderly arrangement of society.

In his discussion in *Twilight of the Idols* Nietzsche expresses particular fascination for a specific manifestation of Indian society to which Manu alludes. In the notion of the chandala, a lowest caste composed of products of mixed marriages, Nietzsche finds a welcome term for the despicable, the despised, the miserable, the wretched, the lowly, the miserable—in short, for everything he associated with Christians, democrats, anarchists, and socialists in his contemporary world.[8] Although Nietzsche's point is that the Hindus developed a morality based on sickness to deal with its outcasts, not unlike the mechanism that he finds among the ascetic priests in Christianity, throughout his last texts the chandala becomes the prototype for the Judeo-Christian heritage itself. What is more, the chandala is viewed as the very opposite of the Aryan.

> These regulations [against the chandala] are instructive enough: here we encounter for once *Aryan* humanity, quite pure, quite primordial—we learn that the concept of "pure blood" is the opposite of a harmless concept. On the other hand, it becomes clear in which people the hatred, the chandala hatred, against this "humaneness" has eternalized itself, where it has become religion, where it has become *genius*. Seen in this perspective, the Gospels represent a document of prime importance; even more, the book of Enoch. Christianity, sprung from Jewish roots and comprehensible only as a growth on this soil, represents the counter-movement to any morality of breeding, of race, of privilege: it is the *anti-Aryan* religion par excellence. Christianity—the revaluation of all Aryan values, the victory of chandala values, the gospel preached to the poor and base, the general revolt of all the downtrodden, the wretched, the failures, the less favored, against "race": the undying chandala hatred of the *religion of love*. (TI 504–5)

This passage is rather suggestive and somewhat ominous in its dichotomizing. Nietzsche identifies "humanity" with Aryan values and opposes these values to a religion that had its origin in the Jewish tradition. Although the brunt of his attack throughout his later works is borne by Christianity, the opposition between Aryan and Jew here and in other passages is striking and can be easily mistaken for political anti-Semitism, a movement and discourse with which Nietzsche otherwise took pains not to be associated.[9] Perhaps more important for Nietzsche's concerns is the way in which the chandala fits into the historical mythology that is his trademark in discussions of ethics and religion. One of the reasons he was so impressed by the "Law of Manu" is because he was able to locate there a mythical origin and a confirmation for his own view of Christianity and its proclivity for establishing a new, more democratic social order. In contrast to Christian religions, which disguise this origin in a false universalism, the caste system of Hindu faith concretizes a real, necessary, and natural relationship among human beings.

We would misunderstand Nietzsche if we believed that he ascribed some sort of higher truth to Eastern religions. As a psychologist (observer of human nature), philologist (careful reader of texts), and a genealogist (researcher into origins and descent), Nietzsche did not believe that any religion could replace science. Before he began to laud "The Law of Manu," he grouped all religious texts together as "holy lies" (*AC* 642). No religion is true in the sense of being able to claim absolute and eternal validity. Indeed, as ideologies that perform the (necessary) function of mediating social relations and natural phenomena to our consciousness, they are necessarily false. What distinguishes Judaism and Christianity from other religions, however, is the purpose and function of the lie. In contrast to Buddhism, Islam, and Hinduism, the Judeo-Christian heritage propagates an interiorized spirituality of rancor and asceticism. Eastern religions, despite their shortcomings, are at least consonant with fundamental truths of human nature, with reality as people live and experience it, and with values compatible with venerated traditions.

Ultimately Nietzsche's views on religion are another aspect of his greater worldview. While writing about Manu he affirms that "a high culture is a pyramid: it can stand only on a broad base" (*AC* 646)—thus recalling his earliest reflections on *Bildung* and the necessity of privilege in his early years. In the initial sections of *The Antichrist* he mentions the overman, who is now just a product of chance occurrence, but who could be consciously bred, while "the weak" and "the failures" should perish.

Here we are reminded that his radically anti-Christian stance is intimately connected with a number of scientific postulates that he adopted earlier in his career. And in almost all of his remarks about religions we recognize that they are tantamount to codification of ethical systems, that these ethical systems are evaluated according to their affirmation or repudiation of social stratification, and that consistently Nietzsche validates those social arrangements that are hierarchical, unequal, and therefore "noble." Nietzsche's anti-theology is not simply anti-Christian, although the brunt of his assault is directed against Christianity as well as against its predecessor, Judaism. It is also a positive doctrine that summarizes cultural, moral, and scientific assumptions and values to which he adhered throughout his mature life.

Chapter 8

The Great Anticipator

The focus of this book has been the ways in which Nietzsche participated in the discourses and tendencies of nineteenth-century Germany and Europe. Nietzsche's views evidence various connections with his times; from his early years as a Wagnerian hoping to revitalize German culture to his critique of the Judeo-Christian tradition, from his concerns with a refurbished educational system to his preoccupation with science, and from his observations on social and political movements of his day to his critique of Wilhelmine morality, Nietzsche developed his thought in active dialogue with his contemporaries. This nineteenth-century Nietzsche, however, is only one part of the Nietzsche story, and it is perhaps not even the most interesting part. There is also the important Nietzsche legacy, the reception of the writer/philosopher in the twentieth century. The enormity of Nietzsche's impact can hardly be exaggerated. Since his death in 1900, he has been associated with almost every major cultural, political, and philosophical movement in the Western world. No other writer has succeeded as well as Nietzsche in impressing such an array of subsequent thinkers. Putatively opposing ideologies have competed for his patronage; traditions that otherwise admit nothing in common find Nietzsche an ally in their endeavors. On the political front he has been considered a promoter of anarchism, fascism, libertarianism, liberal democracy, and—despite his pointed polemics against the most modern manifestation of slave morality—socialism. In the realm of culture he has been viewed as an inspiration for aestheticism, futurism, impressionism, expressionism, modernism, dadaism, and surrealism. In philosophical circles he has allegedly influenced phenomenology, hermeneutics, existentialism, poststructuralism, and deconstruction. The list of major twentieth-century intellectuals who mention Nietzsche in a favorable light would include almost everyone of any import. In contrast to his relative obscurity during his own conscious lifetime, Nietzsche has thrived in subsequent culture and thought—in Germany, in Europe, and throughout the world.

The reasons for this astounding popularity may not have been entirely clear from the foregoing chapters. Much of what Nietzsche propounded in social theory is conservative or even reactionary, and in most cases what he had to say about history, society, and politics is not very developed. His speculative theories, such as "eternal recurrence" or "the will to power," are untenable in the terms Nietzsche presented them and often naive from the perspective of the natural sciences, to which Nietzsche frequently appealed. And his cultural critique, although attractive for many in its broad outlines, is sometimes quirky and usually vaguely formulated. That Nietzsche could fascinate so many diverse groups and individuals must have its origins in something other than a careful and consistent reading of his actual thought. Indeed, there seem to be three aspects that attracted him to subsequent thinkers. (1) Nietzsche touched on a wide array of topics that were interesting and made pithy statements about these topics that piqued the fantasy of eager readers. Observers have often noted that Nietzsche, much like the Bible, is a treasure chest of quotations. As Kurt Tucholsky, the most renowned satirical writer from the Weimar Republic (1919–33), commented: "Who cannot claim [Nietzsche] for their own? Tell me what you need and I will supply you with a Nietzsche citation . . . for Germany and against Germany; for peace and against peace; for literature and against literature—whatever you want."[1] As we have seen, Nietzsche is fairly consistent on a number of topics, but he did change and intensify his views over the years. The result is that writers selecting particular passages can use Nietzsche, as Tucholsky suggests, for opposing positions. (2) A related reason has to do with Nietzsche's historical and intellectual situation. More than any previous writer Nietzsche called into question presuppositions and accepted knowledge. In particular he was skeptical about the tradition of European Enlightenment, and the fact that many twentieth-century thinkers have similarly taken exception to "truths" of the Enlightenment has made him their natural ally. As Steven Aschheim, the author of the most comprehensive study of Nietzsche's influence in Germany, contends, the answer to the fascination with Nietzsche "must be sought in his almost uncanny ability to define—and embody—the furthest reaches of the general post-Enlightenment predicament; to encapsulate many of its enduring spiritual and intellectual tensions, contradictions, hopes, and possibilities."[2] (3) Finally, a factor that should not be underestimated in Nietzsche's popularity is his superb command of the German language. Many of Nietzsche's contemporaries expressed post-Enlightenment thoughts, but only Nietzsche formulated them in such a way to attract hordes of disciples. No matter what he wrote, no matter how abhorrent or how seductive the ideas, Nietzsche remained a consummate stylist. Furthermore, the forms that he chose—usually shorter aphorisms or essay-like ruminations—allow readers to interact creatively with his works. More than traditional essayists, his texts are open and suggestive; frequently, like parables or sacred scriptures, they seem to require interpretation. Without this brilliance of style and this openness of form, Nietzsche would probably not have exerted such a wide-ranging appeal for the twentieth-century mind.

Despite the vast and varied influence Nietzsche's works have exercised on subsequent generations, there are some common tendencies in his reception and some shifts in emphasis over time. Since his mental collapse in 1889 the course of Nietzsche's reception has evidenced three general stages. Until the beginning of World War I, Nietzsche was known mostly as a cultural critic; his reputation was tied mainly to his acerbic assaults on Wilhelmine society and to his advocacy of cultural renewal. Although this cultural dimension continues to be important throughout the twentieth century, with the advent of the war Nietzsche became political. The height of his political reception occurred undoubtedly under National Socialism, where he was hailed as the thinker who anticipated in writing what Hitler had brought into reality. Finally, after World War II there was a need to rehabilitate Nietzsche from his association with National Socialism. The work of purification was carried out chiefly in the name of philosophy: Nietzsche's rehabilitation in Germany, but even more so in the United States and France, was accomplished more on the basis of his putative philosophical insight than his cultural critique or political usefulness.

Critic of Wilhelmine Culture

Nietzsche's earliest reception involves his harsh attacks on German society. Although Nietzsche was not entirely unknown before 1890, the sales of his books and the number of reviews and discussions of his works indicate that his reputation was restricted largely to Wagnerians, former Wagnerians, and a few odd people who came into contact with him or his work more by coincidence than design. It did not take very long, however, for his popularity to soar. By 1896 Heinrich Mann could state that Nietzsche was too much of a modish philosopher to be assessed and understood correctly.[3] Three years prior to Mann's utterance the sociologist Friedrich Tönnies composed a pamphlet entitled "Nietzsche Nitwits," in which he criticized Nietzsche's views on morality and all those who mindlessly borrowed them. And in 1897 Tönnies could write a text rebuking *The Nietzsche Cult,* which had appropriated Nietzsche in the false hopes of liberation.[4] Indeed, perhaps the dominant reading of Nietzsche prior to 1914 relied on the emancipationist rhetoric strewn about his texts. For this reason he was commonly adopted by, and associated with, any individual or group that opposed the status quo. Significantly this identification extended even to the socialists, whom Nietzsche had despised. In a relatively obscure play by Robert Misch from 1902, the son of an aristocratic bureaucrat tells a friend: "Nietzsche is nonsense, father says, a hack and a social democrat."[5] The reason that such a sentence did not seem out of place at the turn of the century was that Nietzsche had already become more of an anti-Wilhelmine phenomenon than a writer whose texts were read and analyzed carefully for their precise meaning. Writing in 1895, Michael Georg Conrad gives some indication of the vaguely oppositional sentiment connected with Nietzsche's works. After a brief citation from a Nietzsche text that speaks of the many daybreaks that have not yet dawned for us, he comments: "With him we stand on the track of ascendant life. With him we have not been entrapped and encapsulated in any abstract ideal, in any paper principles, in any deadly dogma, in any furtively murdering, vampire-like, blood-sucking authority."[6] By the time of Nietzsche's death his reputation in Germany as an iconoclastic thinker and rebel against the norms of Wilhelmine society had spread widely and rapidly.

The promise of liberation from the oppressive social, moral, and political values of a conservative society made Nietzsche especially popular among successive generations of young oppositional movements. Nietzsche was hailed by the anarchist and bohemian wing of the naturalists in the 1890s; he quickly became a hero of the youth movement in Germany, which gained momentum after the turn of the century; and, in the teens, he was especially popular among the poets and playwrights that came to be known as expressionists. Comprised mostly of middle-class sons rebelling against an establishment associated with their fathers and bourgeois propriety, all three of these groups embraced Nietzsche as a liberator and prophet. Nietzsche's reception in expressionism was typical. One of the founding documents of this movement, "The New Pathos" by Stefan Zweig, fashions a version of Nietzsche suitable for a group of young, aspiring, oppositional poets. In contrast to previous artistic creations with their reliance on form, conscious construction, and traditional tropes, Zweig emphasizes feeling, spontaneity, and emotion. In the context of describing a new paradigm for poetry he calls on Nietzsche's "yea-saying pathos *par excellence,*" which produces pleasure, strength, will, and ecstasy. "This poem should not be sensitive and plaintive and should not express a personal grief so that someone else can empathize with it; rather it should be inspired by joy and excess, by the will to produce ardor and passion from joy. . . . The new pathos must contain the will, not to a soulful vibration or to a refined aesthetic pleasure, but to a deed."[7] For the expressionists—and for most of the "bourgeois oppositional" groups—Nietzsche becomes an inspirational figure whose message is one of action and assertion of will. Even critics of expressionism and Nietzscheanism were compelled to recognize him as "the greatest prophet of individualism in Germany" and "the most powerful liberator that German souls have experienced since Luther."[8]

It is only slightly contradictory that the very aestheticism against which the expressionists polemicized also considered itself to be derivative in some respect from Nietzsche's thought. The discrepancy in receptions is partially due to a reliance on different portions of Nietzsche's writings. Bourgeois oppositional groups, like the expressionists, cited rather carelessly and vaguely the many passages containing "revolutionary gestures" from Nietzsche's aphoristic works; more aesthetically inclined authors would point to writings and sections that advocated cultural renewal and artistic quality, in particular *The Birth of Tragedy*. But groups like the George Circle, named for its leader, the poet Stefan George, also read the identical texts differently. Where oppositional groups believed Nietzsche was attacking a philistine society and its moral presumptuousness, George and his disciples found him to be a promoter of elitist values in contrast to the mediocrity of Wilhelmine cultural pretensions. While the expressionists, or at least Zweig in his early programmatic essay, expounded a vitalist message that included an appeal to the masses and the emotions, elitists like George emphasized Nietzsche's anti-democratic doctrine and his hatred of the rampant massification of modern society. And whereas many of the younger enthusiasts for Nietzsche believed that he was the herald of a new age of liberation, the more conservative aesthetes regarded him as a prophet who reinforced hierarchy and who wanted to reestablish an aristocratic order based on artistic and philosophical talent.

The renewal that the cultural elitists desired required a forerunner to justify their own wishes, and accordingly Nietzsche was stylized into an aesthetic prophet. Important for the George Circle was therefore Nietzsche's alleged overcoming of the nineteenth century. There were various dimensions to this overcoming. One had to do with the natural sciences, an activity associated with nineteenth-century thought, but which were considered by George and his cohorts inadequate to capture the genuine spirituality of German culture. Although Nietzsche, as we have seen, had a quite differentiated attitude toward the sciences and a healthy respect for their accomplishments, he was recruited in aesthetic circles solely as the propagator of a new mythology to replace the positivist and scholarly truths propounded by the academic and cultural establishment. Nietzsche was also regarded as someone who was able to overcome the philistinism of German society—or at least as someone who pointed the way toward a new cultural order. In spite of Nietzsche's various disparaging comments about poets and artists, he was viewed by the George Circle as a proponent of visionary poetry, such as Nietzsche and George himself composed. Above all, however, Nietzsche was valued for his separation from the rabble, for his solitariness, and for his geniality. In a poetic eulogy written by George himself in 1900, Nietzsche is called "the thunderer" and "the only one of thousands," who sends his "last dull lightning bolts" on "flat middleland and dead city." Underneath him the masses trot along in a stupor; there are flatterers among them, "vermin that stain him with praise," but the poet waits for them to waste away so that Nietzsche, resplendent, can "face the ages like other leaders with the bloody crown." The poet continues:

> Redeemer thou thyself the most unblessed—
> Burdened with the weight of which fates
> Hast thou never, laughing, seen the land of longing?
> Didst thou create gods but to overthrow them,
> never enjoying rest or what thou built?
> Thou hast destroyed what in thyself was closest
> to tremble after it with new desire
> and to cry out in pain of solitude.[9]

In this poem, and in the other writings of the aesthetic elitists, Nietzsche is stylized, as he often stylized himself, into the lonely sufferer, the prophet unheeded in his time, the noble revaluator of values. Indeed, the general opinion of the George Circle was that Nietzsche's mission was left unfinished, and that it was left to them, the true heirs to Nietzsche's legacy, to complete the transformation of culture he had envisioned.

The Political Activist

Although the views of the bourgeois iconoclasts and the aesthetic elitists were not without political ramifications, Nietzsche's work was evaluated consistently as a political doctrine only with the advent of World War I. Again we find that a different portion of Nietzsche's writings was appropriated, or at least different passages from these writings. Nietzsche's various exhortations to live dangerously, his praise of battle and the life of a warrior, and his constant reference to struggle and overcoming made him in the eyes of both the Germans and the Allies the philosophical prophet of World War I. Although this message could have applied equally to all participants in the war, gradually Nietzschean philosophy became understood, both in Germany and abroad, as an accomplice of German nationalism. Because of Nietzsche's numerous derogatory remarks about Germans and Germany, this transformation was strange and necessitated quite a bit of hermeneutic dexterity. Sometimes his anti-German remarks were simply ignored; at other times the early Nietzsche, who was still tied to the nationalist cause, was enlisted for patriotic purposes; and in still other instances Nietzsche was said to have chastised Germany and the Germans of his own time in order to inspire a future national renewal. The result was that Nietzsche was increasingly harnessed to the very sentiments that were so repugnant to him during his own lifetime. His *Zarathustra,* which had sold so poorly in its first editions, became prerequisite reading for German soldiers: 150,000 copies of a durable wartime edition were distributed to the troops, and 40,000 volumes were sold in 1917 alone.[10] Nietzsche had finally been accepted by the Germans, but ironically as the visionary proponent of a narrow-minded German chauvinism.

World War I thus established an unfortunate trajectory for Nietzsche's writings. Although he continued to have non-German champions as well as German adherents who were not tied to chauvinistic positions, during the course of the Weimar Republic Nietzsche became increasingly identified with the radical right. To a certain extent the intellectual impetus for this shift came from the Nietzsche archives and the indefatigable efforts of Elisabeth Förster-Nietzsche. Her version of her brother and his writings, which she promulgated in numerous books and essays, would have seemed odd to the initial Nietzsche following. She fashioned Nietzsche as a patriotic Prussian who revered the military experience and heroism on the battlefield. Because Nietzschean rhetoric often contained bellicose references, this recasting of Nietzsche was not without some basis in his writings. It was possible, for example, to gather together selected citations from Nietzsche's work, as Hermann Itschner did, to support ultra-nationalist positions.[11] Just as Nietzsche's initial reception had been characterized by opposition to the staid

Wilhelmine society, so too the radical right constructed a Nietzschean image that defied bourgeois complacency and advocated action. The transformation of Nietzsche by the radical right, which occurred during the war and continued through the Weimar Republic, involved, as Steven Aschheim has argued (153), a double revision, one applied to Nietzsche, the other to the right. On the one hand, Nietzsche had to be Prussianized and militarized. But on the other hand, the right had to be loosened from its traditional ties with the church, the aristocracy, and the monarchy. The newly constituted radical right no longer looked exclusively to the past for its inspiration. Rather, it turned to visionaries, like Nietzsche, who seemed to oppose both modernity with its tendency toward democracy and the older order that was visibly decaying.

The proclamation of Nietzsche as a National Socialist philosopher after Hitler's rise to power was therefore prepared by the events of the previous two decades. The visit of Hitler himself to the Nietzsche Archives in 1934 and his attendance at the funeral of Elisabeth Förster-Nietzsche in 1935 are evidence of how completely Nietzsche was absorbed into Nazi propaganda. Indeed, the National Socialists began to claim Nietzsche as their own well before they wrested control of the government in 1933. By 1931 Alfred Bäumler, who had written a respectable book on the philosopher Immanuel Kant, had established the outlines of what would become the Nazi version of Nietzsche. For Bäumler, later appointed to the prestigious position of professor of philosophy in Berlin, Nietzsche was above all an opponent of rationalism and liberalism, and the advocate of power and vitalism. Bäumler did not accept everything that Nietzsche wrote, nor did he try to force everything he said into a right-wing mold. He rejected, for example, the passivity of the doctrine of eternal recurrence and held up in its stead the notion of the will to power. His was a much more differentiated and sophisticated view than other Nazi philosophers or ideologues, who often twisted Nietzsche to fit the whims of party doctrine. For many of these writers, Nietzsche was the herald of a new age, misunderstood in his own times and in his initial impact, but now able to find his authentic home in a racially purified and fanatically German nation. We should note, of course, that even under National Socialism there were some writers who criticized Nietzsche or various positions that Nietzsche advocated. Even one of his strongest proponents, the Nazi hack Heinrich Härtle recognized that Nietzsche's positions on individualism, on the state, and on racial purity did not correspond to present dogma. But in general Härtle and the German state found Nietzsche to be so valuable that they understood their cultural mission in the Third Reich to be applied Nietzscheanism. The National Socialist reception of Nietzsche was not just an academic issue. Aschheim points to "the dense and broad diffusion through which suitably adapted Nietzschean notions became a differentiated and integral part of Nazi self-definition. For its proponents, the Nazi-Nietzschean vision was meant no less than to remold the order of things. Suggestive blueprints for its detailed implementation were to be found at myriad levels of social organization" (240). In education, in law, in eugenics, and in medicine, Nietzsche's thoughts—or perversions of them—became foundational for specific policies. Many of the National Socialists believed that their task was to put Nietzsche's philosophy into practice.

The connection between Nietzsche and National Socialism became so thoroughly established during the 1930s and early 1940s that even writers and scholars outside of Germany began to reinforce this identification. Thomas Mann, for example, who was a great Nietzsche enthusiast before the war, began to associate the philosopher with the fate of the German nation in his later works. In the novella *Death in Venice* in 1912, Mann had adopted the notions of the Dionysian and the Apollonian in his narrative about the infatuation of the aging author Gustav von Aschenbach for a young Polish boy. But 30 years later, by the end of World War II, Mann, living in exile in California, realized that Nietzsche's contribution to German culture extended into a pernicious political realm. The central figure in his novel *Doctor Faustus* (1947), Adrian Leverkühn, who makes a deal with the devil in return for increased powers of creativity, is fashioned according to Nietzsche's biography. His death on 25 August 1940—the same date on which Nietzsche died in 1900—is symbolic for the demise of the German nation. Similarly the Harvard philosopher, Crane Brinton, writing a book on Nietzsche for the series "Makers of Modern Europe" in 1941, discusses Nietzsche's proximity to the then-current situation in Germany. Brinton dissects Nietzsche devotees into two groups: the "gentle Nietzscheans," who tend to downplay the more belligerent and reprehensible passages in Nietzsche's writings, and the "tough Nietzscheans," who revel in the rhetorical flourishes about the superman, war, struggle, and overcoming. Although Brinton recognizes that much in Nietzsche's works does not suit Nazi purposes, he concludes that there is a great deal more that corresponds nicely to their propaganda: "Nietzsche, then, fits into National Socialist needs both in what he damned and in what he praised. He damned democracy, pacifism, individualism, Christianity, humanitarianism, both as abstract ideals and as, in some vague way, actual descriptions of modern Euopean society. He praised authority, racial purity, the warrior spirit and practise, the stern life and the great health, and urged upon his fellow-citizens a complete break with their bad old habits and ideas."[12] There were, of course, still many "gentle Nietzscheans" in the 1930s and 1940s; but from 1933–45 the image propagated by the "tough Nietzscheans" appears to have held the upper hand in Germany and increasingly throughout the world.

The political direction that validated the "tough Nietzschean" interpretation most emphatically was the Marxist camp. Although some early socialists adopted Nietzsche for his oppositional value, and later less orthodox Marxists, like Ernst Bloch or Theodor Adorno, found Nietzsche's position more amenable to their concerns, the dominant party-line on Nietzsche was negative from the very beginning. Franz Mehring, the most influential cultural theorist in the German Socialist Party from 1890 through World War I, considered Nietzsche to be the philosopher of advanced capitalism. He reprimands him for his ignorance of the history of his own times, but in particular for his complete misunderstanding of the ascendant working-class movement. Although Nietzsche represents "subjectively a desperate delirium of the mind," his philosophy is "objectively a glorification of capitalism."[13] The evaluations of subsequent cultural experts from the Marxist camp were occasionally subtler, but not very different in substance. Georg Lukács, undoubtedly the most sophisticated of these experts, brought Nietzsche squarely into the orbit of National Socialism. In his *Destruction of Reason,* which is supposed to delineate "the way to Hitler in the arena of philosophy," Nietzsche plays a prominent role. In the chapter devoted to Nietzsche, entitled "Nietzsche as the Founder of the Irrationalism of the Imperialist Period," his position is defined as quintessentially antisocialist, as a bourgeois foil to the rising workers' movement in the Germany and Europe of his time.[14] Lukács concedes that Nietzsche was vastly superior in intellect to the Nazi rabble who have appropriated him. But he insists that the appropriation by the right wing is not fundamentally improper or incorrect. The views of Mehring and Lukács held sway for almost the entire 40-year history of East Germany, where Nietzsche remained virtually unread and unpublished, until the fall of the Berlin Wall in 1989.

Postwar Rehabilitation as Academic Philosopher

In the Western world, however, the postwar years evidenced a rehabilitation of Nietzsche. The task facing Nietzsche's proponents was a daunting one. Because of Nazi propaganda, as well as various Western accounts that, like Brinton's, reinforced the image of Nietzsche as a proto-fascist, he required considerable preening before he could become acceptable again to the civilized world. The strategy that was most frequently employed to refurbish his image was to fashion him into a philosopher suitable for academia. This task was not very simple for two reasons. First, Nietzsche himself, as we have seen, was poorly informed about the philosophical tradition. He had applied unsuccessfully for an open philosophy position at Basel, but he was not selected probably because of his deficient academic qualifications. His firsthand knowledge of philosophy appears to have been rather meager; except for some areas of ancient philosophy and Schopenhauer there is no evidence of any thoroughgoing reading of the philosophical tradition. His aphorisms occasionally mentioned philosophers or topics in the history of philosophy, but he leaves us no sustained treatise or systematic elaboration of any major problem. Nietzsche thus remained, for good reason, largely unrecognized as a philosopher suitable for the academic world. Second, up until the end of World War II, non-political Nietzscheans had understood him less as a philosopher in the scholarly sense than as a dispenser of general wisdom. He had gained his reputation chiefly as a figure of general culture, and his influence was perhaps greatest among writers of creative literature. His standing among university philosophers was not high, with the exception of the official academic philosophers of the Third Reich, a poor starting point for acceptance in postwar university circles. After the war, one might have simply considered him a "popular philosopher" again, but this label precluded academic respectability and made his writings susceptible to the very sort of politicization that they had experienced in the hands of the radical right and the Nazis.

Two philosophers writing before 1945 who assisted the academic refashioning of Nietzsche in the postwar era were Karl Jaspers and Martin Heidegger. Both had taught at German universities, and together they are probably the chief inspiration for the "existential" view of Nietzsche that emerged in the 1950s. Both produced large volumes on Nietzsche written during the Nazi period, and to some extent each sought to extricate Nietzsche from the vulgarized views presented by his National Socialist proponents. Jaspers portrayed Nietzsche as a philosopher of contradictions and as someone dedicated to the task of philosophy in order to challenge the easy selection of slogans from Nietzsche's works. As Jaspers himself states, he wrote his book with the intention of marshaling "against the National Socialists the world of thought of the man whom they had proclaimed as their own philosopher."[15] Nietzsche is the last great philosopher for Jaspers not because he presents us with a positive philosophy, but because he presents us with a view of philosophizing as a positive activity. In 1937 Jaspers was removed from his position at Heidelberg because of his marriage to a Jewess and his opposition to the Nazis, and after the war he became one of the strongest voices for a renewal of Germany on democratic and ethical principles. Heidegger, who had maintained a friendship with Jaspers until the late 1930s, spent much of the decade from 1936–46 working and lecturing on Nietzsche, and the resulting four-volume work is really a series of lectures and essays from these years. In contrast to Jaspers, Heidegger was a member of the Nazi party from 1933–45 and for a short period in 1933–34 even became Rector of the University of Freiburg; but he too insists that his work on Nietzsche was a sign of opposition to the National Socialist regime. Although his writings on Nietzsche—which emphasize the overcoming of nihilism and metaphysics, the will to power, and the history of being—are certainly much different than the politicized Nietzsche of Nazi ideologues, the very tenor of his arguments often brings him into association with the views he was putatively rebutting.[16] Heidegger is a more difficult case than Jaspers because his writings were more elaborate philosophically, as well as more equivocal politically on key questions relating to National Socialism. But no matter how we may evaluate their efforts, both Jaspers and Heidegger were essential for elevating Nietzsche to a level of academic respectability as a philosopher.

To a certain extent the postwar Nietzsche reception represents a continuation of Jaspers' anti-Nazi, and Heidegger's putatively anti-Nazi, Nietzsche. In order to divorce Nietzsche from his pernicious political appropriation, a similar strategy was followed both in the United States and Germany. Above all Nietzsche had to be dissociated from the right-wing hegemony of the Nietzsche archives and from his sister. Indeed, Elisabeth Förster-Nietzsche became something of a scapegoat for the Nazified Nietzsche of the 1930s and 1940s. In Germany Karl Schlechta, who had worked on Nietzsche editions during the Third Reich, published the first complete edition of Nietzsche's works during the postwar period in 1956. In this edition Schlechta includes all the published writings and completed manuscripts. He excludes, however, *The Will to Power,* a volume of aphorisms put together by Föster-Nietzsche and Peter Gast after Nietzsche's death. *The Will to Power* contains various writings from the notebooks Nietzsche wrote in the 1880s, and the book, as well as the titular concept, became popular among right-wing Nietzscheans. Schlechta presents the reader with this work in chronological, rather than systematic order, under the title "Remains from the 1880s," and thus attempts to negate the centrality of this once important work. Walter Kaufmann, whose book *Nietzsche: Philosopher, Psychologist, Antichrist* dominated the English-speaking reception of Nietzsche for the first three decades after the war, also downplays the political Nietzsche and more openly denigrates the role of Elisabeth (Kaufmann 4–8), but he otherwise employs a different strategy. Like Jaspers, Kaufmann emphasizes Nietzsche as an overcomer of contradictions, and, like Heidegger, he too divorces Nietzsche's philosophy from any biographical or historical circumstances. But unlike Schlechta, Kaufmann places the notion of the will to power at the very center of his analysis. For Kaufmann the key to understanding Nietzsche is sublimation, which acts as a necessary counterpoint to the will to power. Kaufmann's Nietzsche thus does not affirm irrationalism, the "blond beasts," and the great dictators in history, but rather the creative artist and all others who have managed to overcome their impulses and drives through sublimation. This existentially tinged, depoliticized, and "gentle" Nietzsche was perfectly suited for lecture halls and academic conferences. Kaufmann's translations of Nietzsche, complete with commentary, ensured that his Nietzsche dominated the Anglophone academic world until well into the 1970s.

Over the last few decades, however, a new philosophical version of Nietzsche has taken hold of academic interpretations—at least in France and the United States. Replacing the depoliticized, existential Nietzsche is a postmodern or poststructuralist alternative, who is both potentially political and more philosophically elusive. Among the various advocates of postmodern Nietzscheanism the three most important have probably been Michel Foucault, Jacques Derrida, and Paul de Man. Foucault's concern is primarily methodological: his Nietzsche is the inventor of a genealogical method that has the potential to supplant traditional historical approaches. Foucault identifies traditional historiography with the search for origins (*Ursprung*), while he associates Nietzsche's genealogy with the examination of emergence (*Entstehung*), lineage (*Herkunft*), birth

(*Geburt*), and descent (*Abkunft*). In his seminal essay "Nietzsche, Genealogy, History," Foucault elaborates this distinction and demonstrates how genealogy is a superior approach: it depends "on a vast accumulation of source material" and eschews essences and identities, while exploring discontinuities; it "attaches itself to the body," seeking "to reestablish the various systems of subjection, . . . the hazardous play of dominations." In these areas genealogy is the very antithesis of traditional history with its purportedly linear, essentialist, and conventional approach to phenomena.[17]

Derrida's Nietzsche is filtered through the interpretation of Heidegger. Important for Derrida is Nietzsche's opposition to metaphysics, his criticism of naive motifs of enlightenment, and his emphasis on writing as opposed to the spoken word. Derrida's readings of Nietzsche, like Heidegger's, are less an exegesis of the philosopher than an occasion for him to explicate and deconstruct the dominant conceptuality of the Western tradition. In *Spurs,* for example, he uses Nietzsche's texts to emphasize his own philosophical hobby horses: the absence of the complete presence of any sign to itself, the notion of play or free-play in the process of signification, and the plurality of styles.[18] Unlike Foucault, who engages Nietzsche for a putatively emancipatory social science, Derrida appears more aware of the political pitfalls of the Heidegger-Nietzsche philosophical tradition. He notes that the discourse that bears Nietzsche's name served as a legitimizing reference for Nazi ideologues, and that the only political cause that really elevated him to its highest and official standard was National Socialism. But at the same time he insists that the future of Nietzsche's text is not closed; there always exists a potential for a different functioning in his or in any text.[19]

A less politically attentive, American variant to the poststructualist Nietzsche is offered by Paul de Man. Relying on Nietzsche's early remarks on rhetoric, de Man presents us with a Nietzsche sensitive to the undecidabilities of language. The instability of all linguistic utterance becomes for de Man's Nietzsche his seminal philosophical insight. Since according to de Man Nietzsche establishes that all language is inextricably bound to figures and tropes, the traditional notions of the philosophical heritage—identity, truth, causality, objectivity, subjectivity—are no longer able to be trusted. As de Man writes, "the key to Nietzsche's critique of metaphysics . . . lies in the rhetorical model of the trope, or, if one prefers to call it that way, in literature as language most explicitly grounded in rhetoric."[20] The poststructuralist Nietzsche, as presented by Foucault, Derrida, and de Man, is thus neither systematic nor obviously political; he is the consummate philosopher, providing insights into method, linguistic signification, and the operation of tropes.

What stands out in the poststructuralist appropriation of Nietzsche—and in the other appropriations briefly discussed above—are two features. The first is the emphasis on one particular part or portion of Nietzsche's writings. In many cases what we find is that among a given group or direction, certain texts or passages are understood as the center of Nietzsche's thought, and that references to these texts and passages are then repeated almost ritualistically to establish his proleptic or foundational character. For Foucault and his followers the *Genealogy of Morals* is seminal; for de Man and American deconstructors the writings on rhetoric are the focal point; for Kaufmann and liberal American academia Nietzsche's notion of the will to power paired with sublimation are central issues. In each case—and especially for the vulgar right-wing interpretations—Nietzsche is forced into the mold of the person writing about him. We begin to suspect that Nietzsche's appeal has as much to do with the resourcefulness of the exegetes as with what is actually in the texts he produced. Even the foregoing cursory perusal of his impact reveals that a different Nietzsche becomes canonized according to the needs and interests of the particular group of disciples or readers. Throughout the twentieth century, Nietzsche has served interpreters primarily as legitimation for their own concerns. Writers see in him what they want to see, ignoring contradictory passages or even distorting or misreading in an obvious fashion.

The second feature is that Nietzsche is most often dehistoricized. Postmodernists, like other interpreters in the history of Nietzsche criticism, have tended to reinforce the view of Nietzsche as the untimely philosopher, whose genius could only be understood by those living in a wiser and more welcoming epoch. Most participants in the collective reception of Nietzsche have thus bought into the self-fashioned figure of the lonely, solitary thinker, who, like Zarathustra, is compelled to offer his revelatory pronouncements to uncomprehending and unworthy disciples. Part of the appeal of Nietzsche has been that each successive school or generation has been able to flatter itself into thinking that they were the ones who have finally understood what the master really meant. But if the previous chapters of this book have shown anything, it is that no one, however brilliant, including Nietzsche, is really ahead of his or her time—although many often seem to be because there are so many who are behind the times. Nietzsche was certainly ignorant of many of the details of politics and society in the late nineteenth century, but he was keenly attuned to specific discourses in education, culture, ethics, religion, and the natural sciences. Although he was situated on the borders of the intellectual exchanges and never taken seriously, he participated in these exchanges often and repeatedly in his work—in many instances to a far greater degree than this brief study was able to document. By situating Nietzsche in his own world, this volume seeks to contribute to an understanding of what really mattered to Nietzsche when he was thinking and writing. And in the process of contextualizing, however inadequately, it also endeavors to eliminate the ubiquitous and erroneous view of Nietzsche as the proper progenitor of every trend and quirk in the modern and postmodern era.

Notes and References

Chapter 1

1.   The most thorough biographical source on Nietzsche is Curt Peter Janz's three-volume work *Friedrich Nietzsche* (Munich: Carl Hanser, 1978). Perhaps the best biographical study in English is Ronald Hayman's *Nietzsche: A Critical Life* (New York: Oxford University Press, 1980). Parts of Nietzsche's life have been subjected to extremely meticulous attention; for example, his childhood years have been examined in a two-volume, 1100-page study by Hermann Josef Schmidt entitled *Nietzsche absconditus oder Spurenlesen bei Nietzsche* (Berlin: IBDK Verlag, 1990).

2.   Some of Nietzsche's writings were eventually collected together and given the status of a dissertation. He never completed a *Habilitationsschrift*.

3.   William Musgrave Calder III, "The Wilamowitz-Nietzsche Struggle: New Documents and a Reappraisal," *Nietzsche-Studien* 121 (1983): 221. Calder's essay is the most important study of the Wilamowitz-Nietzsche conflict.

4.   See Jaap Mansfeld, "The Wilamowitz-Nietzsche Struggle: Another New Document and Some Further Comments," *Nietzsche-Studien* 15 (1986): 41–58. Mansfeld adjusts slightly the fairly one-sided, but in general accurate, study by Calder.

5.   Föster had committed suicide in June of 1889, when it was discovered that he was embezzling money from the community.

Chapter 2

1.   Nietzsche's published philological writings are collected in the first volume of the second "Abteilung" (Division) of his collected works, cited in the text as *W*. This particular volume was worked on by Fritz Bornmann and Mario Carpitella. The philological writings consist of six studies, some of considerable length, his inaugural lecture at Basel, one edited text, and eight short book reviews.

2.   "The Greek Music Drama," obviously written under Wagner's influence, was a public lecture Nietzsche delivered in 1870 at Basel. See *SW* 515–32.

3.   In conjunction with *The Birth of Tragedy* Nietzsche wrote preliminary sketches for a study on "Philosophy in the Tragic Age of the Greeks." Included in this fragmentary and unpublished work are discussions of the pre-Socratic philosophers.

4.   See E. M. Butler, *The Tyranny of Greece over Germany: A Study of the Influence Exercised by Greek Art and Poetry over the Great German Writers of the Eighteenth, Nineteenth and Twentieth Centuries* (Cambridge, 1935; rpt. Boston: Beacon Hill, 1958); Robert C. Holub, *Heinrich Heine's Reception of German Grecophilia: The Function and Application of the Hellenic Tradition in the First Half of the Nineteenth Century* (Heidelberg: Carl Winter, 1981); and James Brewer et al., "Marx und Nietzsche über Kunst und Literatur," in *Karl Marx und Friedrich Nietzsche: Acht Beiträge*, ed. Reinhold Grimm and Jost Hermand (Königstein: Athenäum, 1978), 98–118.

Chapter 3

1.   We should note that as early as 7 November 1870 Nietzsche had written of his intention to "expose" the essence of the Prussian school system. See letter to Carl von Gersdorff, *SB* 3: 155.

2.   The exact dates of the lectures were 16 January, 6 and 27 February, 5 and 23 March.

3.   Nietzsche wrote on 28 January 1872 to his friend and fellow philologist Erwin Rohde in Kiel: "I am currently holding here lectures 'on the future of our educational institution' and have created a 'sensation' and here and there aroused much enthusiasm" (*SB* 3: 278).

4.   In a letter to his publisher Ernst Wilhelm Fritzsch, publisher of *The Birth of Tragedy,* on 22 March 1872 he estimated his audience at 300 for each of his *six* lectures. Since he delivered only five lectures, his assessment of attendance may also be an exaggeration. In this same letter he began negotiations for a volume to be published by Fritzsch, whose usual fare was music and writings on music, but the project never came to fruition (*SB* 3: 300).

5.   That this scene is a fiction should be obvious. In the first place Nietzsche mentions an informal organization to which he belonged, and his description matches *Germania,* a group from his Naumburg years, rather than the student club, *Bursenschaft Franconia,* which he joined in Bonn. Second, he was never in Bonn on a later summer day, since he arrived there only in the autumn of 1864. Finally, it is extremely unlikely that Nietzsche was ever involved regularly in shooting pistols; neither his disposition nor his eyesight would have permitted this type of activity.

6.   Nietzsche's remarks made in preparation for his lectures go even further in their social implications. "Universal education," he wrote in his notebooks, "is only a prelude to communism: in this fashion education is so weakened that it can no longer grant any privilege. Even less so is it then a means against communism. Universal education, i.e. barbarism, is precisely the prerequisite for communism" (*SW* 7: 243). Nietzsche's view of "communism," of course, was unlike ours; it was probably tied closely to the Paris Commune of 1871, which is one of the few world political events that received mention in his letters (*SB* 3: 195, 203–5). Nietzsche was horrified by reports that important

cultural artifacts were destroyed by the mass revolution in the French capital. This evaluation of the Commune was not the origin, but the confirmation that mass education and genuine culture are incompatible. But Nietzsche also believed that there existed dangers at higher levels of the educational system. The companion extends the general critique of educational institutions more clearly into the upper echelons of learning. Current scholarship, he suggests, is like factory work: the topics are narrow, and the procedures are mechanical. As a result, the more general notion of *Bildung* has atrophied to little more than a journalistic enterprise: "In the journal we encounter the real intention of our contemporary *Bildung,* just as the journalist, the servent of the momentary, has stepped into the place of the great genius, the leader for all times, the redeemer from the momentary" (*SW* 1: 671). Instead of producing genius for the ages, the German educational system currently promotes narrow, pedestrian scholars and superficial cultural achievements. It is threatened from below by the masses, who need to be opposed, and at higher levels by quick and superficial pseudo-knowledge.

7. Nietzsche's notebooks make it evident that his original plan was to write an essay on truth, and that only gradually did he hit upon the topic of history and historical education.

Chapter 4

1. Janz comments as follows: "It is perhaps the tragedy of his life that, because of the lure of the philological professorship, he was prevented from fulfilling his intentions, and later, whenever the thought occurred to him again, he never found the time or the energy for these studies." Janz further notes that because of this missed opportunity Nietzsche only achieved "an unfortunate dilettantism" in the natural sciences. In Curt Paul Janz, *Friedrich Nietzsche: Biographie* (Munich: Carl Hanser, 1978), 1: 319.

2. See Alwin Mittasch, *Friedrich Nietzsche als Naturphilosoph* (Stuttgart: Kröner, 1952), 21–22, 35, 42.

3. The word is used fairly consistently to contrast with other types of "men" in other works. In *Twilight of the Idols* (*TI* 538), for example, it seems to be synonymous with "higher man." In *Ecce Homo,* Nietzsche states that he employs the term to designate "a type that has turned out extremely well, in antithesis to 'modern' men, to 'good' men, to Christians and other nihilists" (*EH* 71).

4. Although there are occasional remarks on Darwin and evolution scattered throughout his works, the most direct and concentrated passages are found in *Twilight of the Idols* ("Anti-Darwin," *TI* 522–23) and in his notebooks from the years 1887 and 1888. Part of Nietzsche's anti-Darwinism may be attributable to the fact that Darwinism was most popular with those on the left half of the political spectrum, in particular with liberals and socialists. These were people with whom Nietzsche did not customarily identify in the least.

5. See Alfred Kelly, *The Descent of Darwin: The Popularization of Darwinism in Germany 1860–1914* (Chapel Hill: University of North Carolina Press, 1981), 23 and 30–31.

6. One of these critics, who apparently exercised considerable influence on Nietzsche's formulation, was Wilhelm Roux, whose *The Struggle of the Parts in the Organism* (1881) claims that Darwin's theory leaves unexplained the internal purposiveness of the creaturely organism. See Wolfgang Müller-Lauter, "Der Organismus als Innere Kampf: Der Einfluss von Wilhlem Roux auf Friedrich Nietzsche," *Nietzsche-Studien* 7 (1978): 189–235.

7. Nietzsche had exposure to the theories of thermodynamics long before his reference to Mayer. At the latest his reading of Friedrich Albert Lange's *History of Materialism* in the mid-1860s would have provided an introduction to the central notions involved in the transfer of energy.

8. For a discussion of his inadequacies the reader should consult Arthur Danto, *Nietzsche as Philosopher* (New York: Columbia, 1980), 203–9. In Nietzsche's time it seems that the notion of "thermodynamics" was not a common one. Lange, for example, refers only to the "law concerning the preservation of energy" (2: 213) without any reference to the word "thermodynamics." In an earlier section he refers to it as the "mechanical theory of heat" (*mechanische Wärmetheorie*) (199–202). Nietzsche frequently used the word *Mechanik* or *Mechanismus* to refer to matters regarding energy and the transfer of energy.

9. The first four books of *The Gay Science* were published in 1882, but the fifth book, which contains aphorisms 343–83, was appended to the work in 1887. Nietzsche's views on perspectivism in *The Gay Science* thus occur at about the same time he wrote the notebooks in *SW* 12.

10. In a later aphorism in *The Gay Science* he calls intellect "a clumsy, glooming, creaky machine that is difficult to start" (*GS* 257).

11. "Reason is a slowly developing auxiliary organ that for an extremely long time fortunately had no power to determine human beings; it worked in the service of the organic drives and emancipated itself slowly to *equality* with them . . . and later, much later to predominance" (*SW* 9: 533).

12. Friedrich Nietzsche, *Gesammelte Werke* (Musarionausgabe) (Munich: Musarion, 1922), 5: 298.

13. For a history of eugenics in Germany, see Peter Weingart, Jürgen Kroll, and Kurt Bayertz, *Rasse, Blut und Gene: Geschichte der Eugenik und Rassenhygiene in Deutschland* (Frankfurt: Suhrkamp, 1988); and Paul Weindling, *Health, Race and German Politics Between National Unification and Nazism, 1870–1945* (Cambridge: Cambridge University Press, 1989).

14. For an overview of Galton's life and works, see Ruth Schwartz Cowan, *Sir Francis Galton and the Study of Heredity in the Nineteenth Century* (New York: Garland, 1985).

15. The biological theory of Jean Baptiste Pierre Antoine de Monet, Chevalier de Lamarck (1744–1829) provided Nietzsche with a welcome alternative to Darwinism. Lamarck emphasized that adaptive responses to environ-

mental changes caused organisms to produce structural changes that could then be inherited by subsequent generations. Although Darwin too believed that acquired characteristics could be inherited, he went further than Lamarck in outlining the mechanism by which organisms survive and change. Nietzsche had more sympathy for Lamarckian evolution because it suggests the exercise of a conscious will and does not postulate the "survival of the fittest" as the chief mechanism for evolutionary change.

16.   See, for example, *SW* 13: 495, where Nietzsche advocates:

An *extra taxation* on inheritance, etc. also an extra taxation on military service of bachelors from a specific age onward and continuing (inside the community)

Advantages of every kind for fathers who put numerous boys [*Knaben*] in the world: under some circumstances a majority of votes

a *physician's certificate* before every marriage and signed by the community leaders: in which several specific questions about the engaged couple and the physicians must be answered ("family histories")

as a remedy to *prostitution* (or its ennoblement): term marriages, legalized (for years, months, days), with guarantees for children

every marriage accountable to and recommended by a specific number of reliable men in the community: as a communal affair . . .

Chapter 5

1.   See, for example, Cosima's letter to Nietzsche from 16 July 1870, in which she writes of the "outrageousness of French arrogance" and adds: "I hope that all of Germany recognizes that the King of Prussia could not and should not have acted differently, and now go with Prussia; perhaps then German unity will be achieved, the hegemony of the Parisian mode will be broken forever, the chignons in flight, the olive tree will rise from the abyss on which Bayreuth's castle lies" (*BW* 2.2: 232–33).

2.   See Peter Bergmann, *Nietzsche, the Last Antipolitical German* (Bloomington: Indiana University Press, 1987), 1–8.

3.   In *Human, All Too Human,* Nietzsche makes it clear that by "Europe" he means not only the geographical Europe, "the little peninsula of Asia," but also America, "the daughter-land of our culture" (*HA* 365).

4.   Nietzsche seems to have accepted the proposition that slavery is necessary for genuine culture. In *Five Prefaces to Five Unwritten Books,* a work that he presented to Cosima Wagner as a Christmas gift in 1872, he writes that although it sounds cruel, we have to admit that "slavery belongs to the essence of a culture" (*SW* 1: 767). Over a decade later, in *Beyond Good and Evil,* he reiterates the same thought. In a discussion about the servitude and bondage of women, he calls slavery "a condition of every higher culture, of every elevation of culture" (*BGE* 189). Considering that Nietzsche is continuously

promulgating a higher culture, it is hardly possible that these statements possess merely descriptive value.

5.   The "Eternal-Feminine (*Ewig-Weibliche*)," translated by Kaufmann as the "eternal-womanly," refers of course to the final lines of Goethe's *Faust*.

6.   Friedrich Nietzsche, *Werke und Briefe*, vol. 1, *Jugendschriften 1854–1861*, ed. Hans Joachim Mette (Munich: Beck'sche Verlagsbuchhandlung, 1933), 254–55.

7.   For a differentiated, sympathetic, and sometimes apologetic account of his anti-Jewish sentiments, written by the director of the Wagner Museum, see Manfred Eger, *Wagner und die Juden: Fakten und Hintergründe*. Eine Dokumentation zur Ausstellung im Richard-Wagner-Museum Bayreuth (Bayreuth: Druckhaus Bayreuth, 1985).

8.   Cited from Ronald Hayman, *Nietzsche: A Critical Life* (New York: Oxford University Press, 1980), 204.

9.   Cited in Alex Bein, *Die Judenfrage: Biographie eines Weltproblems* (Stuttgart: Deutsche Verlags-Anstalt, 1980), 2: 168.

10.   The term "Misojuden" appears in his notebooks in the fall of 1881, shortly after the term "anti-Semitism" had become popular. See *SW* 9: 597 and 649.

Chapter 6

1.   In advancing this claim Nietzsche buys into racist stereotypes about Africans that were disseminated in Europe, in particular as a justification for the slave trade.

2.   Nietzsche himself insists that his third essay is the exegesis of a misunderstood parable from *Zarathustra*: "Wisdom likes men who are reckless, scornful and violent; being a woman, her heart goes out to a soldier." Nietzsche appears to be concerned—or does he feign concern?—that his aphorisms in *Zarathustra* have not been read carefully enough. The inclination of the normal reader is simply to read it and go on to the next one. Indeed, it is difficult to see how one could get through *Zarathustra* if one did not proceed in this fashion, since it is several hundred pages and contains several hundred aphorisms. But Nietzsche insists that one must treat aphorisms in the way that cows treat their food: chew it, regurgitate it, chew it again, and regurgitate it, repeating this process until the aphorism is fully digested. "An aphorism that has been honestly struck cannot be deciphered simply by reading it off; this is only the beginning of the work of interpretation proper, which requires a whole science of hermeneutics" (*GM* 157). Aside from the stereotypical attitudes toward gender contained in this aphorism and perhaps the militaristic rhetoric, this aphorism is of little consequence. What follows on the 60-odd pages of the English edition is less a commentary on this aphorism than an explanation of the title "What Do Ascetic Ideals Mean?"

3.   Wagner's *Parsifal*, which was understood by Nietzsche to be an opera about redemption, was the target of much of Nietzsche's late anti-

Wagner polemic. Nietzsche believed that Wagner had sold out to Christian values, that he had crawled to the cross in his last work. Despite the venomous attacks in texts such as *The Case of Wagner* (1888) and *Nietzsche Contra Wagner* (1895), we can still detect admiration for Wagner. The very fact that he is considered a suitable object for verbal assault indicates his continued significance in Nietzsche's worldview.

Chapter 7

1. Karl Marx, "Contribution to the Critique of Hegel's *Philosophy of Right*: Introduction," in *The Marx-Engels Reader,* ed. Robert C. Tucker, 2nd ed. (New York: Norton, 1978), 54.

2. Nietzsche retained the belief of the antithetical nature of religion—at least those in the Judeo-Christian heritage—and science in his later works. In *The Antichrist,* for example, he interprets the story of the garden of Eden as a sign that science is incompatible with the priestly mentality (*AC* 628–31). "The concept of guilt and punishment, the whole 'moral world order,' was invented *against* science, *against* the emancipation of man from the priest. . . . Sin, to repeat it once more, this form of man's self-violation par excellence, was invented to make science, culture, every elevation and nobility of man, impossible; the priest rules through the invention of sin" (*AC* 630–31).

3. Heinrich Heine, *The Romantic School and Other Essays,* ed. Jost Hermand and Robert C. Holub (New York: Continuum, 1985), 200.

4. Nietzsche draws the connection between Christianity as a teaching of "equal rights for everyone" and contemporary politics in section 43 of *The Antichrist* (619–20).

5. Nietzsche is not completely consistent in his depiction of Christ. In some passages he expresses considerably more admiration for the historical Jesus as someone who introduced a life practice that required following instincts. In these passages Christ abolishes the guilt and sin of the Jewish priests and lives a unity of God and man. Jesus is the bringer of good tidings, not the son of God who reaffirmed a value system of reward and punishment. According to this more charitable view of Christ he himself is not to blame for Christianity: at fault are the Gospels, which distorted his deeds into a belief, his disciples, who perverted his teaching, and the church, which spiritualized his actions and created a new set of internal values (*AC* 610–16). Of particular importance is Paul, who functions in the later part of *The Antichrist* as the very antithesis to Jesus (*AC* 617–19).

6. I am including the world of ancient Greece in the Western tradition because Nietzsche obviously considered Greece part of his own heritage. Recent scholarship has made it apparent that this view is really a result of our own Eurocentric culture. Ancient Greece was part of a Mediterranean world that includes Asia and Africa. It belongs to the heritage of these continents as much as Europe.

7. Nietzsche obviously read the "Law of Manu" in a book by Louis Jacolliot entitled *Les Législateur religieux: Manou - Moïse - Mahomet* (Paris: A. Lacroix, 1876).

8. Actually the chandala seems to be more specifically the offspring of a male Sudra with a Brahmin woman, thus the son or daughter from the combination of the lowest and the highest of the castes. Here, and in other places, Nietzsche appears either to have ignored details or not to have known what the details actually are. In this case he obviously depended on Jacolliot, who describes the chandalas simply as "people of mixed classes and their descendants, chased from their caste by crimes or religious infractions" (Jacolliot 36).

9. Because of Nietzsche's reliance on Manu and his association of Jews and chandala, it is interesting to discover how this association came about from his source, Jacolliot's book. Jacolliot discusses the term *chandala* in a rather long footnote to his text that deals with several matters of significance for his eager German reader in Sils-Maria. According to Jacolliot's account—which has no scholarly merit—the chandalas were a group of outcasts and lawless people that gradually developed into their own nation. In approximately 8000 B.C. the edicts that Nietzsche cites in *Twilight of the Idols* were promulgated with the consequence that the number of chandalas was reduced by about one-half. Four thousand years later they were forced to emigrate because of struggles between Brahmins and Buddhists, an obvious impossibility since Buddha was not born until almost 3500 years later. (He lived from 563–483 B.C.) They migrated into central Asia but also to Persia and settled on the banks of the Tigris and Euphrates rivers. Thus Jacolliot claims that the descendants of the chandalas populate various tribes that come from that region of the world, including the Assyrians, the Babylonians, the Syrians, the Phoenicians, and the Arabs. Included among the descendants of the chandalas are the Chaldeans, who in a further migration established themselves elsewhere in the Middle East and became known as the Hebrews. All of these Semitic tribes can be distinguished because they prefer eating with their left hand and because they submit to circumcision. They are all ultimately examples of an original slave-like mentality that explains their servile attitude and customs. The Europeans, by contrast, as well as the peoples of ancient Egypt, were settled by Hindu migration from the higher castes. These people eat and write with the right hand. The bottom line for Jacolliot is that the descendants of the chandalas are inferior; they can never raise themselves above the vulgarities that are in their blood line, and they can never become as intellectually accomplished as the pure Europeans. What is interesting here is that at the same time that Nietzsche was vehemently opposing the political anti-Semitism of people like his brother-in-law Bernhard Förster, he was simultaneously validating a scholarly version of anti-Semitism.

Chapter 8

1. Kurt Tucholsky, "Fräulein Nietzsche," *Gesammelte Werke* (Hamburg: Rowohlt, 1960), 10: 14.

2. Steven E. Aschheim, *The Nietzsche Legacy in Germany 1890–1990* (Berkeley: University of California Press, 1992), 313. Cited hereafter parenthetically in the text.

3. Heinrich Mann, "Zum Verständnisse Nietzsches," cited from *Nietzsche und die deutsche Literatur,* ed. Bruno Hillebrand, vol. 1, *Texte zur Nietzsche-Rezeption 1873–1963* (Tübingen: Niemeyer, 1978), 106.

4. Tönnies himself admired Nietzsche's early work, especially *The Birth of Tragedy,* where he sensed a communitarian attitude, but criticized the later work as pseudo-liberationist. Tönnies himself is most noted for the problematic distinction between community (*Gemeinschaft*) and society (*Gesellschaft*). The two texts by Tönnies on Nietzsche are collected together in *Der Nietzsche-Kultus: Eine Kritik* (Berlin: Akademie-Verlag, 1990).

5. Robert Misch, *Kinder: Eine Gymnasiasten Komödie* (Berlin: Harmonie, 1906), 12.

6. Michael Georg Conrad, "Jugend!," cited from *Nietzsche und die deutsche Literatur,* 99.

7. Stefan Zwieg, "Das neue Pathos," cited from *Nietzsche und die deutsche Literatur,* 174. Although Zweig was the author of this essay, which was seminal for expressionism, he himself was never identified as one of the central expressionist authors.

8. See Eckart von Sydow, "Der doppelte Ursprung des deutschen Expressionismus," cited in *Nietzsche und die deutsche Literatur,* 197.

9. Stefan George, "Nietzsche," in *Nietzsche und die deutsche Literatur,* 127. I have expanded on the partial translation found in Walter Kaufmann, *Nietzsche: Philosopher, Psychologist, Antichrist* (Princeton: Princeton University Press, 1974), 10–11.

10. The fourth book was originally published in a private edition and did not appear in a public edition until 1892.

11. Hermann Itschner, *Nietzsche-Worte: Weggenossen in grosser Zeit* (Leipzig: Alfred Kröner, 1915).

12. Crane Brinton, *Nietzsche* (Cambridge: Harvard University Press, 1941), 216.

13. Franz Mehring, *Gesammelte Schriften* (Berlin: Dietz Verlag, 1961), 11: 219.

14. Georg Lukács, *Die Zerstörung der Vernunft* (Berlin: Aufbau, 1954).

15. Karl Jaspers, *Nietzsche: An Introduction to the Understanding of His Philosophical Activity,* trans. Charles F. Wallraff and Frederick J. Schmitz (Tuscon: University of Arizona Press, 1965), xiii.

16. Heidegger's work on Nietzsche has been published in English under the title *Nietzsche,* trans. David Farrell Krell, 4 vols. (New York: HarperCollins, 1979–87).

17.   See Michel Foucault, "Nietzsche, Genealogy, History," *Language, Counter-Memory, Practice: Selected Essays and Interviews* (Ithaca: Cornell University Press, 1977), 139–64. The essay originally appeared in 1971 in *Hommage à Jean Hyppolite* (Paris: Presses Universitaires de France, 1971), 145–72.

18.   Jacques Derrida, *Spurs: Nietzsche's Styles,* trans. Barbara Harlow (Chicago: University of Chicago Press, 1978); originally *Eperons. Les styles de Nietzsche.*

19.   See Jacques Derrida, *The Ear of the Other: Otobiography, Transference, Translation,* ed. Christie V. McDonald (New York: Schocken, 1982). The remarks to which I am referring here are drawn from the essay "Otobiographies: The Teaching of Nietzsche and the Politics of the Proper Name," trans. Avital Ronell, 1–38.

20.   See Paul de Man, "Rhetoric of Tropes (Nietzsche)," *Allegories of Reading* (New Haven: Yale, 1979), 103–18.

Selected Bibliography

Primary Sources

Complete Works

Werke ("Großoktavausgabe"). 19 vols. 2d edition. Leipzig: Naumann Kröner, 1901–13. (1st edition 1894–1904). Index, volume 20, added in 1926. The standard edition of Nietzsche's works until it was surpassed by the Colli/Montinari edition. It was compiled under the supervision of Elisabeth Förster-Nietzsche, who used various editors for the separate volumes. Volumes 1–8 contain published works; volumes 9–16 contain the literary remains; volumes 17–19 contain philological writings.

Gesammelte Werke ("Musarionausgabe"). 23 vols. Munich: Musarion, 1920–29. A basically chronological edition of Nietzsche's writings that mixes published works, literary remains, and philological writings.

Werke und Briefe: Historisch-Kritische Gesamtausgabe. 9 vols. Munich: Beck, 1933–42. Discontinued after five volumes of the works and four volumes of letters. Arranged chronologically, the works include only Nietzsche's unpublished writings from 1854–69, the only edition in which the *juvenilia* is currently available.

Werke in drei Bänden. Ed. Karl Schlechta. 3 vols. Munich: Carl Hanser, 1954–56. Index volume added in 1965. First complete postwar edition of the published writings, which are gathered in volumes 1 and 2 along with selected unpublished manuscripts. Volume 3 contains literary remains and selected letters. Index is helpful, but not totally reliable.

Kritische Gesamtausgabe: Werke. Ed. Giorgio Colli and Mazzino Montinari. 30 vols. Berlin: Walter de Gruyter, 1967– . Standard scholarly edition for Nietzsche's works and literary remains. When completed, it will surpass all previous Nietzsche editions.

Kritische Gesamtausgabe: Briefwechsel. Ed. Giorgio Colli and Mazzino Montinari. 18 vols. Berlin: Walter de Gruyter, 1975–84. First complete edition of letters to and from Nietzsche.

Sämtliche Werke. Kritische Studienausgabe. Ed. Giorgio Colli and Mazzino Montinari. 15 vols. Munich and Berlin: Deutscher Taschenbuch Verlag and Walter de Gruyter, 1967–77. Affordable paperback edition drawn from the *Kritische Gesamtausgabe.* Contains all published works and literary remains from the 1870s and 1880s.

Sämtliche Briefe. Ed. Giorgio Colli and Mazzino Montinari. 8 vols. Munich and Berlin: Deutscher Taschenbuch Verlag and Walter de Gruyter, 1975–84. Drawn from *Kritische Gesamtausgabe: Briefwechsel,* this paperback edition contains all letters written by Nietzsche and an index of names and addressees.

The Complete Works of Friedrich Nietzsche. Ed. Oscar Levy. 18 vols. New York: Macmillan, 1909–11; reissued by New York: Russell & Russell, 1964. Only complete edition of Nietzsche's works in English. Translations are generally less reliable than those of individual works listed below.

Individual Writings

In general the translations by Walter Kaufmann and R. J. Hollingdale are preferable to the older translations.

The Birth of Tragedy (Die Geburt der Tragödie, 1872). Trans. Walter Kaufmann, with *The Case of Wagner.* New York: Vintage, 1966. Trans. Frances Golffing, with *The Genealogy of Morals.* Garden City, N.Y.: Doubleday, 1956.

Untimely Meditations (Unzeitgemässe Betrachtungen, 1873–76). Trans. R. J. Hollingdale. Cambridge and New York: Cambridge University Press, 1983. Ed. William Arrowsmith, as *Modern Observations.* New Haven: Yale University Press, 1990.

David Strauss, the Confessor and the Writer (David Strauss der Bekenner und der Schriftsteller, 1873). Trans. R. J. Hollingdale, in *Untimely Meditations.* Trans. Herbert Golder, in *Unmodern Observations.*

On the Advantage and Disadvantage of History for Life (Vom Nutzen und Nachteil der Historie für das Leben, 1874). Trans. Peter Preuss. Indianapolis: Hackett, 1980. Trans. R. J. Hollingdale, as *On the Uses and Disadvantages of History for Life,* in *Untimely Meditations.* Trans. Gary Brown, as *History in the Service and Disservice of Life,* in *Unmodern Observations.* Trans. Adrian Collins, as *The Use and Abuse of History.* Indianapolis: Liberal Arts Press, Bobbs-Merrill, 1957.

Schopenhauer as Educator (Schopenhauer als Erzieher, 1874). Trans. R. J. Hollingdale, in *Untimely Meditations.* Trans. William Arrowsmith, in *Unmodern Observations.* Trans. James W. Hillesheim and Malcolm R. Simpson. South Bend, Ind.: Gateway, 1965.

Richard Wagner in Bayreuth (Richard Wagner in Bayreuth, 1876). Trans. R. J. Hollingdale, in *Untimely Meditations.* Trans. Gary Brown, in *Unmodern Observations.*

Human, All Too Human (Menschliches, Allzumenschliches, 1878–80). Trans. R. J. Hollingdale. Cambridge: Cambridge University Press, 1986. Trans. Marion Faber, with Stephen Lehmann. Lincoln: University of Nebraska Press, 1984 (first volume only).

Daybreak (Morgenröthe, 1881). Trans. R. J. Hollingdale. Cambridge: Cambridge University Press, 1982.

The Gay Science (*Die fröhliche Wissenschaft,* books I–IV, 1882; book V, 1887).
Trans. Walter Kaufmann. New York: Vintage, 1974. Trans. Thomas
Common, as *Joyful Wisdom.* New York: Frederick Ungar, 1960.

Thus Spoke Zarathustra (*Also Sprach Zarathustra,* 1883–85). Trans. Walter
Kaufmann, in *The Portable Nietzsche.* Trans. R. J. Hollingdale.
Harmondsworth: Penguin, 1961. Trans. Marianne Cowan. Chicago:
Gateway, 1957.

Beyond Good and Evil (*Jenseits von Gut und Böse,* 1886). Trans. Helen Zimmern.
Buffalo: Prometheus Books, 1989. Trans. Walter Kaufmann. New York:
Vintage, 1966. Trans. R. J. Hollingdale. Harmondsworth: Penguin,
1973. Trans. Marianne Cowan. Chicago: Gateway, 1955.

The Genealogy of Morals (*Zur Genealogie der Moral,* 1887). Trans. Francis Golffing,
with *The Birth of Tragedy.* Garden City, N.Y.: Doubleday, 1956. Trans.
Walter Kaufmann and R. J. Hollingdale, as *On the Genealogy of Morals,*
with *Ecce Homo.* New York: Vintage, 1967.

The Case of Wagner (*Der Fall Wagner,* 1888). Trans. Walter Kaufmann, with *The
Birth of Tragedy.* New York: Vintage, 1966.

Twilight of the Idols (*Götzen-Dämmerung,* 1889). Trans. Walter Kaufmann, in *The
Portable Nietzsche.* Trans. R. J. Hollingdale, with *The Antichrist.*
Harmondsworth: Penguin, 1968.

The Antichrist (*Der Antichrist,* 1895). Trans. Walter Kaufmann, in *The Portable
Nietzsche.* Trans. R. J. Hollingdale, with *Twilight of the Idols.*
Harmondsworth: Penguin, 1968.

Nietzsche contra Wagner (*Nietzsche contra Wagner,* 1895). Trans. Walter
Kaufmann, in *The Portable Nietzsche.*

Ecce Homo (*Ecce Homo,* 1908). Trans. Walter Kaufmann, with *On the Genealogy of
Morals.* New York: Vintage, 1967. Trans. R. J. Hollingdale.
Harmondsworth: Penguin, 1979.

The Will to Power (*Der Wille zur Macht,* 1901, 1904, and 1910–11). Trans.
Walter Kaufmann and R. J. Hollingdale. New York: Vintage, 1967.

Selections and Collections in English Translation

The Portable Nietzsche. Ed. Walter Kaufmann. New York: Viking, 1954.
Includes *Thus Spoke Zarathustra, Twilight of the Idols, The Antichrist,* and
Nietzsche contra Wagner, plus selections from other writings, notebooks,
and correspondence.

Basic Writings of Nietzsche. Ed. Walter Kaufmann. New York: Modern Library,
1968. Contains *Beyond Good and Evil, The Birth of Tragedy, The Case of
Wagner, On the Genealogy of Morals,* and *Ecce Homo.*

A Nietzsche Reader. Ed. R. J. Hollingdale. Harmondsworth: Penguin, 1977.
Divided topically.

Nietzsche Selections. Ed. Richard Schacht. New York: Macmillan, 1993.

Philosophy and Truth: Selections from Nietzsche's Notebooks of the Early 1870s. Ed. and trans. Daniel Breazeale. Atlantic Highlands, N.J.: Humanities Press, 1979. Only selections from early notebooks in English.

The Philosophy of Friedrich Nietzsche. Ed. and trans. Walter Kaufmann. New York: Modern Library, 1968.

Nietzsche: A Self-Portrait from His Letters. Ed. and trans. Peter Fuss and Henry Shapiro. Cambridge: Harvard University Press, 1971.

Nietzsche: Unpublished Letters. Ed. and trans. Kurt F. Leidecker. New York: Philosophical Library, 1959.

Selected Letters of Friedrich Nietzsche. Ed. and trans. Christopher Middleton. Chicago: University of Chicago Press, 1969.

Secondary Sources

This section of the selected bibliography is weighed heavily toward recent book-length studies in English. A more comprehensive listing of secondary sources can be found in the Reichert/Schlechta bibliography for books and essays written before 1968, and thereafter in the *Nietzsche-Studien.*

Allison, David B., ed. *The New Nietzsche: Contemporary Styles of Interpretation.* New York: Dell, 1977. Excellent selection of essays by neo-Heideggerians and poststructuralists, who have set the tone for much of the Nietzsche reception since the early 1970s in France and the United States.

Aschheim, Steven E. *The Nietzsche Legacy in Germany 1890–1990.* Berkeley: University of California Press, 1992. A nonpartisan review of Nietzsche's fate in Germany, concentrating heavily on the initial half-century of his reception. Especially strong on the nationalist appropriation of Nietzsche.

Behler, Ernst. *Confrontations: Derrida Heidegger Nietzsche.* Trans. Steven Taubeneck. Stanford: Stanford University Press, 1991. Original German in 1988. Study of the interrelations between Derrida, Heidegger, and Nietzsche. Useful review of the American reception of Nietzsche by Taubeneck (159–77).

Bergmann, Peter. *Nietzsche: The Last Antipolitical German.* Bloomington: Indiana University Press, 1987. One of the few American books to situate Nietzsche squarely in his own era. Sensible appraisal of Nietzsche's relationship to the political movements of the late nineteenth century.

Blondel, Eric. *Nietzsche: The Body and Culture. Philosophy as a Philological Genealogy.* Trans. Seán Hand. Stanford: Stanford University Press, 1991. Careful reading of Nietzsche as a materialist. Concern is with culture as a readable text and Nietzsche's relentless opposition to all manifestations of idealism.

Burgard, Peter J., ed. *Nietzsche and the Feminine*. Charlottesville: University Press of Virginia, 1994. Collection concentrating on Nietzsche's figure of woman. Heavily influenced by the work of Derrida, Sarah Kofman, and Luce Irigaray.

Clark, Maudemaire. *Nietzsche on Truth and Philosophy*. Cambridge: Cambridge University Press, 1990. Careful and close reading of Nietzsche's texts focusing on his notion of truth. Clark debunks several popular and careless readings and shows a distinct development in Nietzsche's thought.

Danto, Arthur C. *Nietzsche as Philosopher*. New York: Columbia University Press, 1980. Ambitious attempt to rescue Nietzsche for analytical philosophy. Careful reading of Nietzsche as a systematic philosopher.

Del Caro, Adrian. *Nietzsche Contra Nietzsche: Creativity and the Anti-Romantic*. Baton Rouge: Louisiana State University Press, 1989. Exhaustive study of Nietzsche's contradictory relationship to German Romanticism.

Deleuze, Gilles. *Nietzsche and Philosophy*. Trans. Hugh Tomlinson. New York: Columbia University Press, 1983. Influential study, originally published in French in 1962. Wants to claim Nietzsche as a radical, progressive, and non-dialectical thinker.

De Man, Paul. "Rhetoric of Tropes (Nietzsche)." *Allegories of Reading*. New Haven: Yale, 1979, 103–18. Influential study that focuses on the early essay "Truth and Lies in an Extra-Moral Sense." Nietzsche is seen as the precursor of twentieth-century linguistic theory that finds language itself, as well as its tropes, to be a source of instability.

Derrida, Jacques. *Spurs: Nietzsche's Styles*. Trans. Barbara Harlow. Chicago: University of Chicago Press, 1978. Nietzsche as a proto-deconstructive philosopher. Important for Derrida are the undecidabilities in Nietzsche's texts, the plurality of styles, and the affirmation of free-play in all signification.

Detweiler, Bruce. *Nietzsche and the Politics of Aristocratic Radicalism*. Chicago: University of Chicago Press, 1990. Finds Nietzsche's politics "intriguing and odious." Nietzsche is seen as an advocate of hierarchy and authoritarian rule, since these are preconditions for his ultimate goal: the production of the highest specimens of human beings.

Foucault, Michel. "Nietzsche, Genealogy, History," *Language, Counter-Memory, Practice: Selected Essays and Interviews*. Ithaca: Cornell University Press, 1977, 139–64. Influential attempt to attribute a new type of historical study to Nietzsche in his putative advocacy of genealogy. More a description and validation of Foucault's own method than of Nietzsche's approach.

Gilman, Sander L., ed. *Conversations with Nietzsche*. Trans. David Parent. New York: Oxford University Press, 1989. Translation of *Begegnungen mit Nietzsche*, which appeared in 1981 and was revised in 1985. Contains, in chronological order, reports of meetings and conversations with Nietzsche from his childhood through his sickness. Indispensable source although many of the contributors are unreliable reporters.

Habermas, Jürgen. "The Entry into Postmodernity: Nietzsche as a Turning Point." *The Philosophical Discourse of Modernity.* Trans. Frederick Lawrence. Cambridge: MIT Press, 1987. Nietzsche seen as the first important advocate of a postmodern position. For Habermas, Germany's leading postwar intellectual, Nietzsche began an anti-modernist philosophical trend that winds up in a series of contradictions.

Hayman, Ronald. *Nietzsche: A Critical Life.* New York: Oxford University Press, 1980. Best biography of Nietzsche in English by a writer thoroughly familiar with the primary sources.

Heidegger, Martin. *Nietzsche.* 4 vols. Trans. David Farrell Krell. New York: Harper and Row, 1979–84. Collection of Heidegger's essays and lectures on Nietzsche from 1936–46, depicted by Heidegger as the last metaphysical philosopher. Extremely influential in the poststructuralist Nietzsche reception, these volumes tell us more about Heidegger than Nietzsche.

Hollingdale, R. J. *Nietzsche.* London: Routledge & Kegan Paul, 1965. Study of Nietzsche's life and works by one of his best English translators. Influenced by Kaufmann, Hollingdale similarly places the will to power at the center of Nietzsche's works.

Janz, Curt Paul. *Friedrich Nietzsche: Biographie.* 3 vols. Munich: Hanser Verlag, 1978. Most comprehensive and reliable biography of Nietzsche in any language. Janz finished the project after Richard Blunck died, having completed only the section on Nietzsche's youth. Revised edition in 1993.

Jaspers, Karl. *Nietzsche: An Introduction to the Understanding of His Philosophical Activity.* Trans. Charles Walraff and Frederick J. Schmitz. Tuscon: University of Arizona Press, 1965. Originally published in 1936 in German, then after the war in 1947 with a new preface. Attempting to rescue Nietzsche from his Nazi disciples, Jaspers portrays him as a philosopher preoccupied with critical procedures rather than a fixed doctrine.

Kaufmann, Walter. *Nietzsche: Philosopher, Psychologist, Antichrist.* 4th ed. Princeton: Princeton University Press, 1974. Originally published in 1950; revised for successive editions. Most influential American work on Nietzsche for the first three decades after World War II. Nietzsche is not the brutal proto-Nazi, but the advocate of sublimation and creativity. Useful appendices and bibliography with Kaufmann's interesting, but opinionated, commentary.

Koelb, Clayton, ed. *Nietzsche as Postmodernist: Essays Pro and Con.* Albany: State University of New York Press, 1990. Interesting collection in which a variety of Nietzsche scholars express differing views on Nietzsche's connection with postmodernism, deconstruction, rhetoric, and the self.

Nietzsche-Studien: Internationales Jahrbuch für die Nietzsche-Forschung. Berlin: De Gruyter, 1972– . Yearbook containing important contributions to Nietzsche research. Essays in German, English, and French. Annual updates of Nietzsche bibliography at end of each volume.

Magnus, Bernd. *Nietzsche's Existential Imperative.* Bloomington: Indiana University Press, 1978. Study focusing on Nietzsche's notion of "eternal recurrence." Magnus claims that "eternal recurrence" is empirically false—and Nietzsche knew it to be false—but that it expresses the attitude of those who would overcome nihilism (i.e., the overman).

Mittasch, Alwin. *Friedrich Nietzsche als Naturphilosoph.* Stuttgart: Kröner, 1952. Only extensive treatment of Nietzsche's multiple dealings with science and the philosophy of nature. Dated in its perspective on Nietzsche, it is still valuable for its patient delineation of Nietzsche's remarks on science.

Nehemas, Alexander. *Nietzsche: Life as Literature.* Cambridge: Harvard University Press, 1985. Influential study of Nietzsche as an author trying to create a specific literary image in his writings. Argues also that Nietzsche viewed the world as a literary text.

Pasley, Malcolm, ed. *Nietzsche: Imagery and Thought.* Berkeley: University of California Press, 1978. Interesting collection that contains some essays on Nietzsche's imagery and their influence, as well as a few essays on art and epistemology.

Patton, Paul, ed. *Nietzsche, Feminism and Political Theory.* London: Routledge, 1993. Mostly sympathetic readings of Nietzsche's overtly misogynist and anti-democratic statements.

Pletsch, Carl. *Young Nietzsche: Becoming a Genius.* New York: Free Press, 1991. Interpretive biography of Nietzsche's life until shortly after his break with Wagner in 1876. Emphasis on Nietzsche's growing independence from his intellectual mentors and his burgeoning creativity.

Pütz, Peter. *Friedrich Nietzsche.* Stuttgart: Metzler, 1967. Useful research report divided into discussions of Nietzsche's life, his philosophy, his poetry, and his influence.

Reichert, Herbert W., and Schlechta, Karl. *International Nietzsche Bibliography.* Chapel Hill: University of North Carolina Press, 1960. Revised and expanded 1968. Comprehensive, but now slightly outdated Nietzsche bibliography containing listings arranged in 27 different languages. Useful subject index.

Rickels, Laurence A., ed. *Looking After Nietzsche.* Albany: State University of New York Press, 1990. Neo-Heideggerian interpretations of Nietzsche from French, German, and American scholars.

Schacht, Richard. *Nietzsche.* London: Routledge & Kegan Paul, 1983. Attempt to make Nietzsche palatable to Anglophone philosophers by viewing his achievements in terms of historically relevant philosophical categories. Concentration on Nietzsche's later writings.

———, ed. *Nietzsche, Genealogy, Morality: Essays on Nietzsche's "Genealogy of Morals."* Berkeley: University of California Press, 1994. Rich collection of 24 essays by a variety of Nietzsche scholars of different persuasions, focusing on his ethical theory as articulated in the seminal text, *Genealogy of Morals.*

Schutte, Ofelia. *Beyond Nihilism: Nietzsche without Masks*. Chicago: University of Chicago Press, 1984. Differentiated study of Nietzsche's notion of power; sympathetic to Nietzsche's ontology and critical of his moral and political philosophy.

Solomon, Robert C., ed. *Nietzsche: A Collection of Critical Essays*. Notre Dame: University of Notre Dame Press, 1980. Excellent selection of commentary on Nietzsche from famous philosophers like Heidegger and Jaspers, authors like Thomas Mann and Hermann Hesse, and scholars like Walter Kaufmann and Arthur Danto.

Stern, J. P. *Friedrich Nietzsche*. Harmondsworth: Penguin, 1978. Introductory study in the Penguin Modern Masters Series. Emphasis on Nietzsche's relentless pursuit of freedom and intellectual experimentation.

Strong, Tracy. *Friedrich Nietzsche and the Politics of Transfiguration*. Expanded ed. Berkeley: University of California Press, 1988. Discussion of Nietzsche's relationship to epistemology, religion, politics, and morality. Emphasis on the notion of "eternal recurrence," whose acceptance is supposed to reshape and remold humanity.

Warren, Mark. *Nietzsche and Political Thought*. Cambridge: MIT Press, 1988. Argues that Nietzsche's notion of politics is politically relevant but not politically determinant. Nietzsche as an important figure for postmodern politics because of his situated concept of agency, although Nietzsche himself did not understand or develop his own political relevance. Warren ultimately interprets Nietzsche as an advocate of pluralism and egalitarianism.

Index

Achilles, 20, 123
Adam, 145
Adorno, Theodor, 158
Aeschylus, 23, 25; *Prometheus,* 23
Aestheticism, 149, 153–54
Antiquarian history, 40, 45–47
Anti-Semitism, 80, 97–100, 147, 172n9
Apollonian, 7, 16–25, 28, 30, 157
Archilochus, 21
Aryans, 23–24, 98, 100, 112–17, 146–47
Asceticism, 4, 122–27, 133
Aschheim, Steven, 150, 156–57

Bach, Johann Sebastian, 29
Basel, University of, 5–6, 10, 12–14, 55
Bäumler, Alfred, 156
Bayreuth, 10–11, 15–16, 31–32, 100
Bebel, August, 86
Beethoven, Ludwig van, 17, 29
Benjamin, Walter, 119
Berlin, 50
Bildung, 34–40, 48, 51, 80–81, 107, 147
Biologism, 54, 56, 73–77, 95
Bismarck, Otto von, 13, 82, 84
Bloch, Ernst, 158
Bloom, Allan: *The Closing of the American Mind,* 9
Bonn, University of, 3, 8, 13–14, 55, 80, 96
Breeding, 56, 72–78, 147–48
Brinton, Crane, 157–59
Buchbinder, Friedrich, 2
Buddha, 139
Buddhism, 144, 147
Burckhardt, Jacob, 6

Chamberlain, Houston Stuart, 96, 99
Chandala, 146–47, 172n9
Christ, Jesus, 115, 130, 135, 141–43, 171n5
Christianity, 84, 110, 130–34, 138; origin of, 139–45
Clausius, Rudolf Julius, 64

Colonialism, 83–85
Conrad, Georg Michael, 152
Conscience (bad conscience), 118–22, 142–43
Consciousness, 41–42, 69–72
Corssen, Wilhelm, 2
Critical history, 40, 46–47

Darwin, Charles, 57–58, 60–61, 73; *Origin of the Species,* 57, 60
Darwinism, 57–61, 167n4
De Man, Paul, 161–63
Death of God, 134–38
Derrida, Jacques, 161–62; *Spurs,* 162
Descartes, Réne, 5
Deussen, Paul 3
Dionysian, 7, 16–30, 64, 157
Dühring, Eugen, 100

Eastern religion and philosophy, 4, 20, 139, 144–48
Engels, Friedrich, 9
Enlightenment, 19, 35, 52, 54, 129–30, 150
Eternal Recurrence, 11, 56, 62–67, 92, 150
Eugenics, 54, 56, 73–76
Euripides, 24–26, 114
Evolution, 57–61, 64, 69–70, 75
Expressionism, 149, 152–53

Faust, 123
Fichte, Johann, 2
Förster, Bernhard, 12–13, 93, 96, 99, 165n5
Foucault, Michel, 161–63; "Nietzsche, Genealogy, History," 162
Franco-Prussian War, 6, 10, 30, 80, 112
Franconia, 3, 166n5
Freiburg, University of, 160
Freud, Sigmund, 17, 19, 105, 117, 119; *Civilization and Its Discontents,* 117; *The Interpretation of Dreams,* 17

Friedrich Wilhelm IV (King of Prussia), 1
Fritzsch, Ernst Wilhelm, 7, 24

Galton, Sir Francis, 73, 76–77
Genealogy, 109, 161–62
General German Workers Union, 86
George Circle, 153–54
George, Stefan, 153–54
Germania, 2, 80, 166n5
Gersdorff, Carl von, 3
Gobineau, Count Joseph Arthur, 96,
    98–99; *Essai sur l'inégalité des race
    humaines,* 98
Goethe, Johann Wolfgang, 23, 52, 95,
    123, 130; "Prometheus," 23
Good European, 83–84
Great Politics, 83–85
Gründerzeit (Founding Age of Second
    Reich), 7, 29, 31, 82–83, 85, 97
Guilt, 141–43; origins of, 121–22
Gymnasium, 35–39, 53, 95

Härtle, Heinrich, 156–57
Hegel, Georg Friedrich Wilhelm, 4–5,
    18, 37, 50
Hegelians, 135
Heidegger, Martin, 159–62
Heidelberg, University of, 160
Heine, Heinrich, 134–35; *History of
    Religion and Philosophy in Germany,* 135
Hinduism, 144–47
The Historical, 40–43
Hitler, Adolf, 151, 156, 158
Homer, 18–20, 70, 123

Islam, 144, 147
Itschner, Hermann, 155

Jahn, Otto, 3, 8
Jaspers, Karl, 159–61
Jena, 13, 50

Kant, Immanuel, 4, 17, 26, 104, 135,
    156; *Critique of Pure Reason,* 135
Kaufmann, Walter, 161, 163; *Nietzsche:
    Philosopher, Psychologist, Antichrist,* 161
Kiel, University of, 7

Klopstock, Friedrich, 2
Kösellitz, Heinrich (Peter Gast), 12

Lamarck, Chevalier de, 168–69n15
Lamarckism, 75
Lange, Friedrich Albert: *History of
    Materialism,* 168n7
Language, 71–72, 138
La Rochefoucauld, François, 103
Lasalle, Ferdinand, 86
Leibniz, Gottfried Wilhelm von, 5
Leipzig, University of, 3, 13–14, 55, 80,
    96
Liebknecht, Wilhelm, 86
Lipiner, Sigfried, 97
Lukács, Georg, 158; *The Destruction of
    Reason,* 158
Luther, Martin, 153

Mann, Heinrich, 151
Mann, Thomas, 157; *Death in Venice,*
    157; *Doctor Faustus,* 157
Manu, Law or Tradition of, 144–47
Marx, Karl, 9, 61, 89, 119, 129, 135
Mayer, Julius Robert, 64
Mehring, Franz, 158
Metz, 67
Meysenbug, Malwida von, 11; *Memoirs of
    an Idealist,* 11–12
Mill, John Stuart, 61, 109
Misch, Robert, 152
Monumental history, 40, 43–45, 47

National Socialism, 73, 151, 156, 160,
    162. *See also* Third Reich
Naturalism, 152
Naumburg, 1–2, 13, 91, 95
Nietzsche, Auguste, 1
Nietzsche (Förster), Elisabeth, 1, 11–13,
    91–93, 99, 155–56, 160–61
Nietzsche, Erdmuthe, 1–2
Nietzsche, Franziska (née Oehler), 1, 13,
    91–92
Nietzsche, Friedrich: and classical philolo-
    gy, 2–3, 6–10, 14–16, 31–33, 37, 53,
    102, 111, 130; death of, 13; on
    democracy, 22–23, 73, 81–82, 84,

89, 100; on education, 9, 34–54, 102;
education of, 1–3, 55, 80; on ethics
and morality, 11, 26, 61, 73,
100–127, 137–40; on German culture, 7, 9–10, 26–34, 36, 47–48, 54,
73, 83; on Germany, 81–85, 155; on
Greece, 7, 16–34, 47, 88, 102,
130–31, 143; illness, 1–2, 10, 12–13,
53; on the Jewish Question, 80,
95–101; on Jewish religion and
morality, 114–17, 135, 139–41,
146–47; military service; 5–7, 13; on
nationalism, 79–85, 100, 128, 155;
and natural sciences, 6, 38, 55–78,
102, 129, 148, 154; on religion, 11,
73, 84, 110, 128–48; on women, 1,
73, 79–80, 90–95, 125–26; on workers, 79, 85–90; youth 1–5, 81,
95–96, 128

WORKS
The Antichrist, 12, 83, 139–40, 144,
147
Beyond Good and Evil, 11, 54, 74, 84,
93–94, 108
The Birth of Tragedy, 4, 6–9, 15–33,
35, 112, 153; controversy over,
7–8
The Case of Wagner, 12, 32
Daybreak, 10, 102, 137
Ecce Homo, 12–13, 31, 57, 81, 92,
94–95, 100, 102
Five Prefaces to Five Unwritten Books,
169n4
The Gay Science, 10, 62, 65, 69, 82,
84, 136, 138–39
The Genealogy of Morals, 11, 100,
108–9, 111, 115, 122, 126, 133,
140–41, 163
"The Greek Music Drama," 165n2
"Homer and Classical Philology," 6
Human, All Too Human, 10, 28,
83–84, 92–94, 97, 102–3, 107,
109, 114, 126, 129, 131, 133,
135–36
Nietzsche Contra Wagner, 12, 32
*On the Advantage and Disadvantage of
History for Life,* 10, 40–50, 117

"On the Future of Our Educational
Institutions," 35–40
"Philosophy in the Tragic Age of the
Greeks," 165n3
Richard Wagner in Bayreuth, 10, 15, 31
Schopenhauer as Educator, 10, 15,
50–53
Thus Spoke Zarathustra, 10–12, 56–58,
62–63, 65, 86, 90, 94, 99, 108,
138, 155
Twilight of the Idols, 12, 33, 58–59,
64, 82, 138, 145–46
Untimely Meditations, 9–10, 15, 31,
40, 50, 53, 62
The Will to Power, 161

Nietzsche, Karl Ludwig, 1, 13
Nietzsche, Ludwig, 1
Nietzsche, Rosalie, 1
Nietzsche Archives, 13
Nirvana, 4
Noah, 145
Norddeutsche Allgemeine Zeitung, 7
Novalis (Friedrich von Hardenberg), 2

Odysseus, 20
Overbeck, Franz, 12–13, 99
Overman (*Übermensch*), 11, 56–61, 64,
147

Paraguay, 12–13, 99
Paris, 6, 50
Paris Commune, 112, 166–67n6
Perspectivism, 56, 67–72
Physiology, 69–70
Plato, 68, 102
Poststructuralism, 161–63

Ranke, Leopold von, 2
Realschule, 35, 38
Rée, Paul 11–12, 91, 95–97, 103; *The
Origin of Moral Sensations,* 96, 103;
Psychological Observations, 96, 103
Ritschl, Friedrich, 3, 5, 8, 51
Röcken (Saxony), 1–2
Rohde, Erwin, 7–8, 15, 31; *Afterphilologie,* 8
Rousseau, Jean-Jacques, 52

Roux, Wilhelm: *The Struggle of the Parts in the Organism,* 168n6

Salomé, Louise von, 11–12, 91–93, 97, 99
Schiller, Friedrich, 18–19, 23; *Bride of Messina,* 23; "Ode to Joy," 19
Schlechta, Karl, 160–61
Schlegel, Friedrich, 2
Schlegel, Wilhelm, 2
Schmeitzner, Ernst, 96, 99
Schöll, Rudolf, 8
Schopenhauer, Arthur, 3–5, 7, 10, 14–17, 19, 21, 26–27, 29, 34, 36, 40, 50–53, 93, 129, 159; *The World as Will and Idea,* 4, 27, 50
Schulpforta, 2–3, 8, 10, 14, 34, 55
Second (German) Reich. *See Gründerzeit*
Semites, 23, 98, 112
Silenus, 20
Sils-Maria, 10
Social Democratic Workers' Party, 86, 89, 158
Socialism, 73, 89–90, 100, 149
Socrates, 16, 20, 23–28, 114, 123, 132
Sophocles, 23, 25
Spencer, Herbert, 109
Spinoza, Baruch, 5
Strauß, David, 10, 15; *Das Leben Jesu,* 10
The Superhistorical, 40, 42–43, 49
Superman. *See* Overman

Theognis, 111
Thermodynamics, 64–67
Third Reich, 115, 159, 160. *See also* National Socialism

Thomson, William (Lord Kelvin), 66–67
Tönnies, Friedrich, 151–52; *The Nietzsche Cult,* 152; "Nietzsche Nitwits," 151
Tragedy, 16–27
Tucholsky, Kurt, 150
Turin, 13

Umberto II, 13
The Unhistorical, 40–43, 49
Union of German Workers Organizations, 86

Venice, 74
Versailles, 7
Vischer-Bolfinger, Wilhelm, 8

Wagner, Cosima, 5–6, 80, 97
Wagner, Richard 3, 5–8, 11, 14–17, 26–34, 40, 73, 79–80, 96–97, 99, 123, 149, 151; "Judaism and Music," 96; *Die Meistersinger,* 15; *Parsifal,* 11, 32, 123, 170–71n3; *Tristan und Isolde,* 30
Weimar, 13
Weimar Republic, 150, 155–56
Wilamowitz-Moellendorff, Ulrich von, 8–9; *Zukunftsphilologie,* 8
Wilhelm II, 13
Winckelmann, Johann Joachim, 18, 33
World War I, 151, 155, 158
World War II, 151, 159
Wörth, 6

Zurich, University of, 11
Zweig, Stefan: "The New Pathos," 152–53

The Author

Robert C. Holub teaches German intellectual, cultural, and literary history in the German department at the University of California, Berkeley. An undergraduate in natural sciences at the University of Pennsylvania from 1967 to 1971, he studied comparative literature and German as a graduate student at the University of Wisconsin–Madison from 1972 to 1979. He currently chairs the German department at Berkeley. Professor Holub has researched and written extensively about German culture, literature, and philosophy in the nineteenth and twentieth centuries. His previous publications include *Heinrich Heine's Reception of German Grecophilia* (1981), *Reception Theory: A Critical Introduction* (1984), *Reflections of Realism* (1991), *Jürgen Habermas: Critic in the Public Sphere* (1991), and *Crossing Borders: Reception Theory, Poststructuralism, Deconstruction* (1992). He is the editor of *Heinrich Heine: Poetry and Prose* (1982), *The Romantic School and Other Essays* (1985), *Teoria della ricezione* (1989), and *Impure Reason: Dialectic of Enlightenment in Germany* (1993).

MISSION ON THE HO CHI MINH TRAIL

Nature, Myth, and War in Viet Nam

By Richard L. Stevens

UNIVERSITY OF OKLAHOMA PRESS : NORMAN

BY RICHARD L. STEVENS

The Trail: A History of the Ho Chi Minh Trail and the Role of Nature in the War in Viet Nam (New York, 1993)
Mission on the Ho Chi Minh Trail: Nature, Myth, and War in Viet Nam (Norman, 1995)

This book is published with the generous assistance of The McCasland Foundation, Duncan, Oklahoma.

Library of Congress Cataloging-in-Publication Data

Stevens, Richard L., 1939–
    Mission on the Ho Chi Minh trail : nature, myth, and war in Viet Nam / by Richard L. Stevens.
        p.   cm.
    Includes bibliographical references and index.
    ISBN 0–8061–2768–6
    1. Vietnamese Conflict, 1961–1975—United States. 2. Ho Chi Minh Trail. 3. Vietnamese Conflict, 1961–1975—Personal narratives, American. 4. Stevens, Richard L., 1939–   . I. Title.
DS558.S74   1995
959.704'38—dc20   95-10198
                                                                              CIP

Book designed by Bill Cason

The paper in this book meets the guidelines for permanence and durability of the Committee on Production Guidelines for Book Longevity of the Council on Library Resources, Inc. ∞

1   2   3   4   5   6   7   8   9   10

MISSION ON THE HO CHI MINH TRAIL

To Maria Fernandez Rodriguez
with love and thanks

CONTENTS

List of Illustrations   ix
Overture   3
Introduction   5
Sources   7
Chapters
1. Viêt and the Grim Reapers: The Call
   to Adventure   12
2. Machine in the Forest   46
3. Deep Play in the Belly of the Whale:
   Passage into the Realm of Night   95
4. The Gloomy Wood and the Poison Trees   142
5. Separation-Initiation-Return   181
6. The Road of Trials, or the Dangerous Aspect
   of the Gods   191
Notes   253
Glossary   257
Bibliography   263
Index   267

ILLUSTRATIONS

Photographs
Viêt and an unidentified major ready to   *Following page* 131
    fly recon on the Trail
The author and Viêt before the raid on Triêu Phong
Viêt and the "NVA"
The author on Firebase Ann
Viêt, Ramos, Captain Mao, and a 3rd Battalion advisor
The author near the Ho Chi Minh Trail
The author, Viêt, and ARVN on the old river road
Ramos
The Author and Captain Mao
The "New" Viêt

Drawing
Batman Caper, by Wailehua Gray   129

Maps
Quang Tri Province   14
Triêu Phong VC district headquarters   48
NVA rocket company's camp   97

MISSION ON THE HO CHI MINH TRAIL

Moreover, I, on my side, require of every writer, first or last, a simple and sincere account of his own life, and not merely what he has heard of other men's lives; some such account as he would send to his kindred from a distant land.

—Thoreau, *Walden*

OVERTURE

Hence this life of yours which you are living is not merely a piece of the entire existence but is in a certain sense the whole.

—Erwin Schrödinger, *My View of the World*

This book follows my *The Trail*[1] in examining the role of nature in the war in Viet Nam and revealing more of the mythic substratum. Seven operations spin a tapestry of light and shadow; in microcosms are connections to all the rest.

This is the Viet Nam War, hologram-displayed. "My purpose is not to write histories, but lives,"[2] not so much to argue as to present. The "secret of the Garden," Loren Eiseley and Joseph Campbell remind us, is within.[3]

In the Viet Nam Garden-forest grew the Tree of Life and the Tree of the Knowledge of Good and Evil, and hence, as America, we came, with hubris and great power. This was, though we did not realize it at the beginning, and even less so as time went on, the mythic hero-journey. Separation-initiation-return: this was America's path in Viet Nam, and we are walking it still into our future.

INTRODUCTION

. . . where to begin
if everything is beginning. . . .
—from a poem of El Salvador

Ten years after the war, reading Joseph Campbell's *The Hero with a Thousand Faces,* I realized I had lived in Viet Nam the mythic hero-journey: separation from "the World," which is what we called the United States in those days; travel to a strange and dangerous land; combat with often invisible enemies, some of them within; initiation into mysteries; and return with a message of importance. Later, I realized we had *all* lived that journey, those who went and those who stayed at home; the whole country had walked the mythic hero-path of separation-initiation-return in Viet Nam and was walking it still. And now was the time to share the message.

On missions on the Ho Chi Minh Trail I watched from holes on scarred hilltops as tropical forest turned to gray mush. I floundered through land become bare-dirt upheaval, not a feather or piece of skin left of the birds and animals that had once lived there. In three years in Viet Nam I came to believe we were fighting against Nature and would lose, while the other side was working with Nature and would win, and that there were lessons here on a global scale. I wrote about this in *The Trail.*

Now come the experiences *The Trail* was based on, themes in action, leaf flutter, whispers, footsteps, forest hush. Multidimensional connections lie deep behind these actions, the coming to vast power of the continent-conquering Americans, the irresistible "Drive South" of the Viets, and other ancient movements far beyond that. Time is like a tunnel through the trees, like the Trail as it came down from the mountains and forests bearing young men and women from East and West to a fateful meeting. The roots of this story lie deep in the farthest reaches of space-time and are with us still as part of the Tree of Life today. In the beginning is the end; in the end is the beginning.

Morning in Viet Nam, November 1969: sunrise over the sea, with golden rays streaming over the battered but still beautiful land. In Quang Tri Province below the Demilitarized Zone a series of operations begins which will suck in and claim several human lives, devastate great areas of the green and living world, and send survivors back into life with messages of importance about Nature, war, myth, and death.

SOURCES

I'm on the other side now.
—Việt

There is no telling this story without Việt, and the world of which he was part: raindrops in the forest, mountains, streams, sea, sky. Without Việt, there is no story, just as without Nature, there is no life. Việt was a Việt Công, a VC guerrilla. He was born of frontier Vietnamese moved west into tribal Montagnard country, the Ba Long, or "Three Hearts," Valley, in the time of President Ngô Dinh Diêm. Việt grew up on the edge of the wilderness as a child of the forest and mountains.

At fifteen, Việt became a guide for North Vietnamese Army (NVA) units on the Ho Chi Minh Trail, then a guerrilla fighter running night missions into the enemy-occupied lowlands. He was wounded north of Quang Tri City in 1966 in an ambush by U.S. Marines and was carried sixteen miles by his comrades to a secret forest hospital. He almost died, was evacuated to the North on the Ho Chi Minh Trail, and spent a year in a hospital near Hanoi. Việt recovered slowly and began to help out around the hospital. He liked the work, the caring for others, and decided he wanted to become a doctor. He requested training as a medic, went back to the South on the Trail, and served in the same forest hospital where he had first been treated.

In late 1968, Việt began one of the war's most perilous assignments: one-man courier missions from the forest and mountains of the Ho Chi Minh Trail, across the deadly piedmont and paddies to the dunes, and back to the "Indian country" of the Trail again. Six nights of dropping to listen, smell, *feel* ambushes and mines. Six days of hiding in underground, stale-air, gravelike bunkers. Six days of fear and sweat; six days and nights in Hell. By 1969, Viêt at twenty was an expert on surviving in the world's most dangerous environment: Quang Tri Province, scene of the heaviest fighting of the war.[1]

On November 8, 1969, the Viêt Công Triêu Phong District commander gives Viêt a mission: carry medicines and messages to the guerrilla company hiding in the dunes east of Quang Tri City. Viêt prepares, dressing in a brown NVA shirt and black VC shorts and putting on his lucky hat. He leaves his AK-47 behind; it is too bulky, makes his silhouette too large, and will not help much in an ambush. He takes one Chinese grenade for that, to make some noise and help him get away if he survives the first storm of fire. In a Chinese pack he puts the medicines and documents and his notebook for writing poems, one of his favorite forest pastimes. One poem he has written about his two heroes, John F. Kennedy and Ho Chi Minh.

Viêt looks young for his age, is chunky for a Vietnamese, and has a long, curly forelock that often falls over one eye. He is small, strong, and tireless on the Trail. He flows down the Trail like water; the Dao is natural in him. Baby-faced, cherubic Viêt is master of the sinuous, floating art of guerrilla war.

Viêt walks by day on forest path branches of the vast, living Ho Chi Minh Trail system, then hides and sleeps till night where the ocean of trees meets the grassy, rolling-hill piedmont. Where Viêt goes the Trail goes, each footstep creating a Trail extension, a capillary and nerve ending and new beginning of an immense, interconnected flow.

Viêt walks through the night in the piedmont to Nhan Biêu refugee hamlet along the Thach Han River. Here he lies low, studies the dark hamlet, and signals with a night bird's call. A light comes from the hamlet in reply, and in a moment an old woman emerges from the shadows. She guides Viêt to her one-room, tin-roofed shack, and Viêt hides all day in the tomblike bunker dug into her packed earth floor. The next night the old woman escorts Viêt to the far edge of the hamlet, and he is alone again, crossing the deadly paddy-sea, going around U.S. and ARVN ambushes, and entering the bone-white dunes. Now Viêt brushes out his tracks with a pine bough, bending, brushing, the Trail disappearing behind him, down to the South China Sea.

Viêt enters the water and wades, Ho Chi Minh sandals in hand, waves erasing the Trail. To the north, a fishing village looms, and Viêt passes it, its black doorways gaping, bamboo windows hanging open, and people gone, moved to hot, tin-shack, refugee desolation in the dunes, in the U.S.–Saigon government policy of trying to find the fish by drying up the sea. Viêt wades on, pushing the Trail into darkness. Farther north, at a small grove of dune pines, Viêt turns inland and just before dawn climbs a large sand hill, carefully brushing. At the top he whispers a password, and the dune stirs and opens, a shaft of moonlight penetrating a secret bunker. Viêt crawls in, and the lid closes, sand settling back over the slight disturbance.

Inside, in total darkness and with little air, two invisible voices float. One is the guerrilla company commander, a veteran of years of fighting and living underground. The second is a new recruit from a nearby hamlet, a guerrilla younger than Viêt. Viêt hands his pack to the commander. There is no talk beyond what is necessary, no using up of precious air. All try to sleep jammed tightly together till dark, VC time, comes and they can move again. Being awake is bad—very bad—in the bunker.

Viêt shallow-breathes, sweats in darkness, and tries to

sleep: twelve, thirteen hours. Finally, night comes, and Viêt is on his way, brushing with his pine bough down to the sea, wading south, and turning inland into the dunes again, heading toward the distant mountains, the Trail, sanctuary, and home.

The night rumbles and flashes with American artillery and hides deadly ARVN ambushes and mines. Viêt lies in a ditch beside the old road called by the French the Street without Joy, then crosses fast, like a shadow, a ghost. He stops near a tree-shrouded hamlet and again lies low, watching. Dark houses loom across a paddy, and bamboo blows and clacks in the wind. Viêt gives his night bird's call, and a light comes from the hamlet in reply.

A dark form soon emerges from the night, a man who keeps his face hidden from Viêt and whispers, "*Dên.*" "Come."

Viêt follows the man away from the hamlet and along the brushy banks of a dry lake. The man stops in a clearing near a small, ruined shrine. "The bunker is here," he says.

Viêt wants to talk, wants to stay above ground a little longer. He asks for news of life in the lowlands, of nearby Quang Tri City, where his uncle lives.

"No time," the man says. He opens a bunker near the small shrine and tells Viêt to get inside.

Viêt slowly climbs in and lies down on his back. The lid comes down like the top of a tomb, shutting out light and life. The man goes away, his footsteps retreating. "Shades of the prison-house begin to close on the boy."[2] Viêt lies sweating, still, and awake in the tight grave of his past life. Finally, he sleeps. From here he will rise into a different world.

In the morning, a message arrives at the Quang Tri City office of ARVN Captain Rang, head of the province Special Police, the Vietnamese CIA. Rang calls his American advisor, and soon a U.S. Huey helicopter is cranking its big rotor blades on Quang Tri Citadel pad. The chopper loads Rang, seven

ARVN soldiers, and the American advisor and flies to the shores of the dry lake. Blades whirl, brush whips, and dust flies as the chopper descends roaring U.S. power.

Viêt's story and mine as our lives intertwine are the sources for what follows, backed by tapes I made in Viet Nam; notebooks, maps, and documents, some of them captured, I brought back; a nineteen-hundred-page manuscript I began writing there; and research in the National Archives. Direct-quote conversations after the passage of years are difficult to reconstruct; however, because of the sources mentioned above and the often sharp-etched and heavy impress of memory, I believe all that follow are true to the moment and character speaking, and sometimes are exactly as they occurred. This is true of the visions, images, and dreams recorded, which I wrote down soon after they happened or on awaking.

Now begins the mythic hero-journey, and a fragment of life as it was lived in Viet Nam, with connections to all the rest.

> . . . where to begin
> if everything is beginning
> and returning to live again. . . .

CHAPTER 1

VIÊT AND THE GRIM REAPERS:
THE CALL TO ADVENTURE

Misfortune struck at mounts and rivers,
Even trees and grass suffered.
—Vietnamese poem of the 1700s

In his bunker, Viêt lies in darkness listening to the beat and roar of the approaching helicopter and the landing and running of men. A shout explodes: "Come out or die!"[1]

Viêt lies thinking, heart racing, as more shouts and threats burst in from the green world outside. He slowly pushes open the bunker lid and emerges blinking into the sun, a frightened-looking, moon-faced kid with his hands in the air and a curly lock of black hair falling over one squinting eye.

The ARVN rush forward, throw Viêt to the ground, surround him, and begin beating him with the butts of their M-16s, screaming, "Kill him!"

Hard-faced Captain Rang stands off to the side, smoking an American cigarette and watching. Everything is being done under his direction. He wades into the circle shouting, "Stop!" and throwing the ARVN aside. He has orchestrated his role as Viêt's savior. Rang helps Viêt up and leads him into the trees, tells him not to be afraid, that all he has to do is cooperate. Viêt looks dazed as Rang talks. He nods and answers Rang's questions.

They fly to the dunes, and Viêt guides them from the clump of dune pines to the guerrilla commander's bunker. The ARVN climb partway up the sand hill and lie in a circle around it. Again the shout explodes, "Come out or die!"

The top of the dune erupts, sand and the lid flying. The VC leader jumps out firing his AK wildly in a last burst of rebellion and life. Shooting storms of steel from the prone position, the ARVN cut the VC down in a ripping hell of M-16 fire. The VC's body pitches forward, twitches, and lies still, blood staining the bone-white sand.

More shouts: "Come out! Want to die?"

The young VC rises from the dune looking like a dead man, his hands high and trembling and his face pale. The ARVN move forward and roughly take him and then carefully remove everything from the bunker. They reboard the chopper and fly back to Quang Tri City, where the VC is left at the local chamber of horrors, the Province Interrogation Center (PIC). In a visit to his Special Police office, Rang makes a tape of Viêt saying what he tells him to, and then he brings him to me at the Chiêu Hôi center, where VC who have defected, or "rallied," arrive.[2]

Rang speaks broken English in hard, jerky spurts: "He's prisoner, but I give him to you for now. If he cooperate fully, maybe I make him rallier. I have no troops to go where he knows: Ho Chi Minh Trail."

Rang nods his head ominously off to the west, then hits my wall map with the palm of his hand in the green mountains near the Laos border. "He knows all this: base camps, hospitals, Trail, everything."

The Trail! I look at Viêt. His head is hanging, and he looks sick, half dead. Since I came to Viet Nam I have been obsessed with the Ho Chi Minh Trail; now I see my passport there.

Rang goes on: "He *has* to cooperate, or I send him to military prison. Maybe I do it anyway."

"He might escape from here," I say. "Go back."[3]

"He *can't* go back," Rang says, and he pulls the cassette tape out of his pocket and waves it under Viêt's nose. "I

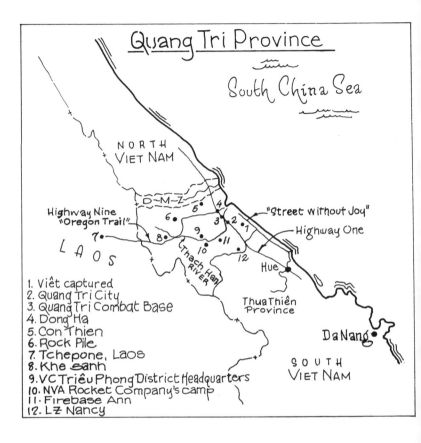

Quang Tri Province

South China Sea

NORTH
VIET NAM

Highway Nine
"Oregon Trail"

L A O S

DMZ

"Street without Joy"

Highway One

Hue

Thach Han River

1. Viêt captured
2. Quang Tri City
3. Quang Tri Combat Base
4. Dong Ha
5. Con Thien
6. Rock Pile
7. Tchepone, Laos
8. Khe Sanh
9. VC Triêu Phong District Headquarters
10. NVA Rocket Company's camp
11. Firebase Ann
12. LZ Nancy

Thua Thien
Province

Da Nang

SOUTH
VIET NAM

broadcast this over mountains, tell VC everything. He can't go back; they kill him for sure."

Rang says hard words to Viêt, then leaves, his jeep bouncing away down the rough road that leads to the Center. I look at Viêt again. He looks different from the many VC I've seen come in from the mountains. He's chunky, moon-faced, almost pudgy looking, with a long, curly forelock falling over his right eye. He looks like a Vietnamese cherub in an Italian

Renaissance painting. I direct him to my big wall map, point to the mountains and forest in the west near Laos and say, "*Cho tôi biêt Duong Mon Ho Chi Minh,*" literally, "Give me know Trail Ho Chi Minh."

Viêt slowly raises his head and looks at me through his hair. "*Tôi mât lâm,*" he says in a suddenly firm voice. "I'm tired. I want to sleep. I'll tell you everything tomorrow." I look at him. I consider ordering him to talk and wonder how far I could go with that. He would never dare refuse if Rang were around. The force seems to leave him, and me. He drops his head again to his chest. "OK," I say. "*Ngây mây.*" "Tomorrow."

I tell one of the ralliers to take him to the barracks to sleep. I watch him go, excitement leaping inside me in conflict with fears that he'll run away in the night or blow the place up, taking my chance for the Trail with him. In the morning I arrive at the Chiêu Hôi center early. Viêt comes right away with what looks like a pirate treasure map. Mountains, streams, two headquarters, a hospital, and an NVA rocket company's camp have been connected by a dashed line labeled "Duong Mon Ho Chi Minh." I feel on fire to go out there and follow that mysterious, curving line.

Over the next several days Viêt and I talk long about the Trail, the bases, the men and the women there. I feel we're becoming friends, the American and the ex-VC. The ralliers begin to call Viêt my "son." I tell Viêt what he must say when we take what he knows to the nearest American Army unit, the 1st Brigade of the 5th Mechanized Division: "When they ask you to guide them on the Trail, you say you will only go if I go, too. And you are not a prisoner; you are a rallier."

I try to get the brigade to launch a reconnaissance operation to verify Viêt's information, but they are huge and ponderous and slow to move, especially because the weather has been bad: it's *crachin* time in the mountains.[4]

One morning in December, I arrive at the center to find that Viêt is gone, taken away for shipment to military prison by Captain Rang. I race off in my Scout and finally find Viêt chained to two VC in a small, nearly airless closet in the province headquarters. Rang is frustrated, too, by the lack of action and wants Viêt interrogated again and then imprisoned. Viêt looks sick, half dead. *"Giup tôi,"* he says weakly. "Help me."

I drive to Rang's office and ask him to release Viêt. "Nothing happening," Rang says. "You Americans not using what he knows. Waste time, waste life. Intelligence old, no good. And I see him all over Quang Tri with you, even go to your house, go to base, go into TOC, talk with S-2. He's VC prisoner. Not supposed to go anywhere, but cooperate."

I lie. I tell Rang an operation is set to go any day now, after one of the headquarters Viêt knows about. He *can't* take Viêt now.

Rang snorts. "Maybe big trap. Too long wait now. And you trust him? Stupid! Once VC, *never* change!"

Rang finally agrees to let me have Viêt back, but only if I sign for him. He writes out an agreement: Viêt is not to leave the Chiêu Hôi center except to guide operations, and I am responsible for everything he does.

"Sign," Rang says.

I sign, hoping I'm not making a big mistake and being blinded by my passion for the Trail.

"Maybe Viêt *kill* you some day," Rang says as he folds the paper and puts it in his desk. "And he better get results soon, or I take him back, send him to prison."

I push and prod the brigade to go. Reconnaissance is not its specialty: big mechanized operations are. And Rang is right: too much time has passed, deadly time—time for leaks and traps to be set. I drive to Quang Tri Combat Base, home of the brigade's tactical operations center (TOC) and S-2 intelligence office. For one month I have been trying to get them to act on Viêt's knowledge—a month of agonized waiting through plans, paperwork, briefings, clearances, and finally, especially, for the weather to be just right.

On December 26, with Rang making ominous noises again and Viêt falling into deep depressions about his future, I get a telephone call from Red Devil, the brigade command. This is the call to adventure I've been waiting for, maybe all my life. A recon mission is planned for liftoff tomorrow to try to locate the Viêt Công's Triêu Phong District headquarters along the Ho Chi Minh Trail, where Viêt was given his last courier mission.

"I don't think you can find this without us," I say.

"But is the rallier willing to go?" the S-2 asks.

"Oh, yes, he wants to—but he says I have to go, too, as his interpreter."

"OK, I'll bump two recon men off the team. You do know you'll be out there in Indian country with only a seven-man team?"

"Yeah, sure, no problem." A strange voice inside my head suddenly says, *What are you doing?*

"The mission is planned for five days," the S-2 says. "You'll have to provide your own gear. It gets rainy out there. Will the rallier be carrying a weapon?"

"No," I say, "he won't."

I hang up in a daze, a fever. I'm going! I race around Quang Tri and get a small-sized American Army uniform for Viêt, but no boots: I can't find size six. He'll have to wear his Ho Chi Minh sandals. Viêt is quiet. One month ago he was a VC; now he'll lead an American recon team back into the mountains and forests of the Trail.

On the morning of December 27 we load our packs with rain gear, water, and C-rations and drive out to the base. My insides are full of butterflies; at last I'm on my way to the Ho Chi Minh Trail. We drive onto the dusty sandbagged and barbed-wired base and park at Pioneer Pad, the steel mesh helicopter landing area of the 1st Battalion, 11th Infantry, a historic Indian-fighting unit. In the distance I see four pack-laden, camouflage-clad black soldiers coming. *Oh, God,* I think, *I'm going to be the only white man on a soul patrol!* Often in stressful times in Viêt Nam, something absurd, even cartoonlike, starts playing in my mind. This time it's the old joke about the Lone Ranger and Tonto. Riding into a canyon, they discover they're surrounded by ten thousand Comanches, ten thousand Sioux, ten thousand Cheyennes, and ten thousand Apaches. "My God, we're surrounded!" the Lone Ranger says. "What do you mean, 'we,' white man?" Tonto replies.

The black soldiers near Pioneer Pad. Now I see it is only their faces and hands that are black, camouflage-painted. Viêt will be the only Indian on this white man's patrol. The recon team leader, a twenty-one-year-old sergeant named Tex, intro-duces his team and then whips out a camouflage stick and paints Viêt and me black: faces, hands, wrists, necks, even our eyelids.

"Black like me," I think, looking at my hands and remem-bering the book of the man who changed colors. Viêt and I are now part of the battalion's Recon Team One, radio call sign the "Grim Reapers." We troop big and armed down to the 1/11 TOC to meet Major Joe Lukitsch, the battalion S-3 operations officer. He escorts us into the underground briefing room, where big wall maps are festooned with colored pins marking known friendly and supposed enemy positions. Waiting there is another black-painted Texan, Captain Willett of brigade artillery.[5]

"Captain Willett will be attached to your team for this operation," Lukitsch says. "If you need artillery support, he'll have a direct line to brigade."

One of Tex's team mutters something, and Tex says, "We usually handle that ourselves, sir."

"I know," Lukitsch says, "but the captain has been sent to us by brigade."

"If we hit the shit you'll be glad I'm there," Willett says.

Willett has what a Foreign Service colleague of mine calls a "smell-shit" expression on his face. He looks too much into being a captain and part of the Green Machine. I smell trouble, especially for Viêt, at whom Willett glares—especially at his sandals—with disdain.

"Mr. Stevens will tell us what you're going to find out there," Major Lukitsch says.

I rise and use the map to tell the story of the various sections of the VC headquarters and the people there as Viêt has told it to me: "old fox" District Commander Huynh, veteran of the struggle against the Japanese, French, and us; young Dr. Son from Hanoi, surgeon at the forest hospital; an English-speaker, also from the North, who writes the propaganda leaflets that appear now and then outside the base.

Willett interrupts: "How do you know all this?"

I feel trouble coming now. I nod toward Viêt and say, "He told me."

Willett snorts with savage satisfaction. "I *thought* so. And how's *he* know?"

I imagine Willett as a nasty, spoiled little kid; then a mean, hazing college frat man; and now an officer probably hated by his men.

"He's been there," I say.

"In what capacity?" Willett says.

Now it comes out—part, anyway. "He was a VC," I say.

"I knew it!" Willett says. "The dink's a VC! And *he's* goin' on this mission?"

Lukitsch has red hair and is built like a running back. And he doesn't like his authority questioned. "Mr. Viêt *was* a VC," he says with a hard look at Willett. "Now he's a rallier. He has cooperated fully with us and has our complete confidence. He has volunteered for this mission, too, and it probably won't succeed without him. I can assure you, Captain, that this operation has been carefully planned in my S-3 shop. If you don't feel comfortable with it, you can bail out now."

Willett slouches in his chair and shoots a killer look at Viêt.

"I'll remind you, too, Captain," Lukitsch goes on, "that you are attached to this team in *support,* with Tex in command. Is that clear to everyone?"

Willett continues to glare at Viêt, while the rest of us say, "Yes." Viêt sits wide-eyed and listening. I wonder if he really doesn't understand any English, as he claims. What can he be thinking of us? We seem already in combat—with each other.

We troop back to Pioneer Pad and load aboard a doorless Red Devil Huey slick with a red diamond on the nose. Tex and I sit in the open doorway with our legs hanging out, like two kids on a carnival ride, while the others jam in on the aluminum floor, packs and backs crunched together and weapons rattling. The Huey lifts off and blasts up the Thach Han River, sails high over the mountains, becomes lost in cloud canyons, and descends over dangerous forest. All is Indian country below, with trees pointing up like spears at the belly of our roaring bird and our soft flesh inside thin metal skin. We rise and fall to false drops on scarred hills, the *crachin* ceiling dropping, pressing us down.

There is no hiding a helicopter landing troops in a large, silent forest. The VC will know we are here, but we hope that pretend-landing false drops will confuse them about exactly where we go out on a hover-jump. Our landing zone has been carefully chosen after several reconnaissance flights by Lukitsch, Viêt, and me and meticulously plotted on Lukitsch's map, but those flights were on clear days and from higher up, and the map is not much help in the clouds. Viêt is airsick as usual and can't assist much, either. Anyway, he knows the place from the ground, not the air.

We're lost in clouds and mist, we can't find our LZ, and Lukitsch is about to call off the mission. We Americans are getting sick, too, with all the rising and falling and engine exhaust smells and roar. We can hardly think. Helicopter noise has invaded our minds and body rhythms, substituting mechanical beat and chop for heart-thump and brain waves. More and more we are part of the Machine.

Below, through a sudden break in the clouds, a circle of old foxholes rings a grass-grown, scarred hilltop. Our LZ! Trees explode in size as the helicopter descends, and Tex and I brace in the doorway and prepare to jump. The chopper nears the earth, air-brakes, hovers beating insanely, and Tex shouts something—I think, "Go!"

I fly through the air, fall on my face, leap up, and run through the roaring, whipping grass. I dive and roll over the crest of the hill, tumble into an old foxhole, and point my M-16 down into the surrounding ocean of trees. Images of marching Birnam Wood in *MacBeth* burst in my mind, and the British advancing up Bunker Hill: stress images with the veneer of my education and the patina of civilization overlying deeper levels of primitivism.

I twist around and look back as the Huey flies away. Alone! I'm alone on the hill! Maybe it was another false drop, or the pilot saw VC at the last moment and quickly pulled away. Maybe Tex shouted "No!" instead of "Go!" I wanted the Trail, but not alone. Not yet.

I hear voices above. It's the team. They're finding each other in the blowing grass. I begin to crawl up, then stop. What if they mistake me for the VC? I hiss though my teeth and whisper, "Comin' up!"

Tex calls us together and we move out fast to get away from the LZ. We enter the forest, fight downhill, struggle, and crash. We get constantly hung up on vines, caught on roots, our big packs snagged, M-16 rifles and bulky radios snared, jungle boots trapped. Viêt is different: he moves through the forest easily, passing up and down our ragged line freeing us from vines, helping us up from falls, pulling us through tangles.

Viêt whispers to me that he wants to lead, to find a trail and follow it. "We'll never get anywhere if we don't," he says. "We'll just crash around out here until the VC find us. Tell Sergeant Tex."

I translate to Tex, and he consults with his team, as he does on all important decisions. "We all say no," Tex whispers. "You don't follow trails in Indian country."

Willett horns in: "Little dink probably wants to lead us into a trap."

Mostly blind, with the vegetation like a great Sargasso Sea all around, we struggle on, fighting the forest each step of the way. Near the end of the day, Tex calls a halt, and we sink down slumped, sweating, and wrapped in green, black paint smudged and streaked on our faces and gone from our thorn-cut and bleeding hands. The radioman reports what we guess is our position under the multiple canopy and then whispers to Tex that Cobra Six himself, General Burke, the brigade commander, is on the horn: "He wants to know why we made only five hundred meters today."

"If he was out here, he'd know," Tex says.

Shadows begin to deepen, the green world turning black. The Grim Reapers set out claymore mines, and we all wrap up in ponchos and lie down on the ground along the banks of a small, dry creek. We look like strange, dark cocoons, meals awaiting some monster spider. Darkness comes, the beyond-black of the multiple-canopy rain forest night. It begins to rain, *crachin* dripping from invisible trees. I pull my poncho over my head but feel the rain running down my back. I squirm around, trying to make myself small, and churn the earth to muck. Cold rises from the ground and comes down with the rain, settling in my boots and soggy socks, and I begin to shake uncontrollably in the first stages of hypothermia. I grew up in Iowa and had an outdoor life, but I have never been this cold. I shake and shiver for hours as the rain drips on, finding ever new ways to run down my neck, chest, and legs.

I pray for, and try to will morning to come so we can get up and move. I open my poncho slightly, hoping to see light filtering down through the trees. I gasp and for a moment don't notice the rain spattering my face. Under the canopy it's still totally dark, but on the ground fallen twigs and leaves are glowing with bioluminescence, living light. I reach out and pick up a glowing twig and hold it before my face. For a while I forget the rain and the cold; my hands aren't even trembling. It's foxfire, luminous fungus, death turning into life. The rain drum-beats on my poncho all night.

In the morning we unroll and stiffly sit and stand on the churned ground looking like New Guinea Mudmen. Viêt still sleeps, rolled up in a ball with large leaves under him and his poncho wrapped tightly around him. He's so quiet I wonder if that's a log in there and he has slipped away in the night. Willett and the Grim Reapers watch as I go over and shake him. He stirs, unwraps, and comes out smiling. He's dry! Clean and dry! Tex and his men shake their heads, nudge each other, grin, and whisper.

"Little guy is good," Tex says.

The Reapers begin to like and trust Viêt from this moment, and Willett hates Viêt more. Viêt and I eat a breakfast of cold, canned C-rations while the Grim Reapers and Willett eat freeze-dried lurps. Viêt reaches in his pack and says, "I can tell what's in C-rations just by shaking the can."

I squat on the ground eating and watch while Viêt closes his eyes and pulls out a can. Sitting on his big leaves he looks like a strange Buddha. He shakes the can and says, "Peaches."

I reach over, take the can, and read. In black letters on olive green it says, "Peaches."

"You saw," I say.

"*Khong phai!*" he says. "Not true! Anyway, I can't read American. I ate plenty of C-rations in the VC. We used to follow U.S. units around, picking up what the GIs threw away."

Việt in the forest is a kind of genius. The Vietnamese have a name for such people: *tho cong,* "earth gods." We struggle on through the jungle, fighting our way forward. Again Việt is up and down our line, freeing and helping.

He passes me and complains about our slow, noisy movement. "We'll never find Triêu Phong this way. We'll only make a lot of noise and wear ourselves out for nothing. Maybe the VC will hear us, too. We have to find a trail and follow it. This is no good!"

Tex turns, with his round face sweaty: "What's the little guy say?"

"If the point finds a trail, let him know."

Willett pushes up. "You sure ain't thinkin' of followin' *him,*" he says to Tex, exaggerating his drawl and shooting a hard look back at Việt.

"Well, now, I might," Tex says, "but I sure ain't gonna consult you."

Two Grim Reapers in front of us come back and stand at Tex's shoulders. One has an olive green scarf around his head, the other a machete at his belt. "Anything wrong?" the Reaper with the scarf asks. Both he and the machete man carry their M-16s as if they were part of them.

"The captain here seems to forget who's in charge of this patrol," Tex says.

"Could be bad if he forgot it was you," the machete man says.

Both Grim Reapers look about nineteen. Willett mutters something, goes back to his place in line, and passes Việt with a mean, sidelong look. I feel big trouble coming. We seem more at war with Nature, and ourselves, than with the enemy, who remains unseen in the great forest-sea.

We fight our way to the top of a hill, and the Reaper with the scarf at the point sends back a whispered, charged message: "Trail ahead!"

Tex and I go forward, and Viêt comes up behind. The first two Reapers part a curtain of green, and we look out on a powerful sight: a trail, winding through the jungle like a snake. We pull back several steps and crouch and whisper.

Viêt is excited: he knows this sinuous tunnel through the trees. He pulls my sleeve to get my attention and whispers, "Tell Sergeant Tex to follow this trail. It takes us where we want to go. It's an American and ARVN trail. They made it on operations here. It goes very near Triêu Phong headquarters."

I think about what Viêt has said before translating to Tex. The trail looks much older to me, the product of centuries, not just the last few years, but then I'm not an expert on jungle trails. I ask Viêt, "Are you sure?"

Viêt looks at me as if he's stunned I'd question him. "Sure I'm sure! This is my place!"

"But what about trail watches, ambushes, mines?"

"*Khong co!*" he says. "No have! The VC have nothing to do with this trail. This trail stays high; theirs are down low. You'll see."

"So it's safe to take this trail?"

"Perfectly safe! I guarantee it! One hundred percent!"

"What's he say?" Tex says.

Willett comes and whispers to Tex, "You're not thinkin' about takin' this trail, are you?"

"I'm thinkin' about consultin' with my men," Tex says.

"Jesus!" Willett says.

Tex confers and comes back. "My men don't like the idea of crashin' around in the brush for nothin' for the next four days and maybe drawin' the VC to us, but nobody wants to walk point on a trail in Indian country, and I sure as hell ain't gonna make 'em."

"Smart move," Willett says.

Viêt pulls my sleeve. "What's everyone saying?"

I translate Tex's words and Viêt's face becomes solemn. "All right, I'll walk point," Viêt says. "We'll never find Triêu Phong if we don't follow this trail."

I translate and Willett growls, "Hell no, he ain't leadin' us nowhere!"

"I make those decisions," Tex says, and he turns to the radioman. "Tell the guys: conference again."

Tex and the Reapers huddle. I wonder what Viêt thinks about all this? He stays apart and spoons C-rations from a can.

Tex returns and whispers, "We'll walk the trail with Mr. Viêt at the point, but my guys say no weapon."

"Walk the trail?" Willett says. "Behind him? This is stupid, Tex! At least whoever walks second has to kill this little bastard if we hit the shit. And we damn well probably will."

"I'll walk second," I say.

I feel I could more easily kill Willett than Viêt. We're deep in the jungle and outside the law. Our journey is within, too, and back into time. Where will it lead? What will we find?

Viêt pulls my sleeve and whispers, "Ask Sergeant Tex for a weapon. I have to have one now."

I dread this: "No, they decided you can't."

Viêt looks at me forlornly and says, "I walk point on the trail with no weapon?"

I fear we could lose Viêt here, that he could become so disillusioned with us that he could go back to the other side, maybe take his chances with them by delivering us. And we will be at his mercy, walking behind him on the trail.

Viêt puffs up his cheeks, blows out a big breath, hitches up his pack, and slips through the jungle to the trail. He parts the leaves at its edge, looks out, and begins walking quickly up it. I follow, then the Grim Reapers and Willett. We walk on the body of the serpent, our boots thudding into its back as it winds and stretches through the forest.

We follow Viêt at a fast pace through the forest all day. He stops often for us to catch up and sometimes disappears for long periods. I begin to fear he's left us for good, but there he is, standing in the shadows beside the trail, looking back. He sees me and hurries on. I first saw Viêt as a scared VC kid in Quang Tri City; now I am seeing him in the forest. He's different from us "civilized" Americans; he is the "other," a Nature-child, as we were long ago in our forest life. I think about our differences. We are camouflage-dressed, black-painted, big; Viêt is small and blends in naturally. We run, do calisthenics, pump iron; Viêt walks, all day, all night, for years. We clump in heavy boots, stumble under high-tech loads, slip, fall, make noise, even on the trail are slow; Viêt is light on his feet, sure-footed, fast. We are lost in an alien world; Viêt is in his home—and we have become totally dependent on him.

Late in the afternoon the trail climbs a high ridge and skirts a broad circle of elephant grass. Ten feet tall and tangled, the grass extends across the top of a hill. Tex calls a halt; this will be our place to hide for the night. We crawl deep into the grass. The heat and humidity are terrific. We stop where the grass is shorter and mash down sleeping places. The shadows are thickening, green going into black. Tex crouches from man to man and we whisper in the dark like criminals.

"You got radio watch from ten to twelve. Wake up the captain."

"Got it."

I lie down in the grass and wrap my poncho around me. I feel no one could find us in here. It starts to rain, and under me

I feel the ground begin to go to muck. It rains all . . . night . . . long.

The next day's climb is hard, down into deep ravines and up the other side. Our uniforms are black with sweat. It's getting harder to keep up with Viêt. Willett comes up behind me, sticks his face too close to mine, and looks at Viêt. "You sure he knows where he's goin'?"

"He knows," I say.

Willett's snort is sharp: "I *bet* he does."

Viêt disappears in front of me again, just melts away around a bend, into the leaves, and down the trail-tunnel through the trees. Long straight stretches pass. I don't see him, and I'm afraid again he's gone back to the other side.

Tex comes up from behind and says, "I wanta call a break. Where's Mr. Viêt?"

"He just went around the next bend. I'll get him."

"We'll be right here, five meters off the trail. Step off to my left at this rock."

Tex tells me the exact distance and place because he knows the jungle eats people like a python does pigs. I hurry up the trail, walking fast once I'm out of sight of Tex. What if Viêt's gone? I begin to jog, making more noise than I want to—but I can't be gone too long. Finally, I see Viêt standing in the shadows at the side of the trail. He frowns and looks about to scold me for the noise I'm making.

"We have to go back," I pant.

"Why?"

"Sergeant Tex called a rest."

"I can rest here. Let them come up."

"You're getting too far ahead. You have to slow down."

"You're too slow, too noisy."

"We better go back."

"The captain doesn't like me. He hates me. Maybe he hates all Vietnamese."

"Maybe not all."

"He hates me."

"We better go back."

Việt pushes past me and leads back down the trail, walking fast. Again I see how natural he is on the trail. He seems not to exert himself much, but moves in a kind of flow. We link up with the others. Việt sits separate and in a moment seems to have forgotten about us as he spoons pears from a C-ration can.

We walk on all day. In the mid-afternoon we climb a rocky ridge above a grass-filled valley. Việt quickly turns back and kneels with me on the trail, and Tex comes up.

"The headquarters security section is down in that valley," Việt whispers fearfully. "Fifteen to twenty NVA with AKs and B-40s. We have to go back now. It's too dangerous to go on."

I translate all but the part about going back. Behind us, Willett spoons grape jam and throws the can into the brush. Tex, Việt, and I wince at the sound, and Việt whispers, "Tell the Americans we have to be very quiet now."

Tex motions everyone off the trail, and we crawl deep into a thicket and whisper.

"We know where the headquarters is now," Việt says. "Our mission is complete. Soon our trail will drop into the valley and cross their trail, the Ho Chi Minh Trail. It's too dangerous to go on."

I translate all but the last part. I can't go back. While I talk with Tex, Việt eats from a C-ration can. He finishes and inexplicably throws the can into the brush, where it makes a small *"ping!"*

Willett whispers, "You little sonofabitch! Do that again and I'll kill you!"

"No you won't!" I whisper.

Tex moves between us and whispers, "Shut up! Everyone cool it. This is what we've decided: we'll go around the security section and look for the other parts of the headquarters."

"There it is," the Reaper with the machete says.

Việt pulls my sleeve. "Are we going back?"

"No, we're going on," I say.

Việt drops his head and looks half dead. Finally he looks up. "I have to have a weapon now."

"I agree," I say, and I translate.

Willett pushes up to Tex's side and says, "Not no, but hell, no!"

"*We* make that decision," Tex says, and he confers with his men. They whisper together and then Tex says to me, "Give him your pistol."

Willett explodes again. "What? You're gonna give the dink a weapon? At least only give him five rounds. That way he can't get us all."

"No way he can get all of us with a pistol," the radioman says, and he fingers his M-16.

"Give him the pistol," Tex says.

I unbuckle my belt and hand it to Việt. He looks at the .38 as if it were a pitiful rag.

"Does he know how to use it?" Tex says.

I translate, and Việt draws the .38, pops the cylinder out, checks the chamber, flips it closed with a flick of his wrist, spins it once around his finger, and drops it back in the holster.

"He knows," Tex says.

Việt leads us through the brush to the trail, and we begin to descend. Our American-ARVN trail has been keeping to the high country, but now it drops because the land forces it to; there is no other place for it to go. Throughout the war we and our allies generally stayed high, following the dictates of our military history and training manuals, while the VC kept low, down along the streams and in the valleys where we rarely dared go. A short distance down the trail, Việt drops to his belly, and behind him we all go down, one by one like dominos. I crawl and worm forward, cradling my M-16. Viêt and I lie looking down the trail, down the tunnel through the trees. At the bottom is an electrifying sight: another trail comes out of the forest to the right, runs over ours, and to the left quickly disappears again in the trees.

"Duong Mon Ho Chi Minh!" Viêt whispers in fear and awe. "Ho Chi Minh Trail!"

The Trail! I see it for the first time. It's fresh and alive, glowing, powerful, snakclikc, growing. In contrast, ours looks cold and old, like a discarded snake skin. You can feel the enemy presence down there, too: they have recently passed and will soon be coming, VC in small groups swinging along easily like Viêt, and NVA battalions heavily armed, looking. Montagnards, the Bru, pass here, too, many of them scouts and guides for the NVA. Much of the Trail is made of the paths used by their ancestors for centuries, pipe-smoking women with big basket-loads, brown breasts bare and swinging, sarongs stretching tight across rolling hips, tough bare feet on the living Trail.

It is like looking forward and backward in time. Soon the VC will pass by, see our trail, and talk about the last time it was used, an American or ARVN operation from hilltop to hilltop along the ridge lines. They'll look at our trail, see us, shout, drop, fire with AKs blazing.

Viêt rises without a sound, the pistol drawn and focused on the Trail. He heads for the bottom of the hill, passing like a ghost-blur through the trees. I rise and follow. At the bottom of the hill, Viêt steps over the Ho Chi Minh Trail. I walk tense and ready to blast. The Trail rushes up at me as I walk fast toward it. Behind me I'm vaguely aware of the others coming. Ahead, Viêt disappears where our trail runs up again into the trees.

I quickly glance left and right. The Trail! Before me, *under* me now. I step over it as Viêt did and hurry into the trees. I

climb, legs pumping, heart pounding, wanting to get away
from it but hating to leave it behind—wanting to lie beside it
for a while, to watch and wait.

Our trail rises fast. Viêt is up in the trees, watching us cross.
We quickly climb, pulling the forest around us, as our trail
continues to rise, heading west. Tex calls a halt on the next
hilltop, and he and Willett begin to argue about where we are
on the map. Willett insists on shooting a "willie peter" white
phosphorus artillery marking round from the base to prove
we're on *that* hill and not *this* one, as Tex thinks. Willett is
dying to shoot something.

"It's not a good idea," Tex says.

Willett disregards him and calls his unit, brigade artillery.
He whispers coordinates and informs us excitedly, "Shot
out!"

We wait. We listen. We hear the sound of a big 155-mm shell
coming. It's like the sound of a flying freight train of death. It
gets louder. Louder. Suddenly it dawns on us: it's going to land
on *our* hill!

We dive for cover, rolling, scrambling for whatever crevice,
tree trunk, rock we can find. We flatten like moles, press the
earth hard as if we were its lover. Our breath is caught, our
lives are suspended: the big steel and chemical death-machine
roars in and lands on our hill just below the crest. Shrapnel and
white-hot streaks of phosphorus fly, burning holes in life. We
rise and look at Willett.

"Pretty damn smart," Tex says. "The VC will never guess
we'd call in fire on our own position. And hey, you must be
right, Captain: I guess we *are* on that hill over there!"

Willett smolders silently and again directs his most hateful
looks at Viêt. Viêt is eating again, spooning in bites of peanut
butter from a C-ration can. He always seems to be eating. I get
a bad feeling and go over to him.

"How much food do you have left?" I ask.

Viêt feels around in his pack. "One can," he says. "No, two."

"Two?" I say. "You've got two cans? We're going to be out here at least two more days and you've got only two cans? I told you back in Quang Tri: we go for five days and eat two meals a day."

"Your Vietnamese was not clear. What you said was go for two days and eat five meals a day. Sounded good to me. Anyway, no problem: the Americans will call for resupply. *Chuon-chuon* will come; I've seen it many times. I've followed many American operations. I know what they do."

"No helicopter resupply," I say. "Not on this mission. To keep it secret."

Viêt makes a face at my use of the word *secret*. Then he gets a sad look and says, "I guess I just have to go two days eating one can a day."

I go over and get my pack. I don't have that much, either; I give him a couple of cans. Tex and the Grim Reapers come over. They give Viêt freeze-dried recon meals, good stuff, far better than C-rations. They load his pack and Viêt smiles. He has more chow now than when we started. Willett glares. More and more he's isolated and burning.

Viêt leads on the rest of the day. We sweat, steam, descend, and climb. We come to a high peak all blasted, bare, and burned on top and name it Old Baldy. Tex calls a break in craters and foxholes. Viêt eats one of his freeze-dried meals, then crawls to Old Baldy's crest, looks down to the west, and excitedly waves me over. "There!" he says.

I look down into a broad, circular valley filled with trees and large "islands" of elephant grass. Death, in us, looks down from Old Baldy.

"There! It's there!" Viêt says again. "Triêu Phong!"

Tex and Willett crawl over. We all lie looking down. We name the valley the Bowl. It's wild and beautiful.

I translate Viêt's description. "The political section is there, economic section there, hospital. . . ."

Tex works with his map as I talk and has his radioman send six-figure coordinates back to brigade. These are mostly guesswork numbers; only Viêt knows where we are, and he knows on the ground, not the map. The Machine needs numbers, though, so it gets numbers.

Willett pulls out his binoculars, glasses the Bowl, and looks excited, as if he can see the VC there. I wish *I* had binoculars. Willett seems changed, maybe by what he has seen. He hands the binoculars to Tex and then me, saying in a friendly way, "Wanta take a look?"

I slowly turn the adjustment knob and watch the canopy come into focus. All I can see are treetops, thousands of interlocked treetops in endless patterns of green. It's like looking at a Seurat forest painting through a magnifying glass, all points and daubs of vibrant green. There is no sign of Triêu Phong headquarters, the VC, *any* human life, or that there has *ever* been human life here.

"Are you sure this is it?" I ask Viêt.

"I guarantee it!" he says. "One hundred percent! We have to go back now. You know where it is. It's too dangerous to go on."

"What's he say?" Tex says.

"More about the sections," I say.

"Ask him if we can get any closer," Tex says.

My mind races. I have to ask Viêt a question I know will bring nods and a positive reply, probably something about food. But I can't do this to Tex. I tell him the truth: "He says we should go back."

Tex thinks about it. This time he's not conferring with his team. Like me, Willett wants to go on. We tell Tex he and his team will just be sent out here again if we don't confirm whether the headquarters is really there and whether it's occupied or not. And coming back to the same place could be hurtin'.

Tex looks over at his men. He decides we'll go on, but just us four. The other Grim Reapers will stay on Old Baldy. Viêt pulls my sleeve. "What are you talking about? Are we going back now?"

"No, we're going on," I say. "We have to know."

Viêt shakes his head and says, "*I* know. We'll all be killed for sure."

Night comes in shadows spreading like giant monsters from the mountains in the west. We crawl into a huge tangle of knocked-down trees, skeletons of those that once grew on Old Baldy. It's a strange, twisted world inside this mountain of blasted-down trees, a monument to man's war against Nature.

We spend a fitful night among broken branches, strange noises twice sending us reaching for rifles and claymore plungers. What is it? Wind moving the snakelike dead branches? Tigers, ghosts, spirits of the trees? I sleep at last and awake after a nightmare of doom down in the valley.

In the morning we crawl out of our hideout, Tex takes one radio, and we set out with Viêt leading, me second, and Willett last. Tex's team stays hidden in the tree-tomb with our packs, the other radio, and the claymores still out. The ARVN-American trail follows a scarred ridge line from Old Baldy to a linked, blasted, and bare peak we name Baldy II. We hide in a bomb hole on top while Viêt crawls to the crest and peers over. He quickly comes back, his face drawn and pale. "Ho Chi Minh Trail!" he gasps. "Just below us. We *have* to go back now."

I don't translate the going back. Tex, Willett, and I rise to go on, but Viêt grabs my sleeve and pulls me back. "We can't go on," he whispers. "Our trail drops into *their* valley now. We'll be killed if we go on."

"*Minh phai di,*" I whisper. "We have to go on. *Minh phai biet.* We have to know."

"*I* know," Viêt whispers, and his head drops.

Viêt pulls the .38 from its holster, looks at it in dismay, climbs out of the hole, and leads the way down the trail in a panther crouch with the pistol pointing Vietnamese belly high. Soon he passes into the trail-tunnel and is swallowed by the trees.

I follow, then Tex, then Willett. Soon we are swallowed, too. The trail is like a tunnel through time, a black-hole passageway into another world. We follow Viêt down. He rounds a bend and disappears. I don't see him on the next straight stretch. I walk on. Still no Viêt. I'm growing ever more fearful that he's gone, back to the other side.

Willett passes Tex and catches up to me. "Where's the dink?" he whispers.

"He just went around the next bend."

Willett softens again and looks with awe at the tunnel ahead. "I have to admit it," he whispers. "He's a brave little shit."

Tex comes up and we whisper, heads together, keeping one eye on the trail ahead. Willett tries to convince Tex we should hit the headquarters. "The brigade will probably never come back here, anyway. Come on, let's hit it, Tex. We can attack from the trees, shoot the place up, scoop up documents, a few weapons. When we get back I'll write you and your men up for medals and you can do the same for me. What do you say, Tex, Silver Stars for you and me and Bronze Stars for your men? Hey, we can even get Viêt a Bronze Star. We can give a dink an American medal, can't we?"

Tex looks disgusted but doesn't say anything. I wonder if he's thinking about the medals. Finally he says, "That's not our mission. Let's move out. I don't want Mr. Viêt thinkin' he's goin' down there all alone."

I start off, and at five-meter intervals Willett and Tex follow. The trail-tunnel opens to receive us. Still no Viêt; I'll have to

tell Tex soon. Viêt has just walked away from us, maybe
stepped off the trail and watched us go by, inches from us as
we walk down the trail.

Any second, I think, ambush will burst from the trees,
leaves will spit death. Or we'll blunder right into the headquarters, dense trees opening to a canopied clearing with shaggy-
thatch huts all around. Hard-faced VC with AKs will take us
prisoner or cut us down. I've got to tell Tex. We have to go
back. The mission is a failure, and Viêt is gone. The Trail, and
the men and women of the Trail, their houses and headquarters, will still be hidden from me, part of the mystery. *I have to
tell Tex,* I think as I walk. *I have to save him, myself, even
Willett.*

Suddenly, Viêt is there, standing at the side of the trail,
almost invisible among the leaves. A small, hopeful smile
lights his face, something like, I think, *We're in this together.*
A wave of relief, even love, flows out of me. Viêt turns and
disappears again, and I walk on, tense-breathing, heart hammering, hands tight and hard on my rifle.

Around the next bend on a short straight stretch the trail
points down like an arrow. Viêt appears, walking quickly back
toward me, looking as if he is being pursued. He karate chops
the air with his hand, comes to me, and points down the trail.
"VC!" he gasps. *"Gan lam!* Very near! They're chopping
wood, just down there." He pulls on my sleeve, and I go with
him quickly up the trail.

Willett and Tex see us coming and halt, their eyes big in
their black-painted faces. We crouch and I whisper-translate
Viêt's words.

"Maybe the chopping's a signal," Tex breathes. "Maybe
they've seen us!" He rises and turns to go back.

"Wait," I whisper. "I want to make sure."

Before Tex can stop me, I walk down and around the bend,
heart hammering, M-16 pointing. I can't go back yet. I have to

hear them, at least. I can't go back on just Viêt's word. I have to get close.

Down the trail I go slowly walking. Suddenly I hear chopping. Slow, rhythmical, lazy chopping. In the tangled tree world a few meters ahead the VC are chopping wood. And either they are in no hurry to fell that tree, or it *is* a signal. Hunger for the Trail turns to desire for self-preservation. I spin around and quickly go up the trail, M-16 now pointing the other way.

Around the bend, I see a strange sight: Viêt and Willett are playing charades. Standing tall on the trail, Texan Willett draws his big Bowie knife, points it down toward the headquarters, takes off his camouflage cowboy hat, grabs himself by the hair, grins horribly, and slowly draws the knife across his black-smudged throat. He's acting out "Let's go down and hit the camp."

Viêt scoffs silently, kneels, and begins to act out "This is what will happen to you." He puts an imaginary B-40 on his shoulder, making sure that Willett gets it. He pats himself on the head, fires, rocks with the recoil, and then becomes the target, sticking out his tongue, bugging out his eyes as if his face is exploding, and shooting out his arms as if his body has been blown to bits. Willett looks sheepish, totally defeated, wiser, and almost likeable again. He concedes with a grin at Viêt, and puts his big knife back in its sheath.

I recover and hurry up the trail. I whisper about the chopping, and they look wildly down, expecting VC to appear any moment. Tex tells me to ask Viêt if he thinks the chopping is a signal. I don't know the word for "signal" in Vietnamese, and I'm trying to think of a way to express it when three sharp explosions burst below and something sounding like a small rocket whooshes up through the trees. Without a word or a backward glance we rush up the trail in a cluster and jump into the bomb hole on Baldy II. Tex whispers into the radio and tells the Reapers what happened, to call the base, and to get ready to move out fast.

I ask Viêt what the whooshing sound was, finally thinking of a way to say "signal rocket." Viêt makes a face as if I am as ignorant as Willett with his suggestion to attack. "It's an AK-47," he whispers. "They sound like that going up through the trees. The VC were probably shooting birds."

Back at the base the Machine stirs and prepares to fire artillery and send troops to our aid, based on reports of our radioman:

> On 30 December 1969, at YD 166429, Recon Team I reported that they found what they thought to be the VC Political Headquarters at YD 164448. The Hoi Chanh indicated that the enemy rest area was located at YD 164438 and a weapons cache at YD 163437. Team I did not observe these areas but reported hearing wood chopping in a valley NNW of their location. The sounds appeared to be coming from vicinity YD 164432. At 301151H December 1969, Recon Team I heard 3 rifle shots from vicinity YD 162433. The Hoi Chanh said that the enemy was probably shooting at birds. B/1–11 and D/1–11 were alerted for helilift RRF. Artillery was alerted and fired on call fires. Gunships and extraction trooplift a/c were alerted. Recon Team I moved out of the area.[6]

We rise to move out of our hole then quickly jump back as the sound of a wooden rifle butt rhythmically bumping against a metal canteen comes closer and closer just below us on the Ho Chi Minh Trail. Breathless, we listen to the sound pass and fade. We rise again and hurry to the tangle of tree-skeletons. The team is ready to go. We sling our packs on and take off, slipping and sliding down Old Baldy.

Halfway down, Tex halts us and whispers, "We'll leave the trail here, head for the river, and call for extraction. Last man in cover our sign."

Tex steps off the trail and is swallowed. You can hear him in there, pushing his way forward. We follow, struggle, and crash. In four hours of fighting we advance only a few hundred meters. In mid-afternoon, we break into a bomb-blast clearing, where ragged trees ring a circle of earth torn from the side of the hill. Down through the trees, huge gray boulders litter an avalanche path to a stream shining silver through gaps in the leaves. There, a tall waterfall drops into a pool. It looks like a jungle paradise.

We climb down, Tex leading; I follow close behind. Near the bottom, I look up. The others descend, leaves in their hats, rifles, packs, black-painted faces. I get a feeling of déjà vu; I've seen this before. Where? In a dream, a movie, through other eyes in another time?

I climb down to the stream and kneel by the pool, dash water on my face, drink from the stream, and fill my canteens from the waterfall. I look around in awe. It feels as if no humans have ever been here. We start downstream, wading in the water and following the flow. Surely the stream will lead to the river, and we can call for extraction from the grassy banks. Here in this narrow valley there is no sky, just myriad levels of leaves and intertwined branches arching overhead.

The stream wanders on with no sign of the river. The valley seems utterly wild and lost in time. I think of a dream I had as a boy exploring Iowa woods, to go where no man, or no white man, had ever been, to see what was over the next hill or deeper into the deepest woods. I look around in wonder and feel that dream fulfilled.

Darkness begins to fall from the invisible sky, and fear rises within; we'll be out here another long, cold night. We wade on, our camouflage uniforms soaked from falls. Tex calls us together and we whisper as water flows through our boots.

"We'll climb the bank and hide out for the night. Last man out of the water, cover our sign."

We struggle up the steep bank, pulling ourselves from tree to tree. We breathe hard and grunt as rocks roll and sweat drips. The visible world is rapidly vanishing; soon we'll see nothing, not even ourselves. We spread our ponchos among roots and rocks and lie down side by side. We wrap up in our ponchos under branches that hang down just above our heads. The stream sings below as the last light disappears.

Tex and I whisper of dreams back in the World, our voices floating back and forth from our invisible bodies. Tex will go back to his girl and school; I'm hoping for Paris as my next Foreign Service assignment. Black raindrops begin to fall from unseen leaves, run down ghost branches, sink into the dark earth. I wrap up tighter in my poncho, anchor it under my boots, and pull it taut up under my chin. Rocks and roots probe my shoulders and vertebrae. I slide down toward the stream and squirm back up the increasingly muddy ground. The night, I know, will be long, sleepless, painful, and cold.

A strange weight begins pressing down on my feet. My mind races through possibilities, with fear starting to work. *Branches,* I think, *bent down by the weight of raindrops? Not likely.*

The weight grows heavier, presses down harder. My mind begins to tumble toward panic and a darkness lit by erratic, inner flashes. The weight moves upward, flowing slowly up my legs. On it comes, stretched now from my boots to my thighs.

Snake! A big snake is crawling up my legs! A long, thick, heavy snake!

The snake's head reaches my groin and stops, and it draws its long body slowly to it, coiling and curling up like a cat on my lap. It lies still and seems to be asleep.

Terror-thoughts flash white-hot in my mind, while my body lies frozen, paralyzed in fear. *Cobra!* I think. *A king cobra is lying on me for warmth! One twitch and it will strike, bury its fangs in my neck, sending poison directly to my brain!*

Suddenly some unthinking force breaks the terror-hold and my body explodes in frenzied action, feet kicking down, hands jerking up. The stretched-taut poncho pops like a trampoline, sending the snake flying into the air. Down it comes all over me, writhing on my face, shoulders, arms, chest. Snake! Snake all over me!

I scream, kick, convulse, and pop the poncho again and again. The snake flies up and down, writhes wildly from my face to my feet. Snake!

In the totally black world, my screams explode like bursts of jagged light. Tex and the others think the VC are cutting my throat or strangling me, and they reach blindly for guns and knives. Tex leaps in the darkness, and we wrestle like maniacs.

"Snake!" I gasp. "Snake! Snake! A big snake crawled up on me!"

"Jesus!" Tex says, as he jumps off to the side. "I hope the VC didn't hear that screamin'."

"I'll take watch the rest of the night," I whisper. "No way I can sleep."

I crawl around and gather up glowing twigs and leaves and arrange them around myself in a circle of living light. I crouch and stand bent under the limbs and leaves, knife in one hand and pistol in the other, waiting for the snake to crawl back across my circle of light. Something begins to play with my mind as I watch and wait, a strange voice like the one that asked, "What are you doing?" when the call to adventure came. This voice says, "It wasn't a real snake."

"Yes, it was!" I answer. "There was nothing more real than the feeling of that weight pressing down, and the writhing all over my face!"

The voice says it once more: "It wasn't a real snake."

I wait and watch all night.

The serpent keeps recurring through the earliest cycles of mythology, always as a central symbol for the life of the universe and the continuity of creation.[7]

Finally my light circle fades and the forest begins to turn gray-black. I wake the others and we continue downstream. For a long time there is still no sign of the river and deliverance. We are still lost in the labyrinth, and the stream is our only thread of hope. We go on, following the flow.

The stream begins to change subtly, then by greater degrees. The narrow valley it has made widens, the trees along its banks thin a little, and there are occasional glimpses of sky. Mud flats appear, and on one there is the track of a big tiger, still oozing from its recent passage before us. We are not alone here.

A broad, muddy pool lies ahead, and across it, the beginning of the grass sea that stretches to the river. We raise our rifles high and wade, sinking waist deep with each step. Warm, dark swamp mud pulls at us, fills our boots with rich jungle soup, worlds exploding in the water, the mud, and us.

When I would recreate myself, I seek the darkest wood, the thickest and most interminable and, to the citizen, most dismal swamp. I enter a swamp as a sacred place, a sanctum sanctorum. There is the strength, the marrow of Nature.[8]

We push into thick, tall buffalo grass, the last man in trying to cover our sign where we leave the stream. We crash and fight forward, worn down by heat and hunger and bleeding from cuts of the razor-sharp grass.

We burst into a small, flattened-down circle where an elephant or water buffalo has been rolling, and Tex whispers, "Take a break."

The Grim Reaper with the scarf steps to the edge of the circle, unbuttons his fly to urinate, and lets out a gasp: "I've got a *leech* on my dong!"

Heedless of VC, hunger, and fatigue, we all rush madly to the edge of the trampled clearing, turn our backs, drop our pants, and frantically search. Our legs are covered with squirming black leeches, writhing as if having orgasms as they suck our blood. We wildly pull them off and fling them away. We're supposed to apply heat or lighter fluid to get them to back out with their infection-causing, chewing heads, but the sight of them is horror-producing; we want those suckers off *now*.

We sit sweating in the grass, slowly pulling on our wet pants, soggy stinking socks, and muddy, lead-heavy boots. We drink our last stream water from tilted canteens and gird ourselves for more fighting through the grass. We have to find a flat, open area for an LZ, and we have to find it soon. We rotate the point and all are soon exhausted, even Viêt showing signs of wearing down. We try to crawl through the grass, but it's impossible; it's far too thick and tangled. We try to ram it down and climb over before it rises, but it grabs us, trips us, knocks us down. We could die here in the grass.

We force our way to the top of a hill above the river. It's flat enough here for an LZ, but we'll have to clear the tall grass. We're too fatigued to machete it down, so we'll blast a clearing with claymores.

While the team sets up the claymores and the radioman calls the base for a chopper, Viêt leads Tex and me to the crest of the hill, points across the river, and says, "Look, my village."

Across the river, wide ruins rise among the grass. Viêt asks me to tell Tex his story, how the VC came and took him one night, how the Saigon government moved all the people out, and how the Americans bombed the houses to ruins. Viêt tells the story of his parents, and I translate—how his father died of sickness in the refugee camp in Quang Tri City and his mother of "sadness" soon after, all while Viêt was away in the forest and unable to return.

"We better get back," Tex says. "They're ready to blow the claymores."

The claymores have to be timed just right. When the mines explode, we'll be exposed in a circle of ragged noise. If the VC don't know we're here now, they will when the claymores blow. We hear the rescue chopper coming. Tex waits, then sends an electric charge through the claymore wires. A hell of flying steel balls and ear-splitting sound rips through the grass, leaving a tattered clearing. The machete man pops a green smoke grenade, and we jump and run as the chopper beats in, wind-whipping the billowing smoke and fragments of grass.

The world roars as we throw ourselves onto the chopper, and we blast away in a burst of joy as the river, the forest, and Viêt's broken village fall away below. We fly high over the mountains, piedmont, and paddies and begin to descend toward the barbed-wire and bare-dirt sprawl of the base with its plumes of diesel smoke and red dust rising. Viêt has taken us into the wilderness and brought us home to civilization again. Now to see what the Machine will do with the intelligence we bring.

> The passage of the mythological hero may be overground, incidentally; fundamentally it is inward—into depths where obscure resistances are overcome, and long lost, forgotten powers are revivified, to be made available for the transfiguration of the world.[9]

Out there, where the snake moves in deep-forest night, the Trail flows on.

CHAPTER 2

MACHINE IN THE FOREST

It is difficult to think of a major American writer upon
whom the image of the machine's sudden appearance in
the landscape has not exercised its fascination.

—Leo Marx, *The Machine in the Garden*

Time, the bandit, passes, and the Machine doesn't move.
Briefings, paperwork, planning, clearances, weather: everything has to be just right. We *had* become the "tools of our
tools"; things *were* "riding mankind."[1] The Machine had
come "between us and life . . . enacting our ignorance of
value—of essential sources, dependencies, and relationships."
It was "unmanning the user," and the user was us.[2]

In 1850s New England, Thoreau already believed he lived
in an "emasculated" country, so much of its wildness had
been lost. In 1970 Viet Nam, and in America, we were still
causing loss—and in the process still losing ourselves.

I knew what it was like to roam the woods looking for
something I loved to kill, to feel its fur or soft feathers in my
hand, see the beauty in its drooping head, feel its body warm
against mine, smell it sizzling on Grandma Stevens's old wood
stove, eat it and feel it become part of me. Wild creature of the
woods—that, I knew, was the real me. It was not just the Trail,
combat, them, that drew me with such force out there; it was
not even "only" operations of the Dark Side. It was the forest,
the mystery and power, the *wildness*. Life without it seemed
nothing—as a boy wandering Iowa fields and woods and as a
man wanting the Trail. It was my "other" that was more me
than my current self.[3] Twentieth-century prairie boy though I

was, still the forest was source of life, self, ancestors, gods. Celts and wild Germanic forest peoples still lived in me, and unknown forest dwellers long before that. The forest was pulling me home; I *had* to go out there again.

Sometimes thoughts about what I was doing passed like shadows across my mind. I knew I could die out there; still there was the urge to go on. More, I had to have more. "Contact! Contact!" Thoreau wrote of his experience with wilderness on Mount Ktaadn in Maine. "*Who* are we? *Where* are we?"[4] We were once forest people who lived in Eden; now we were the Machine, turning the Garden into Old Baldy.

I drive in my Scout out to Quang Tri Combat Base with its raw-wound, red-dirt slash and sprawl. The country people whose thatched houses and green paddies had once been here are now refugees in the tin-roofed camp by the Thach Han River where Highway One runs and my Scout makes dust clouds roll. Beyond the river the deep-purple mountains of the Trail rise like towering waves in the great forest-sea. There the Snake embraces the Tree of Life, leaves his old skin beneath it, and flows away renewed. The Tree of Knowledge is there, too, but I hadn't yet fully encountered it.[5]

I push and prod the Machine to start the operation against Triêu Phong headquarters, but still it doesn't move. The Machine is huge, steel, muscle-bound. Why can't we just go? We "are grown mechanical in head and in heart, as well as in hand."[6]

I drive back to Quang Tri City, pass the central market, and see Viêt talking with an old woman. He looks uncomfortable to be seen, doesn't wave and run to get a ride as usual. He's taking a chance with Rang to be away from the Chiêu Hôi center, and who is the woman?

Doubt strikes hard. The woman must be Viêt's contact with the VC. She's a woodcutter who gathers firewood out at the edge of the piedmont where the forest begins and the Trail

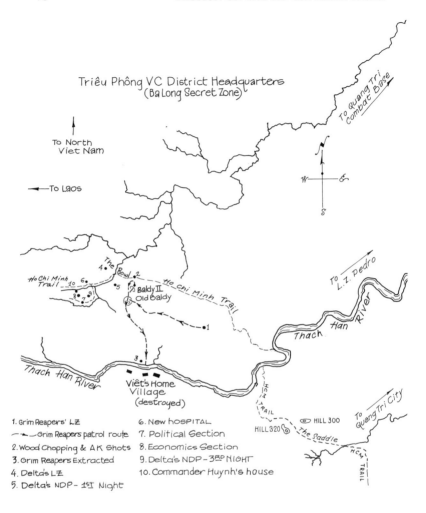

Triêu Phông VC District Headquarters
(Ba Long Secret Zone)

To North
Viet Nam

To Laos

1. Grim Reapers' LZ
—◄— Grim Reapers patrol route
2. Wood Chopping & A K Shots
3. Grim Reapers Extracted
4. Delta's LZ
5. Delta's NDP – 1ST Night

6. New hOSPITAL
7. Political Section
8. Economics Section
9. Delta's NDP – 3RD NIGHT
10. Commander Huynh's house

comes down from the mountains. She'll pass Viêt's messages there, and they'll be waiting for us. The Machine's operation to attack the headquarters will be a disaster, a trap to suck more units in; it will be the worst defeat of the war. Rang now believes Viêt's capture was arranged, the two guerrillas sacrificed to get Viêt into our world. I have to push the Machine to go *now*.

On a gray day in early January 1970 I drive again the dusty road to the base past the riverside refugee camp, where raggedy kids run out to beg and shout, "Sah-lem! Sah-lem! You gimme Sah-lem!"

GIs sometimes throw down C-rations or Salem cigarettes from rumbling trucks and tanks while the ARVN bridge guards eat dust and old men and women wipe their eyes and stare from their shacks. I see a dove sitting here on a roll of dusty barbed wire, the only bird I remember clearly from three years in Viet Nam.

My contact at brigade is the S-2 intelligence officer, "Bad José," nicknamed by his troops after the Jay and the Americans hit song. Viet Nam is a chopper-beat and rock 'n' roll war, mixed with elements from the American frontier, and it is heavy-load, high-power, high-tech.

Bad José is a major, big, barrel-chested, and black. We stand in his small office before large wall maps marked with known friendly and presumed locations of NVA and VC units. "We're moving ahead with plans," Bad José says. "Now if the weather just holds."

I don't tell him about Viêt and the old woman.

"A briefing on the operation is set for tomorrow. I invite you to come. Cobra Six—General Burke—will be there. Look, here's where I've plotted the headquarters."

I'm surprised to see it so definitely grease-penciled on his laminated plastic map. "We weren't that sure of our location out there."

Now Bad José looks surprised. "You all called in these coordinates. You weren't lost out there, were you?"

"Not really lost," I say. "Viêt always knew where we were on the ground, but not on the map. We thought we knew where we were on the map, but not on the ground, and we weren't always right."

Bad José says he'll check the numbers with Tex and Willett.

"Numbers!" I think. The Machine *feeds* on numbers. Numbers tell it where to go and drop its load, when to start and where to stop. We have become "numbers numb," transformed, desensitized by technology, our contact with Nature minimal—or destructive.[7]

I drive the dusty road back to the base for the pre-op briefing. The brigade's briefing room is large, sand-bagged, wood-paneled, and hung with VC weapons. Empty folding chairs stand in orderly rows, and staff officers talk and laugh. I sit in the back feeling smug. An ex-Marine corporal, I feel I'm running, in a way, this army brigade.

The time for the briefing approaches, and tension replaces officer horseplay and talk of drinks tonight at the O club. General Burke has a reputation for meanness, and woe to the briefer who's unprepared or can't answer the general's questions.

At 10:00 A.M. sharp, Cobra Six himself enters, trailed by a tall colonel, his S-3, and everyone snaps to attention. Burke is short, wiry, Napoleon-looking before the latter got fat, and with close-cropped, salt-and-pepper hair. He says, "At ease," and we sit.

Burke sees me and frowns. I can see him thinking, *What's a civilian doing in this briefing? Probably a nosy press man.* He sends the colonel to find out.

"Quang Tri Chiêu Hôi advisor," I say as the colonel approaches, and Bad José adds from across the room, "He was on the recon, sir. He's our contact with the rallier, Mr. Viêt."

Burke shoots me a frosty smile. I can see he doesn't like me much. I never liked officers much, either, when I was in the Marines, or any other kind of authority. I wonder if Burke and I are someday going to clash. He orders the briefing to begin.

The S-1 administrative officer, a major, rises nervously, mounts the stage, and begins to read lists of numbers: numbers of men available for duty, sick, wounded, KIA, coming, going, in the pipeline. Suddenly I remember the livestock reports Grampa Stevens used to listen to from Chicago and Omaha, numbers of cattle, sheep, hogs, and their prices.

Bad José rises and takes the pointer from the S-1. He raps the wall map here and there, hitting colored-pin VC and NVA suspected locations. Burke asks a few questions about electronic sniffer and sensor reports and nods grimly, satisfied.

The tall S-3 operations colonel rises, takes the pointer, and begins to present the plan to attack Triêu Phong headquarters. Now I sit stunned, smug no more. Four hours of artillery, air strikes, and offshore naval gunfire will pound the headquarters to mush before a battalion-sized air assault begins. One kiloton—one thousand tons—of high explosives will blast the grid square of forest below Old Baldy before a thousand men chopper in to see what's left.

Inside I feel a terrible emptiness. What happened to the plan I presented to Bad José for a small-unit raid with Tex and a reinforced team of Grim Reapers? What happened to Viêt's wish to give the VC a chance to "rally" like him? What will Viêt think now when he finds out we're going to obliterate his forest world and the comrades he served with there? More important, what will he *do*?

My mind goes off on another track as the briefing continues with S-4, logistics. Maybe this is actually what Viêt wants, a big operation to suck more troops in. He knows well how the Americans work: he knew this is how we'd do it. Anyway, maybe we never got close to the headquarters, all that ordnance will fall in the wrong place, and the battalion of infantry will land in a trap.

The S-4 passes the pointer to S-5, civil affairs. I still sit heavy in my chair, not listening to how many schools and wells the brigade has built for refugees in the reporting period. "A kiloton of explosives," I think. "Or did he say megaton? Isn't that how atomic blasts are measured?" I see again the Bowl below Old Baldy, the magic Seurat forest, the thousand shades of shimmering green. I think of the people in the headquarters, too: young Dr. Son in the forest hospital, the nurses and medics, the English-speaker, the young women of the drama team. And I know I am responsible. Like Daniel Boone, in my love for Nature I'm going to destroy it.

The weather holds: the mission is on. Viêt and I pack, and Viêt excitedly shows me the battery-powered megaphone he's borrowed from the Chiêu Hôi center, "To call the VC to rally, like me." I don't tell him the details of the operation.

On January 4, 1970, Viêt and I drive to the base and Pioneer Pad. We climb on a Huey slick loaded with soda and beer, sit on the cases, and look out the open doors. With a clattering of steel mesh and in a cloud of red dust, we lift off for LZ Pedro, a battered hill-base in the piedmont, current home of Delta Company, 1st Battalion, 11th Infantry, "hammer" of tomorrow's "hammer-and-anvil" operation.

Viêt is airsick, head hanging, eyes rolling. I feel excitement surging. We're like horsemen of war riding across the sky, sitting on Coke and Bud. Below, scarred, ragged-grass Pedro rises, and the dark mountains of the Trail loom not far beyond. We roar in and beat dust while shirtless men of Delta Company quickly unload the soda and beer.

Viêt and I climb the hill past foxholes and M-60 machine-gun positions to report to Captain Blunt, Delta Company's commanding officer, on top. Bad José has warned me about Blunt: "His name fits."

Blunt stands alone at the top of the hill, staring at the mountains to the west. He's broad-backed and burly, with a completely shaved head, a half-shot-away ear, and another nasty bullet scar across his cheek. His helmet lies upturned on the ground, as if he doesn't need it.

Blunt looks hard at us and gets right to the point: "Brigade sent you out here so I got to take you—but no high-paid civilian and no ex-VC, if he is *ex,* are going to lead my Company anywhere. Now you two go down there and set up with the trackers and dog people, more damn baggage brigade saddled me with. If I want anything from you I'll let you know, but don't hold your breath."

Blunt turns abruptly away from us to stare again at the dark mountains, and Viêt and I go down the hill to set up for the night with the dog people and trackers. The trackers are two lean ex-hillbillies, further trained at the British jungle warfare school in Malaysia. The tracker dog is a black Labrador lying quietly inside a rain shelter. The other dog is King, a huge and formidable German shepherd scout dog that looks like the Blunt of canines.

Viêt wants to pet King, but I warn him back. Buzz, a peach-cheeked kid from Michigan, King's handler, comes over. "Nah, it's OK," he says. "He's real friendly if he likes you."

I look at the huge jaws of King doubtfully, but Viêt extends his hand to the dog's nose and soon the two are romping across the hill together. Buzz looks happy, even proud, as he watches them play, but then he becomes dejected. He begins to pour out his and King's story.

"I wanta take King back to the World with me. Look at him: does he look dangerous to you? He wouldn't hurt a flea if I didn't tell him. The army says scout dogs don't adjust to civilian life. Heck, if a human can adjust, so can a dog. Easier! King's no killer. The army—" Buzz almost can't say it. "—destroys scout dogs. They train 'em that way, then. . . ."

I look sideways at Buzz. He's got tears in his eyes. Viêt and King continue romping across the bottom of the hill.

"I wrote my congressman," Buzz says in a new burst of hope. "I bet he can do somethin', don't you?"

"Sure he can," I say. "No problem."

"I knew it," Buzz says. "They *gotta* let me take him home."

Buzz runs off down the hill to join King and Viêt. They all look alike somehow.

The dog platoon lieutenant introduces himself and looks down at King and Buzz. "It's gonna be bad," he says. "They're not going to let him take King back. No way. I don't know if Buzz can handle it. I'm afraid what he might do."

Viêt, King, and Buzz continue to run and play across Pedro, wind blows through the grass, the sun goes down behind the mountains of the Trail, and Delta celebrates the last night before the operation with sodas and beer. The trackers and dog people invite Viêt and me to sleep inside their rain shelter. Before I crawl inside, I see Blunt still standing alone at the top of the hill. King comes in and lies down between Buzz and Viêt, now and then raising his big head to listen and sniff the air. His eyes look like a lion's, deep, wise, all-knowing. He seems to see beyond us, and he is not afraid.

In the gray dawn I crawl out of the shelter and go stiffly down the hill, as Grampa Stevens would say, to "draw my water." All over Pedro the men of Delta emerge from holes to yawn, stretch, cuss, and spit.

I'm shaking it out when suddenly atop the hill Blunt begins to shout, "Rockets! Rockets!"

A mad scramble explodes all over Pedro. Delta GIs hop one-legged and run pulling up their pants, racing for holes. I leap into a nearby slit trench and land hard on empty cans. Other bodies fly through the air and tumble in on top of me, crushing me down. From above, a young voice screams, "Get down! Get down lower! I'm stickin' out of the hole!"

No one moves to flatten down on the cans any more, and the yelling goes on: "Get down! I'm *still* stickin' out!"

Blunt roars from the top of the hill, "Out! Out! Outa those holes!"

We unpile, grumbling, "What is this, a drill?"

I climb out feeling like a crumpled can. Bad José didn't tell me Blunt had a weird sense of humor. I see Blunt pointing wildly across the river several kilometers to the south.

"Three! Four!" Blunt shouts, as across the river rockets streak up and explode in sheet-lightning flashes far off in the direction of Quang Tri City.

"Five! Six! Seven!" Blunt shouts, then growls into the radio, telling brigade artillery where to put counterfire.

I run up the hill. Viêt is already at the top. We approach as close as we dare to Blunt. Other GIs take up the count: "Eight! Nine! Ten!"

Blunt rages into the radio about the slowness of artillery's response. The NVA are pounding Quang Tri City, making a mockery of the brigade's rocket suppression activities as Têt draws near with its haunting memories of the great offensive of '68.

Finally a salvo of 155-mm shells roars over and lands far beyond the river. Delta GIs hoot, and Blunt curses into the radio, saying, "Put it where I told you, damn it!"

I wonder if Willett's on duty. "Eleven! Twelve! Thirteen!"

Viêt pulls my sleeve and says, "Tell the captain he doesn't need to shoot anymore. There won't be any more rockets. Anyway, the NVA rocket men aren't there. They're probably on that hill over there, watching."

Blunt understands some Vietnamese, turns, and says, "How do you know that, little man?"

I translate Viêt's explanation. "The NVA set up their rockets at night and go. They leave only one man. He sets them off, while the rest watch from far away."

Blunt tugs at his half-shot-away ear and says, "Pretty damn

smart. I wonder how they choose the one guy? I could suggest
some of my numb-nuts lieutenants."

No more rockets streak up.

Blunt looks sharply at Viêt and says to me, "So he led you to
this headquarters?"

"He did," I say. "He also says that the trail at the base of this
hill—the woodcutter's path—goes right there. We could get
on it now and be there for lunch."

"I bet we could," Blunt says, still looking at Viêt. "That's
the way I'd do it, too, if I had a Ranger unit here. He doesn't
speak English?"

Viêt looks uncomfortable under Blunt's hard gaze.

"He speaks a little Russian," I say. "He studied in the VC."

"I bet he did," Blunt says. "What makes you so sure he's *ex*-
VC?"

Stomach-pit emptiness hits, but I hide it. "He was the only
one on the recon who knew where we were," I say. "He could
have done anything he wanted with us, but he took us there and
brought us back."

Blunt pulls on what's left of his ear and doesn't say anything. Finally some inner debate ends, and his words come out
in a rush: "I'll tell you something, Mr. Civilian. This Viêt may
be the greatest little guy in the world, but I'll never trust him
and I'll never let him or you influence the running of this
company in any way. You got that?"

"I got it," I say.

Viêt pulls my sleeve. "What does the captain say?"

I don't tell him.

Blunt goes on, getting more heated: "Now I don't give a
damn how much money you make, or who you're with, the
CIA or whatever. I don't even care if you're the secretary of
defense. I know the little man's right: we could go to this place
on the ground, and I would if I was running this show and had
Rangers with me. But these men *aren't* Rangers, and most

don't want to be here or even believe we ought to be here, and I aim to get them back to their families alive. Now you two get back down there with the dog people. If I want you, I'll let you know."

On our way to the shelter Viêt says, "The captain doesn't like me, I know. He doesn't trust me."

Viêt looks determined—what he might do scares me. Soon he's romping with King and Buzz as if he hasn't a care in the world. But what will he say when he sees what's coming?

Distant rumbling rolls across the hills, and what looks like a wagon train on the Oregon Trail appears, snaking its way toward us. Out of the past it comes, then materializes as a convoy of jeeps, ammunition trucks, towed 105-mm howitzers, and big self-propelled 155-mm guns. My spirits sink. Now Viêt will see what we're going to do to the forest and the people there. The convoy splits into several columns and begins to deploy around Pedro.

Viêt comes running up the hill with King. "Look!" he says. "Big guns! I bet they're going to fire on Triêu Phong! Let's go watch!"

"No, thanks."

Viêt shrugs as if I'm going to miss something big and runs off down the hill with King. They race beside the trucks and cannons, King leaping and barking, Viêt giving the *V* peace sign to the drivers and gunners. The brigade artillery men wave and laugh. In their helmets they look like twentieth-century knights about to joust and knock the forest down.

We have constructed a fate, an *Atropos*, that never turns aside.[8]

To Thoreau the railroad was *Atropos*, one of the Greek Fates, the goddesses who determined the course of human destiny. Belladonna, deadly nightshade, a European poisonous plant, was named *Atropa belladonna* after Atropos.

The artillery sets up and begins firing, hurling its huge chemical and steel loads into the wilderness, and the Earth groans and shakes. I watch Viêt closely for reaction. All I can see is a boy and dog playing. The artillery, naval gunfire, and air strikes pound the forest for four hours.

> Beat! Beat! drums! . . . burst like a ruthless force.[9]

The Machine has taken us into itself. We are now the *Atropos*, deadly nightshade for the world. At high noon the pounding stops, and big Chinook helicopters roar in and land on Pedro. We run up metal ramps, and the Chinooks swallow us, ramps closing, engines revving to liftoff RPM. We fly toward Triêu Phong, piedmont and doomed forest falling away below.

Visions of a thousand tons of bombs form and fall in my mind, explode all at once, tear the green world apart, blow the trees down, churn the bare soil, turn to bits of protoplasm the people of the headquarters. Suddenly I see what I thought Viêt should feel: the guilt was mine, not his. And I found myself hoping the kiloton *did* fall in the wrong place, not yet knowing there was no right place.

We roar in to the LZ, land, and charge off the choppers. In the words of the official report:

> D/1–11 conducted a . . . combat assault which began at 1210 hours and was completed at 1310 hours into a VCI Base Camp southwest of Quang Trì Combat Base (Center of Mass YD 1644). Following the C/A, C/1–11 and D/1–11 conducted an attack toward B/1–11 in a "Hammer and Anvil" operation.[10]

The combat "assault" is this: we charge off the choppers, stumble and fall, hide behind recently thrown up dirt mounds, and dive into shrapnel-shredded patches of elephant grass in mind-numbing helicopter roar.

On bare, bomb-blasted ground, Viêt and I look at each other. Where is the headquarters, the Bowl, Old Baldy? "I've never seen this place before," Viêt says. Atop a shell-crater rim, Blunt is raging. We *have* been dropped into the wrong place—or maybe it is the right *map*-place, but it is the wrong place on the ground. The Machine did what it was told to do: everything went by the numbers—but the numbers, it seems, were wrong.

In the middle of this wrong place Delta Company is trying to find itself, GIs in ragged grass whispering what sound like Abbott and Costello "Who's on First?" routines.

"Psst, hey, you there?"

"Yeah."

"Where?"

"Here."

"Where's here?"

"Here in the grass, dummy."

Blunt roars from his mound of freshly torn earth, "What's all this damn *whisperin'* goin' on around here? Dammit, we're in the wrong place, people! Besides, if Charlie ain't got the message we're here after knockin' on his door with bombs and choppers, he ain't *smart* enough to be dangerous! Now, form up and move out!"

We start off through the torn landscape on a numbered azimuth from the assault plan made at brigade. Soon 1st Platoon sends word it has found a stream and foxholes. Viêt and I hurry down to see.

"*Cûu lâm,*" Viêt says of the holes. "Very old. But tell the captain to follow this stream. It will lead us to some place I know for sure. I guarantee it—one hundred percent."

I translate and Blunt says, "No. You don't take a company down in country like this, you take it up. Anyway, brigade has told us which way to go, and it ain't down this stream."

We flounder on through a torn landscape.

On a break I ask Blunt, "Try to get Viêt and me up in the air. We can find Old Baldy and see how to get to the headquarters from there."

Blunt agrees, and brigade sends a Loach, a light observation helicopter, basically a small plastic bubble with a big rotor on top. Blunt, Viêt, and I run for the chopper. Blunt gets in front beside the black pilot, and Viêt and I jam in the back. The Loach shoots up before we can strap in, and soon we're lost in mist and fog, trying to buckle up and not fall out the open, wind-roaring sides.

It's a mad flight of the bumblebee in the Loach, a wild yo-yo ride over ridges and valleys with gray sky pressing down. Everything is a confusion of chopper noise, bulbous flight helmets falling over our eyes, roaring wind, and loose, flapping straps. The Loach, built to draw fire and get away fast, is a buzzing little demon of maneuverability, speed, and chaos.

Viêt's head is rolling. He's airsick again.

Twisting back, the pilot shouts in his mike, "He better not puke in my chopper!"

Viêt points down, down, down.

Blunt looks back and sees Viêt pointing. "He sees somethin'!"

"No, he wants to go down," I say.

"You're cuttin' me off!" the pilot shouts. "If you hear talkin', stay off the net! You want me to fly into our own goddamn artillery fire?"

Viêt opens his mouth and tries to say, "Down," but his stomach erupts and a cascade of multicolored C-ration vomit pours onto the chopper floor.

"Did he puke?" the pilot shouts into the mike. "If he did, he's gonna clean it up when we get back!"

"Take it to Cindy and head northwest," I say. "And try to get low enough so I can see the ground."

LZ Cindy is an old American hilltop base along the Thach

Han River. The Ho Chi Minh Trail passes around it, according to Viêt, hidden under the trees and in a stream there. I believe I can find Old Baldy from Cindy, following Viêt's hand-drawn maps, the observation flights we had made, and the route we had taken with Tex.

From the river and Cindy we skim misty green hills, shoot over ridges, encounter craggy cliffs face-to-face, rocket straight up, do stomach drops over deep valleys, clear trees and peaks by the skin of our skids. Still we can't find Old Baldy. The ceiling's too low, we're flying too fast, everything looks different.

"What a screw-up," Blunt growls.

The ceiling drops, the fog thickens, and we have to go back. Nature is hiding, protecting Triêu Phong from the Machine's madly buzzing eye.

We land and dash away from the chopper before the pilot remembers Viêt's mess. Blunt radio-talks to battalion, and we move out on a high-ground azimuth, numbers still telling us where to go.

With the platoons rotating the point, we machete-hack through blast- and shrapnel-tangled elephant grass and stumble in bombed, upchucked earth. Weighed down by steel-pot helmets, M-60s, M-79s, M-16s, boots, and big loads, we enter a landscape Titan-torn beyond recognition. This is the wrecked grid square, ground zero of the kiloton. Craters are everywhere, craters in craters, and mounds of dead earth rising from deep pits. We climb and sink deep in skeleton-soil, try to circle the death-holes, fall to our knees, rise, and stumble on.

The trees are totally gone, as if they never existed, and with them has disappeared all animal life. Not a trace of a bird, not a feather; not a piece of skin of tiger or snake; not a frog, worm, or ant. Even the soil looks dead, its billions on billions of microorganisms dead. It is a terrible thought: the earth itself is dead. It is silent here at death-ground zero, except for our labored breathing, boot-suck, radio hiss, and clink of metal and plastic.

We struggle on all afternoon through a land completely ruined. Some hills are knocked down and others thrown up; streams are gone, dammed, and dead. In the bottom of a thirty-foot pit is a lost, muddy pool, once part of a clear, sparkling stream. In it, three fish float belly-up. Viêt clambers down and gets them, while Delta GIs ring the pit and watch. Viêt brings the fish to me, and I hold them in my hands. They look similar to fish I knew back home, sunfish, bluegills, and bass I caught in Grampa's pond, jerking them over my head with a bamboo pole while Grampa smiled and puffed his pipe. Viêt puts the fish in his pack to cook for tonight's dinner.

We stumble on across bomb-plowed ground. The Machine has done its work well. Numbers told it where to hit, and it hit and destroyed. In the late afternoon, out at the edge of the killing radius, we leave the devastation behind and enter a high, rocky area thickly covered with trees. A green cosmos of vegetation is tangled everywhere, underfoot, at waist level, before our faces, overhead. Walking heavy-laden here is like trying to swim with weights through a giant-kelp sea.

We fight forward, machetes slicing a path. Confronted by higher ground, we pause, sweating and steaming, while Blunt calls in recon by fire, artillery to hit ahead in the trees. We sit wrapped in green living patterns of water and earth and listen to shells whoosh over like flying freight trains, the sudden, slight silence, then the big bang of doors slamming on life. Dirty white smoke-flowers bloom over the trees, and we rise and struggle on, heading for our NDP, our night defensive position.

By late afternoon in Viet Nam, every large U.S. unit in the field was in or nearing its NDP. The essential rule was to get to the highest ground possible and prepare for and beware of night. Night was enemy time. We tried, with night-seeing devices and flares, to keep back the night and hold on to the day. A scary feeling crept out at night when NVA and VC time came and the giant shadows of mountains and trees stretched across the land. We Americans were alien to both Nature and night; we were part of the Machine.

Blunt pushes us to the top of a forested hill, and we dig in with much chopping, smoking, and radio chatter. Viêt is lively, making friends with Delta GIs. He borrows a machete and whips up a tight shelter of big elephant's-ear leaves lashed with vines. From another GI he gets a claymore and quickly takes it apart. I watch him with awe and a little fear as he breaks off a piece of the claymore's powerful C-4 plastic explosive, lights it, and makes a white-hot fire over which he cooks the three fish, dries his sandals, and heats a stew of mixed C-rations.

"Tell the captain," Viêt says between plastic-spooning in big steaming bites. "Don't let the men leave anything behind. We used to follow American units picking up all the things they threw away. The VC can make booby-traps out of anything, even empty C-ration cans." He raps a can ominously with his spoon and gives me a knowing look.

Night comes. I lie poncho-wrapped on the ground like the rest of Delta. It begins to rain, and there is no stopping the wet and cold. They fall from the sky in steady *crachin* and rise from the earth in bone-chilling waves. They run in rivulets down the necks of GIs on guard duty and drum on the mummylike shrouds of we who try to sleep on the ground. They come down with each invisible raindrop and in with each breath, filling and chilling from inside out and outside in, settling in our lungs and bones, and turning our skin to mush.

There is no escaping the wet and cold, not even for those of us wrapped in the latest scientifically designed, high-tech rain gear. Inside his leaf shelter, Viêt sleeps, King in there with him. Outside, I lie uncontrollably shaking on the wet ground. I toss and turn, roll on rocks, churn the ground to cold muck. The night seems eternal. I shake and shiver all night long. The thousandth time I unwrap my cold plastic poncho and peek out, hoping to glimpse the light, I see a hint of morning in gray-black drizzle. I stand stiffly, thankfully, look dully around, and smoke even though I don't, trying to warm my hands and lungs. I hold the glowing end of a C-ration Marlboro close to my fingers. My hands look dead, my fingers moisture-wrinkled, puffy, and soft, with big cracks in the skin you can look into but from which no blood comes out. Rain drips from my wrist and puts the cigarette out.

With Delta GIs I stand around and stomp mud-clogged boots, talk, and zombie-stare into the trees. Viêt finally pokes his head out of his shelter, sees nothing is happening, and withdraws inside to cook for himself and King.

We stand around some more while our feet rot inside soggy socks. We can't move until the ceiling lifts enough to let choppers fly. Grounded choppers mean no resupply or medevacs and poor control and communication. The Machine only works well in good weather, and in the forest not always then.

We stand around in tobacco smoke and radio static, listening to the crackling-hiss voices of brigade, battalion, artillery, air. Do the VC radio-talk this much? We stand around and wait for the weather. Viêt stays in his shelter, cooking with C-4 and playing with King.

In the forest with Tex and the Grim Reapers the rain had always stopped at dawn. Now that the Machine is here, Nature seems determined to fight us all day. I wonder as I stand and stomp if it has something to do with the terrible punishment we visited on the forest yesterday. Maybe so many trees have been destroyed it will go on raining forever.

Finally, the sky begins to open. After more radio communications, the 1/11 battalion commander, Lieutenant Colonel

Herndon, choppers in to pick up Blunt, Viêt, and me. We'll try again to find Old Baldy and the Bowl—in a more stable Huey and with a higher ceiling this time.

Herndon welcomes us aboard. He's tall and balding, a kindly family man. He's taken a liking to Viêt and treats him like a son. He's found a pair of small-sized combat boots for Viêt and hands them over. Viêt changes from his sandals while Herndon, Blunt, and I shout back and forth with the pilot.

We fly south through the high, gray sky to LZ Cindy, then slowly and steadily over the stream-Trail system with Viêt not airsick for once and guiding. We arrive above Old Baldy's top, over the tangled tree-tomb and the path to Baldy II. We look down on the Bowl, the beautiful, broad valley where we heard the wood chopping and the AK whoosh up through the trees. The wilderness there, the grid square targeted for destruction, looks untouched, so far, by the Machine.

"*Day!*" Viêt shouts. "There!" And he draws a ring with his finger around the Bowl. "Triêu Phong headquarters!"

Herndon and Blunt excitedly draw grease-pencil circles on the laminated maps on their laps, and we fly back to Delta. On the ground and away from the chopper, Herndon checks more details with Viêt. I translate, and Herndon radios orders for Bravo and Charlie Companies to move. A sudden chill goes through me as I realize Viêt is now directing the battalion. No one but me out here knows that Viêt is not a real rallier, and Rang has predicted this: Viêt's influence with us will grow till he is part of our innermost circles.

Herndon flies off to check Bravo and Charlie's movement toward the targets Viêt has given him, but Blunt doesn't like the way things are developing. He follows Herndon's orders on the general direction of movement but rejects Viêt's advice on going down in the valleys and following the streams. The official report says this:

060615Z January 1970. D/1–11 conducted a Recon in Force operation moving from their NDP (YD 161430) to their south. Enemy contacts: None. Significant events: None.[11]

Our "recon in force" is really a noisy struggle from hilltop to hilltop along rocky and forested ridge lines, with Viêt grumbling, "We'll never find the headquarters this way." On a rest stop, sweating and immersed in deep vegetation, I try again to persuade Blunt to follow Viêt's advice.

Like a Chinese grenade, Blunt explodes in my face: "Look, dammit, this little man may have got battalion to go in the direction he wants, and it may even be the *right* direction, but he ain't leadin' my company *anywhere*. If I was out here like we oughta be with a Ranger unit I would get down in the valleys and snoop and poop and we would find this place, but I sure ain't going to do it with a big, slow, noisy company like this. That's just *askin'* to get our asses shot off and you can bet your little buddy knows it, too. Now you think, Mr. Civilian: when you got a hundred and fifty lives in your hands, you get a little careful about what you do. You understand?"

"Yes."

"Then you get back down the line with your Mr. Viêt and let me run this company."

We struggle on, recon by fire slamming big doors on life and surprise, machetes ringing, men cursing, radios crackling, tobacco smoke wafting in the breeze, white phosphorus marking rounds burning. We are like a huge, disjointed, dangerous, mechanical animal thrashing in the brush, the Machine "sneaking" up on Triêu Phong, one grid square wrecked and more to come.

On another rest stop we sink down sweat-drenched in humid green when suddenly across the jungle-choked valley savage bursts of fire explode, many weapons blazing on full automatic. A thunderbolt of fear rocks me. This is it, what all this has been leading to: Bravo or Charlie ambushed in the springing of the trap, and we're next.

Ahead of me Blunt doesn't bat an eye. He sees my wild-eyed look and says, "Bravo Company, having a mad minute."
Behind me Viêt didn't move, either. He can tell all the weapons firing are American, and he's heard mad minutes before, plenty. He continues spooning in C-rations.

The dog lieutenant explains: "A mad minute is everyone in the company firing full out for sixty seconds."

"Why?"

"Maybe to test their weapons. Maybe scare the VC. Maybe release tension."

"But not to sneak up on anyone," I say.

"There it is," the lieutenant says.

We stomp and hack on. We tear vegetation loose from the earth and trample tender shoots and moss so that a scar wake marks our way, the trail of the Machine. We snake across a hilltop and then are forced down by the land, as the high ground drops sharply into a steep, rocky ravine.

Viêt and I are about halfway down when whispered word comes up the line: "They found something down there."

We climb down in a hurry. Blunt, Buzz, and King are at the point, crouched in the bottom of the ravine. Trees stand all around, expectant. The sky is hidden by canopy.

Buzz is in a fever. "A hooch!" he whispers. "King alerted on it! We would have gone right by!"

King is quiet, poised, watching Buzz closely. Blunt grips his M-16, his big knuckles white in his burly hands. "Pass the word back," Blunt whispers hoarsely to Buzz. "Hold in place and be quiet."

Blunt begins to climb up out of the the ravine, and Viêt and I follow closely. We reach the upper edge, peer over, and quickly duck back down. Looking at us is a small, dark, bamboo-and-leaf hut standing almost invisible under the trees. It looks like a magic house, a place filled with great, supernatural power. This is why we've come to the wilderness: to find this, to fight, kill, destroy—and then return to civilization. The sight of the hut sends a rush of adrenaline through us. It's sinister looking and shaggy with thatch. We rise and quickly look at it again. There's no window, but an open, black doorway from which you can imagine Hell-fire coming out. A fresh-beaten path curves from the doorway into the trees and soon disappears in mystery and danger. In the ravine to our left lies a pile of empty C-ration and Japanese fish cans. The leaves breathe, our hearts pound, and sweat streams from our faces.

Blunt, Việt, and I look at each other. Blunt takes a deep breath, knuckle-grips his M-16, climbs over the top, and begins low-crawling toward the house. Việt and I climb over and follow till we all lie together behind a big rock about fifty feet from the house. Before, the hut had seemed small; now it feels huge and overpowering. The open doorway both lures and repels us with incredible force.

Việt jerks my sleeve and whispers mouth agape, "Tell the captain not to go any closer. Maybe they're waiting; maybe there are mines."

Blunt understands and whispers, "I know that, but I'm not sendin' my men up there, and somebody's got to do it."

Blunt starts to crawl forward, but Việt reaches out, stops him, and whispers to me, "Tell the captain to give me a grenade."

Blunt looks at Việt intently, pulls a grenade from his belt, and hands it over. Việt rises slowly and begins to stalk toward the house in a low panther-crouch.

The hut looks even more sinister now as Việt moves closer to it. The terrible black door could any moment spew orange fire and hot-metal death. Even the earth looks more frightening now, body-rending mine explosion just a heartbeat away.

Viêt walks excruciatingly slowly, silent as a ghost, watching the door, checking out the ground before each step. He's almost at the corner of the house, making an arc through the trees toward the door.

I can't let him go on alone. I rise slowly, quiet as I can, and Blunt rises, too. We all three move toward the house in a strange, slow dance, with the tension so great it seems the air is about to explode.

Viêt reaches the wall and edges along it toward the door. Blunt and I drop to the ground and lie flat, cover him with our M-16s, and hope that if he hits a mine it won't get us, too.

Viêt stays still for what seems a long time at the edge of the door, checking for booby-trap wires and disturbances in the earth. Suddenly he makes a quick move, looks into the house, and then flattens back against the wall, all without a sound. He waits frozen another long-seeming time, takes a deep breath, and steps into the doorway. For a moment he is framed against the black interior, then is swallowed up inside. The magic house has him now.

Blunt and I lie tense, waiting for the burst of bullets or shattering explosion that will send Viêt's broken body catapulting back out the door. Silence hangs so thickly beneath the trees that it seems it, too, will soon explode.

Viêt materializes out of the darkness inside the house. He appears in the doorway again, looking out at us. His face is drawn, as if leeches have sucked away all his blood. He comes quickly to us and whispers, "They just left! And look at this."

He opens his palm. Nestled there is a small glass vial of white powder medicine. "This must be the new hospital," Viêt whispers. "Maybe they moved here after I left. The rest of the headquarters is probably down there, very near." He points down the curving path where it skirts the ravine and disappears in the trees.

I look at the door of the house. "I want to go inside," I say.

Viêt leads me to the house, watching everywhere at once.
We step through the doorway into another dimension. This is
the VC world of Nature, secrecy, and sudden death. My eyes
slowly adjust to the dark. A strong smell of wood smoke fills
my nostrils. I see two levels dug into the earth: everything
slowly comes out of the gloom. Thick thatch hangs and
bamboo poles rise all around. A cavelike hole burrows into the
lower level, the entrance to an underground bunker, maybe a
tunnel system. Firewood stacked in a dark corner lies waiting
near the ashes of a cooking fire. There, too, are a blackened
pot and pan and an old, beat-up wooden ladle. Everything is
simple, natural, used, and full of awesome power.

Viêt pulls my sleeve. I feel in a dream. Everything seems to
be happening slowly, but with almost unbearable intensity.
Viêt points at three bamboo beds on the lower level, and above
them, a taut clothesline where three blood-stained bandages
and a pair of brown NVA pants hang. Beyond them another
doorway opens into the forest, and another branch of the Ho
Chi Minh Trail curves and disappears into the trees.

Blunt comes into the house and looks around like an infidel
intruder in a holy temple. He wants to booby-trap the place and
put ambushes on the doors, but it's getting late and he has to
get Delta into its NDP. He leads us back to the ravine.

Buzz and King are waiting just over the edge. Blunt sends
Buzz back to pass the word, then leads Delta out of the ravine
and up the steep, jungled slope above the house. Darkness is
falling fast; there is no time to get to the top of the hill to set up
a proper NDP.

Buried in dense vegetation, we establish a rough perimeter
and lie down among rocks and roots. It begins to rain, and we
lie shivering all night. The official report tells it like this:

061344Z Jan 70. D/1–11 while conducting RIF operations vic YD
152431 discovered a 12 ft × 10 ft hut made of elephant grass. The

hut contained a tunnel which led to a bunker, 8 ft × 10 ft. The
bunker showed signs of recent use and contained an assortment of
medical supplies. D/1–11 will establish multiple night ambushes
in the vicinity of the bunker complex.[12]

In the morning we stand poncho-shrouded in the cold, gray
dawn, smoking to warm our hands and lungs, exhaling on our
cupped-mush hands, holding burning cigarettes near crev-
assed fingers till drips from our wrists put them out. Under the
trees rise sounds of soft talking, radio crackle, and stamping
of mud-clogged boots, big as if swollen, covering grotesque
cracked toes inside soggy socks. The Machine is stuck in the
mud, mist and fog again keeping choppers grounded. Get hit
now, fall and break something, and you lie in the mud and
wait.

It is nearly 1100 hours before the rain-streaked sky becomes
high enough for the mechanical birds of the Machine to fly and
us flesh-and-blood men on the ground to move. Blunt, Viêt,
and I lead the way down the hill toward the house. Just above
it, Blunt and I hide behind trees and cover Viêt while he goes
down to check it out. He cautiously enters the house, then
comes out fast, looking as if he's seen a ghost. He frantically
waves us to him.

Blunt and I slip and slide down and enter the house behind
Viêt. The NVA pants and bandages are gone. And in the damp
earth just inside the door is the fresh print of a Ho Chi Minh
sandal with a triple-X tread design.

"Jesus!" Blunt whispers.

Outside the door, the Trail is beaten fresh and smooth as it
slants down toward the ravine, daring us to follow. What has
happened here? Didn't the triple-X man know that fifty meters
above his house a mighty American infantry company was
camping? Hadn't he heard us crackling around in the brush up
there, and wheezing, cursing, and coughing? Or did the rain

and wind, the thick forest curtain and the dripping trees, hide us as it hid him? Maybe he knew but didn't care. Maybe he knew we were shivering up there in a tight little circle and had left no booby-traps or ambushes for him. Maybe he watched us search his house and then struggle noisily up the hill. Had he actually slept in that snug, dry hooch while we suffered in the cold and the rain? And now was he tempting us to follow his missing pants and triple-X print?

Blunt sits down on the ground near the hut to think. On his decision ride our lives.

I sit down with him and tell him what Viêt thinks: "He's pretty sure the VC must have moved the whole headquarters to this valley, maybe after he rallied. He thinks this hut is the recovery room, and the rest of the hospital will be down the ravine, maybe three or four more houses. Below that will be the district commander's hut and the political and economic sections. If we follow the Trail—"

"We could get our asses blown off," Blunt says.

Blunt ponders more, sitting crosslegged on the ground. He rises and begins giving orders: King will lead the way down the Trail, then Buzz, Blunt, Viêt, me, and the 1st Platoon; the rest of Delta will move above us on both sides of the ravine.

070615Z Jan 70. D/1–11 continued to conduct a detailed search vic YD 153432 where the bunker/hut complex was discovered on 06 Jan 70.[13]

We descend into the ravine, following King and the Trail from the front door of the house. The Trail branch here is narrow, new, hard-packed, and slippery. We walk slowly and carefully, eyes scanning the thick brush and trees, rifles ready, thumbs on safeties and fingers on triggers. We are ready to fight but fatalistic, too, knowing that if ambushed we can't do much but die.

What hopes we have hinge on fate and King. Buzz claims King's nose is fifty times more powerful than a man's, his ears ten, and eyes five, and that he is trained to alert not only to ambushes but also to mines and booby-traps. I wonder, though: can King smell every buried mine, see a very cleverly hidden tripwire, sense an ambush downwind and perfectly concealed?

The Trail points down the ravine into what looks like the Valley of the Shadow of Death, and we *do* fear evil. Among rocks and trees the Trail twists and turns, leading us deeper.

King alerts! His ears snap forward, his nostrils quiver, and his whole body tenses. Behind him, Buzz hits the ground, pulls King back, crawls to Blunt, and gasps, "Around the bend: *something.*"

Blunt worms forward to the position of King's alert, peers around a bend in the Trail, and crawls back. Ahead are big rocks, the Trail, and tangled vegetation: *anything* could be there. It is not just Delta's lives in Blunt's hands, either, but many more. If we get pinned down, Bravo and Charlie will come in, and then the brigade, and more after that. What begins with us dying on the Trail could become the biggest defeat of the war.

Blunt crawls back to his radioman and whispers quick orders. We are to turn around, leave the Trail, climb to high ground, and rejoin the rest of Delta. Again we struggle along, from hilltop to hilltop along the ridge lines, tearing a path through the forest.

Viêt and I feel low. The Machine's operation seems designed *not* to find the headquarters. If we ever locate the Bowl below Old Baldy, probably all we'll find will be more deserted huts. We're walking away from the Trail, and probably the new headquarters, too. No, not walking—thrashing away is more like it. Nature fights us all the way, making every step a struggle. We are constantly caught in the vines we cut, whipped and slashed by the branches we break. We retaliate with three hundred heavy boots, crushing and killing the small plants that grow close to the forest floor, trampling their bodies and tearing their roots. The forest even retaliates for that, causing us to slip and fall on the bare, slippery ground, banging our knees and elbows.

> 071500Z Jan 70. D/1–11 conducted detailed Search and Clear operations from YD 153432 to vic YD 153427.[14]

Viêt grows more gloomy and complains as he walks, "We've got to go down. Nobody walks up here. Down in the streams, down in the valleys, that's where we'll find Triêu Phong!"

I wonder again about Viêt. Why is he so eager to find the headquarters? To save himself from Rang and prison? To prove himself to Blunt and me? Or to lead us to where the VC are waiting? One thing sure: he knows now, if he didn't already, how bad we are in the forest. We crash on, leaving our scar wake behind. A new trail is forming in the forest, the trail of the Machine.

In the green and black shadow afternoon, we descend once more, forced down by the land. Our point man breaks out of the forest to a fast-running stream, sloshes across, climbs the bank dripping water, steps over a wide path, and continues fighting up into the trees.

Viêt and I reach the stream and Viêt whispers, "Ho Chi Minh Trail! Where are they going? This is *it!* The headquarters is just ten minutes from here."

I look at the Trail, fascinated. The Trail is beautiful here, curving along the stream, carpeted with leaves. It's a mysterious tunnel through triple-canopy forest, made long ago by mountain tribes and by wild animals long before that. It's part of the ancient forest here, like the stream beside it and the trees that arch over it, interlacing their branches and leaves. It seems not an intruder in the forest; like Viêt, it belongs.

Viêt pulls my sleeve and whispers, "We could follow this Trail all the way to North Viet Nam! Tell the captain his men must be quiet now. We're very near!"

I kneel with Blunt on the Trail and whisper what Viêt tells me: "The Economics Section is ten minutes upstream, and the Political Section five minutes more. Downstream the district commander's hut is twenty minutes, and the old hospital ten beyond that."

Blunt pulls at his shot-away ear and thinks. Finally he says, "How does he know these times so exactly?"

I had been wondering the same. To me, this is just another chaotic, tossing wave in the vast forest-sea. How could Viêt know the exact distances from here? I ask him.

Viêt looks around, shrugs, and says, "This is my place."

I remember Viêt telling me how he used to go from section to section of the headquarters to visit friends and play cards. I wonder where those friends are now and what is about to happen to them, and us.

Blunt begins issuing quick orders. The 1st Platoon lieutenant and ten men form behind us. Blunt tells everyone to shuck their packs and check their weapons.

Viêt pulls my sleeve and whispers, "I need a rifle. Tell the captain. This pistol is no good here."

Blunt thinks a moment, pulling his ear and looking at Viêt. He gets an M-16, hands it to Viêt, and says to me, "Does he know how to use it?"

Viêt understands Blunt's question, making me wonder again about his English. As he had demonstrated the .38 for Tex, now he does the same with the '16 for Blunt. He pops out the magazine, looks it over, tests the spring, and slips it back in till it clicks and locks. He jacks a round into the chamber and flips the selector to full automatic.

"Is he going to walk with that thing off safe?" Blunt says.
"Tell the captain not to worry," Viêt says as he hefts the '16.
"I know what I'm doing."

"What all *do* you know, little man?" Blunt says. "Move out."

Viêt steps off in his panther-crouch, M-16 aimed Vietnamese belly high. I follow five paces behind, then Blunt, the radioman, the lieutenant, and the ten Delta grunts.

I'm adrenaline-jolted and rocked by Viêt's image in front of me. Seven weeks ago he was a VC, walking this Trail to play cards with his friends. Now he wears a U.S. helmet, uniform, and boots, carries an M-16, and looks ready to shoot the first person he sees. Has he, too, become part of the Machine?

Viêt suddenly drops and kneels beside the Trail. Blunt and I go forward to him, and he whispers, "The branch to the Economics Section is just around the next bend. We'll go through the trees. Tell the men to be quiet."

Viêt rises and slips like a spirit through the trees. We try to follow like him, but we are not earth gods. Big, we bend, crack twigs, crunch leaves, kick rocks. We get snagged on vines and make noise pulling free. Our gear squeaks, boots clunk, baggy uniforms swish and whisper. Branches twang against our steel-pot helmets, which fall at crazy angles over our sweat-stung eyes and block the flow of forest sounds.

Viêt drops where a line of saplings sprout along a low rise, crawls to the top, and cautiously peers over. He signals to us, and Blunt and I low-crawl up beside him while behind, the Delta men kneel and wait, tensely breathing, sweating.

Across an old bomb-blast clearing, at the edge of a tangle of scythed-down trees, a large, dark, sinister house stares back at us. This is electro-shock in bamboo and thatch, a witch's house in a fairy tale, where fat children are eaten. Beneath the house, a dark, round bunker-eye stares at us evilly. Who is in there, ready to shoot?

Viêt, Blunt, and I squirm down behind the rise and look at each other. We're all sweating. Blunt waves the lieutenant and his men up to the low rise and hand-signals them to spread out and be quiet. We look at each other again. Who's going to make the first move? And what should it be? A movie scene begins to play in my head. This is the old pattern when I'm in extremis. Inside the black-eye bunker two small yellow men sit behind a big machine gun, waiting for us to cross the clearing. We Americans are not deceived, though; we put up a helmet on a stick. *"Kee-rang!"* the bullet ricochets. Now we *know* they're in there.

Blunt and I exchange looks. I feel he's thinking the same thing: Shall we put up a helmet on a stick? Before we can do anything, Viêt puffs his round cheeks, blows out a big breath, gets a strange, fatalistic look on his face, rises, and begins to circle silently through the trees toward the house. When he is halfway there, Blunt and I follow, while the others cover us from behind the rise. It still looks like a movie.

Viêt moves quietly behind and above the house. He hangs on to a tree and looks down through a hole in the roof. Blunt and I catch up with him and we all hold onto trees on a steep slope and look down through the hole. You can see a rickety old bamboo bed and the corner of a weathered table. Behind the house is another pile of rusty C-ration and Japanese fish cans. Everything looks old, very old — old and abandoned.

I look at Blunt. There's a thundercloud look on his face. Viêt shrinks from it and stares down through the hole in the house. He lets go of his tree, catches another, and quietly climbs down. Blunt and I watch as he creeps around the house and cat-walks inside, his M-16 searching. I wonder again: if a mine gets him, will it get us, too?

Blunt and I hang on and watch through the hole. Viêt appears, testing each step, looking intently at the bed and the table. He disappears again. We don't see him for a few minutes. Soon he emerges from the house and climbs to us.

"Cûu lâm," he whispers. "Very old."

"No shit, little man," Blunt says.

"What does the captain say?" Viêt whispers.

"That you did a good job checking the place out."

Viêt makes a face: he doesn't believe me. I don't want to believe, either; the house looks abandoned *much* longer than the two months since Viêt was captured.

"Let's go back," Blunt says. "I gotta get my men into their NDP."

"Wait, the Political Section," Viêt says. "It's only five minutes from where we left the Trail."

Blunt looks up at patches of gray sky through the bomb-thinned trees. "OK, tell him to lead on," he says, "but I bet we'll find the same damn thing: old and abandoned."

Viêt leads us back to the Trail, upstream along it, and then ducking under low-hanging trees where a small, fast stream flows in. We stand in dancing water completely shrouded in branches and leaves.

"This is it," Viêt whispers. "This stream is the Trail to the Political Section. Tell the captain his men have to be very quiet. Don't fall behind. It's easy to get lost here."

Viêt leads us up the stream under boughs and leaves that trail their leaves in water. There is no sign that man has ever passed this way. You can *feel* it, though, as Viêt crouches around each bend as if he expects to meet and shoot someone there.

We turn up an even smaller stream, push leaf-laden branches up and bend to go under. We are totally immersed, lost in an infinitely complex stream system, a passage to the Under-world, with Viêt as our Charon, boatman on the River Styx. We wade on, lives in his hands.

Around a bend, Viêt flattens behind a smooth boulder.

Blunt and I wade to him and whisper with water swirling past our legs.

"It's very near," Viêt whispers. "Just around the next bend."

Again Viêt gets that look: I could die here. He rounds the boulder and wades forward, tense-crouched and ready to shoot.

Around the next bend the Trail rises from the water as if it had been walking on it. It goes boldly up the bank, to . . . nothing. Viêt stands in the water amazed. We move forward and climb the bank off the Trail. In the small clearing under the trees, where the Political Section's house should be, there is nothing.

We approach the site of the house. The jungle around is stupefyingly dense. We look down at the outlines of the house and the dark eye of an underground bunker. The sticks and straw of the house are completely gone, as if carried away by an army of ants.

Viêt looks long and hard at the bunker, then drops and crawls inside, disappearing into the hole as if he were being swallowed by a snake. Blunt and I step back to the edge of the clearing, out of range of a blast. Silence hangs heavy under the trees; the stream sings softly below. What can it be like for Viêt, crawling through the dark belly of the earth?

He emerges sweating and pale and motions for Blunt and me to follow him. We go through the trees just off a narrow path to another powerful sight: a low, igloo-shaped grass hut, shaggy with long and heavy thatch. It's suddenly just there, as if conjured up.

"It's the cooking house," Viêt whispers.

He disappears inside. There are no windows, not even a door, just a slight opening in the thatch. It must be totally dark in there. Viêt soon comes out and says, "They've been gone a long time."

Blunt looks at him hard and says, "I wonder how long you knew that?"

"What does the captain say?"

"He wants to go back now."

Viêt leads us back down the stream system. Doubts fill my head. How long *had* the headquarters been abandoned? Who *was* Viêt?

> 7 Jan 70. D/1-11, guided by a Hoi Chanh, found a 5-bunker complex in the vicinity of YD 151427. The Hoi Chanh said this complex was the Political Control Area. All bunkers were destroyed.[15]

Back on the Trail, Blunt passes Viêt and takes the lead. Deepening shadows give urgency: time to be in our NDP.

The lieutenant catches up. "Sir," he says to Blunt, "shouldn't we go back for our packs?"

I think so, too. Blunt seems headed in the wrong direction, taking the Trail for North Viet Nam.

Blunt looks at the lieutenant with contempt. "We *are* goin' back," he growls, and he stomps on with Viêt close behind. Blunt and Viêt, it seems, are the only ones not lost after the confusing journey down the streams.

Soon we come to our packs lying beside the Trail like headless, limbless men. Viêt pulls my sleeve, his moon face shiny and forelock tumbling over one eye.

"Tell the captain," he says. "The district commander's house and the hospital are just downstream from here."

"If I decide," Blunt says to me, "to follow the little man any more, I'll let you know, and it won't be today."

Blunt leads us up the hill that rises steeply from the Trail. In a long, single line, Delta struggles like a wounded serpent, tearing a bare, muddy path. Platoon and squad formations soon break down as all along the line sweating, gasping men fall out. The company has become 150 individuals, all trying to get to the top. Bodies steam, sweat streams, legs pump, boots tear and trample vegetation. Behind us, the earth is denuded and churned to slick mud. Men stand staggering and fighting for air and sit in the mud, dazed with heat and exhaustion. They fight forward two lurching steps and slip one back.

At the front of the column is a race. Blunt passes the point man, and I stay close behind, determined to prove to Blunt he can't walk me down. Viêt goes around me easily and squeezes in on the heels of Blunt. Now Viêt pulls out to pass Blunt, but I grab his shirt and warn him back with a look.

We reach the top in a close-packed clump, and I veer off to give Blunt space, but Viêt stays near. I think I see a look of respect in Blunt's eyes before he goes panting back down the hill to help his men come up.

Soon the canopied hilltop rings with digging, chopping, and radio chatter. News comes from battalion: guided by Viêt's advice to Colonel Herndon, Bravo and Charlie Companies have found a

> vast complex of bamboo hooches and underground bunkers, the latter both rectangular and triangular and from $10' \times 6' \times 4'$ with $2'$ dirt overhead cover to $12' \times 5' \times 5'$ with logs and dirt for overhead cover, and all showing signs of recent (within 3–4 days) use. . . . The Hoi Chanh passed information to B/1–11 which enabled them to find the Sapper and Security Section, Propaganda and Transportation Section, and the R&R Section. Many of the bunkers were elaborately constructed with underground chimneys and cooking stoves, and as large as $18' \times 15' \times 8'$. Some had elevated bamboo sleeping platforms with insect nets and were furnished with steel-backed chairs. A total of 100 bunkers and 50 hooches were destroyed in the vast base complex.[16]

Blunt calls me over to listen to this come over the radio. "Not quite the harmless place your little buddy said, is it?"

Again I have that empty feeling. "Maybe a big unit moved in since he was here."

"Yeah, sure," Blunt says. "Something else: sensor and sniffer reports indicate a big NVA unit is heading our way. What do you think Viêt has to do with *that*? And think of this: I'll admit the little guy's got guts, but maybe he wants to be first on the Trail and first to check out the hooches because if he meets somebody he knows, he'll have to kill 'em quick before they give him away. Who knows *what* he does inside the bunkers and huts, anyway? Maybe he's hidin' stuff that could be useful to us or identify him. I notice you or me ain't too eager to go in there with him. You don't trust him, either, do you?"

I go back to my part of the hill and lie on the ground thinking of the VC in their shaggy huts. I hope we've at least chased them out in the rain, but I doubt it. All around on the dark perimeter GIs shiver and cough in their mud holes, dreaming of their lives back in the World.

Viêt and King sleep dry in another big-leaf shelter. I try to keep warm by lighting C-ration heat tablets but only succeed in burning more holes for the rain in my new poncho liner. I lie shivering in the mud all night.

In the morning the ceiling lifts early and Blunt calls me to a hilltop conference. He's decided to make one more try with Viêt. We'll go for the district commander's house, the 1st Platoon lieutenant and one squad accompanying. Blunt tells me to brief the others on what we'll find, "*If* there's anything there."

I tell what Viêt has told me. "The commander's name is Huynh. He's about forty, tall and thin. He has a finger missing on his right hand. He's fought the Japanese, French, and us. He lives alone in his hut and runs Triêu Phong District from there. Underneath his hut is a bunker and out back is a cooking house where two women live. Downstream about ten minutes is the hospital, four houses, four bunkers, and six or seven people, one of them Doctor Son from Hanoi. The others are nurses and medics. They're not combat-oriented, and we're hoping to capture them or call them to rally."

"Lock and load," Blunt says. "Move out."

Viêt leads us down the hill, walking off the muddy slash we made yesterday. Near the Trail he kneels in deep bushes and waves Blunt and me to him. "We won't follow the Trail," he whispers. "Maybe the VC are waiting, maybe mines. We'll cross the stream and go through the trees. Tell the Americans to be quiet."

Viêt leads us into the trees, and we struggle through dense vegetation. Soon the stream is lost to us, even its song swallowed. I begin to worry about where Viêt is taking us. How can he know where he's going?

Viêt stops and casts an agonized look back. We're too noisy, too slow. Minutes stretch into an hour. It seems we've gone much too far from the stream. Behind me, Blunt mutters that he's ready to call it off and go back. I wonder if Viêt is lost, too. How can he navigate here? We can see no sun through the canopy, and the terrain rises and falls with no hint of a slope to the stream. We seem to be underwater, swimming in the Sargasso Sea. Blunt whispers that he'll give Viêt just a few more minutes. We sweat and struggle on.

Stream sounds come through the green curtain. Viêt is *not* lost, and he is not like us. He relates to Nature in a different way. I have watched Viêt now on two operations, seen him float over the Trail silent as an owl, slip through the trees like a deer. Now I see his skill at deep-forest navigation. He has walked blindly through a nearly impenetrable curtain, somehow matching the curves of an invisible stream with the vegetation-cloaked undulations of the land. Now he stares at the dancing water as if he knows it and is listening to a message in its rush over rocks.

"Gân lâm!" he whispers. "Very near! We'll walk in the water from here."

Viêt leads us into the stream, and water darkens our uniforms like blood. We hug the far bank and wade forward, M-16s hard-pointed and ready. I strongly feel something's going to happen: this is not going to be a dry run.

Viêt crouches behind a boulder and cautiously peers around the bend. He twists back, face aghast, and waves Blunt and me up. "There!" he says. "The Trail to the commander's house."

Blunt and I look around and duck back. Just ahead, the Trail rises from the water, climbs the bank, and loses itself in the trees. It's very fresh; it has that glow.

Viêt wades forward, '16 on full automatic. I follow, then Blunt, the lieutenant, and the squad. We're all ready to spurt streams of hot metal, projectiles tumbling through meat and blood.

Viêt slowly climbs the bank, senses burning into the trees. He walks parallel to the Trail, checking each step before his foot goes down, parting leaves, peering into the next layer. We follow as quietly as we can, a death-thrust into green.

Suddenly Viêt stops, looks through branches, motions Blunt and me forward. He draws back a curtain of leaves and points. A narrow path leads to a low mound topped by a hole.

The lieutenant pushes up behind us, looks over our shoulders, and whispers, "A cache! Maybe we better see what's inside."

"What does he say?" Viêt whispers.

I translate and Viêt almost chokes. "Open that up and you'll get a surprise," he says. "That's where the VC shit!"

Blunt looks at the lieutenant like he wants to spit. I'm glad I didn't say anything. I thought it might be a cache, too.

Viêt backs away from the path, ducks under a bough, and is gone. I follow closely, then Blunt. A few steps into dense vegetation Viêt drops silently, and Blunt and I crawl to him.

We look across an open space under tall trees. Looking back is another jungle house, this one open all along one side, as if whoever lives there likes fresh air and a view of visitors coming. Outside, a bunker eye stares at us unblinking. I feel my breath coming in rushes and my heart beating against the earth.

"Commander Huynh's house," Viêt whispers in a voice so low it can hardly be heard.

This house is not abandoned. Someone is here, or very near. Inside the house on a low bamboo bed something dark lies still. Blunt sends a series of hand signals to the lieutenant, and the Delta men creep forward and lie in an arc facing the house.

My mind races away again. We seem to be in a play. The clearing is the stage, and the trees are the silent audience. The forested hill behind the house is the backdrop, and the canopy is the ceiling. Opening-night tension is in the air as we players, life's walking shadows, prepare our entrance—brief burst!— on the way to dusty death.[17]

Viêt gets his fatalistic look and begins to rise, but Blunt reaches out and pulls him back.

"Tell him he doesn't have to," Blunt whispers. "He doesn't have to be first every time."

I translate, but Viêt shrugs and answers, "I'm Vietnamese; it should be me."

Viêt rises and begins to ghost-drift through the clearing. Blunt and I follow, spread out so a single AK burst or mine blast, we hope, won't get us, too, and shrapnel-leech our American blood into Vietnamese earth.

Viêt moves silently, eyes and M-16 searching. He stops at the bunker. Blunt and I drop and lie low, protecting ourselves and covering him.

Viêt looks hard at the entrance for what seems a long time, then drops and crawls inside. Who knows what he does, what he feels in there, his life bounded by tight earth walls, the circle of light to the upper world behind him, the passage to the Underworld below. We know nothing of this.

Silence screams, tension explodes as Blunt and I lie waiting for the mind-shattering burst.

Finally Viêt emerges, his face pale, his eyes big, and something brown in his hand. He comes to us streaming sweat, death-life currents flowing. He whispers, "Look, Commander Huynh's pack!"

Viêt pulls out of the Chinese pack a pair of brown NVA pants, a coil of wire, and a glass vial of the white-powder medicine, sulfanilamide, for treating wounds. "His entrenching tool is down there, too," Viêt whispers. "He hasn't gone far, and he'll be back. He would never leave these things behind."

Viêt slings Huynh's pack on his back and approaches the house. He looks all around and then enters, cat-walking across the packed-earth floor. He goes to the bamboo bed and looks down at the dark something lying there. He studies it, then gingerly lifts it and hangs it on his belt. It's Huynh's U.S. Army poncho. I wonder where—and how—Huynh got it.

Viêt points to a machete stuck in one of the house supports and warns us with a ghastly look. It must be booby-trapped.

Viêt comes out, waves Blunt and me forward, and shows us triple-X prints in damp earth. Was it Huynh at the first house? Has the Old Fox been leading us here, and is he again daring us to follow? How many Japanese, French, ARVN, and Americans had he played with this way? Huynh gave Viêt his last courier mission; what was, what *is,* Viêt's role here?

Viêt leads us around the back of the house and points down at a narrow, beaten path that rises into the trees, quickly curves, and disappears. Huynh is up there, Viêt says with a look. You can feel it, too. Huynh and other VC are waiting, maybe watching. Want to meet them? Go up that Trail. It's guaranteed you will not come down.

Viêt steps over the Trail and leads us to a rise that drops to a small stream. Beside the stream and hidden by thick canopy is another house, this one low and shaggy with heavy thatch. "The cooking house," Viêt whispers. "Huynh's two women cooks live here." Blunt and I lie on the rise covering as Viêt goes down and into the house. He comes out fast with another horror-struck look and a flat bamboo basket of greens. He climbs the rise and thrusts the basket in our faces. The greens are freshly chopped and wet from a recent rinsing. Minutes, *seconds* before, someone washed them in the stream. "I want to see in there," I say. Viêt leads me to the house. I step in behind him and stop, with my senses overwhelmed. It's dark inside and strong with wood-smoke smell; the thick leaf walls and heavy thatch roof allow no smoke to escape and rise above the trees. It's dry, too; they slept here last night.

My eyes slowly adjust. I stay still, shallow-breathing, tall American standing where VC women squat and cook. Shapes begin to emerge from the gloom: two low bamboo beds in a corner, a big stack of firewood along the far wall, a blackened pot, a black wooden ladle, and cooking-fire ashes on the floor. I imagine Huynh standing here where I am, looking at the women cooking. Spicy smells rise: rice, *nuoc mam,* dried fish, and jungle greens. It's warm in here; outside, the forest breathes, and wilderness sounds play in the breeze.

I approach the cooking fire, kneel, and put my hands in the ashes. Suddenly my mind bursts with another childhood scene from the cyclops screen. This time it's the *Lone Ranger*, a classic episode. The Masked Man and Tonto are following outlaws through canyon country. They come upon a campfire, with thin smoke curling. Tonto leaps off his pinto horse Scout, puts his hand in the fire, and says, "Unh, coals still warm, Kemo Sabey." Good God, Tonto, *smoke* is still rising! I pull my hand back with the shock of recognition. The ashes are still warm! Viêt stands over me in the dark. *"Di,"* he says. "Let's go." We go out and blink in the light. Leaves flash silver and green, and the small stream sings over rocks. Blunt sits on the rise, legs dangling over. He looks pretty casual up there. Viêt and I climb up and sit with him.

"I want to think," Blunt says, and he stares at the stream and pulls his shot-away ear.

Viêt and I sit quietly, M-16s across our laps. The forest is beautiful here. It's hard to believe we could die now.

Finally Blunt says in a hard voice, "You know what *really* pisses me off about this? After all the damn noise we've been makin' out here, Charlie is still livin' in his hooches right up to the minute we come take a look. And as soon as we leave, he'll come right back and go *on* livin' here while we stumble around in the bush and sleep in the mud and the rain. What pisses me off even *more* is that he's probably up there in the trees watchin' us and laughin'. If I was out here with a Ranger team I'd pretend I was goin' away, and when he came back I'd see who was laughin'!"

"How about getting the trackers and tracker dog?" I say.

"Oh, no," Blunt says. "I told you no dog and no hillbillies are going to lead my company *anywhere*. The dog walks along with his nose to the ground and the trackers with their heads up their asses, anyway."

Blunt is silent for a while, his bullet scar livid under a growing cloud. He stands abruptly and says, "Let's go back. I don't feel like providin' Charlie with any more comedy here."

Viêt pulls my sleeve and says, "Wait, tell the captain to give me two grenades."

"Why?" Blunt says.

"I want to make booby-traps," Viêt says.

"Booby-trap what?"

"The cooking house and the commander's bunker."
Blunt nods toward the cooking house and asks me, "Didn't
he say two women live here?"

"Yes."

"He doesn't have to do that," Blunt says.
I translate and Viêt answers, "I want to."
Blunt pulls two grenades from his belt, looks at Viêt sharply,
and says, "What is it that goes through your mind, little man?"
"What does the captain say?" Viêt whispers.
I don't translate, but I wish I knew, too.
Viêt and I go back in the house. Viêt works fast and
efficiently in the dark. He slips Huynh's pack off, takes out the
coil of wire, pulls off a strip, and bends it back and forth
rapidly till it breaks. He fastens one end to the rim of the
basket of greens and puts the basket in the corner by the
cooking fire. Then he carefully works the pin of one grenade
almost all the way out till it is just hanging, a breath from
killing us both. He attaches the loose end of the wire to the
pin's ring and lodges the grenade in the kindling pile.
Viêt steps backs and admires his work. "Good, huh?" he
says. "When they come back, they pick up their vegetables,
and BOOM!"

My mind jumps back to my last meeting with Rang. He
waved a paper in front of me and said it was an agent's report
on Viêt. Viêt was *not* a medic and courier, as he claimed: he
was a sapper, most feared of all the VC, experts in demolitions
and base penetration. I had blown the report off as black
intelligence, VC-planted to discredit Viêt, or Rang's lies to
send Viêt to prison. I didn't want to believe. Now I wondered:
would a VC medic be this good at booby-trap making? And
more: Why would Viêt do it? He didn't seem like a killer of
women. In fact, he didn't seem like a killer at all. Rang had an
answer for this, too: "*Sure* they choose someone like Viêt for
mission like this, so innocent-looking."

Like a runaway train my mind races on. Maybe Viêt's doing this to prove to Rang he really has changed sides now. Now he can tell Rang, "Even though the Americans screwed up the operation, I got Huynh and his cooks with grenades." There is another possibility, too: Viêt *knows* no one will be killed by his booby-traps. If Huynh and the others are watching, they'll carefully check every place we've been. Maybe the basket of greens hadn't been sitting in that dark corner by the cooking fire. Maybe it had been on the kindling pile or by the door. The women will know right away, find the grenade, push the pin in, and have one more to use against us. The same will happen at Huynh's bunker: *two* more for them! God, would the doubts about Viêt never cease?

"Let's go to Huynh's bunker now," Viêt says. "I've got a great idea for a booby-trap there."

Blunt and I wait outside while Viêt disappears inside the dark hole. He emerges with a big smile: "I hooked it to his entrenching tool. When he takes it to dig—BOOM! He digs his own grave."

Blunt shoots Viêt another hard look and says, "We'll go back now."

Viêt pulls my sleeve and says, "Wait, the hospital. It's only ten minutes from here. I'll show you where I used to work."

Blunt finally agrees. We make a cursory try at erasing all our tracks but don't really think we're fooling the VC. Viêt leads us back to the stream, and we wade in its swirling tunnel through the trees to a scene not of healing, but destruction.

The hospital is gone—burned, Viêt thinks, by the ARVN. All that remains of the place where Viêt's life was saved is a trash heap of old medicine bottles and syringes, the outline of three huts, and, still strangely standing, four bamboo supports for the operating table. Again, everything looks old, very old. Can the jungle age human structures so fast? And where are Dr. Son and the medics now? At the new hospital we walked away from? Again, what is Viêt's role here? The official reports give no hint of all this; the Machine doesn't deal in subtleties:

> At 081430H Jan 70 VIC YD 150428, D/1–11 discovered 2 bunkers 12' × 5' × 5'. The Hoi Chanh working with D/1–11 said these bunkers had been used by a VCI 'Commander' and staff. One of the bunkers contained warm ashes of a campfire. It appeared as if individuals had been in the area within the last 12 hours. The bunkers were destroyed. At YD 156432, D/1–11 discovered 3 destroyed bunkers that had been 12' × 5' × 5'. The Hoi Chanh said that these bunkers had been a hospital complex.[18]

Viêt leads us back to Delta's hill, cigarette smoke, and radio chatter. Bravo and Charlie, still guided by Viêt's information, have continued to make big finds: hooches, bunkers, three recent graves, and tables set with steaming food. One scout dog has been slightly wounded by a booby-trap, unsettling news. King and Viêt get together for a C-4–cooked lunch. Buzz and the trackers are bored: nothing to do.

Blunt calls me over. Sniffers and sensors continue to report big NVA units headed our way. Colonel Herndon has ordered us to a new position, away from the huts and bunkers of Triêu Phong and from hilltop to hilltop along the ridge lines. As soon as he can, Blunt will get Viêt, me, the dog people, and the trackers on a chopper back to the base.

We struggle on the rest of the day over high, forested country. Viêt and I are just two more plodders now as the Machine and the NVA play ultimate-stakes chess in the mountains. Late in the afternoon, Blunt leads Delta to an NDP occupied by Bravo last night: another denuded, trashed hilltop island in the forest-sea. Wooden ammo crates are stacked here and there, and fighting holes fringe the hill's crest like pits in a monk's shaved head. Stretching away in every direction waves of green jungle roll, and choppers begin to come and go, moving the ammo to Bravo and Charlie and making us targets. Suddenly a big explosion rips our hill, setting off a mad scramble for holes. Blunt roars into the radio and learns it's a friendly, off-target marking round.

"Willett again," I think.

Big shadows begin spreading from the high mountains to the west, and the cold chill of VC time creeps across the land. We dig Bravo's holes deeper.

Blunt calls me over. He doesn't like to let it show much, but I feel we're becoming friends. He wants to talk about the war and Viêt: "Tomorrow you and your little buddy'll go back on the resupply chopper with the dog people and trackers, and me and my men will stay out here fighting a lost war, lost because of the no-balls politicians in Washington and the numb-nuts generals in Saigon. You'll be havin' your hot showers and hot chow and hot women, I reckon, and me and my men will be humping the hills and sleepin' in the rain. You know how long it's been since we've had hot showers, clean uniforms? One month! You wouldn't like that, would you? Not even for your big civilian pay."

"I don't make that much," I say.

"Ha!" he says. "Now I'll tell you something about your Mr. Viêt. I'll admit part of what the little man did was OK. He took us where he said he would and he showed a lot of guts checking out the hooches and bunkers. He could take me to a hundred headquarters, though, and I still wouldn't trust him. Once they've been on the other side, they can never be with us. Anyway, what's he got waiting for him when we leave?"

I get a sinking feeling as the sun goes down into Laos. The view from the high, bare hill is immense, profound, and ominous. Darkness is coming, for us and all Viet Nam.

Blunt looks out over the forest and mountains. The last light of day plays across his bullet-scarred face and damaged ear.

"The NVA are coming down," he says heavily. "We're on the way out. What's going to happen to your little friend then?"

I try to sleep poncho-wrapped with my feet pointing down toward the dark forest-ocean. I slide down and worm back up. I start to drift off, and feel the snake again, pressing down on my feet, crawling up my legs. I jerk up in terror and fall back in cold sweat. A dream! Thank God! I try to sleep, and feel it again. The snake—"the symbol of life throwing off the past and continuing to live."[19]

The night seems never-ending. Finally, light comes, and ghostly forms begin to appear, mountains and trees out of the fog and Delta men moving like spirits. I think of the half-cured blind man's words to Jesus, "I see men, but they look like trees walking."[20]

Chopper sound comes from across the mountains like a mechanical heartbeat, distant at first, then coming closer, beating faster, entering our own heart rhythms as it materializes out of the sky, flying toward us in Machine-deliverance. "This is the end," the heartbeat says, overwhelming now as it roars into landing, making everything tornado-fly—dust, feelings, things spinning out of control. The Huey sits vibrating, green locust body trembling with dino-fires, ecstasy-pain of end-beginning.

We run for the chopper and throw ourselves in, jammed on the floor, whooping, laughing with the joy of survival, gravity-defiance, flight.

The mountains and forest fall away as we beat back toward base. We're silent now, lost within. I'm already thinking about the next operation, south of the river this time, where the Trail leads to the NVA Rocket Company's camp—but not with the Machine: Tex, Viêt, me, a reinforced Grim Reaper team. I begin to see it in my mind, back on the Trail again. . . .

then the rushing *Pequod,* freighted with savages, and laden with fire, and burning a corpse, and plunging into that blackness of darkness, seemed the material counterpart of her monomaniac commander's soul.[21]

Who was the commander here? Viêt? Me? Huynh? Or the Machine? We plunge on into darkness, with smoke and dust from the base rising like plumes from a forest bird, like a feathered serpent.

CHAPTER 3

DEEP PLAY IN THE BELLY OF THE WHALE: PASSAGE INTO THE REALM OF NIGHT

*Dewdrops, let me cleanse
In your brief, sweet waters
These dark hands of life.*

—Bashō, 1644–94

Anthropologist Clifford Geertz read about deep play in Jeremy Bentham's *Introduction to the Principles of Morals and Legislation* and wrote about it in "Cockfighting in Bali."[1] Deep play is doing that for which the possible rewards of winning do not seem commensurate with the probable consequences of losing. Man is generally a creature of much deep play, and this leads often to his and the Earth's perdition.

In the valley of Ba Long the Rocket Company has its camp. Viêt draws another pirate-treasure map: river, streams, the Trail, a saddle between Hills 300 and 320, and the Rocket Company's camp.

"We can go this way," Viêt says. "The stream is the Trail; the Trail is the stream. The VC walk in the water here."

I write up a plan and make a big mistake: I leave it in my house and find Viêt looking at it as if reading. Then another blunder: I take the plan to the advisory team to be typed. I tell the chief clerk, an American civilian, "This is very sensitive. Keep an eye on it." Later I find one of the ARVN interpreters reading it alone.

Finally, I drive it out to the base. While I wait to cross the river bridge, a big U.S. tank comes chewing its way across, spitting wood splinters from its steel-tread teeth. Below, the

Thach Han flows by, down from Ba Long and the Rocket Company's camp. Will the NVA be waiting?

The ARVN bridge guard waves me across and I ease my Scout over and through the refugee camp. The kids run out to shout, "Sah-lem! Sah-lem!" and the old men and women stare from the doors of their shacks. I enter the base, park beside a jeep outside the 1/11 TOC, duck into the igloolike entrance, and am swallowed in sandbags and steel mesh. It's like walking inside a strange war-whale.

My feet clunk on the wood planks, remnants of the North American forest shipped on demothballed, World War II victory ships across the Pacific. I push open a door and emerge into a large room with many radios, static hiss, and GIs talking.

Major Lukitsch comes to meet me. "Colonel Herndon's in the field," he says. "Blunt's out, too, on rice denial and rocket suppression. Pressure's on to keep things quiet at Têt."

"That's why I'm here," I say, and I show him the plan. I've designed it, subtly, I hope, to show why the mission must be done my way. Lukitsch reads:

1. The Rocket Company's Camp cannot be attacked by conventional means because its exact map location is not known. Therefore the following is advised . . .
2. Rallier Viêt, Chiêu Hôi Advisor Stevens, and 12 Grim Reapers will go. No packs, one canteen, four rations per man.
3. Go as soon as possible on an odd-numbered day. Mr. Viêt states enemy do not walk this section of the Trail on odd-numbered days.
4. Rallier will lead on the Trail to near the Camp. From here, Team Leader, Rallier, and Chiêu Hôi Advisor will crawl forward to observe Camp and confirm it is occupied. They will return to the rest of the team and night will be spent in the bush near the Camp.
5. Before dawn, all will crawl to the three houses that comprise the Camp. Attack will begin at first light, using LAWs,

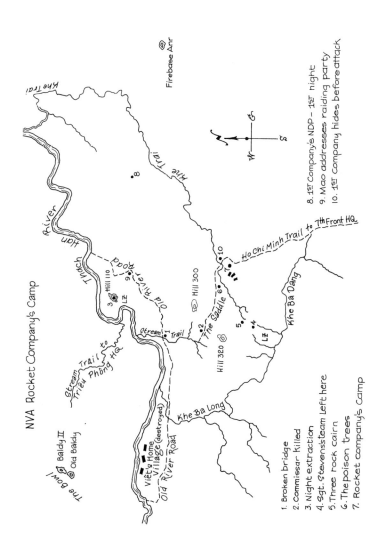

NVA Rocket Company's Camp

The Bowl
Old Baldy
Baldy II

Khe Trai

Hon River
Thach

Stream Trail to Trieu Phong HQ
Old River Road

Hill 110

3 LZ

Viet's Home
Village (destroyed)
Old River Road

Khe Ba Long

Stream
Trail
1

Hill 300

The Saddle 6
2

Hill 320

Khe Ba Dang

8

Khe Trai

Firebase Anr

10
Ho Chi Minh Trail to 7th Front HQ

5
4
LZ

N
W
S
E

1. Broken bridge
2. Commissar killed
3. Night extraction
4. Sgt. Stevens's team left here
5. Three rock cairn
6. The poison trees
7. Rocket company's Camp
8. 1ST Company's NDP – 1ST night
9. Mao addresses raiding party
10. 1ST company hides before attack

M-79s, and M-16s. Documents and weapons will be seized, and prisoners captured if possible. Extraction will be from the grassy area at YD 235376 southeast of the target. Estimated elapsed time of operation: 24 hours.

"I like it," Lukitsch says. "I'll have it retyped and sent up to brigade."

"It has to be soon," I say.

"I know," Lukitsch says, and he spreads his hands. "What can you do?"

Time passes, too much time, time for leaks and ambushes. This odd-numbered day thing is troublesome, too. I ask Việt about it again: "How can you be sure? Maybe they've changed since you were captured."

"They won't change," Việt says, in his comic, old-time orator style. "VC from there have been captured, rallied before. They didn't change. Don't be afraid. We won't meet them on the Trail. I guarantee it one hundred percent!"

Việt comes often to my house, defying Rang's restrictions. He likes to listen to my stereo with the headphones on. "I don't understand the words," he says in a too-loud voice, "but I like the sound."

He has me put on his favorite song, the Beatles' "Maxwell's Silver Hammer," and he grooves along with his eyes closed. Why does it have to be *that* song, I think, about a treacherous little guy who creeps up behind people and bangs them on the head, making sure that they are dead? Should I be bothered by that? Does he understand the words? Why, out of all my records of Creedence, Jefferson Airplane, the Rolling Stones, and the Beatles, does he like *that* song?

I push and prod the brigade to go. As usual, clearances, plans, briefings, paperwork, and weather have to be just right. Worst of all, politics rears its ugly head, as Lukitsch calls with the word, "The operation's off."

"*No!* Why?"

"The pressure's on for Vietnamization, all the way from the White House. Nixon wants to hold U.S. casualties down. Besides, the area of operations south of the river belongs to the 1st ARVN Regiment now. We can't go in there without their OK. Anyway, it wouldn't look good for Vietnamization if we made a big kill in their AO."

"Don't cancel," I say. "Let me try to come up with something."

I drive my Scout south to LZ Nancy, a dusty, frontierlike fort on the Thac Ma River north of the Thua Thien border, and home base of the 1st Regiment of the elite 1st ARVN Division. I ease through rings of barbed wire, park outside the headquarters, and descend to the underground office of the S-2, Captain Anh. Radios connect Anh to his intelligence and reconnaissance teams, some of the best long-range soldiers in Viet Nam, operating now along the vehicle routes of the Ho Chi Minh Trail in and near Laos.

Anh looks up and smiles. He's young, Catholic, and moviestar handsome. He leads me to the regiment's briefing room, and we sit in semidarkness among rows of empty folding chairs. Big wall maps look down, and VC weapons hang as war trophies. We play this little game; Anh is a very mischievous man, a kind of Vietnamese Huck Finn.

"So what, Mr. Chiêu Hôi? You got some information for me?"

"Maybe," I say. "You got some for me?"

"I always got plenty," Anh says. "Where you think you Americans get your intelligence? From us Vietnamese!"

"I know where an NVA rocket company is."

"Only one? I know plenty. Which one you know?"

"You show me yours—on the map."

Anh rises and hits the mountains quickly several places with his open hand; no help there. "All over," he says. "Here, there, wherever you like. Now you tell me."

I've eaten at Anh's house in Quang Tri City. His wife is beautiful and shy, his little daughter a Vietnamese doll. "South of the Thach Han River," I say. "Ba Long." "I know that one," Anh says. "Show me on the map." "You show me first." Anh laughs and says, "OK, maybe you know one. Show me, then I tell you if you're right."

I rise and point to where I think it is, in the broad valley below Hills 300 and 320, from Viêt's maps and our reconnaissance flights over the area.

Anh is interested now. "Close enough," he says. "Anyway, have to be some Vietnamese tell you."

"Mr. Viêt," I say. "The rallier."

"Not rallier," Anh says. "Prisoner. I know all about him. He took you and 5th Mech to Triêu Phong. Didn't get much: no kills."

"He can take us to the Rocket Company's camp."

Anh leans forward. Our little information game is over, and another is about to begin.

"I've written up a plan," I say, and I reach for my pocket.

"No need," Anh says. "I read it later. Tell me everything."

I tell him almost everything. He questions me closely about the camp, the Trail there, the number and location of huts, and where the rockets are hidden.

"There's a problem, though," I say. I tell him about the AO and the pressure on the brigade for Vietnamization.

"No problem!" Anh says. "I loan you four men from my Intel and Recon Platoon, make joint operation. Good for you: learn something from us. And no problem about the AO: we'll loan it back. Easy!"

Anh sits back and smiles. Then he leans forward, looks around the empty room, and drops his voice: "I give you four men: Khai, Bao, Nam, Than—my best. They'll walk point for you: it's better that way. But they have no chance if they meet the enemy. Only if they have surprise. We'll dress them in NVA gear, they'll carry AKs."

My mind races away: back on the Trail with four of the best ARVN, dressed as NVA! "And a uniform and AK for Mr. Viêt," I say.

Anh leans back and smiles: "He doesn't have his own?" I drive to the base and present the plan to Bad José.

"I think Cobra Six might buy it," he says. "But I don't know about the NVA gear. I think there's regulations against it. I'll check and let you know."

"*Soon, it has to be soon.*"

Bad José shrugs and spreads his hands like Lukitsch.

More days of tense waiting pass. It's been three weeks now since we came back from Triêu Phong. Surely the NVA will be waiting.

Khai, Bao, Nam, and Than come to my house. They're amazing guys, these ARVN. Sergeant Khai is the oldest. He's been in the army thirteen years and wounded four times. Sergeant Bao has been fighting eleven years. He's been wounded three times and captured once and escaped, with Than, in the jungle. Corporal Than has been in the ARVN seven years and has been wounded twice, once almost dying. He and Bao were captured on recon on the Trail, and after their escape from the NVA they walked all the way from Laos back to LZ Nancy. Only young Corporal Nam, in the army four years and wounded once, isn't married and a father, and from the teasing Khai, Bao, and Than are giving him, it seems he's about to take the plunge.

Viêt doesn't interact much with the ARVN. He's very quiet around them, unusually so for him. Now and then Khai asks him questions about the camp, and Viêt's answers are always quick and delivered in humble language. I wonder how many times Viêt and the ARVN have fought, killed each other's comrades and brothers? Would they be fighting if we weren't here, or would it all be over now?

Like me, the ARVN are eager to go, and they also worry about the delays. Finally word comes from Bad José: liftoff is set for tomorrow. "But no AKs or VC gear," Bad José says. "The general blew up when he heard. Said something about the Geneva Convention and that he wouldn't have any 'Batman capers' in his brigade."

"'Batman capers'!" I say. "What does he think we're doing, playing games out there?"

"Sorry," says Bad José, "that's the way it is. No VC gear."

I hang up in dismay. How can I tell the ARVN they'll have to walk point on the Trail wearing their own uniforms? What can I say to Anh? This was our deal. And it's what I want to do. I decide to go ahead anyway and take my chances with Cobra Six.

Viêt and the ARVN gather at my house on the morning of January 31 to prepare. I pass out the NVA uniforms and AKs, they dress, and the ARVN begin horsing around. They're like kids going on a picnic.

Viêt tells them what to say if we meet someone on the Trail: "Hello, Comrade! We're from the K-14 Battalion, going on operation today." Then they'll use their taekwondo to capture the VC. They throw punches and kicks and laugh while Viêt and I stay out of the way.

Khai and Bao, who'll walk one and two, practice with Than and Nam playing "real" NVA. "Hello, Comrade," Khai says, and he runs through what Viêt has told him about the K-14 Battalion.

"K-14?" Than says. "We're the K-14!" And they throw kicks and punches like crazy.

"Time to go," I say.

They pile in my Scout, threatening to pop up and scare the police as we drive through town.

I'm scared that they might, and say, "Khong duoc!" "No good! Stay down!"

We approach the checkpoint by the river, where two white-uniformed police with pistols and carbines check vehicles and IDs. A young ARVN is there, too, lounging against the barricade, fingering the trigger of his M-16.

"Police!" I whisper. "Stay down!"

Lying beside me in the front seat, Khai exchanges whispered jokes with the others in the back. They're all giddy, wild since they put on the NVA gear and took the AKs in their hands. Some power, some energy and mischief has passed into them, and seeing how jittery I am only makes them worse. The police wave me to slow down, and the ARVN stares hard at my Scout.

"I'm gonna do it!" Khai whispers. "Watch them faint when they see me!"

"*No!*" I say through gritted teeth. "Stay *down!*"

I think of flooring the Scout and trying to get away in a hail of fire. The "white mice" police and young ARVN would love to shoot an American civilian, I'll bet. I ease slowly through the barricade and breathe again when we're past.

Our next hazard is the river bridge with the dust-eating ARVN guards. Khai and the others stay down this time, and quiet. Standing in the heat and exhaust fumes all day puts the guards always on edge. I wait for a U.S. convoy, then bump across the chewed-on planks. I glance quickly to the left, upstream, where we'll soon go. There the river builds from many streams, the tiger pushes his big paw into the soft mud, and the Trail flows down like a powerful snake.

I drive through the refugee camp. Now we have American MPs to face. The base gate guards will almost surely approach the Scout and ask my business. I swing in under a tall watchtower with an M-60 looking down. I'll have to talk fast, but calmly, before the MPs panic at the sight of my "NVA."

I ease in through the barbed wire. Just ahead the MPs are checking cleaning women and vendors from the refugee camp. The base sprawls out in all directions: dusty roads studded with bunkers and barracks. A young MP with an M-16 approaches the Scout. I stick my face out the window. "Uh, listen, I've got some guys in here dressed as NVA, but it's OK, we're going on a special mission. You can call Major Lukitsch at 1/11. Tell him the Chiêu Hôi advisor is here."

The MP stops in his tracks. He studies me for a while, his jaw clenching and his hand squeezing the '16 as if he's doing wrist exercises.

"It's OK," I say. "We've got lift-off at 0900. Take a look."

The MP looks in the window and recoils. "Jesus!" he says. "You sure those guys are all right?"

"Trust 'em with my life," I say.

"Take 'em through," he says, and he wrist-snaps us forward.

I drive to Pioneer Pad. *Now it comes,* I think. *What will Herndon and Lukitsch do? And will Cobra Six be there?*

On Pioneer Pad twelve black-faced Grim Reapers wait. Not Tex, though: he's on another mission. Sergeant Stevens, a lean, hawk-faced Hoosier, will command this operation.

Stevens welcomes us and paints me up. The Recon Platoon lieutenant joins us; he'll go along, too, drawn by the lure of deep play.

Battalion GIs run for their cameras to photograph themselves with the "NVA." So far, no Cobra Six, but Herndon and Lukitsch pull up in a jeep. Now the *cuc* hits the fan.

Herndon and Lukitsch don't say anything. They shake hands all around, Herndon hugging "his boy" Viêt, Lukitsch wishing he could go—but they don't even mention the general's orders. It's as if they've been enchanted. We've got to get out of here fast.

A radioman comes from the TOC with news for Herndon: "Only one chopper is available, sir. The other has been preempted for a VIP tour."

Herndon rages inwardly and Lukitsch kicks the ground. I feel a terrible sinking; we've got to go *now.*
"It's OK," I say to Herndon. "One team is enough. Send the sergeant and two of his men with me and the Vietnamese. We can do it."
"No," Herndon says. "The general would have my head if I sent only three of my men on a mission like this."
"Just me and the Vietnamese, then," I say.
"No, sorry. I can't do that. We'll have to abort for today."
"Let me use your radio," I say. "There's one possibility. . . ."
I call up Willie, the Black Cat courier pilot. Warrant Officer Willie Williams flies for the Quang Tri Advisory Team in a Huey with a yellow moon and arched-back black cat on its nose. Willie is a very hot pilot and a good friend; he's taken me on many wild rides down the river, flying the bends, skids inches above the water, then roller-coastering the dunes. There's one big problem, though: Willie doesn't consider himself a combat pilot. He flies the lowlands, high when he can, and stays away from Indian country. I catch Willie at Citadel Pad. We don't use radio procedure, just talk.
"Willie, I got a great deal for you."
"Yeah, I'll bet."
I picture Willie standing by the Black Cat, his dark shades on, tall and California-looking in his flight suit, his crew hanging out in the shade of the chopper.
"It's easy," I say. "Just take us out and drop us."
"Where?"
"Ba Long."
"No way; that's Indian country."
"Just a little way in, Willie. You don't even have to land: we'll go out on a hover-jump."
"Get a bird from the Green Machine. Not that they know how to fly."

"We got one. We need one more. Come on, Willie, it's important."

"You can only get one chopper from brigade? Where's all the Red Devil pilots? Sears took away their flying licenses?"

"Come on, Willie, you're not doing anything. Wouldn't you rather fly?"

Willie doesn't say anything. I feel he's thinking about it. He loves to fly.

"There's no danger on the insert, Willie. I guarantee it one hundred percent."

Willie breaks communications. He's talking it over with his crew. He comes back: "You better be right about that guarantee. And get ready for a fast ride and a new record low time over the LZ."

"You got it."

I look around. I should feel happy, but there's still a cloud. One thing could kill everything: the sudden arrival of General Burke.

Willie's Black Cat and a Red Devil Huey roar in and settle on the vibrating steel mesh of Pioneer Pad.

"I don't like the looks of those guys!" Willie shouts out his window at Viêt and the ARVN.

I motion to Sergeant Stevens to load up fast. Half the ARVN load with Viêt, Stevens, and me on Willie's chopper, with the lieutenant and the rest on the Red Devil bird. Behind his helmet and goggles Willie glares at the Red Devil pilot as if to say, "I'm gonna teach you some flyin'!"

I squeeze up between Willie and his copilot. "Let's hit it!" I shout.

Willie mutters something, but the words are chopped and pummeled by the big blades and flung out spinning through the universe. Herndon and Lukitsch salute below and get smaller and smaller as we swing southwest and beat toward the Thach Han.

"Take it low up the river!" I shout to Willie.

"You know me!" he says.

We fly toward deep purple mountains under a silver gray sky. Viêt's head is hanging; I hope he doesn't puke. Now it's up to me; I have to land us in the right place, the LZ Viêt and I chose on our reconnaissance flights, the grassy area near Hill 110 on the old river road. I've got to get it right, tell Willie where we'll go out on our hover-jump.

Willie takes us down over the river, so low his skids seem about to skim the water. He flies the river's curves at more than 100 miles per hour, daring the Red Devil pilot to follow. The world flies by, streaming, roaring. I'm afraid I'm going to screw up.

Too fast! Everything is flying by too fast: river, hills, grass, trees. Viêt and I chose the LZ from high up in a lazy-circling observation plane. Where is the big river curve, the small stream, breast-shaped Hill 110? I'm very afraid. I'm going to screw up and look bad.

There! Hill 110! Wasn't it? It's past in a green blur. Another is coming up.

I take a chance. "There!" I shout to Willie. "The LZ!"

Willie blasts straight for the grass as if he's going to dive right into it. The world roars, energy streams, everything explodes in ear-splitting sound. I move to the open doorway and brace myself to jump. Outside, the grass whips in tornado frenzy.

Willie hits the air brakes and the Black Cat hovers vibrating insensate, defying gravity and other natural laws. I throw myself out, big rotor chopping and slicing above my head. Everything is huge and in ultrafocus, like a giant's world through an immense magnifying glass.

I fly through the air and land in a Medusa-hair tangle of ten-foot-tall, wind-beaten grass. I fall on my face—the momentum is terrific—and am swallowed in a hell of sound. Behind me the others leap out and we all crawl away, struggling through the chaos of noise and snake-whipping grass.

The choppers fly away to false drops upriver and finally their sound is gone. The grass slowly rises, and our senses gradually return, eardrums recovering from the beating and the smell of avgas exhaust fading. We form behind Khai and Bao and force our way through the tangle. Seen from above, it must look as if a huge snake is crawling toward the old river road.

We push against the grass, fall forward, lunge, and crawl. Sweat streams, runs in rivulets down our backs, mixes with blood from slices of the razor-sharp blades, stings our eyes and open wounds. Black camouflage paint runs down our faces and into our mouths; we can taste it, and blood. Our hearts pump and legs drive; the grass resists, as Nature fights us all the way.

Finally we part the last of the grass and peer out on the old river road. The road is a narrow, muddy track through the grass-sea. No vehicle has driven this road for years, and only the VC and NVA walk it. Khai and Bao take the lead heading down the road to the west, Vietnamese and Americans interspersed on both sides, spread out at five-meter intervals.

A terrible image begins to play in my mind as I walk, boots sucking mud. Ambush erupts from the grass, white-orange fire-bursts spitting from the green. We scream and our bodies jerk and dance grotesquely like torn rag dolls; we spin, fall, and lie still in blood-slime. Onto the road our lives run, and we become mud and grass again.

Another image comes, pulsing rhythmically with our march. The road explodes with mines, so easy to lay in the mud. We fly into the air and come down in pieces, blood spuming as from harpooned whales. We scream in Vietnamese and English before death claims us in cold embrace.

On we go, boots sucking with a sound like being eaten, grass hanging down by the side of the road, reaching, taking it back into itself. Ahead of me Viêt points down at the ground and looks back to catch my attention. I pass and see a big tiger track. Not long before, the tiger walked down the road ahead of us and turned into the grass on its own death mission.

"What a lamentable thing it is," Zeus said to the gods on Mount Olympus, "that men should blame the gods and regard us as the source of their troubles, when it is their own wickedness that brings them sufferings worse than any which Destiny allots them."[2]

At the point Khai and Bao drop and lie on their stomachs at the edge of a steep ravine sloping sixty feet down to a fast-flowing stream. We all come up and lie beside them, our bodies laid out as if for counting. An old bridge lies bomb-broken and scattered into the ravine. I lie to Viêt's right and stare down at the stream.

"Ho Chi Minh Trail!" Viêt breathes. The stream is the Trail; the Trail is the stream. Viêt points at another awesome sight. On the far bank many tracks suddenly rise from the water, climb the steep slope, and go on down the old river road. "VC," Viêt whispers. "*Many*, maybe a battalion."

I stare in fear and fascination. It is like being transfixed by a snake.

"Last night," Viêt whispers. "They didn't go down to the river crossing, so maybe they're camping near here."

Nobody moves. Finally Khai calls Viêt and Bao to a conference. While they whisper I look upstream to another fearsome sight: the tunnel made by the stream through the trees where the forest begins and the water comes dancing out. We'll have to enter that black-hole passage into the enemy's world; we'll be swallowed in it. Out of the forest we came long ago, Paleolithic-borne. Now we'll return, powerful, disobedient, and dangerous. This is deep play in the belly of the whale, this is where we'll dip our hands in blood.

Khai looks at Bao with the same fatalistic look I've seen come over Viêt. How many times have Khai and Bao looked at each other this way, knowing this moment may be the last? Khai adjusts the strap of his pith helmet, slings his AK across his back, goes over the edge, and begins climbing into the ravine. Bao follows, searching for foot- and handholds, then Than, Nam, and Viêt.

It's my turn. With each man down, the earth wears away, rocks and dirt tumbling to splash in the stream and muddy the water. It will be very difficult for the last man. Khai enters the water and approaches the tunnel with Bao close behind.

I make it and step into the stream as the last Grim Reaper starts down. One by one we leave open sky behind, enter the black hole, and wrap the forest around us like a womb. "Who goes to the mountains returns to his mother," Nguyen Du wrote in the Vietnamese epic *Truyên Kiêu*. We penetrate deeper.

Anxious eyes search enveloping leaves, black-painted hands grip cold-steel guns. Boots in the current, slippery rocks; I fall, and Viêt turns and warns me with a look. We Americans are too noisy, too slow. Walking up mountain streams in tropical jungle is not a normal part of our lives. Where are the concrete highways, chemically treated water, and land mostly stripped of trees?

We plunge deeper into the forest. We seem to be running both away from and toward something. We wind ourselves tighter in the great living tapestry and in the tense web of war. Bright moss shines on rocks polished by eons of flowing water, yet the forest looks young, like us.

Tiny air bubbles race each other down small waterfalls, float, eddy, spin, and vanish. Ferns bend from the stream banks, catching droplets of water. Vines hang, wrap themselves around trees, and reach for the light. Life pulsates, flows in interconnected rhythms and patterns, as we push on against the flow.

We bend and drink the cool, living water. We and the stream are exchanging fluids. Falls in the stream darken our uniforms like blood. The water cools our skin, fills our eyes, and sings in our adrenaline-laced brains. We climb toward Olympus, Prometheus-armed with steel and fire.

Viêt is nimble as a crawdad, balancing with his AK, jumping from rock to rock. His NVA uniform is still dry except from sweat. Sergeant Stevens behind me goes down, and his M-16 clacks on a rock. Viêt turns and warns us with a frown, then goes on leaping, balancing. The stream-tunnel is a cyclotron up which we hurl our atoms. We shall become as gods, just as the serpent said to Eve.[3] Denied return to the Garden, we shall *force* our way back in—and destroy Eden doing it.

Excitement surges back from the point. The Trail appears, abruptly rising from the stream, shining sandal-packed on the bank, rounding the stump of an immense tree broken and fallen across the water. The enemy battalion recently walked here, passing the trunk and then dropping back into the water.

Ahead, a huge boulder makes a pool deeper than our heads. We inch along a narrow ledge, fingers gripping, bodies pressed against the rock. VC and NVA pass here, including women warriors, and Bru mountain tribeswomen, too, baskets on their backs, breasts brushing living rock.

> Who will prefer the jingle of jade pendants if
> He once has heard stones growing in a cliff?[4]

We descend into the water, baggy camouflage pants heavy-hanging, water-prints dripping from the ledge into the pool, and small silver fish darting to investigate the signs of our passing. We are stiff forms in a world of sinuous shapes. The forest here moves in patterns like Vietnamese spirit-women in a sensuous dance. Vines and trees intertwine, leaves interlace, wind sighs, branches groan, birds and insects sing. Life streams in wondrous array as forward we go, weapons hard-pointed. The stream flows around and beyond us.

An electric wave passes back from the point; on a small gravel bar are charred sticks and ashes. Last night young NVA sat around this fire, brown faces in dancing yellow light, cooking manioc roots. Where are they now, waiting to kill us? Ahead, the stream widens and a small fragment of sky appears above a long gravel bar. The trail crosses the bar, twenty steps for boots to breathe, slosh, and ooze. Viêt points at more man-sign: propaganda leaflets, every one torn in two. This is unusual: the enemy uses our leaflets for toilet paper. Viêt picks up one, safe conduct pass on one side and B-52 raining bombs on the other. The leaflets look as if they have been ripped in anger at this airborne littering of the forest floor or the sight of the B-52 dropping destruction on the land. Are the leaflets a message to us?

The time has now come . . . when we will listen or we will die.[5]

The Trail drops into the stream. Seeing Viêt and the ARVN ahead makes me feel as if I've walked up behind an NVA patrol. Soon their last man will turn, see me, and fire. Viêt disappears beyond the bend. I look back: Stevens is around the bend to the rear. I'm alone in the forest. The first time I flew over the Trail, with Air America in '66, I had this fantasy; it just started to play itself out as my head lolled against the window and I looked down at the forests and mountains of the Central Highlands, and I knew the Trail was down there. The plane's engines start to sputter, and the pilot looks back, concerned. We go down and make a soft landing in the trees. The others get away in another direction, and I'm alone in the forest. I find the Trail, I hide beside it, I watch the VC pass.

I shake my head and try to clear the vision. Fantasies like that can be dangerous.

Alone with the spirits of the forest and the past, I round the bend and see everything changed. Khai and Bao crouch with

Viêt behind a boulder gesturing to me wild-eyed. Nam and Than are now at the point, lying and aiming their AKs around the next bend. I wade up fast and crouch in the shelter of the boulder, while behind, Sergeant Stevens hand-signals his men to take cover along the banks of the stream.

Khai and Bao look as if they've seen the Abyss. They both whisper excitedly at once, in bursts I can hardly understand: "We almost walked into them! Maybe a battalion!"

I look upstream, expecting to see NVA coming.

"Very near!" they whisper. "Talking, chopping! They must be camped up there!"

I listen hard but hear only the rush of the stream.

"We better go back," Khai and Bao whisper, and Viêt concurs. "Go back downstream and call in Phantoms, gunships, artillery."

Visions of the Machine in the forest form in my mind, explosions in the trees and dirty white smoke flowers blooming. Torn land, going back: I don't *want* to go back. Viêt looks at me in anguish: he knows I'm thinking about going on.

"Give me that," I say to Viêt, and I point to his NVA helmet. "And your AK."

Viêt says as I put on the helmet, "You don't look much like an NVA."

"I want to make sure," I whisper. "I want to see. You can stay here."

Khai and Bao exchange looks; they don't want to return to where they heard the terrible sounds. Viêt edges into the brush and sits down; he's not even considering going.

Khai rises. "We'll take you there," he says, and he and Bao look at each other again. This could be the end.

Khai leads, then Bao and me. I pull the helmet low over my forehead. I know I don't look much like an NVA; I just want a split-second advantage if we meet them. And I don't want to go back.

The tranquil waterway leading to the uttermost ends of the earth flowed somber under an overcast sky—seemed to lead into the heart of an immense darkness.[6]

I wade forward, every sense about to burst. We round one bend and then another. The forest presses in from all sides and hangs heavy overhead. I'm alone on a short straight stretch, then see Khai and Bao wedged between two boulders beside the stream, looking back with fearful faces. I wade up and squeeze in between them.

"Here's where we heard," Khai whispers in a voice like death. We listen hard. I hear the rush of my blood and the dance of water over rocks. Khai and Bao begin to look uncomfortable.

"We heard them here, we did," Khai whispers.

I believe them, but I also know what tricks the forest can play. Finally, a distant sound comes through the thick green curtain: slow, lazy chopping, and voices—maybe—floating on the wind.

"They were closer before," Khai says. "And there were many. We're not lying."

"I know," I say. I try to reassure them; they feel they've let me down. What is it like for them up here? If I felt hyperalive and terror-struck five men and several stream-bends back, what is it like for Khai and Bao here on the constantly moving point, the thin red line, the razor's edge between life and death?

"I want to go on," I say. "I'll walk point if you want."

Khai's fatalistic look comes again; Bao also wears a death mask. "No," Khai says. "We'll go first. Bao, go back and bring up the others."

Khai and I wait. The chopping comes floating on the stream again. It sounds high up the slope that drops to the water, maybe over the ridge.

"It was closer before," Khai says. "It was."

The others catch up, and Khai leads on. The stream begins

to change. Its banks narrow, its bed tilts up, and its flow tumbles faster. Everything looks younger here, closer to the source. Filled with fear, I feel a kind of ecstasy, too. I'm irresistibly drawn on, deeper into wildness.

> Nature was here something savage and awful, though beautiful. I looked with awe at the ground I trod on, to see what the Powers had made there, the form and fashion and material of their work. This was that Earth of which we have heard, made out of Chaos and Old Night. Here was no man's garden, but the unhandselled globe. It was not lawn, nor pasture, nor mead, nor woodland, nor lea, nor arable, nor waste-land. It was the fresh and natural surface of the planet Earth, as it was made forever and ever. . . . There was there felt the presence of a force not bound to be kind to man. It was a place for heathenism and superstitious rites, —to be inhabited by men nearer of kin to the rocks and to wild animals than we . . . here not even the surface had been scarred by man, but it was a specimen of what God saw fit to make this world. . . . What is this Titan that has possession of me? Talk of mysteries!—Think of our life in nature,—daily to be shown matter, to come in contact with it,—rocks, trees, wind on our cheeks! the solid earth! the actual world! the common sense! Contact! Contact! *Who* are we? *Where* are we?[7]

Suddenly, the Trail appears, rises boldly from the water, climbs the bank, and curves like a question mark into the trees. Khai, Bao, and Viêt whisper standing in the water while Than and Nam keep watch. Like a sinister, awful power, the Trail comes out of its tunnel in the trees, runs down to the stream, and disappears, flowing like a spirit down to the river and on to the sea, where it rises again, blown back to the mountains and beginning it all again while we stand in the water and break the flow.

Viêt whispers with eyes wide that the Trail will climb to the saddle between Hills 300 and 320, drop to the second stream, and go on to the camp. "We have to be very quiet now," Viêt says. "Tell the Americans."

Khai begins to climb the bank on the Trail, then Bao, Than, and Nam. I follow after Viêt. I feel the Trail under my boots, pulsating up my legs. My heart pumps nitro bursts with each electromagnetic surge. My blood rushes audibly—too loud! My boots scuff heavily, my feet feel made of lead. My body bulks too big for the forest; I shrink up inside and grip my gun. My thoughts roar, my breath chuffs, my eyelids click—too loud! My synapses are lit up all over, my nerves flash electric across the gaps, my eyes burn into the multiple Salome veils of green. Whose head will be on the platter tonight, who will divide the kingdom?

Viêt looks back and frowns: we're making too much noise. Here no stream-rush hides our passing, no wind ripples the leaves. In the deep, rocky stillness our wet camouflage clothes whisper and our body-sounds echo inside our fevered heads. The stones, the trees—they're watching, passing the warning to the Rocket Company's camp: enemy coming! Prepare!

The Trail slants steeply as it climbs toward the saddle. We shift rifles from right to left hands, balance, poise, lean into the curves, try to look at both sides of the Trail at once, wince at the sound of brushed branches, booted rocks, click of metal on plastic. The trees shiver as we pass: the Angel of Death is coming near.

Viêt seems to float up the Trail like a ghost, without effort, without sound. He rounds the next bend and is gone. I look back. I'm alone on another straight stretch, Stevens not yet appearing behind. The forest is still, breathless.

Suddenly the world erupts in savage firing around the bend, heavy automatic hammering shattering the silence, ripping leaves and man. I dive to the ground without thought, just pure action, and bury my face in dirt and leaves as the heavy firing continues, tearing the jungle to tatters. My mind explodes up around the bend: Viêt and the ARVN, dead! Viêt! Viêt is dead!

I see their bodies riddled. God, why do they keep shooting? They're dead!

Now they'll be coming for us! I begin low-crawling backward down the Trail like a crab. I twist and see Stevens and behind him the lieutenant doing the same, all of us blown back by the force of the firing.

Again in my mind I see the bodies punctured—by .50-caliber, it seems, the sound is so heavy. God, why do they keep shooting?

I look up. Movement on the Trail ahead. NVA! No, Viêt! Viêt comes backing down the Trail, firing his AK from the hip into the jungle in bursts. Viêt has killed the ARVN! And now he's coming for us!

Viêt turns and sees me lying on the ground. He waves me up, saying, "Advisor, come!"

I think, "Now it's *my* turn." But I scramble up anyway and run, with the same feeling of doom I've seen in him. Now is *my* time: here comes the steel, tearing through the gut. Death is coming for *me*.

I run around the bend and then stop as if hit by a hammer. Ahead a tableau of death electric burns in the forest. A man lies twisted on the Trail, blown back by a terrific force. Khai stands over him, and for a moment everything is still. I feel the scene seared into my mind: leaves, Viêt, Khai, the dead man, the Trail etched forever in the skein of time, and yet in a way already gone, flying in light waves out through the universe. The Earth seems stopped, everything frozen: trees, light, life, sound. Then Khai begins to throw up in the bushes, the forest vibrates, and the Earth turns again. Now everything begins to happen at once.

Viêt and I run up to Khai, and Sergeant Stevens comes up and peers over our shoulders. The lieutenant appears behind the sergeant, and other Grim Reapers keep anxious watch behind.

"Where are Bao, Nam, Than?" I say.

"I'm sorry," Khai gasps. "We wanted to capture him. We tried, but he went for his pistol the moment he saw us. He knew we weren't NVA."

I look down at the man, trying not to see his face. "Where are Bao, Nam, Than?"

"Chasing the VC," Khai says. "There were at least four more. They ran back down the Trail. We met them right here, like this." Khai holds his hand in front of his face. Tough veteran Khai, who's seen more death than most morticians, looks as if the life has been torn out of him, too.

"I'm sorry," he says again. "We didn't want to kill him."

"I shot him, too," Viêt says.

Khai looks hard at Viêt. "No, Bao. Not you."

I glance down at the dead man again, trying not to look at his face. At first I see no wounds. He has straight black hair swept back as if by the shock of contact. He looks about forty. He's lean, strong, and brown, a Trail man. He wears a khaki shirt and black shorts. His legs are muscular—now I see a wound. His right leg is horribly twisted back, and below the knee is a big black hole with, behind it, blood-smeared bone sticking out. His head is turned slightly, cheek nestling against the earth. His presence is powerful among us.

Bao comes running down the Trail, a Soviet officer's leather belt and holster flopping at his waist. He's wild-eyed and streaming war-energy: "Come on! Let's go get them!"

Khai starts to run up the Trail with Bao, but I grab his arm and say, "No! Maybe ambush! Bring Nam and Than back."

Khai and Bao run up the Trail and are swallowed by the vibrating trees. Sergeant Stevens and I look at the dead man. Everything still seems to be happening at once, kaleidoscope pieces falling fast.

"We've got to search him."

Stevens and I kneel on opposite sides of the dead man as if

we were praying. Neither of us wants to look at his face, touch the warmth in his skin, or let his spirit get into our brains. Somehow we begin going through his pockets, reaching into the dark recesses of his shirt and shorts and pulling out a pen, notebook, knife, and vial of sulfanilamide. Behind me, I'm vaguely aware of Viêt gathering everything up.

Something is lodged deep in the dead man's left shorts pocket. I try not to feel the warmth as I grope in the terrible warm dark, my fingers reaching down his hard thigh on the other side of the thin cloth and closing around something metal. Trembling, I draw it out, hold it in both hands and pry it open. It's a tin of cooked rice, densely packed, and still warm from a fire, probably at the Rocket Company's camp. In the rice I see the man.

"We've got to get his pack off."

Now we have to work near his shoulders. We try not to look at his face or touch his skin. His head hangs forward as we pull and tug. We can't get the pack off.

"We'll have to turn him over."

We roll him face down on the Trail, strip his pack off, and dump its contents on the ground. More vials of sulfanilamide spill out, a pair of NVA pants, and a U.S. Army poncho. Behind me, Viêt gathers everything up.

A leather thong around the dead man's neck is attached to something hanging against his chest. I tug and pull but can't get it out. He's lying on it, pressing it against the glowing, packed earth of the Trail.

"We have to roll him again."

We try again not to look at his face as we roll him on his back. I insert my fingers under the thong and feel the warm, smooth skin of his neck. I pull but the thong is stuck.

"Give me your knife," I say to Stevens.

I saw at the thong, trying hard not to hurt the dead man's neck. The thong finally parts and I pull out a large leather map case in waterproof plastic. I dump everything on the Trail. Viêt gathers up letters, Hanoi newspapers, and documents in code. One thing more: I pull it out and Stevens and I stare in horror and fascination. It's a notebook with a large color picture of Ho Chi Minh's face on the cover. In Ho's forehead, just above the right eye, is a bullet hole. This is the shot that killed him.

I hold the notebook and look at the hole. The dead man had walked the Trail with Ho's picture over his heart. Uncle Ho, dead just a year, had lived on in this forest man—had continued walking the Trail that bore his name and would go on living and walking here long after we were gone.

The ARVN run back down the Trail and whisper breathlessly over the dead man's body. "The VC ran away! Come on, let's go get them!"

Sergeant Stevens, the lieutenant, and I think it's a bad idea. "Let's get the hell outa here," the lieutenant says.

I translate to the Vietnamese: "We're going back now!"

Stevens and I roll the dead man's body off the Trail and into the bushes, trying not to look at his sharp brown face for the last time. Then we scoop up the medicine vials and throw them into in the jungle.

"He's got the documents," the lieutenant says, pointing at Viêt. "I saw him stuffing some in his shirt and throwing others away. He said they were no good, at least I think that's what he said."

This is troubling, like the VC walking here on an odd-numbered day, but I can't deal with it now. We take off running down the Trail, Americans leading, Vietnamese behind. We balance with our rifles, leap over rocks, and twist with the bends, heedless of boot-clumping noise, the ten commandments of gun safety, and five-meter interval of march. This is not a controlled descent; it is more like flying.

Images flash in my mind as I run behind the sergeant. I see the VC burst into the Rocket Company's camp with news of the killing. The counterrecon teams quickly form, burning with vengeance and thirsting for blood.

> And Caesar's spirit, ranging for revenge,
> With Atè by his side come hot from hell,
> Shall in these confines with a monarch's voice
> Cry "Havoc," and let slip the dogs of war.[8]

We run down into the stream and whisper wild-eyed, with water swirling around our legs. "Why do you stop?" Viêt says. "We have to go on. Maybe they're coming after us now."

The lieutenant wants to climb into the trees, look for an open area, and call for extraction. Stevens and I also don't like the idea of going back the same way we came: surely the VC will be waiting. The ARVN pile up behind us, want to know why we've stopped, and cast fearful glances back up the Trail.

"No good!" Khai says. "We have to keep going. Move fast!"

The lieutenant radio-talks to a Barky FAC, a forward air controller in a light observation plane. The Barky can see what looks like a grassy area to the west. We'll take to the trees and try to make it and get out of the forest before night. Viêt and the ARVN protest; they want to race darkness down the stream and call for extraction from the river. We overrule them. Our point goes upstream a few meters and plunges into the trees.

"Last man in, cover our sign," Sergeant Stevens says.

Viêt and the ARVN come along grumbling. "Big mistake," Viêt mutters behind me. "Too noisy, too slow. The VC will catch us for sure."

We fight through the green tangle as shadows deepen. Viêt goes up and down our line, freeing us from vines. The ARVN follow sullenly. I begin to see Viêt is right: we'll never make extraction before dark. But why is Viêt so eager to go back down the stream? Surely the NVA will radio ahead and wait in ambush where the stream rushes out of the trees and the bridge lies broken by the old river road.

We pull ourselves from tree to tree to what seems to be the top of a hill. The lieutenant talks again to the Barky FAC. The pilot wants to get a fix on us so he can guide us to the grassy area. "Find a break in the canopy," he says, "and put out air panels."

Sergeant Stevens lays out fluorescent orange squares of cloth under a small gap in the leaves. The pilot still can't see us, so the sergeant moves the panels to another break in the canopy. Viêt and the ARVN complain that the plane overhead is marking us for the VC.

The Barky sees the air panels and radios that the grassy area is still two ridges away. The plane drones on, drawing sound-circles around us.

"We have to go on." Viêt says. "Keep moving. And tell the airplane to go away."

We crash across the top of the hill and fight our way down the other side, with darkness falling all around. We break out into another stream, a thin, silver black thread in the enfolding dark green tapestry. We stand in the water and whisper. Viêt pulls my sleeve, his eyes wide and moon face shining.

"We have to follow this stream," he says.

"No good," I say. "It probably flows back into the Trail-stream."

"It does!" he says. "Near here. We've got to get out of here tonight. We have to follow the streams."

Khai and Bao agree. I translate to Sergeant Stevens. All around us, Nature is going into night mode with the great turning of the Earth. Stevens and I agree with Viêt, but the lieutenant wants to get into an NDP. The other Grim Reapers back up Stevens.

"OK, go," I say to Viêt, and I cast my eyes downstream, where the water curves and vanishes.

Viêt and the ARVN take off fast-wading, nearly running,

jumping from rock to rock. We keep pace as best we can, all making headlong flight downstream. Just as Viêt said, we soon meet the Trail-stream. Now we'll go back in our own continually flowing away footsteps, back down toward the river, down to meet death? There is a certain sound of boots going upstream; downstream it is different. Instead of forcing our way against the current, we're racing it, sliding down cascades and landing in frothy pools. All around, the jungle world reaches, draws us into its spreading net of night. Ahead of me, Viêt seems to float over water and stones like a dragonfly. Ahead of him, Nam, the last ARVN not wet from falls, goes down with a splash and jumps up streaming.

I focus on my feet and the rocks passing below, some bald, others with long, bright green moss like goddesses' hair flowing. Sometimes images of what happened flash in my mind. Who was the dead man? I heard Viêt say, "Dr. Son," when he was going through the documents, but Dr. Son was young and from Hanoi; this man was older, with many years in the forest. The Soviet officer's pistol marked him as someone important, that was for sure. Like Stevens and me, Viêt seemed not to want to look at the dead man, yet he tried to take credit for killing him. I fall again and scramble up streaming.

It's almost dark in the stream-tunnel. Black trees lean and branches reach like giant spiders as the web of night is woven over our heads. The stream flows like black blood. All the world is turning the color of our painted faces, and soon there'll be no streaks or smudges, not a wrinkle in the seamless black.

The lieutenant splashes up behind. "Tell them to stop," he pants, jerking his eyes to Viêt and the ARVN. "It's too dark to go on. We gotta get into the trees, set up our NDP."

Viêt hurries back to see why we've stopped, and the ARVN look back in anguish: What now?

Stevens wades up and we whisper with the lieutenant about the NDP.

Viêt explodes: "We're almost there! Don't stop! Five minutes more and we'll be out of the forest."

Stevens and I agree with Viêt, while the lieutenant tries to convince the other Grim Reapers. We continue to whisper about the NDP.

"We've got to go now!" Viêt whispers. "We can make it! Call in helicopters and go back!"

Stevens tells the lieutenant, "You can do what you want. We're going on."

We all take off after Viêt and the ARVN. It's almost completely dark. The stream-tunnel in full night must be a terrifying place, where gods and titanic forces seethe, ghosts and spirits creep and moan, and the tiger and snake move in the black witches' cauldron.

Viêt falls. He loses his balance on a slippery rock and splashes into a foaming black pool. At least I know he's human. He gets up fast, glances back at me with an embarrassed look, and goes on jumping from rock to rock.

Suddenly I see ahead a circle of light like the exit of a burial cave. Khai goes through, ready to shoot, then Bao, Than, Nam, and Viêt. Now the ambush will explode, I think, from the high banks and the broken bridge, spurts of fire from the black grass, hot metal flames licking, penetrating us.

I stumble toward the light circle, pass through the opening, leave the forest's protective shroud, and emerge under a forbidding gray-black sky. Open sky for choppers to fly. But surely the VC are waiting, following. Yes, waiting for the choppers. *Then* they'll cut us down.

Everything moves slow-fast, boots heavy, legs and heart pumping, mind moving in molasses-time, brain flashing in white-heat explosions. The open sky is a joy-burst, but fear hangs down like the broken bridge, the heavy sky, and the head-bent grass.

Viêt and the ARVN lead us climbing the sixty-foot bank to the river road, pushing powerfully with slim, hard legs. We cling exposed like insects on the steep slope, our backs exposed to bullet streams from the opposite bank. *Now* the VC will open up, I think, and watch us pirouette and slow-motion fall, spouting red like whales to crash in the water and slowly bump and bob downstream.

I grab gnarly roots and rocks, grasp thick tufts of grass, and pull myself past the tumbled-down bridge. I boot-thrust into earth, breath rasping. My hands pull, claw, dig as I balance, teeter, drive up, fear-burning. I am so exposed! My back is so easy a target, camouflage cloth and skin so thin, flesh so soft for penetration. Soil and rocks fall away, and grass clumps go with them, choking the stream. We're making a new trail up the bank for the NVA to follow. One by one we throw ourselves over the top and flow fast like ghosts down the old river road.

The sky is heavy with an impending thunderstorm. The grass beside the road blows, bends, and reaches. The images I had before of ambush and mines play themselves out again in my mind. Somewhere near here the tiger walked; now where does he stalk and wait?

Viêt fast-leads toward Hill 110. He knows good landing zones; so do the NVA. The night goes black with no stars. The storm is nearing, building, wind whipping the grass in a supernatural pagan dance. The world is full of spirits, *mana,* revelations. Down and up the road goes, almost a mile to Hill 110. The hill rises before us now like a sacrificial pyramid.

Viêt, Khai, and Bao whisper at 110's base, then begin to climb, pushing through grass, AKs jutting forward. *This* is where the NVA will hit—when the choppers come roaring in for us—in Hammurabi's ancient law of retribution, only the NVA will take many for one, and two helicopters, too.

We are dark, thick shapes forcing our way up breast-shaped Hill 110. Everywhere man advances, everywhere Nature retreats.

In ragged-patch grass on top, where bombs have long ago scythed away life, we kneel and whisper. Sergeant Stevens gives quick orders, sends Grim Reapers and ARVN to form a perimeter, and gets on the radio to ask why the delay in our request for extraction.

Bad news comes in static crackle. The Machine says no to a night pull; it's too risky, and the thunderstorm is about to break.

Stevens hides his anger but lets his fear show and voices as real our ghost-suppositions: "Be advised we believe we are being pursued. We may not last till morning."

Over the radio in the clear Stevens has put the onus on brigade: if they don't come to get us tonight and we die, it will look very bad for them. The Machine is silent for a while, emitting nothing but snakelike hiss. I imagine scrambling, calling, requests going as high as Cobra Six.

Finally the radio comes to life again, as someone pushes a faraway squelch button: "Grim Reaper Seven, Red Devil Two. Be advised one bird is on the way. Repeat, only one chopper is available. You'll have to go out on two trips."

Stevens whispers as he puts the radio down, "That means the second trip people could be in a hurt. Only one fair way to do it: last in means first out. Who came in on the last bird, get ready to take the first trip out."

"Roger that."

I crawl through the grass to tell Việt, Khai, and Bao. Nam and Than will go out on the first trip with the lieutenant and four Grim Reapers. The rest of us will be alone on the hill for an hour after being marked by an inferno of sound.

I lie by myself in the perimeter wondering if I'll die tonight. I see in my mind the VC creep up, slam a B-40 into the returning chopper, and drop us all in twisted metal and flames. We become another burnt offering to Moloch and all the ancient war gods, smoke rising like a signal from the scarred hill, Nature suffering again from the deep play of man.

I lie aiming my rifle into the night, looking with burning eyes, listening headache hard for man-sounds. I think again of the dead man lying in the leaves. Who will find him first, NVA or the tiger? Chopper sound comes from across the river, Machine-heartbeat growing louder, telling the NVA where we are. They'll rush through the night to get us, running, surging up the hill. Grim Reapers move and whisper in black as the lieutenant forms the first team and big gaps appear in our perimeter. Nam and Than come to Khai and Bao, bend, and whisper good-bye. The radioman sets up a special recon strobe light which begins flashing and stabbing the night in strange, swinging patterns. First sound and now light mark us.

I crawl to Stevens and whisper, "Do you think that's a good idea?"

"It's not supposed to give away our location on the ground," he whispers. "I know what you mean, but we gotta do it. Anyway, when that Huey comes in, the NVA're not gonna have any doubts about where we are."

The light fantastic bounces wildly around the sky, and the chopper roars in like a big black monster materializing out of the storm. The noise sweeps over and envelops us, blasting away our senses. Down the Huey comes, rotor wind whipping the grass. I squirm low and tight against the earth, brace myself to shoot, fight wildly in frenzy, die screaming over the Machine-sound. *Now,* in unbearable chopper roar, the NVA will leap from the grass and pour hot fire and molten metal into us. Life ends, death begins. My mind whirls away in the strobe-flash black storm-gathering night.

The first team runs for the hovering chopper, Vietnamese and Americans throwing themselves in, flying away, banking sharply for the river, distant heartbeat finally fading. They made it. We lie in the grass and wait, and what seems like a long time passes. The night is full of wild and ominous Nature sounds. Distant thunder rumbles like artillery; sheet lightning flashes like rockets exploding. The wind blows cool on sweaty brows; ears and eyes burn into the grass. The pressure builds; soon, it seems, the night will split into jagged fragments.

Sergeant Stevens and I crawl together and whisper.

"Maybe the chopper's not coming back."

"I'm stayin' off the net. The NVA counterrecon teams have radio directional finders."

"Maybe we better head for the river, hide in the grass for the night, and try to walk back in the morning."

"Let's hope the chopper comes."

We decide to wait a little longer.

Below us the river is large and thick like a glowing snake in the lightning flashes. We lie hard-pressed against the earth as Nature's night symphony plays above us, clouds, wind, and thunder. We lie on the grass-sea edge of one of the last great wild forest areas in the world and wait for the Machine.

Finally the sound of the chopper comes. Technonoise rises, overwhelms our listening into Nature. If the NVA rush us now, we'll hear only the last heartbeat of the Huey. Man's sound rules now in the rumbling belly of the whale. I imagine the VC moving in fast-forward through the grass, hard-bodied brown men suddenly bursting from the thunderous black curtain to kill us and the chopper on top of the hill.

Stevens sets off the wild-flashing strobe, and the chopper forms out of the night like a great glowing insect. It beats the air furiously, carbonized dinosaur-world burning prodigiously at white heat, blasting back into Nature in eardrum-deadening noise and toxic smoke. Behold, Machine-deliverance!

We jump up and run, senses bursting in flash-time. We hurl ourselves into the Huey, the door gunner grabbing our belts and hauling us aboard. The pilot pulls away, banks hard, and beats for the river.

Jammed and tumbling together on the floor, our every mole-

Batman Caper, by Wailehua Gray.

cule strains with the chopper for the margin of space between us and the ground that says, "Safe! They can't get us now."

We burst with joy, shake hands, slap backs, laugh, roll across the sky with the lightning and thunder. Life! Victory! We're heroes! And we're *alive!*

The dead man's pistol is a strange, alien thing here on the hurtling chopper. It comes from another world, out there. So do Viêt's and the ARVNs' NVA uniforms and AKs, but they have been in our possession for some time and turned to our service. The Soviet pistol comes new from out there; it's fresh with the feeling of *them*. It is in a way the man who died, hanging now like a scalp at Bao's belt.

The chopper's crew begin shouting bids at Bao over the roar: they want the pistol. The pilot joins in, and the price quickly goes to $250, a fortune for an ARVN. Bao shakes off all the bids, confers with Khai, unbuckles the belt, and hands it to me.

I don't understand; I wasn't even bidding. I guess Bao wants me to look at it, maybe so I'll make an offer. I hold it. The belt is brown, with a red star on the metal buckle. Khai gestures to me to pull the pistol out. I open the flap of the holster. Like the belt, it's leather and well-made. Attached to the side of the holster is a small sheath for an extra magazine and another for a cleaning rod. Everyone looks as I pull the pistol from the holster and hold it in my hand. I feel it pulsing with enormous power.

"Three hundred big ones!" the crew chief shouts to Bao. "I'll give you three hundred in green when we land!"

Bao shakes his head. I didn't know he knew English. I look at the pistol in a kind of daze, oblivious to the pounding chopper beat and shouted, rising bids. The pistol is beautiful, black, magic, and deadly. It's a K-54, with *CCCP* and a black star on the grip. What kind of journey brought it to arrive now in my hand? Across the Soviet Union on the Trans-Siberian Railway, down through China to Kunming, across the North Vietnamese border, and south at the belt of the dead man on the Ho Chi Minh Trail? How many bullets had it fired, how many men had it executed with a quick shot to the head? I slide it back in the holster and hand it back to Bao.

Bao shakes his head; he doesn't want it. I try to give it to Khai. "No!" Khai shouts. "We give it to you!"

I don't understand. I try again: Bao, Khai.
More shouts: "No, for you! We give it to you!"
I'm still dazed. Why me? I don't get it. They could get big
money for this. It strikes me as very un-Vietnamese; I wonder
what they want from me?
"Put it on!" Khai shouts. "See how it looks!"
Immersed in mystery, I wrap it around my waist and fasten
the red-star buckle. It feels good, the leather holster at my
side, the pistol heavy at my hip, the power of the dead man
entering me. Who was he who held it in his hands, sighted his
brown eye down its black barrel, squeezed his finger, and felt
it buck in his hand? It had hung against his hip; now it's
pressed against mine. It had bounced with him each step down
the Trail; now it flies with me in an American helicopter. That
man was dead because of me, because I got out of Viêt what he
knows and protected him from Rang, because I pushed and
prodded brigade, because I went to Anh to save the operation,
because I insisted to Khai that we go on. If not for all that, the
dead man would still be walking the Trail—and perhaps using
the K-54 to kill Khai, Bao, Viêt, or me. How will *I* use the
pistol now, and when will I join him, and what will we say to
each other when we meet?

I ride through the sky in a dream. Black camouflage paint
streaks my Celtic-Teutonic face like the coal across Industrial-
Revolution European skies, like soot streaks in the rivers, too,
as my peasant-farmer forbears steamed off for America's blue
skies, blue waters, and open land. In the darkness gleam the
eyes of Asians: the snake, the tiger, the ghost of the dead man,
and all their long line. We beat on, chopper into the exhaust-
smoke darkness, back to the base and the Machine.

The reaches opened before us and closed behind . . . seemed to
lead into the heart of an immense darkness.[9]

Viêt and an unidentified major ready to fly recon on the Trail.

The author and Viêt before the raid on Triêu Phong.

Viêt and the "NVA."

The author on Firebase Ann.

Viêt, Ramos, Captain Mao, and a 3rd Battalion advisor.

The author near the Ho Chi Minh Trail.

The author, Viêt, and ARVN on the old river road.

Ramos

The author and Captain Mao.

The "new" Viêt.

CHAPTER 4

THE GLOOMY WOOD AND
THE POISON TREES

In the midway of this our mortal life
I found me in a gloomy wood, astray
Gone from the path direct; and e'en to tell
It were no easy task, how savage wild
That forest, how robust and rough its growth,
Which to remember only, my dismay
Renews, in bitterness not far from death.
Yet, to discourse of what good there befell,
All else will I relate discover'd there.

—Dante, *Inferno*

We land on Pioneer Pad and are greeted by Herndon and Lukitsch like heroes. Other 1/11 GIs gather, too, to see the "NVA."

"Where's my boy Viêt?" Herndon shouts among the tumult, and he and Viêt embrace like concerned father and returning warrior-son.

Husky Lukitsch beams and shakes hands all around. Success! One important VC was killed, valuable documents and one K-54 were seized, and all are back safely. Everyone eyes my K-54, and more offers of big bucks fly, but I reject them all. Inside, I'm strutting; outside, Mr. Humble. Joy burns bright, life explodes on dark Pioneer Pad as the rescue Huey lifts off and flies away, exhausts orange red against the black sea of night. Does my mind fly out to the forest, to the dead man lying in the leaves? Through tiger or in shallow grave, he returns soon to the jungle.

Viêt pulls the documents out of his shirt and hands them

to a translator from military intelligence. I start to ask Viêt about the rest, but a jeep driver pulls up with a message for Herndon: "The general wants to see you, sir. Major Lukitsch, too."

A dark cloud passes over our celebration: this could be big trouble.

"Maybe he wants to congratulate us," Herndon says hopefully. "You better come, too," he adds to me. "He probably wants to hear all about the operation."

"Not *all*, I hope," Lukitsch says.

Whatever spell was on Herndon and Lukitsch at our departure is off now as flashbulbs pop, GIs taking pictures of Viêt and the ARVN. We climb into the jeep, Herndon riding shotgun, Lukitsch and me in back. The dead man's pistol rides heavy on the right.

"If he asks me, I'm not going to lie," I say.

"I wouldn't want you to," Herndon says.

"Maybe he won't ask," Lukitsch adds.

I feel powerful, invincible. I'm bursting with an urge to tell the general, throw it in his face: "Yes! we defied your orders and dressed as NVA, and that's why we're alive and he's dead, and no! we aren't playing games out there."

"He'll find out anyway," I say from the dark back of the jeep.

"Let's hope it's after I'm back in the World," Herndon says. He's near retirement.

"Or in another life," adds Lukitsch, who has several months to go in Viet Nam and years to go in his military career.

We talk of other things. The driver gears down and crunches to a stop in a parking area by a sandbag mountain, General Burke's office, the minotaur's lair. Here lives the mind of the Machine.

A tall captain, looking incredibly squared away for Viet Nam, comes out of the passageway leading into the bunker.

"The general's aide," Herndon says, sotto voce, as we disembark from the jeep.

The captain leads us down the passageway, our boots clunking on the wood floor. Herndon enters first, then Lukitsch, then me. Wiry Burke rises from his desk and shakes our hands in a crunching grip. Except for his salt-and-pepper hair, Burke looks made of steel, like the tanks of his mechanized brigade. The captain steps in behind us and closes the door.

Burke smiles flint hard and waves us to chairs set up in a scimitar curve facing his desk. "Good operation," he says to Herndon. "Let's have the story."

Herndon nods to me and says, "Sir, since Mr. Stevens was there, I'll let him give you the details."

To my left, Lukitsch looks uncomfortable in his metal chair.

I begin to tell the story. Mostly I praise Viêt and the ARVN to the skies.

Burke interrupts. "We had people out there, too, didn't we?" he asks Herndon.

"Oh, yes, sir," Herndon says. "Two teams from our recon platoon. They did an excellent job, too. But Mr. Stevens is right: Mr. Viêt and the ARVN were really superb, crucial to the operation. We plan to put them in for Bronze, maybe Silver Stars."

Burke starts to say something, but a side door opens and an olive green Hermes, a spec 4 clerk, comes in and hands the captain a message.

"First read-out on the documents, sir," the captain says.

"Let me see that," Burke says.

Burke reads the Military Intelligence Detachment's initial report.

311645H Jan 70, YD 211386. Reinforced Recon/Killer Team VI accompanied by a Hoi Chanh and 4 ARVN from the 1st ARVN Regiment Recon Company ambushed 5 VC/NVA dressed in gray uniforms and pith helmets. The point man, who was carrying a pistol, medical supplies, numerous documents, and hot food, was killed. The Recon/Killer Team pursued the remaining enemy after the body was searched. Heavy movement was detected in the area of the contact and a Barky FAC, under gathering darkness and a tropical thunderstorm, covered the extraction of the Recon/Killer Team. One VC/NVA KIA, one pistol, two magazines, one diary, one leather belt, one poncho, one holster, and medical supplies were captured. The documents captured revealed that the individual was a Political Officer for Trieu Phong District.[1]

Burke discusses with Herndon and Lukitsch the details in the report and speculates on what more will be learned from the dead man's letters and other documents still being translated. My mind races away: "Political Officer for Trieu Phong District." I know who the dead man is! The political commissar is the Communist party leader assigned to all major VC and NVA units as counterpart to the military commander. This man was Viêt's political commissar! Viêt has told me many times about Têt in the VC—how he always cried for missing his family but had to hide so the commissar wouldn't see. "What would happen if he did?" I asked. "He would scold me," Viêt said, "maybe begin to doubt me, watch me, who knows?" Why didn't Viêt tell me who the man was? And was this why he, too, didn't want to look at him?

The pistol hangs heavy at my hip. How many political "errors" had it rectified?

Burke's gravel-hard voice cuts into my thoughts: "I want to hear more."

I'm burning to jerk everything into the light. I don't want to get Herndon and Lukitsch in trouble, but Burke will hear from someone: better to hear it from *me* and *now*.

I wax eloquent about the importance and impact of the operation; how we sowed doubt, fear, and confusion out

there; and how that could lead to more valuable ralliers like
Viêt.

Burke cuts me off again. He doesn't like hearing this from
me, a civilian. And he has smelled a rat. I sense more unease
in Lukitsch to my left.

"I can see sowing *fear* out there," Burke says. "But there
was no doubt or confusion about what we did. We went out
there and hit 'em where they live."

I feel it coming now. The long confrontation building with
Burke is about to explode.

"Oh, we sowed plenty of doubt and confusion," I say. "It's
like if you and your troops were getting shot at here on the
base, maybe on the way to the club or the mess hall."

"*Fear,* maybe" Burke granites. "Not doubt; not confusion.
We know who's doing it, and we go after 'em."

"They saw no Americans," I say. "We were down the
Trail."

"They saw ARVN," Burke says. "They heard American
weapons."

"No. They heard no American weapons."

Burke seems to levitate from his chair. He grows several
inches taller but remains sitting. His words come out like
marching Prussians: "What-kind-of-weapons-did-they-
hear?"

"AK-47s," I say. "Only AKs."

Still in levitated position, Burke traverses right like the
killer snout of an M-60, aims hard at Herndon and Lukitsch,
and says, in a voice exploding with anger, "What were my
orders? What did I say?"

Lukitsch is catatonic. His mouth is open, but nothing comes
out. He's rigid in his chair as if pinned there.

Herndon coughs and says something literally true but
absolutely incredible: "Uh, your orders were no black pajamas, sir, and those men weren't wearing black pajamas."

Burke can scarcely contain himself: "What-were-they-wearing?"

"Uh, NVA uniforms," Herndon says. "NVA gear."

"Jesus Christ!" Burke says, and he turns to Lukitsch. "Is that what you thought, too, Major? That 'no black pajamas' meant NVA uniforms are just fine? Is that what you thought?"

Lukitsch's face is red. He doesn't know what to say: he's damned both ways.

I feel I have to ride like a hero to their rescue. I dare to interrupt Burke's tirade. "I take full responsibility," I say. "I told Mr. Viêt and the ARVN to wear those uniforms. I felt it was the only way—"

Burke traverses back to me and blasts: "Let me tell you something. *I* am responsible for *everything* that goes on in this brigade. You are responsible for *nothing*."

Burke swings away from me as if I were an insignificant bug and bores in again on Herndon and Lukitsch: "You two will understand one thing: I command this brigade. My orders will be obeyed *to the letter,* or I will find officers who *will* obey. You understand?"

Herndon and Lukitsch nod like schoolboys and chorus, "Yes, sir."

Burke relaxes his jaws slightly. "In spite of that one deficiency," he says, "it was a good mission. Let's do more of it. But no enemy gear. Understand?"

"Yes, sir," Herndon and Lukitsch say.

Burke rises and we all stand. The captain makes a move, and we begin to shuffle toward the door. Suddenly the ceiling seems far too low, the walls too close. I want to explode out into the night.

Burke stops us at his desk. He pulls open his top left drawer, takes something out, and says to me, "We have a little token we give to our friends."

Burke steps around his desk and pins a metal red-diamond insignia to the collar of my camouflage shirt. It's the insignia of the 5th Mechanized Brigade. Burke's hard, lined face and bristly crew cut are near my shoulder as he works the metal points in and fastens the plastic stays. "There," he says, and he steps back and holds out his hand. "You're an honorary Red Devil now."

"I'm very honored to be one," I say, and we shake and try to crunch each other's hand bones.

The captain escorts us through the sandbag tunnel. The night is cool. Except for the pain in my hand, I feel I'm flying.

In the morning when it's light and safe enough to travel Highway One outside the base, I drive Việt and the ARVN back to Quang Tri City. We say our good-byes. It's a strange feeling—we've been so much a part of one another's lives. We plan to meet soon; Khai and Bao say they have something they want to ask me. I wonder if it has to do with the pistol?

I go home and put the AKs in my closet with the K-54. The NVA gear and my camouflage clothes I leave for my maid, Ba Thuy, to wash. I strip and try to wash the remnants of camouflage paint from my face and hands. "Out damned spot! Out, I say!" Lady Macbeth said in similar circumstances. I look in the mirror. I still see the face of the dead man.

Soon the Trail calls again and I cross the river, drive back to the base, and pull up in a cloud of dust before the 1/11 TOC. I duck into the opening and walk down the sandbag tunnel, boots thudding the chemically treated wood floor. The K-54 bulks at my hip, and the Red-Devil diamond is on my collar, blood-spot on camouflage green.

The radiomen look up when I enter, and one jerks his thumb to Lukitsch's office and says, "The major's in—wait'll you see what he's got in there."

Lukitsch rises from his desk with a smile. Behind him on the wall is a big full-color poster, Batman and Robin leaping, and the words, "Biff! Bam! Pow! Another *Batman* Caper!"

"Like it?" Lukitsch says. "One of my radiomen did it. Everybody heard about the general's chewing."

"No lasting damage?"

Lukitsch spreads his big hands. "I'm still here. The colonel, too. I can always go back to school, I guess."

I spread my map and present my plan. "We still don't know if the Rocket Company's camp is there, exactly where it is, or if it's still occupied. I suggest we take one team," I begin to point it out on the map, "land here above the Khe Ba Dang, climb this west ridge, and go down into the valley of the Khe Trai. We'll follow the stream to the Trail-crossing, I estimate two or three hours. From the crossing it's only ten minutes to the Rocket Company's camp."

"But recon only," Lukitsch says. "No raid. I don't think the general's ready yet for that."

"Recon only: no problem."

"Mr. Viêt's ready to go?"

Inwardly I take a breath. This is a crucial part of the presentation. I don't know if Lukitsch will go for this. "He's not going this time. I promised him he wouldn't have to go out during Têt. He's going to his uncle's house."

Lukitsch looks at the map and then me. "You sure you can find this place without him?"

"I know I can. He's told me all about it and we've done recon flights. All we have to do is follow the stream."

"Damn, I wish I could go," Lukitsch says. "I hate these staff jobs. OK, I'll try to sell it to brigade. But I emphasize: recon *only*. No more 'Batman capers.'"

"Not to worry," I say, and I look up at the poster and smile.

There's a big surprise: Lukitsch calls soon to say the recon's on. "One team, one chopper, three days. In and out. Locate the camp and confirm it's occupied. Sergeant Stevens's team will go; Tex is on R 'n' R."

I drive to the base and park near the dusty huts of the Recon Platoon. Stevens is alone in his hooch, sitting on his cot at the back writing a letter and listening to Johnny Cash's "Folsom Prison Blues" on his big tape deck. He looks up as I walk toward him. I'm dressed in my usual visiting attire, camouflage and K-54.

"It's on," I say.

"Damn!" he says.

Energy flows like lightning bolts between us.

"When?"

"Tomorrow. Lukitsch is calling you over for a briefing at ten today. I wanted to talk to you first." I unfold my map on his cot. We kneel on opposite sides of the bed like kids saying their prayers, or as we had knelt while searching the commissar's body. I tell Stevens the plan and trace it on the map with my finger.

He looks up, his hawk face sharp. "You sure we can find the camp without Viêt?"

"No problem," I say. "Just follow the stream. We've flown over it, too."

"Not *too* many times, I hope."

I look around; still no one in the hooch. I lower my voice. "I've got this idea; the fewer on the approach to the camp, the better."

Stevens lights up; he gets it right away. "Like how few are you thinkin'?"

"Like two."

"Damn!" Stevens says. "Quieter on the approach, faster on the getaway!"

"There it is."

"Hey, what do you say if it looks good, we hit the camp ourselves? The brigade'll probably never go back anyway, or if it does, it'll screw it up."

"You got it."

Stevens's enthusiasm takes a sudden dip, then rises again. "My team's not gonna like it. They'll wanta go, too. I won't tell 'em till we're out there—don't you tell anyone, either. Brigade would never go for it; Cobra Six would have a shit fit."

"Not to worry," I say.

"Know what?" Stevens says with his riverboat grin. "This sounds like another 'Batman caper.'"

I drive back to Quang Tri City and the *crachin* mist returns to the mountains, delaying the operation. My misgivings rise, lunar cycles turn, and Têt comes with its shadow-fears of 1968. Têt is the best time of the year for Vietnamese, but since '68, also the most fearful. Viêt is delighted to have his first family Têt in four years, and he invites me to his uncle's house for the first, most special day of Têt visiting.

I dress in my best civilian clothes and drive to the uncle's house, a small, poor home by the river, newly cleaned for Têt. Viêt comes out to meet me. He's dressed Vietnamese cool in new clothes and is wearing dark sunglasses on a cloudy day. Behind the house the river flows big from the recent rains in the mountains. Viêt is feeling good, the happiest I've seen him.

We sit, and uncle serves Têt cakes and Cokes with ice. Viêt knows something is about to happen, but not, I hope, exactly what.

"Sure I don't have to go this time?" he asks.

"Sure!" I say. "I guarantee it. One hundred percent!"

We laugh and sip our drinks. Uncle brings more special Têt food and offers me American cigarettes and beer. Viêt has been getting "black bag" money from the advisory team's S-2 for the intelligence he provides and the weapons we seize, but this Têt spending is far beyond that.

Viêt lapses into memories about past Têts in the VC, when he used to hide from the commissar and his mother and father were living. The more he talks, the more he sinks into a somber mood. Finally he says bitterly, "My mother and father should be living, they should be here. They died too young, away from their home, torn from their land." I don't stay long. I feel a kind of unease here and that both Viêt and the uncle are glad I'm going. Viêt walks me out to my Scout, puts his sunglasses on, and looks up and down the street. He's changing. I can see it in his clothes. He's smoking, too, and looking a little pudgy. He's dealing in the black market now; he gets me to buy him things at the PX that he sells for big profit. He's got other Americans doing it, too—GIs he's met on operations.

At the Scout on the empty street I see a flash of the old Viêt. He grabs my arm and says, "Thanks for not making me go on this operation. Being with Uncle at Têt—it's the best thing that's happened to me in five years."

"Be careful of Rang," I say. "You're taking big chances around town."

"I'm not afraid of him." he says in his comic voice. "I'm not afraid of anything. Besides, I know he's gone to Huê for Têt."

Suddenly Viêt gets serious and grips my arm hard. "Be careful on this operation. You won't have me to take care of you this time—and maybe they'll be waiting."

He looks upriver toward the distant mountains, hidden now in the mist. He drops my arm and the new Viêt returns: "Uh, can you buy me two more cases of Coke and three of beer, any kind? I can pay you in green; I got plenty. And two cartons of Salems and two Winstons. Just for Têt, you know."

I drive to Ba Thuy's house for more Têt visiting. Thuy lives in La Vang, on the south side of town, where the NVA rockets have been falling. Thuy is twenty-three, small, svelte, and attractive, a widow, like the legions all over Viet Nam. Her husband was an ARVN sergeant, killed by the VC near Da

Nang. His picture is on the family altar; he looks handsome and full of life. Their daughter, four-year-old Minh, is all dressed up in her new Tết clothes. She's a fatherless child, like the legions all over Viet Nam. Thuy serves Tết cakes and warm Cokes and apologizes for not having ice. She has neither a stove nor a refrigerator in her small, packed-earth house. We sit at a low table and talk and listen to Vietnamese music on the radio. The house has been recently cleaned for Tết, floor swept, mats aired, everything washed. Outside, colorful chickens scratch where Thuy has thrown rice husks.

I give little Minh new money in a red envelope, and Thuy brings betel leaves and nuts on a tray; this is the first time for me to try. I chew, laugh, feel my face turn red and warm, and get a little high. Minh plays with her toys on the floor. The next day I go to war.

Stevens and I meet on Pioneer Pad with four members of his team. We paint up black and board a Red Devil Huey. Herndon and Lukitsch shake our hands, wave, and diminish in size as we lift off and head for the river.

LZ Pedro passes below, abandoned to the wind, ragged grass, and war junk. Around its base the woodcutters' path curves and heads west toward the mountains. In a rush I think of Viêt and the old woman at the market, Thuy's cooking fire, the wood-smoke smell of VC huts, and baking Tết cakes. East the path leads to the populated lowlands and the maze of paddy dikes, hamlet paths, and market roads; west it becomes part of the labyrinthian Ho Chi Minh Trail system. Much of the history of Viet Nam could be seen on that woodcutters' path curling around Pedro.

The river appears in the distance like a giant silver serpent. The Red Devil pilot stays high, and Stevens and I keep our feet in as we beat toward the valley of the Khe Ba Long. We near the LZ below the west ridge, and our hearts begin to trip-fire faster, excitement mounting, adrenaline flowing, energy pulsing with the Huey's power. We grip our weapons hard; death is in our hands and in our future.

I guide the pilot up the Khe Ba Dang to a bomb-blast clearing. The trees explode in size as we descend fast, everything—noise, smells, feel of cold steel in our blackened fingers—magnifying, our minds exploding with brain cell fusion-fission, fear-desire bursting.

The door gunners tense behind their M-60s as the clearing expands with fearsome force. The chopper air-brakes, hovers, whip-lashes the grass. We jump out, free-fall into the wildly beating roar-world.

I hit the ground, fall on my face, and wriggle like a leech into the grass. I lie aiming into the surrounding trees, breathing hard and trembling. The chopper flies away to false drops elsewhere, taking its noise and connections to the Machine. Now it's just us and Nature and, somewhere out there, the enemy.

Stevens whispers us together and leads into the trees. We hide and wait for our senses to return after the helicopter beating, then begin climbing the ridge, pulling the forest around us like a shroud. We immerse ourselves in the wilderness. On the border of death, I feel hyperalive.

We penetrate the forest further, pulling ourselves from tree to tree. We stop often and listen hard, trying to quiet breath and heart sounds. All around us Nature whispers, sighs, passes secrets of the forest world, a seething, life-rich tapestry in green.

We climb to the top of the west ridge and crawl into a tangle of bushes.

"You guys set up here," Sergeant Stevens whispers to his team. "Me and Mr. Stevens are going on."

"Hey, no way," the Grim Reapers say. "We wanta go, too."

"We'll come and get you if we find something good," Stevens says. "Set up here and lie low. Don't tell 'em anything back at base. We'll just go down in the valley, check out the place, and come back. It should only take," he turns to me, "three, four hours?"

" 'Bout that," I say. "It can't be much more than a klick away."

"This is hurtin'," one of the Reapers says.

"For sure we'll come get you if we decide to hit the camp," Stevens says. "Now put those claymores out."

Stevens and I strip off our packs and belts and take only our rifles and a few extra magazines in separate pockets so they won't make noise. We take neither food nor canteens. We'll be back for lunch, we think, and on our way we'll drink from the streams. Stevens takes a new-model miniradio, designed especially for recon teams, and a small pen-flare gun with twelve pen-sized signal rockets.

"I'll walk point," I say.

"I'll take it on the way back," Stevens says.

We crawl out of the bush hideout and are immediately swallowed. The team is gone; they could be in China. Leaves extend to depths unknown. "Beneath each deep, another deep opens," Emerson wrote. I think of Viêt. Which way would he go? Down in the valleys, follow the flow.

I fight forward with Stevens close behind. We can't get separated, not more than three or four steps. Open space appears ahead, and I stop in thinning trees and look across a huge, burned, bomb-strike clearing. It's like a giant graveyard for knocked-down trees. It must have happened a few years ago: shimmering green saplings are rising among the charcoaled tree hulks.

It's too open; we'd better go around, fight through the dense growth and half-fallen trees at the edge of the clearing. It's a long way, too; the clearing is huge. Straight across the clearing the forest sings seductively, like the Sirens to Ulysses: "Come on, try it."

"Shall we take a chance?" I whisper.

"Let's go for it," Stevens says.

This is not a good sign: early in the mission, and already we're making mistakes. I take a deep breath and step into the clearing. I feel vulnerable under the sky. Stevens waits, then steps out behind me and offset slightly to the left. We walk slowly, eyes searching. All around the burned and broken forest looks and breathes, *"J'accuse."*

I pick my way around blackened tree trunks and climb over shrapnel-gouged tree bodies, giant, peaceful victims of war. I slip between saplings and crush tender plants. I feel as if I'm walking across a stage set with Nature-cadavers. If the VC see us now, we're dead.

I'm sweating and breathing hard. With my eyes I measure the last agonizing steps before I reach the far side of the clearing. Calypso, daughter of Atlas, kept Odysseus seven years on her island before he finally rejected her offer of immortality and continued on his journey home. The last steps are just ahead: I hold back the urge to race into the trees, plunge into their tight embrace. Each step is an agony; Viêt would have gone around.

We bury ourselves in the forest, and behind us Calypso sings in the wind. She lets us go, to live for now. We continue on our death mission.

I lead on down the slope, hoping to find a stream. Suddenly I see something brown coming toward me. NVA! My heart leaps into my throat; I drop to the earth, and lie aiming and shaking. Brown-uniformed NVA, low-crawling toward us. The counterrecon killer teams must have heard our landing, calculated our course, perhaps tuned in on the team's transmissions to base. Now they'll take revenge for our killing the commissar. Now we fight and die.

I twist and look back at Stevens. He can see from the way I dropped and the horror on my face this is *it*. I see it again, the low, brown form coming relentlessly closer. My breath comes in spasms; soon I'll have to shoot. Fear tremors wrack my body: today I die!

Twenty feet in front of me the brown form emerges from the green. It's a deer! A beautiful, miniature deer. God, I want to laugh and cry. A *deer*! It's a buck with a large rack of antlers, slowly browsing, stretching its neck, searching among the leaves. It looks like an American white-tail deer, but it's very small, not much bigger than a dog. And there's something perfect about it. It's wild, free. I *love* that deer! There's something magic about it, beyond normal reality.

The deer passes slowly and is soon swallowed again in green.

Stevens and I rise and look at each other, eyes wide in our black-streaked faces. We feel invisible, wild, part of the green world, too. Our whispers are no louder than the wind in the leaves.

"We must be moving good if not even the deer sees us."

"There it is."

Ahead the forest thins a little and we see a cut, a crack in the earth. We slip through the trees and look down into a narrow ravine. It points like an arrow down into the valley. "Come, follow me," it says. "I'll take you where you want to go."

Stevens attempts to call the team on the miniradio. We can't be more than five hundred yards as the crow flies from their position, but the radio can't penetrate the layers of vegetation. We get nothing but static.

"Piece of shit," Stevens mutters.

We're on our own now even more, cut off from the team and from the Machine. Isn't this how we wanted it? To be beyond the law? We descend into the ravine and look up its rocky sides to the trees that arch over us. We're completely hidden, enfolded in the earth, lost to all except ourselves.

The rocks under our boots are dry, but soon dampness comes, just appears, as if water is being squeezed from the earth. The moisture becomes a trickle, then a flow. Now, we believe, we are in the valley's stream system. Following the flow as it grows will take us, we think, to the stream crossing near the Rocket Company's camp. We don't need Viêt, we can do this ourselves. Don't we both come from pioneer stock? We go on hidden in the ravine, like invisible phantoms of death.

A small stream emerges from low-hanging vegetation to our right and joins our flow, confirming, we believe, that our plan is a good one. We're still hidden in the ravine and under the multiple canopy, but we must be now in the headwaters of the Khe Trai, the main stream down the valley. It feels as if no humans have ever been here, not even Montagnards.

Where the two streams join and flow off to the left, our ravine ends. Now we'll walk in the water, deeply immersed in branches and leaves.

"We better mark this place so we can find our way back to the team."

"Good idea."

We build a cairn of three rocks leaning together so they'll look natural to any would-be pusuers, but recognizable to us. We take one last look back at the cairn and try to imprint the whole chaotic jungle scene on our midwestern American memories. The rocks barely stick up out of the forest-floor growth. Will we ever see this place again? It could be bad—very bad—if we miss it.

We enter the stream, duck under heavy boughs, and round the next bend. The cairn, like the past, is gone. We're pointed ahead toward our future, like our rifles as they search the banks. Our lives are now bounded by the walls and ceiling of the stream-tunnel and the flow beneath our feet. This is our world, of fecund life and sudden death.

More streams flow in from left and right—so many streams, so many decisions to make going back. We try to remember the turns and branches, the way to the three-rock cairn. Maybe coming without Viêt was *not* so smart.

I slip on a water-smooth stone and fall, throwing my right hand high to keep my rifle dry and landing full force on my elbow on a rock. I jump up fast, exploding with pain and streaming water and blood. My blood flows downstream and flies downwind in scent molecules. I think of the tiger. Is it downstream now, lapping water with its big tongue? Downwind, sniffing the air? Did it eat the commissar, and will it now eat me?

Stevens looks around, M-16 following his eyes. The fall made too much noise. We wade on, carefully round each bend thinking we'll see the NVA squatting beside the stream, filling their canteens. It's farther than I thought. More streams flow in from left and right, and the main stream builds in flow and power. It's more than three hours since we left the team. Stevens and I are like microbodies in a great life-stream.

We pause and drink, scooping, lapping the water and looking around like wild animals as the stream rushes into us. Here the snake flows across the stream, and the deer looks up, hunted, like us. Where is the Trail? Time and distance are growing between us and the team. I think back through the stream-labyrinth; I don't think we'll ever find the cairn. We are like specks of floating plankton in an immense jungle-sea.

> Land in a swamp, march through the woods . . . feel the savagery, the utter savagery . . . all that mysterious life of the wilderness that stirs in the forest, in the jungles, in the hearts of wild men . . . it has a fascination, too.[2]

We hide behind a boulder and whisper as small silver fish dart around our legs, discover we're not edible yet, and go away.

"Maybe we missed the Trail," Stevens says.

"I don't think so. The way Viêt described it there's a big tree on the right bank, and the Trail is visible on both sides of the stream."

"You sure this is even the right stream?"

I look at the water. I remember how Viêt listened to the stream as if he heard a message in it; I hear only a babble over rocks. I remember Viêt looking at the water as at an old friend; it's all strange to me.

"This is it," I say. "It's got to be."

We can see no farther than the next bend. Life is often like that. The banks are impenetrable green curtains, and to search for the sky is to try to look up through a strange, constantly moving ceiling, more phantasmagoric than any ever designed by Arab or Moor. We are in a lost, wild world. Nature reigns here.

Around a bend we flatten behind a big rock. Man-sign! Someone has recently been walking along the stream, cutting young willows along the left bank with a sharp knife. There are no tracks, just fresh-cut saplings oozing sap-blood like fallen boy soldiers. The impression is of someone wading, idly swinging a machete, slicing the young willows and letting them lie. Why? Who? Is it a sign?

We can't stay here, and we don't want to go back. I round the boulder first, then Stevens. We wade on, ready to shoot and run. We focus on the banks, the cut willows, the foaming water ahead. My thumb is on the selector switch of my rifle, ready to punch from S to F, safe to full automatic, in the racing milliseconds before the death of someone.

Around the next bend the cut willows end. No sign that the machete man climbed the bank, no sign of him walking downstream. Who was it? What does it mean?

Many more bends come and go and still no Trail. Doubt gnaws like our growing hunger. Why didn't we bring some rations? Are we in the right stream? Is this even the right valley? If only we could see the skyline, Hills 300 and 320, we'd know where the saddle is and where the Trail comes down to the stream. Even if we started back now, we couldn't make it to the team before dark, assuming we could find the cairn *and* them in the tossing jungle-sea. We're dealing with the great questions now: Where did we come from? Where are we? Where are we going? We're dealing with survival.

What's sure is that we'll be out here tonight with no food, no ponchos, no radio, and no Trail. The day begins to turn black in the spaces between the leaves. We crouch at bankside and whisper, Stevens looking upstream, I looking down. Words float in stream-rush: "We'd better hide for the night."

"Let's crawl up a ways and look for a level place."

I lead the way up the bank through the tangle. Snakes writhe and tigers bite through skulls in my mind as I reach ahead into the green unknown and pull myself up. *Anything* could be in here. I wriggle through leaves, dragging my stomach and thighs along the ground, toes and forearms immersed in spidery growth. I push branches aside and peer through to layer on layer, row on row.

I'm hoping for a small miracle, a relatively flat place where we can sleep, even a *big* miracle, an open area where we won't lie wrapped in branches and vines like some giant python's dinner. The stream-song vanishes, swallowed by dense vegetation.

Suddenly I break into a flat, open space. Stevens crawls up beside me; he can't believe his eyes. We look across a dark, level place beneath several scattered trees of the same species. The ground is strangely bare here, like a desert island in the rolling sea.

We rise and look around as darkness fills the clearing. There's no deep green bed in which to snuggle up with vipers or poison spiders, some clear area around if the tiger or python comes, and, strangest of all, no leaves to rustle, no twigs to crack, no brush to crunch if we toss in our sleep. Who knows how close the NVA might be?

I motion to Stevens I want to talk and cup my hand to funnel the whisper into his ear: "I'm going to crawl up a ways, try to see something."

"Don't get lost."

I walk quietly to the edge of the clearing. I want to make one last try to see where we are before it's completely dark. Maybe there'll be another miracle like these spaced-out trees and I'll be able to see the saddle. I have to know we're in the right valley, at least. We can't go on long without food, and there's another time problem: tomorrow, if they haven't already, the team will have to report us missing and the Machine will start flying search missions, alerting the VC.

I bend and push into the brush. I duck under branches, drop, and finally have to crawl. I squirm forward, hoping for a *quick* miracle. I look back: Stevens and the clearing are gone. I note carefully the direction I'm crawling; I could easily get lost here. I wouldn't dare call in more than a whisper, either—and the forest swallows sound. Stevens, maybe fifteen meters away, could be in another world.

I worm forward, hoping for more spaced-out trees and a break in the canopy. Leaves and branches brush my face like spindly-legged beetles. I push up slightly, crane my head, cradle my rifle, and wince when my sore elbow hits the ground. The blood has dried my sleeve hard as a board. I wonder how far the tiger scents blood?

Where is the sky, *something*? Soon I'll have to turn and crawl back down the closing black tunnel behind me. A little more, just a little. I wriggle, rise to my hands and knees, and crawl. I feel like a bear or giant baby.

My head breaks into the clear: sky above, and open space to left and right. My body is still wrapped in vegetation, and my

head is sticking out over—I turn it left and right—the Trail!
My head is sticking over the Trail!
I duck back fast and lie hard-breathing inches from the
Trail. I try to quiet my breath, heart, and blood-rush and rein
in my stampeding mind. The crossing must be around the next
bend. I want to squirm forward—just a little—and look at the
Trail again. Wait, Stevens! What if he coughs, sneezes in the
clearing, comes looking for me?

I crawl back to the clearing. Stevens is sitting on the
ground, M-16 across his lap. I signal a fast "Quiet!" then
crawl to him and whisper, "The Trail—there."

Stevens stares where I'm pointing. Someone's coming!
NVA are coming, marching on the Trail.

We grip our rifles and stare into the surrounding black wall.
I can hear my heart booming, nerves crackling, eyes grating in
their sockets. "Shut up!" I want to shout at my body. "The
NVA will hear!"

We stand paralyzed, listening to the rhythmic slap of Ho
Chi Minh sandals and the tinkle of metal canteens against
wooden AK butts. Ghosts of the forest are passing nearby on
the Ho Chi Minh Trail. You can feel them as well as hear,
coming in a wave of awesome power.

We stay staring, not breathing. Outside, I'm rigid; inside,
like jelly. A throat tickle could kill here, an itchy nose destroy.
Is life so insignificant that it could end this way? Where was
the body's instinct for survival?

The NVA death-wave passes on down the Trail, headed for
the stream crossing and the Rocket Company's camp. There
they'll cook their rice and sit around the fire as the commissar
had done, and tomorrow we'll crawl up and kill them.

Stevens and I exchange fearful looks. We dare not talk at all
now, nor make the slightest sound. With infinite care we sit,
lay our rifles beside us, and lie back like zombies in their
coffins. We lie like dead, arms folded across our chests. We

dare not move or even sleep. Who knows what dreams may come to cause us to thrash and cry out?

A tickle begins to work way back in my throat. Of course! It always happens at moments like this. It builds and threatens to burst out in a cough. I'm *dying* to cough. I grit my teeth, try to reason with my throat, order it to be calm and quiet. Does it *want* to return to the earth?

My nose begins to itch. Of course! A sneeze threatens to explode. I carefully move my sore-elbow arm and apply hard-knuckle pressure under my nose. I *order* you not to sneeze.

Hunger gnaws at my innards like a pond full of beavers dam-building at night. My stomach growls; there's a wolf in there. Beside me, Stevens fights his own body-battles.

We lie rigid in utter black, invisible to all except those who sense with other than human eyes and live their lives in deep-forest night. Everywhere around our bare clearing a great jungle symphony plays, and life cycles spin and end-begin as night creatures move, mate, and feed.

Something begins attacking us with a terrible itching, biting, and burning. It feels like we're being devoured by tiny, invisible, mad-making beasts. And we're like Gulliver chained: we can't move or fight back for fear of noise. The invisible creatures are lighting us up all over with fierce, painful fire spots, and we can do nothing. The beasts increase their attacks, everywhere biting, burning, torturing. We have become, in Nixon's words about the United States if it "allows itself" to be defeated in Viet Nam, like "pitiful helpless giants."

We begin to take chances. We fight back. We sit up and try to grab the beasts through our clothes. Nevermore! Not one! The creatures must be amazingly fast or have special night vision that allows them to escape our hand sweeps and hammer-and-anvil, finger-thumb squashes. I try ambush, wait with killer fingers poised, ready to grab and crush. If I could get just one, feel it pop between my fingers. . . . I wait silently, hand under my shirt, poised and ready. When I feel the biting, I'll—there! Nothing! There! Nothing again! Nothing!

How can they get away each time? I do blind, frenzied sweeps, search and destroy; I grab with pumped-up power. Never, *never* anything. This goes on all night.

We suffer twelve hours of torture in black before silver gray spaces appear under the trees. Stevens and I are nearly insane, and now, as day begins, what seemed impossible—that the burning and biting could get worse—rises to a crescendo. At least now we'll see them, grab them, kill them.

We tear off our camouflage jackets and green T-shirts and wildly search our burning skin. Nothing! They *are* invisible. And now, with our torsos exposed, the burning and biting rises to an even greater fury, roaring like a forest fire all over our backs and chests.

Suddenly, it dawns: the trees! The trees are raining poison on us. That's why the strange, bare-ground clearing: nothing grows here, nothing comes here but us. Heedless of noise and the NVA, we dash madly into the surrounding jungle, roll on dew-wet ferns and grass, scrape our bodies with sharp sticks, and wipe ourselves with big elephant's-ear leaves. We're becoming wild, falling back into ancient ways, civilization just a recent, thin veneer. Remove our boots and camouflage pants, and we would look indistinguishable from charcoal-blackened Teutonic tribesmen from the time of Tacitus.

A sharp roar from the jungle stuns us into catatonia. The tiger! We grab our rifles and look around wildly. It's been waiting for us to leave the clearing. We can see at most arm's length. Any moment, from any place, it could explode in orange and black from the green.

My camouflage jacket still lies in the clearing, its sleeve bloody hard. We wait, listen, fingers curled around triggers. The roar—more like a giant cough—bursts again, farther away this time. It's moving, maybe waiting till tonight, when we'll be away from the poison trees and considerably weakened.

We recover our shirts, wipe them with leaves, and whisper.

"Let's head for the stream and find the camp fast."

"It's that way, isn't it?"

"I thought we came up *that* way."

"Look for which way is down."

We scuff quietly around on the ground. We're swimming in green up to our waists, and the land gives no hint of a slope to the stream. We try Stevens's direction to the left, then mine to the right. No drop to the stream becomes visible, no sound of stream-song floats through the trees.

"Let's go back to the clearing and try from there."

We push through vines and leaves. Where *is* the clearing? We can't be more than twenty steps away. We try another direction. No clearing. Now we could be forty steps away.

Panic begins to claw like the tiger at the back of my mind. We're getting deeper into trouble, and if we lose it here, we're done. We came thinking to bring death; now we're about to find it.

"Let's forget about the clearing, concentrate on the stream. Try that way."

We try one way, then another, short stabs so we don't get too far, feeling with our feet for sloping ground, listening hard for water over rocks, watching for the tiger's rush.

"The ground's sloping down," I whisper.

We push through the green curtain and hear the stream, its beautiful silver song. We descend eagerly and soon we can see it in flashes through the trees.

To the right is another small clearing, an old bomb strike growing back in deep vegetation. At its far side, a tall, white-barked tree stands almost alone, rising above the canopy. I look at the tree and get an idea.

"I'm going to hang my shirt up there," I whisper, "to mark the Trail crossing from the air. With the Rocket Company just across the stream, we can get a good fix on it, too." Stevens looks at the tree. "Make sure the NVA can't see it." "I'll get it up high." We wade through thigh-deep growth to the tree. I hand my rifle to Stevens, strip off my camouflage jacket, drop it in the grass, and begin to climb. Stevens stands at the base of the tree, looking up and all around, his hawklike face intense.

I climb high. The tree is almost dead, wounded by a chunk of shrapnel to the heartwood, the hole allowing the entrance of killer fungi. I pull higher, remembering Dad's advice: never trust all your weight to only one limb. I climb through dead branches and empty space where once the upper-canopy world sang with abundant life.

I hug the trunk with my thighs and grip with black-painted fingers. I climb to near the treetop, hold on, and look around. Above, the sky is blue and gold, the sun back at last. Below, the stream snakes through the forest, sparkling diamond-bright through gaps in the leaves. Across the stream, hidden in the ocean of trees, is the Rocket Company's camp and the Trail. I must be looking at them now, and soon we'll be there.

Hanging on with one hand, I peel off my olive green T-shirt and cling to the trunk. I tie the shirt to a limb; it looks good. It should be easy to spot from the air and almost impossible to see from the ground,

I climb down carefully, muscles flexing. I drop to the ground and Stevens and I look up at the shirt. You can see it a little, but it's not likely, I think, that the NVA will leave the Trail and come to this clearing. The shirt looks like a small flag flying up there. Now we'll be able to locate the camp on the map from the air and feed the numbers to the Machine.

We push through to the stream, kneel, and drink, water running down our chins. We drink more, trying to drown hunger. We've been without food twenty-four hours now, and we have to find the camp fast. We Americans are not used to going without food often, three squares daily, snacks and sodas when we want and machines always handy to dispense them. And the longer we're out here, the more dangerous the brigade will become to us. Soon, surely, the rescue birds will start droning over the valley, round and round over the trees, telling the NVA we're here.

We wade around the bend in tight crouches, expecting to see the Trail. Nothing. It must be around the next bend. No. We wade on. No again and again. Something is wrong: how could we miss it? Are we *still* to fail?

With each step we're farther from the shirt and the team, and more carbo-deficient. We'll have to turn back soon. God, we can't go back as failures.

Around the next bend we see the Trail, rising from the right bank past a tall, thick-trunked tree that looks like a cottonwood. We're ten minutes from the camp.

We wade forward and see a chilling sight: churned mud on the right bank, where the Trail leaves the water and disappears into a curving tree-tunnel. We wade several more steps, then stop, turned to stone. On a flat rock near the left bank is the water print of a Ho Chi Minh sandal. Seconds before, NVA crossed here.

We wade across the stream and hide on a small gravel bar under a weeping willow. We squat and whisper, keeping wild eyes on the crossing.

"What'll we do?"

On the right bank is the Trail to the camp. The churned mud on the bank still shines, radiating bone-breaking power.

"Goin' up that Trail could be hurtin'," Stevens whispers.

"Anyway, we don't know where the camp is. We could walk right into it."

We look at the left bank, where the water print dries on its rock and the Trail angles up toward the saddle.

"You think they heard us coming?"

We look into the green wall at our backs. Through there is the camp. But where? Crawling we would make big noise, maybe get lost, maybe crawl right into their camp, our heads sticking into their semicircle of huts, the looks on all our faces almost comical before the killing starts.

We decide to stay here and ambush whoever crosses the stream. We separate a little and sit cross-legged on the gravel bar, rifles across our laps. We'll shoot, dash out, grab AKs, strip map cases and documents, run upstream, and bury ourselves in the wilderness.

The stream flows by, singing its song. We look through the willows and wait as hunger and American impatience grow. The willows blow and trail their leaves in the water, making skimming traceries of silver, green, and gold. We sit like camouflaged Buddhas or big toads, rifles *Pietà*-cradled. I look at the big cottonwood. What has it seen in its long life here of the dramas of Nature and man, and what will it see today?

The willows form a lovely curtain, a living veil. I look through it and see in my mind the NVA come, AKs across their backs. We shoot them and they fall. It's a beautiful day; the *crachin* season seems over at last. Hunger chews at our stomachs and our brains.

Voices come through the green curtain. We sit bolt upright, look at each other, ready our rifles to fire. Now it comes, maybe the end. The voices float in the stream, sparkle in the breeze, and fall silent. We crouch together and whisper, squatting with our elbows on our knees and our rifles pointed in opposite directions.

"Must be from the camp."

More voices come: singing and laughter.

"It sounds like a party."

"It's the third day of Têt."

Women's voices come through the curtain. Soft, light women's voices, floating on the wind. Women are in the camp. We squat together again and whisper.

"What do we do if *women* cross?"

"Woman can kill you easy as a man."

We separate again and sit watching the stream. In my mind I see them come, black hair falling from beneath their hats, AKs across their hourglass backs, wading interspersed with the men. Do we shoot them and they fall, bodies bumping among the rocks? How do we live with that? Do we not shoot at all— but what if they see us? Do we shoot the men and try not to hit the women and hope they run away? Or do we shoot them?

A rifle shot cracks from behind our backs, and we dive on our stomachs on the gravel bar and lie twisting our faces among rocks and water. Everything is sharpened in detail and immense. No more shots come. What to do now? We low-crawl together and whisper.

"Sounds like it came from the camp."

"Closer."

"Whata you think it was?"

"Maybe the NVA shooting birds, maybe a signal."

"Maybe they're tryin' to trick us with the women's voices and party sounds. Maybe the killer team's creepin' up."

"We know where the camp is now, and that it's occupied."

"Mission accomplished."

This is important: mission accomplished. We're *not* failures.

"Let's get outa here."

We rise and stand under the willows, and Stevens quickly takes the point.

"Lucky him," I think. "Last in, first out."

Stevens passes through the willow curtain, enters the water, and begins wading upstream without another look back. I wait three steps, and no one shoots Stevens from the trees. I step through the veil, willows brushing my shoulders. It looks like forever to the first bend upstream. I'll be exposed for minutes with my back to the crossing, and now it's *my* body I see in the stream.

We push into the current. I wade fast but try to be quiet; I feel like I'm sweating blood. Panic claws up my spine and threatens to bite into my brain. Now the NVA will cross the stream, see us, shout, and shoot. Now! I twist back in horror, expecting to see them. I try to will myself around the bend. Stevens makes it. I never wanted anything so much as just to turn that bend. I strain forward, heavy and in slow motion as in a dream. I feel my back is about to be punctured by AK bullets as I wrap myself around the bend.

We go on fast, feeling pursued. How many boot prints did we leave on the gravel bar, what impress of our sitting, how many kicked rocks in clear water heading upstream? How good are their trackers, and how soon before they come up behind us? Or will they hang back and let us lead them to the team?

Streams come in from left and right, far more than we remember. With each one we face a decision: Which way back to the cairn? Everything looks different going upstream. We stand in the water and whisper.

"I think we're lost."

"We could go back to the last branch."

"I wasn't even sure about it, were you?"

"We might meet the NVA, too."

"I heard something back there, I know I did."

"They gotta be comin', we better keep goin'."

We wade on, take branch after branch, look back, and hide behind rocks watching straight stretches, sweating, hearts pumping. We hear ghost-sounds of pursuit and voices— maybe—floating on the wind. We drink, our faces in the water, still trying to drown hunger. We're fast running out of energy and time; we could wander in the stream-system maybe one more day. Which of us will go first? We have to do something different fast, and we whisper as water swirls past us. "Let's take to the trees, try to get up high, see something." "I wonder why there's no planes flying. Maybe the team didn't report us missing?" "Maybe the NVA got 'em. Maybe there's no team." We look up. A slope falls steeply into the stream. We can see only a few inches. Anything could be up there, or nothing. "You ready?" "Better drink plenty. This'll be the last water we see for a while."

Hard struggle is coming, fighting and crawling up through dense tangles with no guarantee we'll be able to see the river, Hills 300 and 320, or *anything*. But what else can we do? We bend and drink like wild animals for the last time. Soon we'll be running on will alone; how much we have of that and fate or luck or God will determine if we live or die.

Stevens climbs up into the thick growth and is swallowed in green as if by man-eating plants. Somehow it's as if he never existed. I follow closely, covering our sign where we leave the stream. We fight up the steep slope. We are like tiny tube worms in the sea. We crunch and kill, leaving our drag marks and scent-sign, sweat-surging through the trees.

Penetrating the jungle here is like delving into a mystery from which there is no issue but death or rescue to another world. No clearing opens, no level terrain signals the top of the hill. Each decision cuts off the past; there's nowhere to go but on and up.

I hear something behind, reach and grab Stevens, and motion "Someone coming!" We lie breathing tensely, staring into the green curtain. There! Someone, something moving. It stops. Forest-sounds come. Maybe they are hanging back, waiting. We can't wait. We have to go on. We have no time.

We fight to what seems to be the top of the hill. We can see nothing. Only leaves, myriad levels of leaves, leaves beginning at our noses, running down the lengths of our arms, crawling up our legs. How long before we become leaves and the vines bear us up, our skeleton-bodies hanging in the trees? We fight down the hill. We worm and wriggle, burrow and crawl. We sweat and struggle bruised and bleeding to the top of the next hill. Still nothing. No sky, no view, just leaves and more leaves. We fight on down the other side, reaching inside for the strength to continue. What is that something that wants to struggle on while our bodies cry out, *Let me lie down and rest, transform, feed the forest, return?*

Thorns gash us where others have already torn the skin open, rocks and roots bruise previously bruised elbows and shins, leaves slice our black-streaked hands, noses, and cheeks, and our knees are rubbed raw from crawling. Blood- and sweat-smell stream from us; surely the tiger is following. We're stumbling tired, hungry, thirsty, and starting to get careless about noise. Is even the *something* giving up now?

We drag ourselves up another hill. We feel time's winged shadow hovering near, ghost-bird in the trees. We have eaten the forest all our lives; now the forest will eat us. I push to the hilltop, part leaves, and see another miracle: a tree standing almost alone, rising up through the canopy like a magic beanstalk. It has lower limbs; it looks climbable. Maybe it goes up to a view of the sky.

"Boost me up," I whisper to Stevens.

He makes a step with his knee and I pull to the first limb. I drive myself up into the labyrinth of limbs. Below, Stevens winces at the boot-on-bark noise and looks around for the ghost-pursuers.

I begin to flow like a snake through the writhing branches, patterns of water in wood and flesh. I climb high and Stevens disappears. I'm immersed in the tree; it's the only world I see. I look up and climb higher. I see sky begin to appear through gaps in the leaves. Hope brings energy, and I drive myself higher as the limbs become smaller and the trunk sways more in the wind.

I trust limbs I shouldn't, risking all for a view of the sky. I stand on the last limbs I dare, feet close to the trunk, hands reaching, raising myself up. My body squeezes a diminishing trunk, and my head rises through the upper canopy. I cling tightly in the top of the tree and look far away to the horizon. Stretching away in every direction are trees and more trees, and mountains like waves in the great forest-sea. I'm stunned by the sight. This is Quang Tri, the DMZ province, battered in places like the face of the moon—and yet from this hilltop tree, all I can see are beautiful mountain-forest waves. And suddenly I realize we never can win. We never can blow the top off every mountain, scrape every valley, defoliate every tree. We're fighting against Nature and will lose; they're working with Nature and will win.

I look all around. I see no river, no Hills 300 and 320, no saddle. And why are no planes flying? The forest is vast, awesome, and silent; the sky is high, gray, and empty. The world seems devoid of human presence, yet I know the NVA are down there, living like Tom Sawyer and Huckleberry Finn, while we crash around trying to find them.

Two hills away I see what looks like a small grass island atop a densely forested peak. If we can just get there—but can we find it navigating under the canopy, and do we have the strength to make it?

I try to imprint in my mind the route there. My eyes run down the hill, up the next, then down and up one more. I begin to climb down, seeking new limbs and handholds in the tree-world below. If we miss the grass island, it's over. The forest will be our tomb, the trees our bodies rising. I snag the seat of my pants on a broken stub, lose my balance, and grab on as the pants rip out, exposing my green shorts. I drop to the ground, ragged and wild, and whisper my message to Stevens. We make our plan, whispering and looking around us and feeling hope rising, riding over the hunger and fatigue. "We'll shoot sight lines from tree to tree starting from this one, and just keep going in that direction." We stay close and try to keep focused. We fight downhill, use trees as guides, and shoot azimuths with our eyes. Our lives have become a series of short, sharp struggles between two very limited points, with no assurance of anything beyond.

We get hung up and help each other through. The first hill leads down into a rocky ravine, with no water in the bottom. We slide into it, scraping our legs on sharp stones. We climb up to a point we fixed on the rim, go over the edge, and fix on a tree. The slightest deviation now means a big miss later on, with no way to find the island again. We're fighting the jungle, heat exhaustion, hunger, and dehydration. How long will it be before we lose the ability to focus on direction, before we lose the physical strength to struggle forward, before we lose our will, when even the *something* ceases to care?

We struggle to the top of the second hill, where there's no glimpse of sky or anything else to tell us if we're going wrong. We go over the side and down, push, dig deep, *will* ourselves beyond. I remember now the motto of my high school class: "Climb, though the rocks be rugged."

We fight up the third hill. This *has* to be it, the last chance for us now. We crawl, bend under branches, climb over decaying tree bodies rich with moss, ferns, and young trees. Ahead the forest thins a little, and we see grass, and above it, sky. We did it! We surge forward, break free from the forest, spill into the open, and look wildly around. We're on an island in the sky, jungle-ocean stretching in every direction.

The clearing is an old bomb strike, trees blasted into nonexistence at the center and half fallen outward at the edges, the craters overgrown with grass. *Still* no rescue planes are flying; we feel like the last men on Earth.

We listen for ghost pursuit. Either we have lost them or they are waiting. We sink back into our holes. Our minds are going as our bodies search desperately for resources. We're tattered like castaways, blood- and dirt-smeared. We converted into wild men; now we're beginning to convert to forest. Except for our bones and maybe our spirits, the forest will quickly take us back into itself.

The wind blows, the grass sighs, and the sun glows from behind the high, gray dome. We're in a world totally without man-sounds except for our breathing. We lie back and look up at the sky for a sign. Far out on the frontiers of perception, we hear something. A faint hum, a plane.

We stand up and frantically scan the sky. Far off over what could be the west ridge, an O-2 Skymaster observation plane floats in lazy circles. We strip off our camouflage jackets and wave them in big semaphoring arcs, and Stevens takes off his T-shirt, too, so we're both bare-torsoed. The plane continues to bank and circle.

"Maybe he's lookin' for the team," Stevens says. "Maybe he don't know anything about us."

We wave like mad and cast anxious glances into the trees. The Skymaster floats on. There's something so remote and impersonal about the small plane up there, so detached from the earth, the forest, and us.

"Maybe he's a drone," Stevens says.

"If he can't see us half-naked and wavin' like crazy on this bare peak, how can he see the NVA down under the trees?"

We're starting to get angry at the pilot as he continues his lazy circling. We want to shout, break the terrible silence: *Look! Look here, damn you! It's us!* He continues banking and circling.

"We'd better use the pen-flare gun."

We've been avoiding this. We wanted to wait till the plane comes closer or, better, not use it at all. Once we fire a flare, every NVA in the forest will know where we are. The Skymaster banks; it looks like it's going away.

Stevens whips out the small tube and pulls a pen-sized flare from the plastic-ring twelve-pack. The pen-flare gun looks like something you could get in the 1950s for seventy-five cents and a Kix boxtop. Stevens drops the flare down the tube, inserts his finger into the metal ring on the side, pulls it down and lets go, releasing the firing pin. The flare whooshes up, arcs across the sky, and explodes with a flash, a *pop!*, and a puff of smoke. Suddenly I feel naked, the trees all around like NVA looking. The plane floats on, banking and circling.

"He didn't see us!" Stevens says. "Jesus, is he *blind*?"

He loads up again. There's no holding back now: this is *it*. "Take the bull by the horns, boy," Grampa Stevens used to say. "Take the bull by the horns."

Whoosh-pop! The second rocket streaks through the sky and bursts in another sharp flash and puff of smoke. The pilot floats on. Prometheus, chained to a rock, has his *eyes* torn out as well as his liver!

Stevens fires again and again, while I shoot agonized looks into the surrounding trees. The NVA must be coming fast now, or are already here and waiting for the chopper.

Whoosh-pop! Whoosh-pop!

Stevens is firing *at* the plane. "I wish I could hit that bastard," he says. "Put it right in his damn cockpit!"

"If he *does* see us," I say sarcastically, "he'll probably think we're NVA, and call in the Phantoms and artillery."

Nine, ten, eleven flares; we're down to the last.

Stevens pulls the flare off the plastic ring, drops it in the tube, and says, "This is it."

The flare arcs up, taking what hopes we have with it. He sees it. The plane banks sharp right and comes our way, leaping over mountains, ridges, valleys, streams. We wave our shirts fast as he dives on our hill in attack approach. I see the smoke rockets under his wings. "Good God!" I think. "He's going to hit us with a smoke rocket."

We keep waving like crazy as he zooms low over us, wagging his wings. We can see his face clearly, looking down. He climbs fast and flies away, far away, gone, till there's not even a distant hum.

"Do you think he knew who we are?"

"I just hope he didn't think it was an NVA trick. We're gonna be in a world o' hurt up here if he calls in the heavy stuff."

Again it's us and the jungle. Nature sounds return, and beyond them a terrible silence that covers the forest and sky. Has he gone for the Cobras and Phantoms instead of a rescue chopper? We keep an eye on the trees and whisper about what to do.

"We better make up a story," Stevens says. "We weren't lost. We took to the hills because the NVA were after us. We *had* to come up here and signal for extraction."

"Sounds good to me."

We lie back in our holes and scan the sky. We feel lost and abandoned, human wreckage on a lonely, wild island. Will we ever see civilization, the World, our families again? Finally, out of desolation and from far away, comes the familiar heartbeat sound: chopper on the way.

"Make it look good!" Stevens says.

We roll on our bellies and aim our rifles down through the grass at the marching trees, as if the NVA were coming. The chopper roar grows as ancient dino-forests combust, and two Cobras blast over the hill. The sharklike gunships hover, feint, swing their rocket-pod snouts at the trees, daring the ghost-NVA to incarnate. We see the pilots bulbous-helmeted and tense behind their controls, riding their weapons systems, ready to spurt hot, exploding metal.

Into the Cobras' roar-beating world comes a Huey rescue bird flying straight toward us. The right door gunner is hanging in the open doorway, no helmet on and his shirt open and flying loose from his pants as if he has run from some other activity on radio flash: *Two missing Americans sighted on hill!* This is usual for rescue crews: flying fast into the jaws of Hell.

Stevens and I aim into the trees and bunch our muscles under us, ready to jump and run. Adrenaline is roaring and crackling through our bodies; no hungry, no tired now, buddy. The Huey booms in, whips the grass into a frenzy, sends dust tornadoes flying. The Cobras continue to spin and feint, defying gravity and the NVA. The Machine is here. It has a heart for its own and a lust to kill the other.

The flying-shirttailed door gunner looks wild, crazed as he stands in the open door, ready to shoot great bursts of M-60 bullets, death-spit into the trees.

"Come on!" he shouts and gestures as the chopper hovers over the center of the clearing.

We jump up and run. Now is when the NVA will hit, drop the Huey and us with B-40 blasts, then run from the total unload of the vengeance-seeking Cobras, inferno on the hill and in the forest, gloomy wood lit with hellfire.

We run, *fly* through the grass, throw ourselves in and are hauled aboard by our belts, the door gunner jerking us in as if we were no heavier than flies. Then back to his M-60 he goes, wild-looking into the trees, shirt flying, chest bare as the pilot pulls away and banks hard for the river. We're saved!

Stevens and I whoop and laugh, roll on the floor, clutch the seat supports, hold on to anything we can as the Huey climbs and the Cobras cover our engine-straining withdrawal. Joy-bursts of life and flight build on adrenaline highs as we beat beyond ground-fire range and fly toward the river.

We look out the open doors and fall silent, lost in our own thoughts now as the forest falls away below. My mind spins like whirlpools in the stream down into the trees. Tall, mysterious, Hills 300 and 320 regally march below, like noble forest ancestors passing. Down there is where the commissar fell, and the saddle, and the Trail, angling toward the stream, the crossing, the big cottonwood tree, the weeping willows, the water-print rock, and the tunnel going through thick vegetation to the Rocket Company's camp. Down there, too— somewhere—is the three-rock cairn, the arrow-ravine, and the beautiful miniature deer. My shirt is there, flying like a flag, and the tiger circling the poison trees. I think again of the revelation from the hilltop tree, one of the great lessons of Viet Nam. Now to share what we have seen: good-bye Nature, hello Machine. We fly high back to base to link up again with civilization.

Aujourd'hui, maman est morte. Ou peut-être hier, je ne sais pas. ("Today Mother died. Or maybe yesterday, I don't know.")[3]

CHAPTER 5

SEPARATION-INITIATION-RETURN

Give me to sing songs of the great Idea. . . .
—Walt Whitman, *By Blue Ontario's Shore*

Separation-Initiation-Return is the essence of the hero-journey. The Magic Flight, or the Escape of Prometheus, is a phase of that journey, as is the Refusal of the Return, or the World Denied. We see them all now, as Shiva and Kali dance.[1]

The Machine talks, radio-crackles through the pilot's headphones, and he shouts back to Sergeant Stevens and me, "Major Lukitsch is on the horn. The team's back. They're OK! He asks if you want anything."

"*Food!*" we shout back.

We laugh and whoop, filling the chopper with wild emanations. We're dirty, ragged, glowing, crazy. The wilderness is still on us, in us. We look like Tom and Huck; the NVA are Indians. And we are headed not to "the Territory ahead of the rest," but back to civilization.[2]

"And a chopper!" I shout. "We need a chopper, too! We'll tell him why when we get there."

The base comes up in the distance in smoke and rectangular lines, big fuel bladders like bloated intestines, spindly-legged watchtowers, and razor-wire gates. The painted frontiersman on Pioneer Pad expands in size as we descend and land rattling on it.

Lukitsch greets us like heroes, man-shakes our hands, and jeeps us to the mess hall. Stevens and I are still flying, and all we want to do is tank up on chow and soar back out to spot that shirt. Lukitsch agrees; he'll come along, too, in the chopper with his map. We tromp into the mess hall, feeling like giants. Lukitsch tells the dirty–T-shirted mess sergeant, "Take good care of these boys," then drives off to radio a chopper. The mess sergeant brings us lunchmeat sandwiches on white bread and "artificial" milk in cardboard cartons. *This* is what heroes eat? I bite and try to chew but can only coax one hard swallow of the nothing-on-it bread and fat-heavy, sodium nitrite–laced lunchmeat past my heightened systems. I glug the reconstituted quart of milk down, though, spilling some on my chin. We Iowa boys can almost always drink our milk.

Stevens's Adam's apple is big, like Ichabod Crane's. After a choke and a hard swallow or two, it starts bobbing up and down like apples at a Halloween party as he gets his sandwich going. I give him my sandwich, too, and he gives me his milk. We're ready to go back.

Lukitsch comes jeep-rolling up in a cloud of dust and with a long face. "It's a no go," he says. "Brigade choppers are all committed."

"Again!" I say. Visions of VIP hordes flying like locusts all over the province grind in my mind. "Let's go over to the TOC. I'll call Willie." I can't come down, I don't want to come down.

Lukitsch escorts us to his office, where a rattlesnake-sounding field phone sits beneath the Batman poster. I crank the phone and hear a voice in a bored black accent say for the thousandth time today, "Red Devil Operator One, sir." There were GIs who spent 365 days in Viet Nam inside windowless rooms answering the phone.

"Quang Tri Citadel, please," I say.

Willie comes on the line. Before I can ask, he says, "The answer is negatron."

I talk fast, words tumbling out like clowns. "No, it's nothing, Willie. We just fly out and find my shirt."

"*What?* No way."

I can see Willie in his flight suit, thinking of hot rods, flying, girls, and surfing. I talk faster. "There's no danger, none at all. We just fly high, spot the shirt, mark our maps, and come back."

"Where is this shirt?"

"Ba Long."

"No way. That's Indian country."

"Just a little way in, Willie. Come on, it's important. You don't want to sit around all day doing nothing, man. Come on, let's fly! Nothing bad will happen: I guarantee it one hundred percent!"

"Where are you?" Willie says heavily. I hear that fatalism in his voice like I've seen in Khai and Viêt. Willie knows this is not smart: he could get killed. He doesn't have to do it, but he's going to, anyway. Maybe it's the flying he can't resist. Everyone probably has something.

I hang up and beam the good news to Stevens and Lukitsch. "We're on! Back to Ba Long!"

Willie fires up the Black Cat, and the instruments start to talk. The beat rises as the engines warm, big rotor blade chopping and small back blade slicing the air in heavy avgas exhaust. The Huey begins to get light on its skids, vibrates as Willie plays with the controls, he and his copilot studying the dials, looking at the surrounding stone Citadel walls, intercom-talking to each other.

The Black Cat lifts off, raises its yellow moon over the craggy gray walls and stagnant, green-moss moat. The old fortress reaches back to other ancient struggles for the land, rice, and the people. Below, antennae like giant insect feelers rise, and trucks, ammo crates, and the flag of South Viet Nam get smaller and smaller as Willie flies into the future.

The Black Cat chuffs over the river, the dust-eating ARVN guards, and the refugee camp with kids running out, flies crawling in the noses and eyes of babies cradled in their little sisters' arms, racing for a shower of candy and C-rations thrown down from a passing convoy. Puffs of exhaust blast out behind Willie to settle in the river, mix with the convoy dust, fall in the worm- and life-rich paddies, and crawl with the flies in the babies' eyes. A little girl in ragged dress, baby in her arms, looks up as Willie flies by. You get a unique perspective up here: far but not close. The little girl is remote, an upturned face, a fly-speck in the eye.

Willie beats on toward the base and begins to descend over a winding creek where brown-faced buffalo boys look up from their herding among cropped-grass grave mounds. Here ran the old Hanoi–Saigon railroad, VC-bombed long ago, now swallowed by the base, by razor wire and mine fields, where GIs keep watch from sandbagged bunkers, sweeping their M-16 sights and M-60 snouts past the buffalo boys and among the silent tombs.

Willie lands on Pioneer Pad, rattling the frontiersman. Stevens, Lukitsch, and I climb on fast before Willie can change his mind.

"You guys look like hell!" Willie shouts.

Lukitsch and I squeeze in between Willie and the copilot, while Stevens hangs on in the open door. Lukitsch shows Willie his map of Ba Long, where he's drawn a large circle around the presumed location of the Rocket Company's camp. Willie shakes his head. He doesn't like the wild, ripped look of Stevens and me and the "Probable NVA Base" grease-penciled on the laminated plastic covering Lukitsch's map.

"It's OK!" I shout. "We'll stay high. They won't want to shoot and give away their position. Just one pass, so we can see my shirt."

Willie withdraws inside his insect-head helmet and begins to play with the controls. Lukitsch and I move to join Stevens in the open doorway, and we watch the base fall away as we beat toward the river. Back to Ba Long, to the magic wilderness world of dancing streams, secret trails, strange trees, and ocean-rolling peaks.

I wish to speak a word for Nature, for absolute freedom and wildness.[3]

In the distance the river appears, winding like a giant serpent down from the jungle-cloaked mountains. LZ Pedro passes below, and the piedmont grass-sea changes to forest, where the rice-culture tide of human population has not yet flowed. Below us now is a remnant of the primeval forest world, marked only here and there by war scars. We beat on, engines bursting with power.

I guide Willie up the valley of the Khe Ba Long, the way we had come in the Red Devil chopper. Out the door I see the ruins of Viet's home vllage. It seems he is always here, like a spirit looking over my shoulder. I call Stevens up beside me. I want to make sure about the route we took up the west ridge and where we left the team. We see the LZ, and below begin to pass, silent and hidden and as in a dream, all the places we struggled through, with leaves in our faces, vines around our ankles, leeches chewing, insects biting, sweat stinging our open cuts and eyes. Now we float over it, remote, detached, enveloped in reinforced metal and Machine power.

We guide Willie over the west ridge and down where we walked submerged in the arrow-ravine. Below, totally hidden under the trees, are the myriad streams of the vast system in which we were lost, and, barely visible, a thin, snakelike line down the valley, a slight break and overlapping in the canopy, that marks the Khe Trai. Along that stream my shirt is hanging. We all hang on in the blasting wind, looking for it.

I see right away this will be harder than I thought. The forest floats by placidly too far below with no hint of *any* small clearing, let alone one with an almost-alone white-barked tree and an olive drab T-shirt. In a few quick heartbeat moments we fly the two and a half kilometers from the west ridge past Hills 300 and 320, and Willie banks for the river and home.

"Wait, go around again, Willie!" I shout. "And lower! We got to get lower!"

"Negatron!" Willie shouts back, and he shakes his big helmet, turns thumbs-down like Caligula, and beats on toward the base.

I squeeze up next to him and shout, "Just one more time. Come on, a little lower. We'll see it this time."

Willie knows it's not smart to fly over the same place twice, and not lower, especially if down there is a known NVA camp. But to my surprise he suddenly banks left, circles back along the river to the west ridge, drops to a lower altitude, roars down the arrow-ravine slope as if he were speed-skiing, and blasts over the valley. Willie is not immune to the seductive enigma of deep play, especially when it involves flying.

Flashes of rare silver burst in leaf gaps below, brief hits of the stream through the trees. We ride our aluminum dragonfly, holding on and looking down with composite eyes. Nothing. No clearing, no tree, no shirt. Willie banks for the river and home.

"One more time, Willie!" I shout. "Just one more. We're still too high. Take it down *low. Really* low. We'll see it this time."

Willie turns thumbs down again but banks hard left for the river and the ridge. Maybe his gesture means more than "No," and he's saying to himself through gritted teeth, "OK, I'll take it back again and low, just to show you what a stupid idea this is!"

Willie roars down the slope hardly clearing the trees. If the deer is still there, he's surely crashing through the tangles in panic. Birds, even insects, explode away, frantically trying to escape the noise, and the tiger races for some deep, secret hideout. Trees flash by in a green streak. No clearing, no tree, nothing. Now we're *too* low, and everything is passing by before we can see or even think. Wait! There! Not the shirt, but—wasn't it? The big cottonwood tree. Willie heads for the river and home.

"One more time, Willie! On the opposite bank. We think we saw the Trail crossing. Take it *upstream* this time, on the other side."

"Damn it!" Willie shouts. "Isn't that where the camp's supposed to be?"

"Don't worry about it." I shout. "They won't shoot and give themselves away."

With a Dürer *Apocalypse* death face, Willie banks sharp right. It seems he's doing this in anger. He crosses the stream and comes blasting back up. Stevens and I hang out the open door, and Lukitsch kneels between us, the map on his knee, his grease pencil poised. There! Yes! The big cottonwood tree.

"Mark!" Stevens and I shout, and we point wildly.

Lukitsch grease-pencils a big X on his map. We must be right over the camp . . . now! Suddenly the air around the speeding chopper explodes as big, streamlined pieces of hot metal stream up from the trees, burrowing holes in the atmosphere. The NVA are shooting at us with antiaircraft fire.

Whether through training and conscious thought by Willie, or fear-shocked pure action, the Black Cat goes crazy with evasive maneuvers, rolling like a tomcat fighting, left-right as the air around us continues to crack with the passage of the big bullets.

Stevens, Lukitsch, and I are flung around like rag dolls on the metal floor and almost fly out. We wedge ourselves in the open doorway and under the seats, grabbing each other and the seat supports, anything we can clutch, as the Black Cat rocks and hurtles on. What would it be like to tumble out into the streaming green world?

The door gunner rides his M-60 like a bucking bronco, ripping long bursts down into the trees and straight up in the air as Willie throws hard rolls. Heavy slugs from Asia and America shoot up from the ground and down from the sky, cutting leaves, splitting branches, burrowing into the heart of Gaia. Willie flies as hard and fast as he can, fights for altitude over the river, then beats grim and hunched over the controls back toward the base.

In the back, Stevens, Lukitsch, and I celebrate. It was another Magic Flight,[4] an Escape of Prometheus, Black Cat–aided and with Willie as a reluctant Hercules. Now, back to the base, that transplanted fragment of the World, to prepare to return to the forest and the Trail, our initiation not yet complete, more enemies to face, more lessons to learn, more messages to receive, and the Rocket Company still out there, with some antiaircraft protection. Dust plumes and scarred red earth come up in the distance: the Machine and civilization again.

We land and get out fast. Willie quickly walks around his Black Cat, tenderly touching its metal skin, checking for bullet holes. "That was big stuff," he shouts after us. "If just one of those had hit it would have been all over. Never again! *Never!*"

Sergeant Stevens heads for the huts of the Recon Platoon for a shower, clean clothes, and hot chow, then over to the club to drink and think, and later, to his cot, to lie reliving everything while listening to Johnny Cash.

Lukitsch and I walk rapidly to the TOC, talking mile-a-minute, still adrenaline-buzzed. I feel I could walk forever, fly. We duck into the narrow opening, go down the sand-bagged tunnel, and burst into the radio room. Lukitsch's men are glad to see him back. He and I crowd into his small office, feeling far too big for it, like Superman bursting out of his clothes. Batman and Robin still leap down from the poster as Lukitsch spreads his map on his desk.

"I suggest a raid," I say excitedly. "Small team, two choppers. We go the way Stevens and I did, but with Viêt to lead us from the Trail crossing to the camp. Soon, though, it has to be soon. Maybe tomorrow."

Lukitsch deflates, and I see in his face it's over: no more operations with the Machine. "It won't be soon," he says, "and maybe not ever. I don't think the general will go for another mission like this. He was very worried about losing one of his boys out there. And the brigade's given the AO south of the river back to the 1st ARVN Regiment. It's their war, I guess. We're on the way out."

I drive back to Quang Tri City thinking about the 1st Regiment. I'm not crazy about going out to the Trail with an all-Vietnamese unit, but who else is there? I think about Viêt. If Rang is right, Viêt's mission could be leading to this: destroy ARVN's best regiment and suck in the whole 1st Division. Of course! With U.S. forces leaving, the NVA will turn their attention to the ARVN, especially their elite units. Destroy the best and break the will of the rest. I feel filled with misgivings, but I have to go out there again.

> The spider turned him round about, and
> went into his den,
> For well he knew the silly fly would soon be
> back again:
> So he wove a subtle web, in a small corner
> sly,
> And set his table ready to dine upon
> the fly.[5]

I pull up to my house exhausted. Everything's catching up to me now. I drag myself out of my Scout, put my rifle in the closet, undress, and leave my bloody, ripped clothes for Ba Thuy to wash and mend. I look at myself in the mirror. I'm black-smeared, bruised, scraped, and haggard. I look like a

Cro-Magnon after a mammoth hunt. "What am I doing?" I ask myself. I rationalize that going after the Trail could help shorten the war and that would save a lot of lives. But I'm not fooling myself; I know why I go out there.

Man . . . never perceives anything fully or comprehends anything completely.[6]

CHAPTER 6

THE ROAD OF TRIALS, OR THE DANGEROUS ASPECT OF THE GODS

We have not . . . to risk the adventure alone; for the heroes of all time have gone before us; the labyrinth is thoroughly known; we have only to follow the thread of the hero-path. And where we had thought to find an abomination, we shall find a god; where had thought to slay another, we shall slay ourselves; where we had thought to travel outward, we shall come to the center of our own existence; where we had thought to be alone, we shall be with all the world.

—Joseph Campbell, *The Hero with a Thousand Faces*

I drive alone the dusty road that leads to LZ Nancy.[1] In the distance, Nancy rises like a goddess on her hill above the river, looking down where so many armies had passed: Viets, Chinese, Cham, French, Japanese, American, and unknown peoples long before, marching and killing. In an age before man, Nancy had risen through the warm, shallow waters of the South China Sea to stand rich with life and cloaked with vegetation, catching the rain from the clouds and sending it back down the river to the sea. Now Nancy was devoid of all vegetation, and the only life evident on her was man-life, war-life. Nancy had been scraped, blasted, burned, built on, wired, mined, polluted, and defoliated. Once a verdant vestal virgin, Nancy was a brown war-hill now, a Hell-hill, as mighty Mars swung his sword and fiery, blood-swilling Huitzilipochtli demanded more sacrifice.

I pause at Nancy's gate while a young 1st Regiment ARVN in U.S. helmet, uniform, and boots, and with an M-16 in one hand, drags the barbed wire open. Dust plumes behind my Scout as I drive up through more rings of wire to regimental headquarters at the top of the hill, where the South Vietnamese flag flies and howitzers point west at the Trail. I park beside two ARVN jeeps and descend to the underground, S-2 office of Captain Anh. I don't get the usual friendly, teasing greeting; Anh is hunched tight over a radio, and I freeze and listen. He's talking to Khai, whose team is lying low near the Trail near the Laos border, observing many NVA trucks pass. Troops are walking by, too, and Khai's voice comes back from out there strained, whispered, and broken by static and fear. Anh and his radioman, a corporal, exchange worried glances.

"Go off the air," Anh says. "Don't take any more chances."

Anh tells the radioman to get him if anything happens, then leads me to the briefing room. We sit in near dark and talk. The rows of empty metal chairs make me think of dead soldiers gone to their graves. I wonder if Khai will sit here again?

Anh metamorphoses from grimness, and regains his mischievous twinkle. He eyes the K-54 at my belt and says, "I wonder why Khai and Bao gave that to *you?* Better they give to their commanding officer: *me.*"

I shrug and think of saying, *I guess I'm just a likeable guy.*

"I heard you buy them things at the PX," Anh says. "They got some business going with Viêt."

I'm surprised that he knows this, but I shouldn't be.

"It's OK," Anh says. "Their army pay is very little, hardly enough to buy rice for their families, and prices always rising. Even me, it's hard to live—and the VC make nothing."

We think soberly about that last for a moment, then Anh brightens again as the cycles turn and the present reminds us we're here. "So what you got for me?"

I try to tell him the story of the last operation, but he interrupts: "I know that already. So what you got *new* for me?"

"The Rocket Company is still there. We can hit it."

"How you know it's there? You see it?"

"We heard it."

"Not same thing. You got to get close, like my teams. See, touch; then you know."

"We got close," I say. I feel like a kid whom no one believes. I want to shout, "Yes, we did! We did it! We got close!"

Anh leans back and smiles, "So what you want from me?"

My plan pours out in a rush: "Two teams. We go the way Stevens and I did. I can lead; Viêt will take over on the approach to the camp."

Anh shakes his head. "No good. Maybe you get lost. And Viêt doesn't know that way; he knows on the Trail. Anyway, we have no choppers for insert."

I feel my stomach drop, and I remember Willie flying the dunes and pulling the Black Cat high into a deliberate stall and the bottom falling out.

Anh laughs; he loves to play me like a yo-yo. "No problem. We go talk to my colonel. Maybe we don't need choppers. Walk!"

Both hope and fear hit: we're going, but a long walk means high chance of ambush.

We walk through a passageway to Colonel Thuong's office. "Now it begins," I think, "the maddening delays: briefings, planning, paperwork, clearances, weather, and probably far worse with the ARVN. We advise them, don't we?"

"Monsieur Chiêu Hôi," Thuong says, rising from his desk and extending his hand, the Vietnamese shake more a touch than an American crunch. "*Il y a longtemps. . . .*"

Thuong and I know each other slightly; he likes to speak French. He motions for us to sit and sends a sergeant for tea. We small-talk in French a few minutes, then Thuong says to Anh in Vietnamese, "What is it?"

Anh describes the situation and points it out on the map.

"Here's where it dies," I think gloomily, "or begins to be spread far and wide."

The sergeant comes in with tea on a tray, and Anh keeps talking. I wonder about the sergeant as I watch him pour; he's hearing everything. I wonder about Thuong, too, even Anh. Maybe going with the ARVN is a big mistake.

Thuong asks Anh several quick questions. I can't follow, and they're not translating. I hear units and commanders discussed. Thuong interrupts. He's heard enough. "It's over," I think. "This is the end."

"Good operation," Thuong says in English to me. "I give it to 3rd Battalion, my best. You go tomorrow. Today better, but they are finishing other operation."

Tomorrow! I stumble in French trying to tell him I've been there on recon and have a good plan to hit the camp, that we can. . . .

Thuong waves his hand impatiently: "No, no. You go talk to Major Toan, 3rd Battalion commander. He will go, not me. *He* will make plan."

I drive back to Quang Tri City flying. No paperwork, briefings, planning, delays for the weather? Just *go*? This is great! But who to get to go with me? I don't want to be the Lone Ranger with an all-Indian unit. Stevens can't go, nor anyone else in the brigade. I know: Ramos. Ramos is *dying* to go out there.

I drive to the Mai Linh District compound near Quang Tri City to look for him. Sergeant Eddie Ramos, from Puerto Rico and New York City, recently married and on his third volunteer tour in Viet Nam, is an advisor there. Ramos looks amazingly like the Cuban rebel Che Guevara, though with a more *loco* look and with darker skin and eyes. I find him on radio watch in the Mai Linh TOC, feet up on a table, reading a paperback and listening to Armed Forces Radio rock 'n' roll over the province-net hiss. He looks up and flashes a dazzling smile. Ramos has a perpetual energy-dynamo look of "*Peligro!*" — "Danger!" — and "Let's do it!"

He looks around like he's planning something illegal. "Hey, *'mano,*" he says. "*Qué pasa?* What's the scoops? Time to get nice?"

We talk in a kind of code, some Spanish, military, and Vietnamese slang and a few words of our own invention. We're partners in crime—nothing major, mostly rebellion against authority and stealing time.

"Op's on," I say. "Indian country. Want to go?"

Ramos throws down his book and jumps up, his chair falling over behind him, his black eyes glowing like coals in a fire. "So, *qué?*" he says in his husky voice. "What you got?"

I begin to tell the story. I feel nervous inside; I'm rocking up on my toes as I talk. I'm hardly aware of where I am, part of me intensely staring at Ramos, part of me already out on the Trail. The words come out in a rush, like water over rocks.

Ramos moves around the table and is in my face before I can finish. He looks like toro and matador combined. "I'm goin'!" he says.

"You think your captain will let you?"

"Hey, I'm *goin',*" Ramos says. "*Tú me necesitas.* You tell him. You need a radioman, weapons man, bodyguard, whatever. *Dung roi!* Damn right! Come on, you go talk to him."

Ramos rushes out to find a substitute radio watch and drags me to see his captain, the district senior advisor, a man, unfortunately, I don't know well. He's a recent replacement for Captain Ollie, who was badly wounded as a result of the Rocket Company's last attack on Quang Tri City, the one Việt and I saw with Blunt from LZ Pedro. To get rocket fragments for the daily briefing, Captain Ollie, a fine black athlete; the young engineer advisor, Lieutenant Gilbert; and an ARVN interpreter inexplicably walked into a marked mine field around an ARVN base. Lieutenant Gilbert and the interpreter were killed, and Ollie, the last we heard, was in danger of losing his leg. It seemed the Rocket Company didn't need to score hits to cause casualties, and they could terrorize simply by shooting some now and then, showing the people once again we couldn't protect them, no matter how high-tech and powerful we were and how many troops we had around. Wasn't that reason enough to go out there after them?

The captain is in his office. I put on my best Foreign Service front and say, "Captain, I'd like to request that Sergeant Ramos accompany me on an operation. It's very important. I need a radioman, one that knows the Vietnamese well. We're going with the 1st ARVN Regiment. It's a good combined mission, good for Vietnamization."

The captain is new, while Ramos and I have been in Viet Nam a total of almost six years. "You want to go on this mission, Sergeant Ramos?" the captain asks.

"Yes, sir," Ramos says. "Mr. Stevens needs a radioman, and I know the 1st Regiment. I been out with them plenty."

"Where is this operation?"

"Ho Chi Minh Trail." I look around as if I can't say much about it, as if the walls have ears.

"How long?"

"Maybe three days."

"Maybe four," Ramos says.

"OK," the captain says. "But be careful out there."

Ramos races off to prepare, and I drive around Quang Tri City looking for Viêt. I find him at the house of one of his business contacts, carrying cases of soda and beer through a narrow alley to a small truck. His new Honda motorbike leans against a crumbling wall.

Viêt is sweating and puffing; he looks like he's gaining more weight. I help him carry the cases and recognize them as the ones I bought him recently at the PX, plus some others, probably Khai and Bao's share. We load the truck and then talk apart in low voices. I tell him we're going, and he wipes his brow and looks at the truck. What can he say? Têt is over, time to go back to the war.

"Let's meet tonight at seven for ice cream by the river," he says. "Vinh is coming—after he takes his girlfriend home. Don't worry, I'll be ready to go tomorrow. Any place you want. Any time."

Viêt doesn't ask where, and I wonder if he already knows. I go home and put rain gear, food, grenades, and ammunition in my pack and then drive to the café by the river. Vinh, my former interpreter, is waiting at an outside table when I pull up in my Scout. He looks up quickly and then checks all around.

Vinh, like Anh, is Vietnamese movie-star handsome, but while Anh is mischievous and laid-back, Vinh is intense and full of nervous energy. Like Ramos, Vinh is always darting his eyes furtively around, but with Ramos it's for misdemeanor, while Vinh has the look of a serious felon. He is, too, in the view of the Saigon government, anyway: he's a draft dodger; he doesn't want to get killed in an endless war.

Four ARVN are sitting at an outside table, and Vinh moves away to one near the street. The cafe owner, I think and hope, pays the VC not to bomb the place. It's a starry night, with a breeze off the river. I look around, wonder where Viêt is, and can't stop the image that comes: Viêt passing the word to the woodcutter woman, "Leaving tomorrow. Alert all units in Ba Long."

Vinh leans across the small table and talks low in jerky, nervous English. He's twenty-two and enrolled as a student at Huê University, his dodge since he stopped working for me and the advisory team. He could be picked up anytime by the ARVN, though, dragooned off the street and taken to training camp. In a few weeks he'd be a lieutenant, and soon after that, probably dead.

"I'm worried about Viêt," he says. "You got to talk to him."

I lean toward him over the table and talk low. "You mean the black market?"

"No, the way he talks—he's going to get in big trouble, maybe drag me in, too."

I lean closer. The ARVN are talking loud and flirting with the young waitress. "What kind of talk?" I say.

Vinh looks around, eyes darting at the ARVN and quickly away. "About the VC," he says. "About the North. About how good they are, and how bad life here is."

A motorbike coming fast and loud cuts into all our conversations. The ARVN look hard at Viêt as he parks the new red Honda. He's dressed in Saigon cowboy style, with tight pants, white shirt, and dark glasses. He greets us, shakes hands lightly, and sits down. The waitress comes right away, and we order sherbet and Cokes with ice.

Vinh tries to loosen up a little. "He's got a girlfriend," he says to me in English, then repeats it in Vietnamese.

"*Ba lap!*" Viêt says. "You bullshit!" He's learning a little English.

"Is she beautiful?" I ask Viêt.

"Very," Vinh says. "One of Quang Tri's best."

"*Ba lap,*" Viêt says again.

Viêt is embarrassed, but likes it, too. He looks happy in a way I haven't seen before. He leans back and looks around as if he owns the place. The ARVN continue talking nearby, and the waitress brings our sherbet, glasses with ice, and Coke in cans from the PX.

Vinh drums his fingers nervously on the table as Viêt begins to talk excitedly in a not-too-quiet voice: "Today I saw buffalo boys in the graveyard by the base. They should be in school. But they'll never go, never! You know why? Their parents have no money to send them. No money! In the North, you don't need money to go to school. School is free. Everyone goes, even the poorest."

Vinh darts a quick glance at the ARVN, huddled over their small dishes of ice cream. This kind of talk can be deadly. Vinh reaches out and squeezes Viêt's arm. "Brother Viêt," he says. "Don't talk so loud."

Viêt lowers his voice, but only a little. He seems totally lost in what he's saying, possessed by it. "You know what I saw at the hospital here, too? No one cares. No one cares unless you have money. Oh, then the doctors will come, and the nurses, too, maybe even the hospital director. But no money? No attention! The VC have nothing in their hospitals compared to here, but they care. Sometimes that's all we had to take care of the wounded. But it's the most important. We cared! Here it's just money."

Vinh reaches over to me and says in English, "You got to stop him."

The ARVN are starting to notice us, lowering their voices and trying to hear.

"Brother Viêt," I say, and I squeeze his arm. "Eat your sherbet. And tell us about your girlfriend."

Viêt's eyes fall to his dish and he begins to scoop. He has a kind of crazy look. All those years in the VC, all those endless days lying in the tight grip of the earth in underground, tomblike bunkers: What has he seen, what has he done, and what kind of strain is he going through now?

Vinh quickly says, "Maybe he's going to get married soon."

"You big *ba lap,*" Viêt says.

Viêt runs his spoon around his bowl, chasing the last sherbet as if he's just come in from the mountains. He drains his Coke, says good-bye, and heads for his Honda. I watch him and think: behind the dark glasses and underneath the flashy clothes, he's still a true believer.

Ramos and I meet later. We have to persuade Willie to fly us to Firebase Ann, home of the 3rd Battalion, because Anh has no chopper to get us there and Ann is beyond the frontier in

Indian country, where you don't even think of driving. We park at the MACV compound and go into the barracks, where GIs in underwear stroll the halls and tape-deck music plays rock, country, and soul from the small, plywood cubicles of officers' quarters. We stop outside Willie's room.

"Better let me handle this, *'mano,*" Ramos says. "He's not gonna be too happy to see you, *cabrón.*"

I wait outside, listening to Sam and Dave rock down the hall, where they meet Steppenwolf and Merle Haggard coming out of other rooms. *Playboy* pictures are everywhere, like icons in a Russian church.

Ramos comes out sooner than I expected, with his black eyes flashing. "*Sin problema,*" he says, "We got our flight *mañana,* man!"

"He knows I'm going?"

"Hey, I don't want him to cancel at the last minute; I gotta tell him *todo.* Anyway, you know me: I'm an out-front *hombre,* man."

"How'd you get him to go?"

"Not important now; I tell you later. The important thing is, we're goin'."

Early in the morning, Ramos, Việt, and I meet at Citadel Pad. Ramos is full of energy and *feliz;* Việt is silent and gloomy. He's thinking of his girlfriend and is afraid of the ARVN; he says Ramos and I won't be able to protect him out there.

Willie and his crew roll up in a jeep. Willie shoots me a grimace, then says to Ramos, "Remember our deal."

We board, and the Black Cat soon captures our hearing, olfactory sense, brain waves, and heart rhythms. We're part of it now, part of the Machine again. Việt is already airsick. We fly over the old Citadel walls, swing southwest, and head for Ann. Tile and tin roofs of Quang Tri City pass below, and conical straw hats bobbing, upturned faces, the marketplace, small trucks, and buses rolling. The city shades into the countryside, paddylands, and sky, and all along the western horizon, the mountains and forests, our boar's tooth and tiger-fang Bali Hai. Ramos and I strain forward, eager to get there. Viêt's head is hanging, rolling; he looks half dead. We roar over the silent green world. Within us there is the wild firing of nerves across the gaps, the spinning and tumbling of atoms; without, there is chop and beat of engine and rotor, whirling elementary particles in both the micro- and macroworlds. Behind is Creation, from which we're still streaming, and ahead is . . . what—collapse, incineration, decay? We are coming to hurt Mother Earth—not intentionally; we aren't even thinking about that. We are just men living, acting out ancient impulses, long ages of warrior inside the mask.

Willie flies high over the piedmont and the woodcutters' paths leading to the forest. This is no joke, no game, no caper: people are going to die. We are like gods of an ancient time, riding thunderbolts across the sky.

In the distance Ann rises like a sacrificial pyramid. Willie radio-talks, gets the Australian advisor with the 3rd Battalion, and shouts back at us, "Hey! They been takin' rockets today!"

Fear and excitement hit like lightning. Ramos jumps up and grabs the open doorway looking out, his moustache fierce in the wind. Bare, defoliated Ann now looks like a frontier outpost surrounded by hostile Indian country. It is the last ARVN island in a rising NVA sea.

Willie circles Ann high above antiaircraft range. No one is visible. There are trenches, bunkers, sandbags, and wire, but no people. It's as if we're flying to a lost outpost, a ghost ship on the forest-sea.

"They been catchin' rockets *recently!*" Willie shouts.

Below, an ARVN jumps out of a hole, pops a green smoke grenade on a terraced pad cut out of Ann's side, and jumps back into his hole. Willie roars for the cloud of billowing green smoke, while Ramos, Viêt, and I prepare to jump.

"Get out!" Willie shouts as he hovers above the pad, his rotors catching the smoke as if it were magnetized and then flinging it away.

We leap out and run for the nearest hole. Halfway there, the mighty *Whoosh!* of an NVA rocket roars over and slams into the forest just beyond Ann's base, knocking trees down as if by the incredible noise. Willie shoots away downslope, going for speed then altitude as he sails over the forest and beats like hell for home.

An ARVN leads us fast up through a labyrinth of wire, terraces, mine fields, and killing zones to an immense log, steel mesh, and sandbag bunker near the top of the hill. We push open a heavy door and step into a dark cave of musty smells and dimly seen forms moving in the gloom.

We stand for a moment letting our senses adjust. Voices come out of the shadows, none of them directed at us. Weapons and ammo crates are everywhere. If the NVA over-run Ann, this is where the last, desperate struggle will be fought to its bloody end. Radios hiss, and Vietnamese language rises, falls, and makes explosive sounds. Viêt shrinks up and moves behind Ramos and me, his back against the heavy door. A rotund major emerges from the sea of faces; behind him is a lean, sharklike captain.

The major holds out his hand: "I am Toan. This is my XO, Captain Mao."

Mao, the battalion's executive officer, stands back so he won't have to shake hands. He looks beyond Ramos and me and hunts Viêt with his eyes. "Come with me," he says. "I want to talk to you."

"Yes, Captain," Viêt says in a small voice.

I suddenly fear for Viêt as he moves around Ramos and me and follows Mao to a far corner beyond cases of grenades and armed, tough-looking ARVN. I can barely see them there, Mao talking and Viêt nodding.

"So," Toan says to me and Ramos, "you will join my battalion for operation. My 1st Company will go, my best. You leave tomorrow. Now they are coming back from last operation."

I try to tell him about Stevens's and my recon and my plan for the operation, but he cuts me off. "Don't tell me; waste time. Captain Mao will lead; *he* will make plan."

My spirits sink. Mao looks hard and unfriendly to me; I feel he doesn't like Americans. He might cut Ramos and me out of the operation. The Australian major and two Americans, a lieutenant and a spec 4, appear behind Toan.

"These my advisors," Toan says. "You need something, you tell them." He joins Mao in the corner, and now I can't see Viêt at all.

"We're not really advisors," the major says in a heavy Aussie accent. "There's nothing we can advise Toan and Mao on. You learn from them."

Toan and Mao bring Viêt back. Viêt looks ashen. He moves again behind me and Ramos.

I try to explain about the recon and my plan for the operation to Mao, but he quickly interrupts: "I don't speak good English."

"*Français?*" I ask.

He shakes his head.

I try Vietnamese but get nervous. Mao lets me sputter for a while, then says, "You been to this camp? I don't think so. You don't know the way. *He* knows." He looks hard over my shoulder at Viêt. "And now I know. Anyway, to make plans here is no good. Make them out there." Mao's eyes go to the door and through it, to the forest and mountains.

"He know very well what to do," Toan says, and he looks at Mao. "Already he led thirteen raids on NVA camps, *night* raids. Nobody else do that. Two nights ago he led my 1st Company on night raid, kill twenty-three NVA. Maybe more this time. No more rockets hit my base."

Toan laughs, and except for Mao and Viêt, the rest of us laugh with him. Mao continues staring hard at Viêt and through him, out the door. Viêt looks down, seems gone. It's stuffy in the bunker and smells of sandbags, damp earth, *nuoc mam,* and sweat.

No more rockets come in, and I say to Ramos, "Let's make a little exploration."

Viêt starts to go, too, but Mao says, "You stay. I want to ask more questions."

Ramos and I push open the door. It's good to be outside, to feel fresh air on our faces. We climb to the top and take pictures of each other. How long do we have to live as we snap the shutter, how many minutes, hours, years?

From up here Ann looks even more like a sacrificial pyramid with carved terrace-steps descending. Down at the bare base where the last wire ends, a broad, defoliated death zone begins and then the first vegetation, long grass blowing in the wind, and not far away, the forest and more hills. Tomorrow we'll be out there.

"I'm not sleeping in that bunker," Ramos says. "I don't feel *good* in that place, man. *Muy malo!*"

"I'm going for the chopper pad," I say. "Nice and flat, fresh air, deep trench if more rockets come in."

"You s'pose Viêt's OK?"

We return to the bunker to get our gear. Viêt decides to stay inside for the night. Mao has gone to meet 1st Company in the forest, and Viêt is making friends with a few of the ARVN. He likes the bunker's rocket protection, too.

Ramos and I go into the outer world again. The breeze is cool on the high hill as the sun drops toward Laos. We're only about five kilometers from the Rocket Company's camp here, through dense forest and complex terrain. I wonder how Mao's going to get us there and if he'll take my suggestions, follow my plan.

We spread our ponchos on the chopper pad and break out our rations. We trade a few, mostly end up with what we like, and chow down. We're feeling good, excitement building higher with the knowledge of tomorrow. A fog begins to materialize from the forest and move toward Ann. It's like the breath of the trees, like sea smoke. Ramos and I watch in awe. It's both beautiful and frightening. It comes closer, creeping through the grass toward the death zone.

"It's going to cover the hill."

Like ghost-spirits marching, ancestor warriors streaming from the trees, the fog comes, silver gray through the elephant grass, crossing the death zone; nothing can stop it. Ramos and I back away from the pad's edge as it rises up Ann, sit down on our ponchos, and wait. The fog rolls over us and we become strange shadows a few feet away, then almost hidden from each other. We're in it, part of it now. It seems to be lit from within, a kind of glow. Our voices pass back and forth like spirits.

"This is weird, man."

"It's like there's nothing else but—this."

"You got it."

In the morning the sun shines through the fog in rays like golden arrows. We cook C-ration chow with heat tabs, and Ramos brews coffee in his canteen cup. All over Ann, ARVN emerge from bunkers and holes, and warm smells and wood smoke waft over the hill.

"Check this out," Ramos says.

To the southwest near the forest a long line of men comes out of the trees: 1st Company, back from killing NVA. The Aussie major and the two Americans join us with their packs and weapons.

"We're going with you, mates," the Aussie says. "Major Toan finally agreed. Rare thing for him, and Mao almost never. They look bad if they lose an advisor." Viêt arrives with Biên, a friend he's made from Mao's staff, an entourage part aide-de-camp and part bodyguard. Biên looks about fourteen and is the company clown, one of those naturally high-spirited and funny guys who's always laughing and joking around. We all troop down to join 1st Company. They're in the defoliated death zone, waiting for resupply.

Mao in the distance is talking with a tall, hard-looking lieutenant, 1st Company's commanding officer.

"Lieutenant Anh," the Aussie says. "No relation to Captain Anh and almost no resemblance. You won't find many lieutenants like him in *any* army."

Anh looks at us and doesn't smile. Another tall ARVN joins Mao and Anh. He's weathered and scarred but has a kindly look, like Colonel Herndon.

"First Sergeant Bê," the Aussie says, "and a finer man you'll never find. He's like a father to these young ARVN."

Bê approaches, welcomes us to the company, and says to Viêt in a gentle voice, "The captain and the lieutenant want to see you, little brother."

Viêt looks at me as he goes off behind Bê, and I follow. Mao and Anh do not look happy to see me tag along. Bê tries to lighten the mood by introducing Anh, who barely acknowledges me and begins to question Viêt in a harsh, demanding voice. I feel he's showing me Viêt is his now, and I am nothing here.

Viêt answers in a small voice, giving more details about the Rocket Company's camp. Mao and Anh move away to confer, and Bê moves to Viêt's side to reassure him. Suddenly I wonder: is Viêt, so terrified looking, actually leading us all like lambs to the slaughter?

Ramos moves among the ARVN, making friends. "Hey,

'mano!" he calls to me. "Come meet these guys! These are some *hombres, man!"*

Helicopter noise sweeps over us, and a Chinook appears like a giant locust in the east. It roars in, lands, and blasts us all with Agent Orange–laced dust. Young ARVN rush out and throw off rice bags, ammo crates, a box with live chickens inside, and packages of sun-dried shrimp. The Chinook flies away, the ARVN load up, and we're ready to go.

Mao sends Bê with orders: "The captain wants all advisors in the middle of the column, behind Headquarters Section. Viêt—to the front with Captain Mao."

Our long green line of 125 men snakes around the bare base of Ann and heads toward the elephant-grass sea and the forest to the north. Big hills covered with vegetation look down on us as we leave. I know the NVA are watching from up there: they must monitor all movement in and out of Ann. We walk on an old woodcutters' trail till we're out of sight of Ann, then turn into the elephant grass. Now I see part of Mao's plan: he'll lose us from sight in the elephant grass.

We struggle and beat against the grass; we're soaked with sweat and steaming. We climb one hill and then another. The grass-sea seems endless, overwhelming. We mash it down and try to move forward before it rises. A blade rips the bridge of my nose; another slices the back of my hand. We climb hill after hill like a giant serpent thrashing.

The order of march soon breaks down. These ARVN are tough jungle men, but Mao is pushing us beyond limits. Ahead of me an ARVN crashes down with heat exhaustion, and the medic rushes up from behind. Other ARVN lurch to the side, gasping, till the medic comes to them, too, and in the process Ramos and I make our way closer to the front. Viêt and Mao are not far ahead of us now, with two men from the point element. Mao is fiercely driving, challenging, and Viêt is right on his heels. Behind Viêt, a young ARVN from Mao's entourage with a live rooster riding on his pack stumbles, refocuses on Mao's back, and keeps pushing himself on. My shirt, pack, and pants are drenched with sweat and heavy. Behind me, Ramos is breathing irregularly, a bad sign. Ahead, the ARVN is stumbling again, another warning of heat exhaustion. The brightly colored rooster cocks its head to look at the ARVN and then the ground, as if it can sense its ride ending. I push myself, concentrating on keeping up with Mao and Viêt and trying not to let Ramos's ragged breathing or the ARVN's stumbling affect me. Mao pushes ahead of one of the point men and is second in line now, with Viêt right behind.

The faltering point man suddenly catapults backward, as if all the grass he has been pushing against has recoiled to show him who's master. He sits dazed in the tangle.

"Medic up!" Mao shouts. He sees me and Ramos and frowns. He doesn't like us up here, and I'm determined he won't walk me down.

Mao takes the point, with Viêt second. Behind me, Ramos is in trouble. His breathing rhythm is completely gone, and he's stumbling as if he's drunk. I hear him gasp something in Spanish and fall with a crash of gear and rifle. He struggles to his hands and knees and begins to vomit in the grass.

Viêt rushes past me to Ramos's side. He takes Ramos's rifle, pulls off his pack, and helps him lie down. The ARVN medic appears, and he and Viêt administer first aid. Viêt stands and slings Ramos's pack and rifle on. Ramos looks up, weak and embarrassed. He tries to get Viêt to give back his rifle and gear, but Viêt keeps it and says, "Just till you're strong again. You'll carry mine someday."

I try to get Viêt to give me something to carry, and finally he hands over Ramos's rifle. We hurry to catch up, Viêt falling back into Mao's wake. Three steps ahead of me, the ARVN is staggering and losing it fast. The rooster shifts his feet nervously on the pack, cocking his head so his red wattle falls across one eye and then the other. The ARVN takes one more wobbling step and pitches forward. The rooster spreads his wings, rides the fall down, and still stands on the pack while the ARVN lies flat on his face as if dead. The rooster turns his head left and right, looking curiously at the ARVN and seeming to say, "Does this mean I have to walk now?"

The medic appears from behind, sweat streaming, and kneels at the ARVN's side. How many miles has the medic walked up and down our ragged line? Mao exchanges quick words with him on the soldier's condition, then pushes up the hill like a demon. Viêt and I continue hot on his trail, *all* of us possessed.

Mao drives himself to the hilltop and stops where the grass is short and there is a view of the river. Viêt veers off to give him space; I stand close, trying not to breathe hard.

"Where's your friend?" Mao says, with challenge in his words.

"Back there with your men," I say.

Mao smiles; he liked that riposte. OK, I'll be myself around him now. He looks at Viêt, and I see a certain respect in his eyes.

The young ARVN with the rooster struggles to the top of the hill and looks at Mao with chagrin. Mao reassures him, saying, "You're doing good. It happens to everyone."

More ARVN sweat and stumble up, and all look anxiously at Mao. Mao is like a god to them. To the northwest, between two grass-covered hills and beyond a broad belt of forest, we can see the river shining silver in the sun. Mao pulls out a map, orients it to the hills and the river, and studies it carefully. Now I think I see more of his plan: he's taking us to the old river road, then up the Trail-stream. Going the same way we killed the commissar doesn't sound good, and I start to go over and tell him, but Anh comes up and they confer apart. We rest on the hill, hidden in the grass, till everyone is accounted for and rested enough to continue.

Mao leads through another grass-sea to a stream with forest rising on the other side. I drink, dash water on my face, and fill my canteens. With my face near the water, I look upstream. I know these waters! This is the Khe Trai, it *has* to be. Upstream only a few kilometers is the Trail crossing and the Rocket Company's camp. I splash across the stream to Mao.

"I know this stream," I say.

He looks annoyed and says nothing. My Vietnamese falters and starts to desert me.

"I think it's the Khe Trai," I say.

"I *know* it is," Mao says.

"We could follow this stream. On our recon here—"

"Really? You came here? You saw the camp?"

"We could follow this stream to the Trail crossing."

"You sure you know this place? You know the way from here to there? Maybe you'll get us lost."

"It's not good to go the same way we went—"

Mao interrupts again. He doesn't like to hear me say I've been here before, as if he's the only one who comes out here.

"Sure? You've been here before?"

"Yes. I've been on three operations now after the Rocket Company."

"Then maybe you better go my way. Your way is no good."

"We could follow this stream," I say.

"'This stream!'" Mao snorts. "This stream is many streams. If you really have been out here before, you know that."

He turns and vanishes into the trees. I imagine him in there, swimming like a shark through the vines and leaves.

Waiting for my place in line to pass, I kneel and plunge my hands into the water, feeling the current pulse against my wrists. I look upstream and picture NVA at the Trail crossing, stepping on the flat rock and going into the tunnel by the big cottonwood tree. I *know* I could lead us up there and find them.

Ramos passes by and says, "Let's hit it."

We push through the forest toward the river all day. In the late afternoon, Mao calls a halt on top of a hill. Through a break in the trees on the far side, we can see a big, snakelike curve in the river, soft silver gray under the darkening sky. Mao stands alone on the highest point of the hill, studying his map and the river. Around him his retinue works quickly. Viêt's friend Biên strings a hammock between trees and ties a poncho over it, while the rooster ARVN digs a deep hole nearby and rigs more rain gear. Other ARVN prepare a cooking fire and dig more holes around the crest of the hill. Anh and Bê are everywhere, directing the hum of activity and occasionally conferring with Mao.

Mostly Mao lies in his hammock, hat over his eyes. He looks asleep, but frequently he sits up, studies his map and the river, then lies back again. Not far away, and a little lower, Viêt, Ramos, the advisors, and I break off our Mao-watching and set up our shelter, snapping shelter halves and ponchos together, then tying the corners to bushes. We crawl inside, mash the ferns and forest-floor plants down, take off our boots and socks, and arrange our packs and rifles for sleeping. All around the sound of ARVN digging continues.

Viêt is in one of his manic moods after the depression of the bunker on Ann. "We're not digging holes," he says, "because we're not afraid. We're not afraid of the NVA! We're not afraid to die!"

"Not true!" I say, imitating him. "We're not digging holes because we're tired, and because we're planning to jump in the ARVNs' holes if the NVA attack."

"I got first crack at Mao's," Ramos says. "Looks nice and deep. Dry, too, with that rain gear over it."

"I wouldn't advise it," the Aussie says. "And definitely not Anh's. Better to take your chances with the NVA."

I lie back and stare up at our thin poncho roof, then twist on my side and look at Mao. He's lying back again, hat over his

face, map still in his hand. He seems the complete professional, warrior nonpareil. I feel safe with these ARVN. If the NVA
attack, they'll beat them back; they won't sleep on watch, and
they know what they're doing. I feel safe in the forest, too.
Even if the NVA have followed us—and Anh at the back of the
column has guarded against that—the heavy canopy protects
us from the high-angle fire of rockets and mortars. Soon the
spirit-fog will materialize, too, and hide us in its moving
shroud. We're even going to sleep dry tonight.

There's just one problem, one *big* problem. The smell of
chicken cooking is wafting toward us from Mao's part of the
hill. We all sit up and stare. Around Mao his entourage is
preparing a feast, while we have cold cans of C-rations to look
forward to.

"*No puedo,*" Ramos says. "I can't handle this, man! He
knew the wind would blow the smell to us. That's why he had
Bê tell us to set up here!"

More excruciating smells blow across the top of the hill,
and Ramos's nostrils flare. "Shrimp soup, too! And rice! *No
puedo!*"

Night flows out of the west, sweeps down the big bend in
the river, and crawls with the fog toward the top of our hill.
Someone is coming, a tall form walking, more like swimming, through the waist-deep vegetation. Bê bends low and
looks in our shelter. His old soldier's face is surprisingly
gentle. He has a courtliness about him, too, that belies his
peasant past and hard, war-scarred body. In formal Vietnamese he says astonishing words: "The captain invites you
for dinner."

We scramble like hillbillies for our boots and stomp over to
Mao's hammock. A fire glows here, dancing light against dark
trees, and ARVN shapes move around it like shamans. Mao is
sitting up and staring down at an amazing sight: a red tablecloth spread on the grass and neatly set with eight plastic

bowls, small saucers with slices of red and green chili peppers floating in *nuoc mam,* chopsticks, and teacups. Biên passes us with a large pot from the fire and puts it in the center of the tablecloth. Anh comes out of the night, wild-looking, firelight dancing on his face, while Bê oversees the last preparations.

Mao slides out of his hammock, turns to us for the first time, and says in formal Vietnamese, "Gentlemen, please, I invite you to eat." Both Mao and Bê have the courtliness, as if they have slipped from some Vietnamese feudal time of noble and retainer.

We plunk down in the grass. Viêt is subdued. He wouldn't have been invited if he weren't with us, and he especially avoids looking at Anh. Mao says something, and Biên brings a big blackened pot of steaming white rice. Mao concentrates on the arrival of the food, seeing that everything is done just right.

Mao waves his hand over the setting and says, "Please begin."

Mao shows us what to do: use chopsticks to take pieces of chicken or shrimp, dip them in the *nuoc mam,* and let them hover dripping over the rice. We eat and talk quietly. Firelight dances on our smiling faces, and our stomachs glow. Mao talks and everyone listens. Much of what he says is in English—he knows more than he has let on—and much seems directed at me, as if I represent an audience he wants to reach, some message he has to deliver.

"We don't like the military food you Americans give us. Mostly it's canned food, dead food. We like our food, Vietnamese food."

"It's very delicious," I say.

"That's why we sell, trade what you give us and buy our own food. How can we march and fight on dead food? Vietnamese food is alive."

"It's very good," I say. "I'll take some more."

"Good," Mao says. "Eat plenty. It's good for you."

Anh excuses himself to check ambush positions, and Bê directs the serving of tea. All around, the silent black trees look down, and the fire begins to burn low. At the edge of our magic tablecloth, bioluminescence begins to put on its nightly show. We rise, thank Mao, and walk slowly back to our part of the hill. A path is forming between us and Mao. We crawl into our shelter, take off our boots, and lie back with our feet on our packs. Rain begins, small drops boy-soldier drumming on our roof. Far off in the mountains artillery rumbles like thunder, big doors closing on life. I sleep, dry for once, and for the first time, too, on a mission out here, I don't dream of doom and death. I can't capture the dream on awakening, but I know it was good: it has left me with a kind of glow.

In the early-morning fog, no one moves, for a new danger threatens: rain has collected in several sagging bulges in our shelter roof, and with the wind blowing the bushes around, our dry night could suddenly end with a cascade of water dumping in on us and on our packs, socks, and boots.

I reach up and touch one of the big bulges and cup it in my hand. It feels like a milk-heavy breast, but cool, with the night still in it. I roll two together and make a bigger one. I can do this; I'll save us. I roll another in and make a huge one.

"*Cuidado, coño!*" Ramos says.

I almost lose the biggest one where our ponchos are snapped together. This is not as easy as I thought; the bulges seem to have a mind of their own and don't respond to my desire for control. I begin to roll the huge one toward the edge of our shelter, but it joins with another and threatens to get away and Niagara in on us. It hovers like a thing alive near a break in our roof.

"Stop!" Viêt says. "Don't move! I'll do it!"

Viêt carefully crawls out of the shelter, twisting like a yogi to avoid the ropes and the springy branches where they're tied.

He begins to ease and guide the pendulous udder, looking like he's done this before, picking up smaller ones on the way till he has them all together. The bulge now is immense. When he feels he has control, he moves fast and decisively and sends a great cascade of silver water over the roof's edge away from our boots.

"Yes!" he says. "Viêt does it again!"

Bê comes out of the morning fog, bends low, and looks under our roof. "The captain says we leave in fifteen minutes."

We scramble for our packs and boots, take down our shelter, and eat quick cans of Cs: cheese, "John Wayne" crackers, and hard, dark chocolate. We swig fast drinks of stream water, stow our canteens, and clomp over to Mao on the mashed-grass trail, crushing more of the now-extinguished bioluminescent twigs and leaves. They'll come on again after we're gone, converting death to life.

"What'd I tell you?" Ramos says. "No waiting for the weather, just go. These guys are *hot!*"

Bê intercepts our rush toward Mao. "The captain wants you to stay in the middle of the column," Bê says. "Behind Headquarters Section."

Ramos says low in my ear, "I got a bad feeling about this, *'mano*. I think Mao's tryin' to cut us out of the action."

We push through the forest, mostly downhill, Sisyphus over the edge. Mao drove us hard yesterday to have an easier time today, a slight calm before the fire storm. In the early afternoon we emerge onto the old river road. We're downstream from Hill 110, and there's no doubt about it now: Mao intends to take us up the stream-Trail, and this is not an odd-numbered day. He sends word back: he wants Viêt up.

Viêt looks at me and goes. Wind blows through the grass, and our line jerks forward. We walk up the road, watching both sides, rifles ready to blast. We walk where the tiger walked, where we walked to kill the commissar. The pendulum swings, you reap what you sow, action-reaction, karma. The good dream of last night is gone; this could be disaster.

Ahead, the point stops, and halt rolls down the line. Orders from Mao come whispering back from man to man: "Stop here, hide in the grass, eat, and rest. Viêt up."

Viêt goes, and I follow. I want to influence Mao's plan and be part of it, too. Mao frowns when he sees me come but motions me and Viêt to sit with him in the grass at the side of the road. Members of his entourage keep watch, Biên ahead and the rooster ARVN behind. The rest of 1st Company is hiding in the grass; they seem to have disappeared from the planet.

Mao questions Viêt on details of the hike from here to the camp. How far is it to where the Trail leaves the stream? How many branch streams? How far to the Trail crossing, the camp?

Mao sends Biên with a message: he wants nine volunteers for a raiding party. Quickly, twelve ARVN come forward, and Biên sends three back with a joke that's beyond my Vietnamese. Biên and eight young ARVN present themselves to Mao. Biên flashes me and Viêt a grin and the *V* peace sign.

Mao arranges the nine on the road in three columns of three, then puts Viêt in front of the first team, Biên in team two. All kneel on the road and look up at Mao.

Mao begins to speak, and I realize I'm witnessing an ancient tradition, the prebattle oration by a famous commander. I don't think Alexander, Caesar, and Napoleon were more respected, even worshiped, by their men than Mao is by these young ARVN.

I understand some of Mao's speech: "I want men who are intelligent first, then brave. Be careful and don't hurt your brothers. You will enter the camp behind Viêt: team one, to the first house, team two, to the second, team three, to the third. Viêt will place each team for attack. Team three will begin, with grenades and rifle fire into the house. All open up when you hear team three. Viêt will make sure the teams are out of each other's line of fire."

"Yes, Captain," Viêt says, looking up from one knee as if he were an aspirant knight awaiting the touch of the sword.

Mao kneels in the road, calls the raiding party around, and begins to draw the camp with his finger in the dirt. As he draws, he asks Viêt about the placement of the houses, the number of NVA in each, weapons, and the location of rocket caches.

"The rest of us will be just five minutes behind you," Mao says. "When the attack begins, we'll soon be there. Remember, I want men who are intelligent first and brave second. Any questions?"

There are a few, and then Mao tells the raiding party to eat and rest. He walks away and I go after him.

"Captain," I say, "Sergeant Ramos and I want to go on the raiding party."

"No," Mao says. "No good. This is for Vietnamese to do."

"We want to; this is why we came."

"No. You're too big, you make too much noise, you don't speak the language well. You'll get in the way, maybe get hurt. I'll be in big trouble with my colonel if I let an advisor get killed."

"We want—"

"No. No good."

Mao turns away, and I decide to retreat. I'm not giving up, but I'll bide my time, only how to tell Ramos? I try to avoid him while I think, and I slink off in the grass not far from Mao. Like a heat-seeking sensor, Ramos finds me out.

"OK, qué?" he says. "When do we go? What's the plan?"

I don't say anything; I'm still trying to think.

"So? What did he say? How come you didn't get me up there, man? I need to be briefed."

"He says no advisors on the raiding party."

"*What?* Hey, I didn't come out here just for a walk in the sun, man." The more Ramos talks, the more he blazes, words exploding from his black moustache: "You tell him I'm goin', man. I'm goin'! Hey, I tell him myself!"

I grab his arm and say, "No, wait, you'll piss him off more if you go raging over there. I'll talk to him."

"You *better,*" Ramos says. " 'Cause I'm *goin'.*"

I go to where Mao sits with Viêt beside the road, both drawing now with their fingers in the dirt. Mao looks up. He's not used to having people enter his world unless he summons them.

"Captain," I say, "please take two Vietnamese off the raiding party, maybe two with children. Put Sergeant Ramos and me on. We really want to— "

"OK, OK," Mao says impatiently. "One of you can go— and you decide which one."

Mao turns back to Viêt and the dirt-glyphs on the road, signaling that the conversation with me is over. I walk back down the road. Ramos waits, eyes blazing, jaw clenching.

"Well, *qué?*"

"He said one of us—and I have to choose."

"And you chose yourself, right?"

Ramos doesn't wait for an answer—he knows. "Doesn't matter," he says. "I'm *goin'!*"

We wait a long time in the grass. It's evident now: Mao is going up the Trail at night. This is why he isn't worried about the odd-numbered day or going the same way; he's going to walk up the Trail at night. I shiver with the realization; it will be black as Hell in the stream and under the trees. We won't be able to see *anything.*

Late in the afternoon, Bê passes the word: "We leave in fifteen minutes."

I break out my camouflage stick and paint up black. Ramos paints, too, then Viêt. Biên comes over; he wants to paint. All the raiding party paint. It's becoming like a magic ritual. We paint up to make ourselves invisible, impervious to NVA bullets. Mao and Anh first look askance; now they ask to paint, too.

I turn up my collar, button the top button of my camouflage jacket, stuff my pants tight into my socks, and retie my boots. I sit in the grass cradling my KAR-15, a special short version of the M-16, slender vines and young bamboo growing up around me, green-bayonet grass hanging like the sword of Damocles over my head, small plants with white flowers blooming between my legs. If I laid down here and didn't move, the grass would soon eat me. Ramos takes my picture and I take his. In mine I have a lost-in-time stare; I'm thinking about tonight and if I'll be alive in the morning. He looks like a panther about to spring from the grass.

We step out on the old river road, and I feel swept along by a dark, ancient wave. We are warriors on the march, seeking the enemy; the blood of many lands is in us and on our hands. We walk west toward the setting sun. Each step is like a life.

At the point, Viêt and Biên reach the ravine and lie on the bank looking down the sixty-foot drop to the stream. Mao comes up and lies beside them. The column halts, advisors back, everyone standing half-hidden in the grass. Our rifles are ready, and grenades bulge in our pockets like bull's balls.

Viêt and Mao whisper, and then Mao says something to Biên. Biên slings his rifle across his back and goes over the edge. Viêt waits a moment and follows him down. I move forward and lie beside Mao. With each man down the descent becomes more difficult, handholds and footholds wearing away, the route eroding fast.

Halfway down, a young ARVN falls, a chunk of torn-away earth tumbling with him. The ARVN turns slowly in the air—

Mao and I see his expression clearly—and crunches down on his back on the rocks in the water with a sickening sound. His helmet flies off, clangs on a rock, rolls on its side, and begins filling with water.

The ARVN's face explodes with pain, then—I swear—he sees Mao looking down and the pain goes away, at least temporarily. He apologizes to Mao with a look for falling and says—again, I swear—with his eyes, "I'm sorry I fell and made a big noise, Captain, but at least I hung on to my rifle."

He stands, looks around him, picks up his helmet, pours out the water, puts it on, and catches up to his place in line. Viêt and Biên head into the stream-tunnel and vanish, and one by one we say good-bye to open sky. Now the journey through the Underworld begins.

The stream curves sensuously down from high in the mountains, and we sink deeper into the jungle's embrace. We plunge up the forest's dark, fluid channel, black-green velvet closing around us and welcoming us home. Ahead on a straight stretch night begins to swallow ARVN like small fish, each in his turn. Behind, Ramos and the Aussie vanish into black. I wade forward, filled with darkness and stream song. Soon I disappear, too, lost even to myself, inside some great night-being. Each of us wades forward blindly, alone, toward death.

I stumble up black waterfalls, feel my way like a blind man around huge, smooth boulders, step into deep, invisible pools, and feel the cool water rise to my chest. I put my feet into empty space, slip on rocks, and splash down in foaming water.

I stop and listen, heart beating. My blood rushes like the stream, and the two seem to flow together. Beyond that, I hear only a great deafening emptiness and my mind shouting into the void, "Alone! No one! Darkness!" I feel like the only human in a world of eternal night.

I wait standing in the water. Surely Ramos will soon come up from behind. I'll hear him breaking the flow, stumbling, falling, cursing in Spanish. We'll reassure each other: we're together, connected, on the right path. He doesn't come. No one comes. There are no man-sounds in the stream at all. Where are the rest? I have to go on. I hurry forward, slip and fall, rise and wade on.

I grope ahead with fear growing strong in the back of my mind. What if I've gone off on a branch stream? I could wade here forever lost, part of the Vietnamese wandering souls, dead far from home and no one to pray and burn incense for me to guide my spirit back. I bump into someone, a rigid man shape in stream-rush.

"Who's that?"

It's Mao. His voice floats like a ghost above the water.

"Stevens," I whisper.

"Advisor!" Mao says. "You said you came this way. We need you now."

Other ghost-ARVN whisper with Mao. They've lost contact with Viêt and Biên at the point. Another stream flows in here, and a mistake could be fatal for us all.

"Which way?" Mao asks me.

I frantically search the memory-caverns of my mind. Left, I'm sure we made all lefts when we came this way before—but I wasn't paying that much attention then. I had Viêt to guide me.

"Which way?" Mao asks again.

I sense the other ARVN waiting. Behind me, Ramos and the rest must be wading forward. Ahead, Viêt and Biên are probably waiting for us to catch up. I feel everything depends on me, everyone's life is riding on this decision: right or left?

"Left," I say. "We have to go left."

"What? I don't think so," Mao says. "From Viêt's map I remember right here."

An ARVN spirit-voice floats: "I have a flashlight, Captain."

"Give it to me," Mao says. "I'm going to use it fast. Everyone look quickly on the ground where the streams meet."

Mao cups his hand around the light, bends low, and shines it on the ground. Suddenly the material world is here: black water, rocks, and ARVN searching. "Here!" Mao says. His light stops abruptly on fresh-broken reeds. Viêt has left us a VC sign: the reeds point right. I feel like a fool.

Mao switches off the light, and his voice comes out of the darkness, floating on the stream with a certain satisfaction: "You sure you were out here before, Advisor?"

I'm glad it's dark; still I feel lit up with shame.

"Stay close," Mao says. "Don't get separated. Two men stay here to guide the others."

We wade forward blindly. I try to stay close behind a someone I think is Mao. It's more like a presence, a spirit ahead, than a man, just *something* in the water. We walk on maybe half an hour. Time becomes lost in black emptiness. Finally I bump into someone: Mao again. He's whispering with Viêt and Biên. They've found where the Trail leaves the water.

Mao warns us sharply in a state of excitement: "I'm going to shine the light. Look fast."

Mao hits the bank with a brief flash of light, and the Trail jumps out of the dark like a cobra. Striking, in one shot, burning into the brain, the Trail boldly rises from the water where we flew down in hot, wild feeling of pursuit, the commissar's ghost chasing us. Now we'll go back up there and beyond. It seems the most forbidding place in the world.

Mao whispers to Viêt, "Take the raiding party 125 steps up the Trail and wait for me. Understand?"

"Yes, Captain," Viêt says.

I stand close to Mao and try to learn. He whispers to an

ARVN, "Go downstream to the junction and wait. Tell me when the others start coming."

"Yes, Captain."

We stand in the water and wait. Minutes pass, and an hour. The forest remains locked in impenetrable night, and Mao becomes more worried. He sends another ARVN downstream to the junction, and another long time passes. Mao begins to talk to me—maybe he has no one else. He's afraid something has happened to the rest of the company, fully two-thirds of our men. No gap in the line could have opened this wide. Someone behind me turned up the wrong branch and took everyone with him, or maybe the NVA put someone in the line to lead them astray. They've been swallowed by the jungle and the night.

"You wait here," Mao says to me. "I'm going back."

I stand with water running through my boots. I think of the others. Will we hear the sound of their slaughter from here? Or will the NVA wait till morning? Another long hour passes. I shift my soggy feet as the forest breathes. I want to see the Trail again, stand where it rises from the stream. I wade to where Mao's light hit and gasp. The Trail is glowing!

Lit by bioluminescence, the Trail looks like a giant snake with luminous vertebrae lying in the jungle, winding up through the trees. A path of death, the Trail is life, too, death being consumed by the living.

Mao returns; he's found the others. "Someone," he says in an ominous tone, "led them up the wrong stream."

Mao, Anh, and Bê arrange us in a close-packed line, advisors in the middle. One hundred twenty-five steps up the Trail, Viêt and the raiding party are waiting. Mao's orders come whispering back: "Stay close. Move forward."

We lurch ahead, stumble into each other, feel the Trail beneath our boots. Now the Trail looks like the Milky Way flung through a black sky, our bodies blocking most of the glow. We look like a strange death-Machine flying through the galaxy.

Our line jerks to a halt. Our point has reached Biên and Viêt, and our rear guard is out of the stream and on the Trail. Mao comes back, whispering, "Pick up twigs and leaves. Attach them to the man in front of you."

I feel as if I am in a kind of dream as I pick up shining bits of jungle and put them under the pack straps and in the helmet cover of the ARVN in front of me. Behind me Ramos is doing the same to me. I get more and put them in my front, too, in my belt and buttonholes.

Mao goes up the line, glowing with twigs and leaves, whispering encouragement and orders as he passes, and touching us on the shoulders: "Stay close. Be careful. Be quiet. Don't lose sight of the man in front of you." When he reaches the point, another whispered order comes back: "*Di.*" "Go."

The movement ripples back in a long wave, and we flow up the Trail. We are the snake now, our vertebrae glowing. We walk most of the night, stopping often to listen, the blood pounding in our ears, the forest so intensely silent that it seems like a shout inside my head. We stop, too, for Mao and Viêt to whisper kneeling at the front of the column. We start forward again, boot-scuffing, night-sweating, glowing.

Somewhere we pass the curve where I crawled backward like a crab, blown back by the AKs hammering. Just beyond, we pass where the commissar fell, blown back, too, in the other direction, by AK bullets. I feel the Trail level out and begin to descend. We are in the saddle between Hills 300 and 320. We're heading for the stream crossing now. I try to walk softly while inside my body and mind distant echoes of supernovae explode. The Trail is angling, paralleling the Khe Trai but staying high. We stop and stay standing for a long time. This is not one of our listening stops or Mao and Viêt's huddles.

Mao comes down the line steaming with anger. He stops by me and whispers fiercely, "Viêt lost the Trail. It just stops—a blank wall. He says he doesn't know why; it wasn't this way before. I'll find out what he's up to in the morning."

I fear again for Viêt's life, and ours. Mao stomps off down the line to find Anh, and soon word comes up from the rear: "Get off the Trail to the right. Ten steps, no more. Hide, sleep. No noise."

I do a right face and step off the Trail, hand waving in front of my face like a blind man. My mind is reeling as my body lurches. This *has* to be the Trail. But how could it just stop? Is this the trap we've been walking toward in all these operations? Leaves brush my face, and snakes writhe in my mind. Who knows who—or what—is in here? Seven, eight, nine steps, stumbling on roots and rocks. What cliff edge or deep hole could be here? What viper's nest, python's tree, cobra's pit? Ten steps; I stop. Left and right are glowing ghost-men, Viêt and Ramos.

Viêt comes to me very afraid. "I don't know why the Trail ends," he whispers. "It just stops. It wasn't like that before. I'm not lying."

"Shh!" an ARVN whispers. "The captain said no noise!"

I scuff around in the vegetation at my feet, hoping to scare away harmful crawling things. I lie down, sink back into the hard and soft forest-floor world. Nothing seems to be worming under me; nothing seems to be slithering above. Holding my rifle like a baby on my chest and breathing deeply, I try to quiet my strobe-lit mind and make it as dark and calm inside my head as it is all around in the invisible trees.

Viêt's voice comes again out of the night: "I don't know why the Trail stops; I'm not lying." He sounds very afraid.

For the second night in a row I have a good dream, this time of my girlfriend in Quang Tri City, the voluptuous singer Cô Hông, "Miss Rose." For a moment on awaking I feel I'm with her, then I open my eyes to the embrace of the jungle. To left and right Viêt and Ramos appear as night retreats slowly, goes through shades of lightening gray and dark green emerging from black. Mao comes swimming through the vegetation like a shark, with hard-faced Anh in his wake, both looking as if they haven't slept all night. Viêt stands up to face Mao, and Anh moves to block me from interfering.

Mao says to Viêt in a rough voice, "Time to find the Trail."

"Yes, Captain," Viêt says, and he looks past Anh at me with his fatalistic look. I wonder if this will be the last time I see him?

I move around Anh and say to Mao, "If he can't find the Trail, no problem: I can lead us to the crossing. We can go down this slope, follow the stream—"

Mao looks at Viêt and says, "*Di.*"

Viêt goes off through the leaves and vanishes, Mao and Anh close behind. Anh pauses once, looks back at me, and then disappears in the trees.

"I hope he finds that Trail," Ramos says.

Viêt leads Mao and Anh back to the Trail, looks left and right, and steps cautiously out of the trees. Biên and eight ARVN fall in behind at five-meter intervals, all carrying their rifles ready to shoot. Boots ramrod against the Trail as they move to where last night's march ended. Viêt walks in his panther crouch, his M-16 off safe and aimed belly high. Tension seems about to split the air, like a sudden lightning strike.

Viêt arrives at a wall, a chaotic jumble of vegetation. Here the Trail suddenly ends where vines hang strangely, like hangman's ropes from broken gallows. Trees lean oddly here, too, as if pushed half over, and many are dying. Broken branches are everywhere, dangling from trees not of their kind, festooning the vines and littering the forest floor.

Viêt crouches at the edge of chaos. Now he knows what happened. Mao and Anh come up and kneel with Viêt. Viêt whispers, then leads them back along the Trail, carefully searching. Soon he finds what he's looking for, a break in the vegetation. He steps over low grass and ferns onto a new Trail, a narrow, snakelike line of recently trampled growth circling the zone of strangely hung vines and leaning, dying trees. There is a feeling, palpable in the spreading dawn, of something yawning and terrible ahead.

Viêt, Mao, and Anh go tentatively down the new Trail a short way, then Mao calls them together and whispers, and leads them back.

"Pass the word," Mao says to Biên. "Hide for the day, rest, eat. No fires, no cigarettes, no noise."

Mao and Viêt approach Ramos and me through the green sea. "It wasn't his fault he lost the Trail," Mao says in English. "Now we know what happened."

Ramos leaps like a tiger, his eyes blazing. He's been threatening this. "Look, Dai-Uy," he says, using the Vietnamese word for captain, "you gotta put me on that raiding party. I didn't come out here to—"

"OK, OK," Mao says quickly. "You can go. Now hide, eat, rest. No noise."

Mao turns away and vanishes, and Ramos and I stand looking at the rapidly closing hole he made in the wall of leaves.

"Hey, that was easy!" Ramos says. "I told you, 'mano: I'm goin'!"

Now I'm sure of it: Mao is planning to cut us both out. I resolve to keep my eye on him. Every minute around him, I'm learning. In their own way and in their worlds, he and Viêt are both masters of war.

"What happened?" I ask Viêt.

"I'll tell you later," Viêt says in a worn-out voice. He looks drained again, back from another trip along the thin line between life and death. He lies down, pulls his poncho over him like a shroud, and is soon asleep.

In a few minutes Bê emerges from the trees, bends down, shakes him, and says, "The captain wants you again."

Viêt gets up and goes, and Ramos and I don't see him the rest of the day. We try to sleep as gray turns to green under the trees and the temperature climbs.

When the light in the forest begins to fade, Bê comes through the leaves with a message from Mao: "Move back to the Trail. No noise."

We stand in a long line on the Trail. Electricity cracks from man to man and inwardly like lightning. Soon we will fight, maybe die. Mao goes down the line, whispering, touching our shoulders, transferring something of himself to us. He returns to the point, where Viêt and Biên wait, and his word comes back: "*Di.*"

We head for the green wall and step off to the left on the new Trail. Mao lets the forward part of the line pass, then gets in ahead of me. "I'll show you why Viêt lost the Trail," he says.

We skirt the zone of strangely hung vines and leaning trees and enter a region even more chaotic. Here it looks as if a great storm has passed through, leaving stripped limbs, leaves carpeting the forest floor, and vines strewn on the ground like dead pythons. Some incredible force has swept through here, shaking the forest.

"Look closely," Mao says, "and think about this."

We enter a world of sheared-off limbs and raw-wound branches oozing sap. Here it seems as if a giant axe has been swung through the forest by an executioner of titanic powers. Big, broken-off trees lie crashed, and jagged stumps stand slowly bleeding. It feels as if Mao is leading me through Hell.

The new Trail leads to yet another zone. Here, mangled, gashed, and twisted tree bodies lie everywhere, like immense, crushed yarrow sticks fallen in the gods' last apocalyptic throw of the *I Ching*: forest goes, doom comes for Nature and man. The Trail winds among bare ground and tree corpses and circles the edge of a huge pit. The Trail goes around the big crater, passing through the zones of destruction and heading toward untouched forest beyond, but Mao leads me to the rim of the pit.

"The Americans did this," Mao says, as we look down into the crater.

There's nothing here where once rich, tropical forest life played out its ancient story, nothing—just a gaping death-hole. How many tree species once lived here, how many ferns, grasses, insects, birds? Were miniature deer browsing here when the bomb hit, the doe and her fawns? Were there monkeys chattering in the trees? Was the tiger lying here, suckling her cubs? It's as if a great piece has been torn from Gaia's side or ripped from her green breast.

"The brigade has been bombing, firing artillery in here." Mao says.

"I told them not to after our recon."

"Seems like they don't listen to you," Mao says in English. "They do what they like, shoot from far away. Hit nothing, only tell the NVA: we know you're there, we're coming. Stupid! Maybe we die for that, end up in there." He looks down into the pit.

Behind us 1st Company passes, and we catch up to our places in line. Beyond the blast radius, the old Trail and intact forest appear again. Something is working on my mind, the image of the ARVN circling the pit and the Trail going beyond.

The Trail drops now like an arrow through thick vegetation, heading for the stream. Late afternoon green fades fast toward the falling of the black curtain. Somewhere near here the poison trees stand in their bare clearing and my shirt flies in the white-barked tree like a small green flag. Our boots thump where sandals slap. Who will feed the Pit tonight? We slant down between rocks and leaves, with the feeling of death heavy in the air.

The sound of water comes through the trees as the Trail parallels the stream. We see it now, water dancing over rocks with a black-diamond sparkle. The big cottonwood is just ahead, thrusting its roots deep beneath the stream. Will we die here where Stevens and I planned to kill?

I step for the flat crossing rock, put my boot print in water where the sandal print was, look fast at the willow veil and the gravel bar, and think of the voices that came through the trees, women's soft, high laughter among them. Will there be women in the camp tonight, and what will happen to them?

Mao stands in the water near the flat rock, watching us cross, whispering courage. Our eyes meet, and I see compassion in Mao for us all.

"This is where we came," I whisper, indicating with my eyes the willow curtain. "We could hear the camp from here."

I see that Mao believes me now. He passes the word: "Be extra quiet now, brothers."

Viêt, Biên, and the raiding party enter the tree-tunnel on the far side of the stream, each man pointing down as he goes, signaling for us to look. I pass the place and see fresh-cut greens eddying near the bank and barefoot human tracks with mud still oozing. Minutes, perhaps seconds ago, someone was rinsing wild greens here, probably for jungle soup. Did he—or she—have so many he left these, or did he leave quickly, running down the Trail as Viêt approached the crossing? Is he now bursting into the camp, breathlessly saying, "Enemy coming"?

Mao catches up with Viêt and whispers, and new orders come: "Everyone off the Trail to the left. Twenty steps. No noise. Hide, sleep, wait."

Ramos and I stick close to Mao; Viêt remains with Biên and the raiding party. They're set apart, special, what Ramos and I want to be. Mao's men tie his hammock to trees in near total dark, while Ramos and I look for places nearby. When he calls for the raiding party, we plan to be there. Mao climbs in his hammock and looks asleep, hat over his eyes. Ramos and I lie down on rocks and roots, scrunch around, and try to get comfortable. I'm lying held tightly in the fork of a big root; Ramos has a rock poking his spine.

Bê comes to us, bends down, and whispers, "The captain says we attack the camp at 0300. He says you rest, sleep. We'll wake you when it's time."

"No way *I'm* sleepin'," Ramos whispers after Bê leaves. "Mao's not cuttin' *me* out, not *this vato, cabrón.*"

In seconds Ramos is snoring. The night is utterly black now and filled with power. I try to stay awake, too, but the desire for sleep sometimes overwhelms even survival. I surrender and sleep, embraced by the tight *Y* of the root. Again I have a good dream. It's about a beautiful girl, a mystery girl. It's not a sex dream. We're just together, having fun. I awake wondering if I'll meet her someday.

The root reminds me where I am; Ramos still snores nearby, and it feels later than three. Someone's coming through the trees. Bê bends low and shakes me: "*Di.*"

I get up quickly, wake Ramos, and we stumble through the trees toward the Trail. ARVN stand there like ghosts in a close-packed line, shining twigs and leaves in their helmets and belts. Their packs are hidden beside the Trail, and their weapons are hard in their hands. Soon we'll strike the camp.

Ramos looks at his watch; it's 0330. "Damn!" he says.

We pick up twigs and leaves, attach them to each other, and wedge into the line where Bê tells us, about halfway back from the point.

Mao comes up the line, touching and whispering: "The raiding party is five minutes ahead of us. When we enter the camp, be careful of your brothers. Be intelligent first and brave second. Put your hand on the shoulder of the man in front of you, and don't break the connection. *Di.*"

We step off in a wave. My KAR-15 is in my left hand, my right grasps the shoulder of the ARVN ahead, and Ramos clutches my shoulder from behind. Ramos doesn't complain now; this is enough. Soon we'll fight, maybe die.

We move slowly up the Trail but at hyperspeed inside, nerves exploding, blood rushing, breath suppressed like love-gasps at night. I imagine us ambushed on the Trail, black trees erupting with streaks of fire, our bodies dancing, falling, heads twisted, eyes wide, faces in the dirt. One last thought, one silent cry of "Mother!" — and then the darkness of the pit.

High overhead, through a rare break in the canopy, the moon breaks out of clouds and shines down in a river of light. The goddess moon, sailing fast in a stormy sky, looks down on the Trail and makes it glow like the path of a flaming arrow. Our line moves along the Trail as if we were the arrow itself, loosed from Diana's bow and hurtling toward destiny. The moon fades then comes again as the clouds fly like ghost riders in the sky. Suddenly a terrible hole opens in Nature, is ripped in life itself, as what seems like every weapon in the world opens murderous fire. "Viêt!" I think, my mind bursting. "Viêt is dead!"

Savage, sickening streams of gunfire and dull, nauseating grenade explosions continue just ahead, jagged red tearing into black. The raiding party is being slaughtered, and we will be next.

A jolt of power hits our line as the chain-saw fire continues to rip. Something electric comes from Mao and passes from man to man through our linked hands and shoulders. The force surges back in a wave and explodes within each of us as it goes, accompanied by a single word, shouted, exploding, also emanating from Mao: "Di!"

The ARVN ahead of me takes it up: "Di! Di! Di!"

The chant jumps me. My mouth is open and the word is bursting in my head, but no sound comes out. I feel wrenched, swept along. Behind me, Ramos takes up the chant, shouting hoarsely, wildly, "*Di! Di! Di!*"

We charge forward toward the hell of war noise, chanting, pushing and pulling each other on like ancient warriors, like a Death train. There is no doing the seemingly safe, the smart, the sensible — diving for the ground, lying low, retreating. We surge ahead to wrestle with Satan.

"*Di! Di! Di!*"

Mao leads us into a small clearing lit with flashes and rocked with explosions. Ahead of me our line splits as Mao directs men left and right. Men run, dive, and shoot at thick black houses shaped like mushrooms that appear and disappear in explosions. This *is* Hell, right here. High overhead the moon goddess rides, but no one looks but the dead.

I dive into the grass and lie wildly pointing my rifle at the houses. ARVN to my right deliver such a storm of fire it seems it will cut the trees down. Everywhere around the clearing fire and steel stab and burn, and the night is ripped with man's war power.

Beside me to my left Anh stands like a fiend, blazing his M-16 from the hip, his face wildly lit by his own muzzle flashes. He looks like he wants to shoot *himself* out there, pouring fire into the night.

One mushroom-house begins to burn, red flames against giant trees. All the world, all time, is here, reduced to this cracked fragment of insanity and intensity, chaos before cosmos, darkness and fire of the Pit.

Suddenly, earth takes shape as man. To my right a thick, black form leaps up from the grass and runs wildly for the trees.

Anh swings his M-16 and shouts, "NVA! Capture him alive!"

ARVN jump from the grass and run after the zigzagging form as everything appears and disappears in strobe flashes. An ARVN shoots up a flare, and it whooshes, pops, and drifts down under its little parachute, hissing fiercely with chemical fire, swinging in the wind and making immense, grotesque shadows dance around the clearing.

An ARVN launches himself in a flying tackle at the running form, and bodies collide and crash to the earth. The ARVN leaps up quickly, and more ARVN swarm around then jump back as the NVA screams, kicks, and lashes out on the ground. The ARVN circle the frenzied form as if it were a poisonous snake. Finally two ARVN jump, grab the screaming man's arms, and drag him across the ground.

"Prisoner! Prisoner!" the ARVN shout, and they wrench the NVA's arms around and tie them tightly behind his back.

Someone shoots another flare and more Shiva-shadows dance with the giant trees and mushroom-houses. Ramos appears where Anh was, wild-eyed and sweating, and Mao seems everywhere, shouting now, and Anh, too, "Cease fire! Cease fire!"

A cry slices through the noise and confusion, a young voice screaming, "It hurts! It hurts bad!"

Ramos and I run to the sound as another flare streaks up. We see a dark form writhing in the grass. It's Biên. He lies near the smoldering house, knees drawn up like a fetus, one bloody hand clutching his head, the other holding his knee, and blood running out between all his fingers.

The ARVN medic runs up, drops to his knees, quickly pushes Biên's sleeve above his elbow, sharply slaps the skin with the tips of his fingers, and, as if he has done it a thousand times, jabs in a morphine syrette. Biên immediately goes limp, no more pain till later, maybe a lifetime of it. Ramos and I look on in anguish. Funny, cheerful little Biên, where is your teenage bravery and clowning now?

Mao appears, asks the medic quick questions about Biên's chances, and is gone again, shouting, "Cease fire!" at the last wild burst.

Ramos and I race over to the prisoner. He's kneeling, head hanging, hands tied tightly behind his back. He's chunky, barefoot, and wears NVA pants and a shirt hanging open. I get a cold, empty feeling; something terrible is about to happen. A big artillery flare whooshes over from Ann and bursts high above the clearing. Even bigger shadows dance now as the flare hisses and sways beneath its parachute, coloring everything strangely yellow and black. The prisoner trembles and looks sick. All seems huge, ghoulish, horror-struck. Death stands to the left and slightly behind us, waiting with folded arms.

Anh bursts through the circle around the NVA. "A goddamn prisoner!" he shouts, "I'm gonna kill the sonofabitch!" He raises his rifle high above the NVA's head, screaming, "I'm gonna beat this bastard to death!"

Suddenly Bê explodes into the circle, throwing ARVN aside and grabbing Anh. "No!" Bê shouts, and he wrestles Anh away. "No! Don't kill him!"

Anh stomps away muttering darkly and takes the circle of ARVN with him. Bê sits down beside the prisoner and takes out a cigarette.

"Don't worry, little brother," Bê says in his gentle voice, "I'll take care of you."

The NVA is shaking convulsively. He dares a sidelong glance at Bê.

"What's your name?" Bê says, and he lights the cigarette and begins to write in a small notebook.

"X-Xuân," the prisoner says.

"Xuân, eh?" Bê says. "I have a cousin by that name. Where you from, Xuân? Want a smoke?"

Bê begins to put the cigarette between Xuân's lips, but Mao bursts out of the shadows behind us, pulls out his .45, jams it against the side of Xuân's head, and begins to shout questions: "What's your unit, you bastard? How many were here? Where did they go? Where are the rockets?"

Xuân cringes and flinches with each word as if they were blasts from Mao's pistol. He mumbles something I can't understand.

"*Liar!*" Mao screams. "I'm going to shoot you dead!" Suddenly Ramos and I see it, and we look at each other with eyes wide. Mao's acting! Anh must have been, too, but he's good at it.

Bê grabs Mao's arm and jerks the .45 away. Xuân looks pulled like a puppet between life and death. "*No!*" Bê shouts, and he puts his body between Mao and Xuân. "We don't kill prisoners in this unit!"

Mao jams his pistol in his holster, spins, utters Viet Nam's worst insult, "*Du ma my!*" and vanishes into the flare-lit night.

Bê sits, puts the cigarette between Xuân's trembling lips, and says, "Where you from, brother?"

"Q-Quang Binh," Xuân says. Quang Binh is Quang Tri's neighbor province just north of the DMZ.

"All right!" Bê says. "We've got several boys in the unit from there. They came south with their families in '54. I'll introduce you later. Maybe you'll know some."

Xuân looks at Bê with desperate hope. This talk of home. . . .

"You married, Xuân?" Bê says.

Xuân's eyes light even more. His wife. . . .

"Kids?" Bê says.

"One — a boy," Xuân says. His face shows that a part of him is there, with his wife and son in their small home in the village surrounded by fields, and there is no war. The cigarette dangles from his lips and his eyes are far away.

Bê prepares to write: "What did you say your unit was?"

Anh explodes out of the night with incredible force, sticks his M-16 in Xuân's face, and shouts, "What this? A prisoner, smoking? I'll blow his goddamn head off!"

Bê jumps up, knocks Anh's rifle away, and puts his body in front of Xuân. "No! This is my prisoner! You won't hurt him!"

"*Du ma my!*" Anh growls, and he turns back into the shadows.

Bê sits down. "Now what was that unit, brother?"

Xuân talks, quickly answering all Bê's questions: "I'm the assistant commander of an antiaircraft platoon. . . . In the South three months. . . . Twenty-three years old. . . . Moved in here after the Rocket Company left. . . . Because the Americans were firing artillery and dropping bombs in the area, and flying reconnaissance. . . . The rest of my platoon left for political study three days ago. . . . Don't know. . . . Someplace on the Trail. . . . Don't know. . . . The commander said he would send a messenger with instructions."

Bê gets up with his notebook and goes looking for Mao. Flares continue whooshing in from Ann seven kilometers to the east, each arriving as the last is burning out. Ramos and I move up beside Xuân, and he looks at us and blanches as if we were devils. This is the first he has seen that there are Americans here, and he has been told in training that Americans torture and kill prisoners. We look wild and primitive in the flare light and with our smudged black paint, too—Ramos like a pre-Columbian Carib Indian, the man-eating fires burning, and me like a sooty Druid stoking the sacrificial flames. Xuân's eyes search frantically for Bê.

"We want to talk to you," I say in a friendly voice.

"I don't understand American," Xuân says.

I can see he's blocking us out. "Why don't you understand?" I say slowly and as clearly as I can. "I'm speaking Vietnamese."

Xuân looks at me curiously, then stares desperately into the night for Bê.

"What's your child's name?" I say.

Like Bê, I get him talking about home. Home and family are refuge and sanctuary for his mind. I'm not interested in military intelligence now, anyway; I'd rather hear about his life back home and out here, and especially what he was doing on the third day of Tết. He tells me about his village, his parents, his wife, and son. Then: "You were here on the third day of Tết?"

Xuân looks at me curiously again. I can see him thinking, "What is he after?" Finally he decides the question is harmless. "Yes," he says, "I was here."

I feel bursting inside. This is hot. "Were you having a party here then?"

Xuân looks from me to Ramos. Ramos is leaning forward, concentrating on following the language, his usual *energía loca* contained within but radiating from his sweat-streaked face. Xuân looks quickly back at me.

"Yes," he says. "We were having a Tết party."

I can hardly hold it in now. My Vietnamese comes tumbling out, words falling over each other. "Did you shoot at an American helicopter that day?"

Xuân looks scared again. He's wondering whether to tell the truth. "Yes," he finally says, and then quickly, "but we missed."

I whoop and slap Ramos on the leg, clap Xuân on the back, and say, "That was me! You shot at me! Isn't this great!"

Xuân looks lost, like he's fallen into the hands of crazy men.

Mao emerges again from the night. He doesn't look at Xuân, but talks quickly to Ramos in English. "Medevac chopper's coming for Biên. My English is no good. You talk him down."

Ramos jumps up and we follow Mao to the center of the clearing. The Aussie and Americans have gone back with a detachment of ARVN for our packs. No more flares fly in from Ann; they have to save for a possible attack there. We stand like ghosts under the small hole in the canopy. It doesn't look big enough for the chopper to get down. Biên lies in the grass softly moaning.

"What do you think?" Mao says.

"We can do it, Dai-Uy," Ramos says. "Gimme that radio."
Surely the NVA will counterattack, I think, probably when
the chopper comes. But how will the pilot find us in the vast
forest-sea? The house has burned out, its thatch too heavy and
wet to blaze for long.

We hear the sound of a chopper from far away. The medevac
crews are miracle men; *they* are the real heroes. Inside their
helmets the crew races the moon across the cloud-flying sky,
and the heartbeat sound grows louder. They don't know Biên,
don't know his laugh and his baby face, but they're coming.

Ramos talks on the radio, and an ARVN readies a green star
cluster signal flare. The Huey roars over the trees and the
ARVN shoots the flare. The flare arcs up and bursts in a
shower of glittering, fiercely burning green stars, and I shudder, thinking of the NVA and the guns of Xuân's antiaircraft
platoon.

Ramos talks and the chopper descends toward the hole in
the canopy. The flare burns out, and the world plunges back
into black. The sickening sound of metal slicing into wood
explodes in our minds as if it is cutting into us, and branches
start flying and falling all around. The chopper's going into
the trees.

Inside the chopper chaos bursts as the big rotor blade slices
the treetops off like some immense lawnmower and the pilot
and copilot fight for control. Ramos's shouts burst through the
night, "Take it up, take it up, you're too far to the right!"

The pilot rises above the trees, hovers, and checks his
instruments. "We'll try to get low enough to lower a jungle
penetrator," he radios to Ramos. "I'll have to turn on my belly
light."

Now we'll be illuminated in a steady flood from the Huey's
powerful belly light. The chopper descends, monster on a
mercy mission. We gird ourselves for more hits in the trees

and a crashing bird, but Ramos radio-talks and guides the pilot to delicate maneuvers. The belly light streams down and turns us into shining targets.

Ramos looks up and talks fast, directing the Huey through the hole in the trees. The rotor hits again, and pieces of wood fly like shrapnel, but the pilot holds steady and keeps on coming. Ramos's upturned face as he guides the chopper is bathed in light. He looks transported, exalted. This is his finest hour.

The crew chief, his insect-head flight helmet on, appears in the open doorway of the chopper, talking into his mike and looking like a visitor from another world. He begins lowering the jungle penetrator, a folded aluminum chair on a long, thin cable. The chopper beats wildly in its hole in the trees, hovering, the penetrator coming down, all the way to the ground.

Ramos drops the radio, runs to Biên, and helps the medic strap him into the chair. Biên looks bad, his head wrapped like a mummy's and blood soaking the bandage around his knee. Poor Biên—is his young life of laughter, wind blowing in waves across the rice, and pretty girls in the moonlight by the river finished? For now the morphine god has him; he's not concerned about his future.

Ramos returns to the radio and talks to the chopper, and Biên begins to rise, the torsion of the cable making him twist strangely in the river of light coming down from the Huey's belly, the shadow-monster trees trembling and everyone waiting for the NVA to hit. Biên rises like a deus ex machina in a stage play, head hanging, telling his story in silence.

The crew chief grabs the chair and hauls Biên aboard, and the pilot takes the chopper up and switches off the light, plunging us into darkness again. The chopper flies away, and Biên is gone; we remain with the forest and the night.

Mao orders his headquarters section to another part of the clearing, and Ramos and I follow. Việt is still out there somewhere, hunting NVA. Reports come in from the raiding party, and Mao is disturbed at the results: only two NVA killed, a major discrepancy between Viêt's description of the camp and what his men are finding, and no Rocket Company.

"In the morning I'll find out what happened," Mao says darkly. "You two sleep now." He goes off and we don't see him the rest of the night.

Ramos and I lie in the grass but can't sleep. ARVN come and go like ghosts, the moon flies down the sky, sometimes breaking free from the clouds and the canopy, and tall trees bend and dance. We seem to be in a world of Nature spirits and lost, wandering human souls.

Finally gray dawn begins to emerge from black, and Ramos and I tour the camp, trying to relive what happened. The first house squats at the edge of the clearing, almost invisible among the trees. The moon goddess flies high again, and we travel the Trail between death and life.

Viêt emerges from the black tunnel in the trees, the raiding party behind him. The first house looms ahead, and Viêt emplaces the first team for attack. Viêt leads to the second house, Biên and his team close behind. Here the moon seals the fate of men, saving some and killing others. The camp cook is sitting outside early, looking at the moon. Beside him on the ashes of yesterday's fire is a big blackened caldron of jungle greens, more soup to cook for the day. What is he thinking about as the goddess moon flies high across the sky? The moon over his family in the North, his home village among the moonlit fields? Something moves; maybe there's a sound. He sees the ghost men of the raiding party, and they see him. A hell of M-16 fire bursts, and the cook is blown back over his caldron, spilling the soup into the earth.

The first team thinks the attack is on, and they assault their house, riddling it with M-16 bullets and throwing grenades down in the bunker. The night becomes an inferno of noise and death hail as the second and third teams, still together, pour fire and grenades into the second house.

In the third house, Xuân starts awake in terror at the first shots. He dashes from the bunker where he has been sleeping, bursts out of the house, sees muzzle flashes and explosions all over the camp, dives into the grass, worms forward, jumps up, and begins running for the trees.

"NVA!" Anh shouts beside me. "Capture him alive!"

From a fourth house—Viêt hadn't mentioned a fourth house—five NVA run barefoot into the trees, crash through to the Trail, and race down it to the south in the direction of the huge NVA base area in the Laos salient.

Ramos goes into the first house and down into the bunker. I look inside the door. The house is bullet-ripped as if hornets had been attacking it, the thatch torn and hanging, the bamboo punctured and split. Ramos comes out of the bunker as fast as he went down, hurrying up the earthen steps. This is beyond the considerable death he has seen in his years in Viet Nam, and concentrated, Hell in a small place.

"It looks bad down there, 'mano,'" he says in a hushed voice. "One NVA, splattered all over the walls."

We go to the second house. The cook lies dead on his back on the ground. An ARVN has put a handkerchief over his face. His slim legs stick out of brown shorts, and his NVA shirt is pulled up around his chest, exposing his stomach. No wound is visible, but what can be under that handkerchief?

Beside the cook the overturned caldron still spills its mess of jungle soup on the ground. A tall ARVN comes by, looks down, and says, with a mixture of bitterness and pity in his voice, "This is what we feed to pigs."

Ramos looks in the cook's house; nothing much is in there. We go to the third house, where Xuân burst out running. Outside, 1st Company men are piling NVA gear, and a magic pyramid of power objects is growing as ARVN bear them from all over the camp. Atop the pile a big Panasonic radio sits.

Bê comes by and says, "Take what you want."

We begin going through the pile. There are NVA knives and a bayonet, two AK-47s, North Vietnamese stamps and money, canteens, cooking gear, ponchos, belts, uniforms, an NVA hat. Ramos finds a vial of mysterious liquid, opens it, takes a quick whiff, and thrusts it under my nose. I snort, choke, and blow, and Ramos laughs, teeth flashing white in his brown- and black-streaked face. It's chloroform, the NVA's anesthetic. I take a few things: the bayonet, a belt, the hat. Ramos stuffs his pockets and shirt full.

"Take more than you want," he says. "That was the deal I made with Willie: souvenirs for a ride."

Ramos finds a treasure: the sight and big bullets for Xuân's antiaircraft gun. The sight looks like a well-made toy, a small wheel with a crank and a little plane that travels across a wire crosshair and shows the gunner where to shoot. I remember Iowa State Fairs in the 1950s, with crosshair-sight machine guns that shot blips of light at Japanese Zeros and German Focke-Wulfs. I turn the crank and watch the little plane traverse its wire and wonder if Xuân looked through this to shoot at us in the Black Cat.

I test the blade of the NVA bayonet with my finger and turn it over in my hands. Where has it been? Who — or what — has it killed? Has it butchered a wild pig, dismembered a monkey, disemboweled a forest bird? What factory in China, Eastern Europe, or the Soviet Union turned it out; where was the iron mined? What men and women watched it go down the assembly line; what languages; what music did it hear? What taxes were taken to pay for it; what government office instituted this instrument of blood and death? Now it's mine; I stick it in my belt. Who will get it next?

The ARVN who carried the rooster comes to Xuân's house and says, "The captain invites you to eat."

We hurry to the middle of the clearing. The red tablecloth is spread on the grass like a magic carpet, and Mao is already seated. Soon Bê, Anh, the Aussie, and the other Americans come, and Mao's men serve noodle soup and tea. Without Biên, the gathering is subdued.

Mao eats silently and solemnly for a time, then begins another oration, part in English, part in Vietnamese, directing it mostly at me: "The kill was no good: there should have been many NVA here, and five escaped to fight again. Maybe they will shoot down my helicopter or bring a big unit back to kill *us*. Biên was wounded, I don't know by whom. Maybe someone was not intelligent. Viêt lied about the fourth house, too, where most of the NVA slept. He says they built it since he was here, but I don't believe him."

Viêt comes across the clearing wild-eyed and sweating with the raiding party behind him, the last man looking back anxiously toward where they've just emerged from the trees. Viêt shoots me and the food quick glances, then begins a rapid-fire exchange with Mao. Something about "NVA" and "very near."

Mao and Anh grab their '16s and jump up. Mao begins giving orders, and his entourage drop their cooking duties, take up their rifles, and form in a line behind Viêt. Mao and Anh insert themselves two ARVN back from the front.

Ramos and I rise and say, "We're going, too."

Mao is in too much of a hurry to argue. He says something aside to Bê, and Bê tells Ramos and me to fall in behind him. Bê gets into the line halfway back, and we start. We're already breathing hard, the spicy soup still warm in our mouths and heavy in our stomachs. Viêt leads us to where the Trail leaves the camp and heads south, our green line flowing through the trees like a powerful Death serpent.

Viêt and the raiding party have observed NVA coming back toward the camp. Our boots hit the Trail, as Viêt, at the point, goes around a bend. The forest shivers, leaves in tremolo. Halfway back, Bê, Ramos, and I walk down a straight stretch. Suddenly shooting breaks out ahead, AK and M-16 fire ripping back and forth. We hit the dirt, then Bê leads us forward. We soon see that Mao has not only put us in the rear element, but he has also left a wide gap between us and the point.

A breathless ARVN from the raiding party comes running back to Bê: "The captain wants you up right away."

We run up the Trail to a knot of excited men around Mao. Viêt and the point met the NVA on the Trail. The NVA fired first but missed, and Viêt and the ARVN hit one NVA in the arm. The NVA ran back; there is a clear blood trail.

Mao organizes pursuit and details Bê to escort Ramos and me back to the clearing, no questions asked, no complaints allowed. This is as close as Mao will ever let us get to the action. We go back and find Xuân sitting surrounded by a circle of ARVN, and we join in to listen.

Some of the ARVN are from Quang Binh, Catholics who came south in '54 when the country was split. They're catching up on news from north of the DMZ. Xuân is smoking, one ARVN occasionally taking the cigarette from his lips so he can talk and breathe. Another ARVN is feeding him, and many have contributed from their rations; there's a pile of food beside him. There's no evident animosity here; the ARVN and Xuân, last night mortal enemies, this morning are talking like brothers.

Bê bends down, unties Xuân's hands, and says, "Better?"

Xuân rubs his wrists, looks up, and says, "Many thanks, Uncle."

What is it like for Xuân, jerked back and forth between death and life, his future currently limited to this clearing, two of his comrades dead nearby and drawing flies? Bê sends the ARVN off to perimeter guard, and Ramos and I move in beside Xuân. Xuân looks at the departing Bê with anxiety; he's still swinging from hope to fear.

I ask Xuân more about his family. I want to make friends, get to know him. There are a few details, too, about his story I don't believe. He tells us more about his home village, what the war is like there, the people living underground to hide from U.S. bombing attacks. I ask again about his position in the antiaircraft platoon. He's proud of his rapid rise to assistant platoon commander.

"Where did the rest of the platoon go?"

A shadow passes across Xuân's face. He knows he shouldn't answer this. "I don't know," he says, and he looks again for Bê.

"You're the assistant commander," I say, "and you don't know where your platoon went?"

"No."

"Where are the antiaircraft guns?"

"The platoon took them."

"They went to political study and they took the guns?"

"Yes."

"They didn't leave any here?"

"No, they took all."

"Then why is this here?" I nod to Ramos. He pulls out the sight and shows it to Xuân.

"It was broken," Xuân says.

"It's not broken now," Ramos says, and he turns the crank. The little plane travels across the wire.

"I fixed it," Xuân says.

I change the focus. "How was your life here? What did you eat?"

Xuân tells us of life in the camp, the rain, the loneliness, the party at Tết with people trying to be happy but missing home so much it hurt, ". . . and the food was bad here. We only had green soup most of the time, terrible stuff, sometimes a sweet potato, and almost never any rice. We had very little to eat of anything."

"Oh?" I say, credibility deserting me again. "Then why are you so . . . ?" I want to say "chunky," but don't know that word in Vietnamese, so I substitute "fat." Xuân is not really fat, and the conversation's taken an absurd turn. "Fat" in Vietnamese is a comical word, pronounced "mup" in a heavy, almost growling tone. The exchange would be comical if there weren't the sense of tragedy hovering over Xuân's fate. Xuân looks at me astonished. Fearing to be cut up and roasted by the Americans, he's now being asked about his weight.

Bê comes with something in his hand. "It's Xuân's diary," he says. "Look at this."

Bê hands me the diary. Xuân's writing is beautiful, with initial letters and tone marks in flowing style. I can only read a little. Most seems to be about his wife and son, like a letter to them. Finally I get to where Bê's weathered, life-rich finger points, and I read into my own past: "On the third day of Tết we shot at an American helicopter that flew three times over the camp. Results unknown."

Bê takes the diary again: "The captain will want to see some things here."

Ramos gets on the radio; we're ready to go back. He calls up Willie at Citadel Pad, but Willie doesn't like our location.

"We got good stuff," Ramos says in his best *bandido* voice. "Plenty, too."

"Let's hear it," Willie says.

Ramos goes down the list of our lesser souvenirs.

"Not good enough," Willie says. "Walk back."

Ramos ups the ante, but leaves out the antiaircraft sight.

"Still not good enough," Willie says. "You're holdin' out on me."

"Hey, I didn't know you was Chinese, man," Ramos says.
"Let's hear it," Willie says.

Ramos grits his teeth and grinds out the words: "The sight for an antiaircraft gun."

"I want that!" Willie says. "And security on the LZ, the hat, the belt, one knife, and the antiaircraft rounds."

Ramos and I grimace: we'll both pay for this trip back to civilization. Mao radios that he wants us to take Xuân and that his men have found an LZ not far from the camp. Viêt comes out of the forest; Mao wants him to return, too.

"But not yet," Viêt says. "Something I have to do. . . ."

Viêt looks wild, like he's running on adrenaline. Like most of us, he hasn't slept all night, and he has been out there. He talks excitedly to Bê, convinces him of something, gets three ARVN, and disappears into the trees in the direction of the Trail.

I know what he's doing; Rang told him before the operation that if Viêt brought him a rocket he would make him a rallier at last. Rang was smirking; he didn't think Viêt had a prayer—or probably even the intention—of bringing him a rocket. I could see Viêt was serious, though; whether it was to try to save his freedom and his life or to further a double-agent mission was what I didn't know.

In the forest Viêt bends and pushes through the leaves, his moon face shiny with sweat. He walks slowly, stops often, and studies the ground. He looks intently into the trees and examines the bushes and the world all around. You can see Stone Age Asian hunters in him. Behind him the ARVN come, in *their* faces the long procession far back into time.

Ramos and I wait in the clearing, and on the far side we see a commotion: Viêt staggering from the leaves with something huge and heavy on his shoulder.

"Rocket!" Ramos says, and we jump up to go look.

Viêt carries the six-foot rocket to the center of the clearing, bends his knees, rolls the rocket down his arm, and places it gently in the grass. It lies there radiating death power—destroyer of houses and cities, killer of soldiers and babies in the night.

Viêt wipes his brow and puffs out his cheeks. "I'll put this on Captain Rang's desk." he says, a note of threat mixed with his usual comic touch, *shooting* it there a distinct possibility, from the menace in his voice.

"Willie's not gonna like this," Ramos says, looking down at the rocket.

Bê comes with news: the Black Cat is on the way, and a squad will escort us to the LZ. Xuân stands waiting, a rope around his neck. An ARVN hands me the other end; Xuân looks like he's in shock.

I take the rope in my hand and recoil inwardly as if it were a snake. It's about six feet long back to Xuân. I look at him and try to catch his eyes. I want to say something, tell him it'll be all right, even if I don't believe it. "Don't be afraid," I say. "They won't hurt you. Maybe the war will be over soon."

He stares blankly and doesn't respond. He's gone, maybe back to his village again. The squad steps off and we fall in, Ramos with the souvenirs, Viêt staggering under his rocket, and me leading Xuân. Something is passing through the rope between Xuân's neck and my hand, some pulse, some flow. Two lives beat there. We're connected forever.

The forest envelops us, leaves brush us in good-bye as we walk on a mashed-down path made by the ARVN to the LZ. The vegetation thins ahead and the squad splits, ARVN taking positions in the trees. We look across a huge, rectangular clearing. This is no bomb strike. It was made by Rome plows. The giant bulldozers have been out here, phalanxes of them, scraping a great tract of forest away. The bare-earth clearing stretches across a hill and disappears to the east beyond a gray horizon. Good-bye forest, hello civilization.

"No problem about Willie finding us here," Ramos says sarcastically.

Xuân stands staring, mouth agape, the hope he had felt in the camp not even a memory now. I look at him. I want him to run away, dash into the forest and freedom. I drop my end of the rope, but it still hangs heavy around his neck. Armed men are everywhere, too; he wouldn't get two steps. Maybe he'll live out the war in prison, I think, go back someday to his wife and son. Now he looks lost, torn away from everything he loves and belongs to, half dead. I can believe now that Viêt's mother died of sadness.

I look at Viêt standing sweating by his rocket. He and Xuân resemble each other: the same round face, the same chunky build. Forest men for long ages originally, then rice cultivators for millennia, they're probably from the same ancient tribe, with a long history of rebellion against foreign invaders, following lords, generals, and party leaders to war on and kill each other. They look like they could be brothers.

The sound of a chopper comes, and I pick up the rope and feel Xuân flinch. Ramos pulls the souvenirs from his shirt, and Viêt bends and wrestles the rocket onto his shoulder.

"Stand back a little in the trees," I tell Viêt. "Wait till Willie lands."

Ramos radio-talks, and an ARVN pulls the pin on a green smoke grenade and tosses it into the clearing. The Black Cat booms over the bare-dirt horizon and chops, blowing exhaust, toward us. The arched-back cat against the yellow moon appears, the big rotor spinning, Willie and his copilot in their helmets. Helicopter noise takes over, and all our world rolls into it.

The green smoke whips away in billows as Willie descends and sits lightly on the scraped earth, vibrating and beating. We emerge from the trees in a strange procession, Ramos first, waving the souvenirs, then me, leading Xuân and shouting, "Hey, Willie! This is the guy who shot at you!" and finally Viêt, lurching from the trees, balancing the big rocket.

Willie shakes his fist and wags his finger out his window as if he's saying, "No way! Negatron!"

We load up fast, Ramos brandishing the souvenirs and squeezing up to show them to Willie, me helping Xuân in, and Viêt gingerly laying the rocket on the chopper floor. Whatever else I felt on boarding with Xuân, it turns to joy as we blast off. We laugh and shout in another spin of the wheel. We're alive and flying.

The forest falls away below, and we disappear within ourselves. It seems an age ago I lifted off Pioneer Pad with Tex and the Grim Reapers and then with Blunt and King from LZ Pedro. How long does it seem for Viêt since Commander Huynh gave him his last courier mission and his new life began? Xuân stares, sick with emptiness and fear-paralyzed, and Ramos leans back and looks up and far away—to New York City, no doubt, and his beautiful Puerto Rican wife.

I look down at the trees and think about the Trail. I feel it's over, these operations in the mountains and forests. Now the scene will change to where the Trail comes out in the paddy-lands, where light and shadow play among the hamlets and tombs and where Viêt, Ramos, and I will continue to hunt the NVA.[2]

I think about Viêt. With all the doubts about him, he was always there, leading every mission, taking us out and bring-ing us home, even when he stayed back at Têt. He was our guide on the hero-path, our earth god calling us back to the forest. Who else was he, and what would happen to him now and after we left? I shudder as I look down at the forest, floating so silently and placidly below. We killed down there, we ripped holes in Nature, we created the Pit.

The journey along the Trail was within, too, through the labyrinth of our minds. In many ways it was a trip into our own past, and the thread was the hero-path. We are all on it now, too, traveling between life and death like the little plane on Xuân's antiaircraft sight. Inevitably there will come that moment when we will all be in the crosshairs and Death will unfold his arms, step forward, and say, "It's time."

The Black Cat beats through the gray sky. I feel a terrible emptiness and loss, knowing this is the last time. Down there is Eden, Indian country, the land beyond the law and the place of beginnings. Down there are the poison trees and the sparkling stream, the Trail and the commissar's grave. Nature spirits live down there; the wilderness is their only home. You can see them in the glowing twigs and leaves and hear them in the rain at night. They live in the magic animals, too, the miniature deer, the tiger, and the snake, and temporarily in magic, powerful people like Mao, Xuân, Anh, Bê, Biên, and Viêt. What would happen to them now? One day we'll all meet as mist on the mountains.

The base comes up in the distance smoking, the Machine working, eating the land. Through life the Trail runs, connecting, and the hero waits within us all, to guide us along the path. I crawl through the trees in my mind again, edge along the ledge above the deep pool, look down into the water, leave the Trail, and try to hide my sign. Nature is trying to break through, spirit voices out of time. "What next?" I think, as the chopper begins to descend. I think again of the Pit, and of the Trail going around.

NOTES

Overture

1. Richard L. Stevens, *The Trail: A History of the Ho Chi Minh Trail and the Role of Nature in the War in Viet Nam.*
2. Plutarch, *The Lives of Noble Grecians and Romans,* "Alexander."
3. See Loren Eiseley, *The Firmament of Time;* and Joseph Campbell, *The Masks of God: Creative Mythology.*

Sources

1. More Americans died in Quang Tri than in any other province.
2. See William Wordsworth, "Ode: Intimations of Immortality," lines 67–69, in *Complete Poetical Works of William Wordsworth.*

Chapter 1. Viet and the Grim Reapers: The Call to Adventure

1. For the call to adventure, see Joseph Campbell, *The Hero with a Thousand Faces,* "The Hero and the God," 36.

"Come out or die!" would be "Vao di! Muon chêt?" in Vietnamese. The reader will be able to determine when Vietnamese is being spoken, even though the speech may be rendered in English. I have placed some, but not all, of the Vietnamese tone and pronunciation marks, partly to give a flavor of the language and partly to indicate my incomplete knowledge of the language at the time.

2. Chiêu Hôi was called by the Americans, who conceived and financed the program, "Open Arms." Its purpose was to induce VC and NVA to "rally," or defect, and then use them and what they knew against their former comrades. The VC and NVA were badly hurt by the program and went to great lengths to get revenge, both during and after the war. I was then the Chiêu Hôi advisor in Quang Tri. The Province Interrogation Center sat off by itself in a field and was the local chamber of torture and horror. Like Rang's branch of the Special Police, it was advised by the U.S. Central Intelligence Agency.

3. Security at the Chiêu Hôi Center was primarily for defense against

outside attack. The ralliers were fairly free to come and go, remaining because they didn't want to leave, were afraid to go back to the VC, or were plants. The program was, by its "Open Arms" nature, very easy to penetrate.

4. *Crachin,* French for "drizzle," characterized the winter months in the mountains of Quang Tri, when more rain could fall in a slow, steady drip than in the so-called rainy season. And rain dictated the pace of U.S. operations.

5. I'm not sure now of the captain's last name.

6. MACV, *Operational Report,* 1/11, 5th Mechanized Division, 1 Feb. 1970, NAS. "Hoi Chanh" means "rallier," "RRF" is "Rapid Reaction Force," and "a/c" is "aircraft."

7. Lewis Thomas, *The Lives of a Cell,* 144. The snake was probably a python. Guided by heat sensors in its head, it probably crawled up on me for warmth, a not-unheard-of behavior among pythons.

8. Henry David Thoreau, "Walking," in *The Selected Works of Thoreau,* 616.

9. Joseph Campbell, *Hero,* 29.

Chapter 2. Machine in the Forest

1. See Henry David Thoreau, "Economy," in *Walden;* and Ralph Waldo Emerson, "Ode, Inscribed to W. H. Channing," 11:50–51.

2. Wendell Berry, *The Unsettling of America: Culture and Agriculture,* 91–92; and Emerson, "English Traits" (1856), in *Essays and Lectures.*

3. See David Maybury-Lewis, "The Shock of the Other," in *Millennium: Tribal Wisdom and the Modern World,* 1–34.

4. Henry David Thoreau, "Ktaadn," in *The Maine Woods.*

5. See Genesis 2:9–10, 15–17; 3.

6. Thomas Carlyle, "Signs of the Times" (1829), in *Critical and Miscellaneous Essays.*

7. The "numbers" quote is from Chester Cooper, *The Lost Crusade: America in Vietnam.* For another view of human beings transformed by technology, see Henry Adams, *The Education of Henry Adams* (1907).

8. Thoreau, *Walden.*

9. Walt Whitman, "Beat! Beat! Drums!" in *Walt Whitman: The Complete Poems.*

10. MACV, *Situation Report,* 1/11, 5th Mechanized Division, 05 1405Z Jan. 1970, NAS. "C/A" means "Combat Assault." "VCI" is "Viet Cong Infrastructure." "YD 1644" is a map location. "B/1-11" and "C/1-11" are the other companies involved in the operation.

11. MACV, *Operational Report,* 1/11, 5th Mechanized Division, 1 Feb. 1970, NAS.

12. MACV, *Operational Report,* 1/11, 5th Mechanized Division, 1 Feb. 1970, NAS.

13. MACV, *After Action Report FULTON SQUARE,* 1/11, 5th Mechanized Division, Box RG 338, USARV, Vietnam, 1970, NAS.

14. MACV, *Operational Report,* 1/11, 5th Mechanized Division, 1 Feb. 1970, NAS.

15. MACV, *After Action Reports FULTON SQUARE,* 1/11, 5th Mechanized Division, 1970, NAS.

16. MACV, *Operational Report,* 1/11, 5th Mechanized Division, 1 Feb. 1970, NAS.

17. See Shakespeare, *Macbeth,* V.v.23–24.

18. MACV, *Operational Records,* 1/11, 5th Mechanized Division, Fulton Square Daily Situation Report, 1–18 Jan. 70, NAS.

19. Joseph Campbell with Bill Moyers, *The Power of Myth,* 45.

20. Mark 8:24.

21. Herman Melville, *Moby Dick.*

Chapter 3. Deep Play in the Belly of the Whale

1. For the subtitle to this chapter, see Jonah in the whale, Isaiah 4:27; Melville, *Moby Dick;* and Campbell, *Hero,* 36. Clifford Geertz, "Cockfighting in Bali," is in his *The Interpretation of Cultures.*

2. See Homer, *The Odyssey,* first words.

3. See Genesis 3:5.

4. Lao Tzu, *Tao Te Ching.*

5. Thomas Berry, *The Dream of the Earth.*

6. Joseph Conrad, *Heart of Darkness.*

7. Thoreau, "Ktaadn," *The Maine Woods.*

8. Shakespeare, *Julius Caesar.*

9. Conrad, *Heart of Darkness.*

Chapter 4. The Gloomy Wood and the Poison Trees

1. MACV, *Operational Report,* 1/11, 5th Mechanized Division, 1 May 1970, p. 5, NAS.

2. Conrad, *Heart of Darkness.*

3. Albert Camus, *L'Etranger* ("The Stranger").

Chapter 5. Separation-Initiation-Return

1. On Separation-Initiation-Return see Campbell, *Hero,* 36 and passim.

2. See Mark Twain, *Huckleberry Finn,* last words.

3. Thoreau, "Walking," in *The Selected Works of Thoreau.*

4. Campbell, *Hero,* 37 and passim.

5. Mary Howit, "The Spider and the Fly, A Fable," in *One Hundred and One Famous Poems.*

6. Carl Jung, *Man and His Symbols.*

Chapter 6. The Road of Trials, or the Dangerous Aspect of the Gods

1. See Campbell, *Hero,* 36, 97.

2. See Richard L. Stevens, "Where the Trail Came out in the Paddylands," manuscript for forthcoming book.

GLOSSARY

1/11. Shortened battalion designation, in this case the 1st Battalion of the 11th Infantry Regiment.

.38. A .38-caliber revolver.

Agent Orange. Code name for the defoliant commonly used by U.S. forces in Viet Nam to strip jungle vegetation.

Air America. Aviation service of the U.S. Central Intelligence Agency during the Viet Nam War period.

AK-47, AK. Standard NVA-issue 7.62-mm automatic rifle patterned on the Soviet model, used also by the VC.

AO. Area of operations.

ARVN. Army of the Republic of Vietnam, or a member of that army.

Avgas. Aviation fuel.

Bali Hai. In James Michener's *Tales of the South Pacific* (1947), an island symbolizing mystery, beauty, and sensual allure.

B-40. Rocket-propelled grenade launcher, and its grenade, used by the NVA and VC.

C-4. Common plastic explosive, highly explosive when set off by a detonator but slow-burning when ignited by a match or cigarette lighter flame.

Chieu Hoi. The program to induce VC and NVA to defect, "rally," or "return" to the GVN side. The information and the weapons that they brought were often valuable when used against their former comrades. Means "Persuade to Return" in Vietnamese; called "Open Arms" by the Americans, who conceived, financed, and "advised" the program and pushed it on the often-unwilling South Vietnamese, many of whom didn't trust the "rallied" ex-VC and North Vietnamese. I was the U.S. civilian advisor to this program in Quang Tri Province in 1969–1970.

Chuon-chuon. The VC name, meaning "dragonfly," for helicopters.

Chinook. Large troop- and cargo-carrying helicopter.

Cobra. Heavily armed AH-1 attack helicopter.

C-rations. U.S. Army combat rations, supplied in cans.

Dai-Uy. "Captain" in Vietnamese.

Dao (Tao). In Taoism, the flow of creative energy in the universe.

Di. Vietnamese for "move," "go."

District. Administrative and geographic division of a Vietnamese province, comparable to a U.S. county.

DMZ. Demilitarized Zone established by the Geneva Conference of 1954 to separate North and South Viet Nam.

Drone. Remote-control aircraft.

FAC. Forward air controller; pilot of a small, light airplane like the O-2 Skymaster who directs rescue or recovery operations and fighter aircraft attacks on ground targets.

Gaia. In Greek mythology, the goddess of the Earth. The Gaia hypothesis of today is that Earth is alive, a living system.

GVN. Government of (South) Viet Nam.

Hermes. In Greek mythology, the messenger of the gods.

Hero-path. The mythic hero-journey as seen by comparative mythologist Joseph Campbell in *The Hero with a Thousand Faces.*

Ho Chi Minh sandals. Sandals made from rubber tires, worn by VC on the Ho Chi Minh Trail.

Ho Chi Minh Trail. Secret network of paths and roads snaking from North Viet Nam into Laos, Cambodia, and the South, generally through mountains and dense forests, used by the VC and NVA to win the war.

Hooch. U.S. soldiers' slang for "hut."

Huey. UH-1 utility helicopter.

"Indian country." VC and NVA territory. Generally the mountains and forests of the Ho Chi Minh Trail. See "Oregon Trail" below, and Frederick Jackson Turner, *The Frontier in American History* (1920), on the U.S. frontier as a line continually moving westward. Viet Nam and the American West became mixed in the war, and *are* mixed on the mythic level.

J'Accuse. French for "I accuse," and the title of a book by Emile Zola about the Dreyfus Affair.

K-54. Soviet-made semiautomatic pistol.

KAR-14. Automatic carbine, a short version of the M-16 rifle.

Klick. GI jargon for kilometer.

LAW. Short-range surface-to-surface or air-to-surface missile.

Loach. LOH light observation helicopter.

Lurps. Long-range patrol rations.

LZ. Landing zone.

M-16, '16. Standard U.S.-issue automatic rifle, 5.56 mm, also used by ARVN troops.

M-60. Standard U.S. 7.62-mm machine gun, mounted on helicopters and carried by ground troops.

M-79. Single-shot U.S.-issue grenade launcher.

"Machine," or "Green Machine." The U.S. military in its impersonal, huge, technically powerful, career-oriented, and sometimes seemingly all-encompassing sense, as in "part of the Green Machine." Here also a dominant force in thought and history beginning with the scientific revolution of the 1600s, and gathering force through today. Then there is the mythic Machine, in contrast to Nature. "Beneath each deep," Emerson wrote, "another deep opens."

Mad minute. One minute of intense, undirected automatic fire by an infantry unit for the purpose of covering a withdrawal, securing an area, or confusing the enemy.

Mana. Hawaiian-Polynesian word for spiritual energy, power.

Medevac. Medical evacuation aircraft or flight.

Myth. Myth is the voice of the Earth, speaking through succeeding generations of human beings. Myth is the questioning of humanity, trying to understand its origins and itself. Myth is the secret opening, the goddess awaking, stretching, whispering through time.

NDP. Night defensive position.

Nuoc mam. Vietnamese fermented fish sauce.

NVA. North Vietnamese Army, or a member of that army.

O-2 Skymaster. Light observation aircraft commonly used by forward air controllers.

"Oregon Trail." Highway 9 in Quang Tri from Dong Ha to Khe Sanh, scene of some of the heaviest fighting of the war; part of a pattern of "reincarnating," in nomenclature, at least, the vanished American frontier in the war.

Phantom. F-4 fighter-bomber aircraft.

PIC. Province Interrogation Center.

Point. Lead man or element in a patrol.

Political Commissar. Political counterpart of the military commander in VC and NVA units; responsible for political correctness and moral discipline. One of the most important VC/NVA positions.

Province. Administrative and geographic division of Viet Nam; similar to a U.S. state.

PX. Post exchange, the variety store of an army base.

Quang Tri. Northernmost province in the Republic of Viet Nam; also the province capital.

R 'n' R. Rest and recreation, a short leave in a noncombat area.

Recon by fire. Firing into an area in an attempt to get the enemy to reveal his position, or to determine friendly locations.

RPM. Engine or helicopter rotor speed in revolutions per minute.

S-1. Administrative office or officer.

S-2. Intelligence office or officer.

S-3. Operations office or officer.

S-4. Logistics office or officer.

S-5. Civil affairs office or officer.

Sapper. Soldier trained in infiltration and demolitions.

Shiva. One of the major Hindu gods. Kali is his consort and a principal goddess.

Slick. Troop-carrying helicopter.

Spec 4. Specialist 4th class.

TOC. Tactical operations center.

VC. Việt Công guerrilla organization, or a member of it.

VIP. Very important person.

White Mice. South Vietnamese police, so called because of their white uniforms.

Willie peter. White phosphorus incendiary artillery ordinance often used for marking because of the white smoke it produces.

"Word." Important information; orders; latest on a significant situation, as in "What's the word?" Often has a grave, deep, even sacred sense: "Did you get the word?"

"World." Viet Nam–era American slang for the U.S.A., as in "back in the World," or "How many days before you go back to the World?" The mythic connection should here be seen.

XO. Executive officer.

BIBLIOGRAPHY

Adams, Henry. *The Education of Henry Adams.* New York: The Modern Library, 1931.

Bentham, Jeremy. *Introduction to the Principles of Morals and Legislation.* New York: Hafner, 1948.

Berry, Thomas. *The Dream of the Earth.* San Francisco: Sierra Club Books, 1990.

Berry, Wendell. *The Unsettling of America: Culture and Agriculture.* New York: Avon Books, 1978.

Campbell, Joseph. *The Hero with a Thousand Faces.* Princeton, N.J.: Princeton Univ. Press, 1949.

————. *The Masks of God: Creative Mythology.* New York: Penguin, 1968.

————, with Bill Moyers. *The Power of Myth.* New York: Doubleday, 1988.

Camus, Albert. *L'Etranger.* Englewood Cliffs, N.J.: Prentice-Hall, 1955.

Carlyle, Thomas. "Signs of the Times." *Critical and Miscellaneous Essays.* New York: Belford, Clarke, n.d.

Conrad, Joseph. *Heart of Darkness.* New York: New American Library, 1983.

Cooper, Chester. *The Lost Crusade: America in Vietnam.* New York: Dodd, 1970.

Dante. *Inferno.*

Eiseley, Loren. *The Firmament of Time.* New York: Atheneum, 1962.

Emerson, Ralph Waldo. "English Traits." *Essays and Lectures.* New York: Viking, 1983.

————. "Ode, Inscribed to W. H. Channing." *The Norton Anthology of Poetry.* Rev. ed. New York: Norton, 1975.

Geertz, Clifford. *The Interpretation of Cultures*. New York: Basic Books, 1973.

Genesis 2:9–10, 15–17; 3.

Homer. *The Odyssey*.

Howit, Mary. "The Spider and the Fly, A Fable." *One Hundred and One Famous Poems*. Comp. Roy J. Cook. Chicago: Contemporary Books, 1958.

Isaiah 4:27.

Jung, Carl G. *Man and His Symbols*. Garden City, New York: Doubleday, 1964.

Lao Tzu. *Tao Te Ching*. New York: Penguin, 1963.

Mark 8:24.

Marx, Leo. *The Machine in the Garden: Technology and the Pastoral Idea in America*. London: Oxford Univ. Press, 1964.

Maybury-Lewis, David. *Millennium: Tribal Wisdom and the Modern World*. New York: Viking, 1992.

Melville, Herman. *Moby Dick*. New York: Modern Library, 1926.

Plutarch. *The Lives of the Noble Grecians and Romans*. S.v. "Alexander."

Schrödinger, Erwin. *My View of the World*. Trans. Cecily Hastings. Cambridge: Cambridge Univ. Press, 1964.

Shakespeare. *Julius Caesar*. III.i.270–71.

———. *Macbeth*. V.v.23–24.

Stevens, Richard L. "Love Is Light." Manuscript in author's possession.

———. *The Trail: A History of the Ho Chi Minh Trail and the Role of Nature in the War in Viet Nam*. New York: Garland, 1993.

———. Viet Nam documents and maps in author's possession.

———. Viet Nam tapes in author's possession.

———. "Where the Trail Came Out in the Paddylands." Manuscript in author's possession.

Thomas, Lewis. *The Lives of a Cell*. New York: Bantam, 1974.

Thoreau, Henry David. *The Selected Works of Thoreau*. Boston: Houghton Mifflin, 1975. Includes *Walden* and *The Maine Woods*.

Twain, Mark. *Huckleberry Finn*. New York: Dodd, Mead, 1953.

U.S. Department of Defense, Army, Military Assistance Command

Vietnam (MACV). *After Action Report FULTON SQUARE*. Box RG 338, USARV, Vietnam, 1st Bde, 5th Inf. Div. HQ, 1970.

———. *Operational Report for the Period Ending 31 Jan. 1970*. 1/11, 5th Mechanized Division. 1 February 1970.

———. *Operational Report for the Period Ending 30 Apr. 1970*. 1/11, 5th Mechanized Division, 1 May 1970.

———. *Situation Report*. 1/11, 5th Mechanized Division. 05 1405Z. January 1970.

Whitman, Walt. *Walt Whitman: The Complete Poems*. London: Penguin, 1986.

Wordsworth, William. "Ode: Intimations of Immortality." *Complete Poetical Works of William Wordsworth*. Ed. Andrew J. George. New York: Houghton Mifflin, 1932.

INDEX

Abbott and Costello, 59
Abyss, 113
Adrenaline, 68, 76, 111, 179
Agent Orange, 207, 257
Air America, 112, 257
Alexander the Great, 216
Angel of Death, 116, 235, 252
Apocalypse (Dürer), 187
Armed Forces Radio, 194
Atropos, 57—58

Baldy II, 35, 38, 65
Bali Hai, 201, 257
Ba Long Valley, 7, 95—96, 100, 105, 183—85
Batman, 102, 148—49, 151, 182, 188
Beatles, 98
Bioluminescence, 23, 42, 214—15, 223—24, 231
Black Cat, 105—7, 183, 187—88, 193, 200, 243, 249—50, 252
Boone, Daniel, 52
Bowl, valley of the, 33—34, 52, 59, 65, 73
Bravo Company, 58, 65, 67, 73, 82, 91—92
British, 21
Bru, 111
Buddha, 23
Bunker Hill, 21

Caesar, Julius, 121, 216
California, state of, 105
Caligula, 187
Calypso (nymph), 156
Campbell, Joseph, 3, 5, 191
Carib Indians, 237
Celts, 47, 131
Central Highlands, 112
Central Intelligence Agency (CIA), 56, 253n.2
C-4, 63—64, 91, 257
Cham people, 191
Chaos, 115
Charlie Company, 58, 65, 73, 81, 91—92
Charon, 78
Chiêu Hôi Center, 13, 15—16, 47, 52, 253n.2,3, 257
China, 130, 191, 243
Crachin, 15, 20, 22, 63, 151, 169, 254n.4
C-rations, 23—24, 26, 29, 32—33, 49, 60, 63—64, 67—68, 77, 82, 184, 205, 212, 215, 257
Cuba, 194

Dao (Tao), 8, 258
Dark Side, 46
Delta Company, 52, 54—55, 58—59, 62—66, 70—74, 76, 80, 85, 91, 93

Demilitarized Zone (DMZ), 6,
    174, 236, 245
Dogs and handlers, 53—54, 57,
    88. *See also* King
"Drive South" of Viets, 6
Dürer, Albrecht, 187

Earth gods, 24, 76
Economics Section (VC), 75—76
Eden, Garden of, 3, 47, 111, 252
Eiseley, Loren, 3
Emerson, Ralph Waldo, 155
Eve and the Serpent, 111

Firebase Ann, 199—201, 204—5,
    207, 235, 237—38
1st ARVN Division, 189
1st ARVN Regiment, 99, 144, 189,
    191, 196
1st Battalion, 11th Infantry, 18, 64,
    96, 104, 142
1st Brigade, 5th Mechanized Divi-
    sion, 15–16, 100, 131, 144, 147–
    48, 150, 182, 189, 229
1st Company, 3rd Battalion, 1st
    ARVN Regiment, 203–6, 216,
    229
Foreign Service (U.S.), 19, 196
French, 19, 82, 86, 191, 193—94,
    203

Gaia, 229, 258
Geneva Convention, 103
Germanic peoples, 47, 131, 165
Greek Fates, 57
Grim Reapers, 18, 22, 51, 64, 93,
    104, 110, 117, 122, 126—27,
    154—55, 251
guerrilla company commander, 9
Guevara, Che, 194

Hammurabi, 125
Hanoi, Viet Nam, 7, 19, 83, 120,
    123, 184
Hercules, 188
Hermes, 144, 258
Hero-path, 3, 5, 11, 251—52, 258
Hero with a Thousand Faces
    (Campbell), 5, 191
Highway One, 47, 148
Hill 100, 107, 125, 215
Hills 300 and 320, 15, 100, 115,
    161, 172, 180, 186, 224
Ho Chi Minh, 8, 120
Huckleberry Finn (Twain), 99,
    174, 181
Huê, 152, 197
Huitzilpochtli, 191
Huynh, VC District Commander,
    19, 75, 82, 85–86, 90, 94

I Ching, 228
Indian country, 8, 20, 26, 181,
    183, 195, 200—201, 252
Iowa, state of, 23, 40, 46, 182,
    243

J'Accuse (Zola), 156, 258
Japanese, 19, 82, 86, 191, 243
Jesus, 93

Kali, 181
Kennedy, John F., 8
K—14 Battalion, 102
King (scout dog), 53—54, 57,
    63—64, 67, 70, 72—73, 82, 91
Kunming, China, 130

Labrador, black (dog), 53, 88
Laos, 15, 92, 192, 204, 242
Leeches, 43, 44

Lone Ranger, 18, 87, 194
LZ Cindy, 60—61, 65
LZ Nancy, 99, 191
LZ Pedro, 52, 54, 57, 153, 185,
    195, 251

MacBeth (Shakespeare), 21, 148
Machine (Green Machine), 19, 21,
    34, 39, 45—50, 58—59, 61—
    67, 71, 73—74, 76, 91, 93, 105,
    113, 126—28, 131, 143, 154,
    157, 162, 167, 179—81, 185,
    189, 200, 224, 252
Mad minute, 67, 259
Mai Linh District, 194
Malaysia, 53
Mana, 125, 259
Manioc, 112
Mars (god), 191
Medusa, 107
Michigan, state of, 53
Minotaur, 143
Montagnards, 31, 158
Moon goddess, 232—33, 241
Mother Earth, 44, 201
Mount Olympus, 109, 111
Mythic connections, 3, 5—6, 46—
    47, 93—95, 109—11, 114—15,
    119, 123—26, 128, 131, 142,
    156, 159, 161, 173, 191, 201,
    205, 215, 223—24, 232—35,
    237, 240—41, 251—52, 259

Napoleon, 216
National Archives, 11
Nature, 5—6, 25, 27, 35, 43, 50,
    52, 61, 63, 70, 73, 83, 184—85,
    191, 228, 232, 241, 249, 251—
    52
New England, 46

New York City, 194, 251
Ngô Dinh Diêm, 7
Nguyen Du, 110
Nhan Biêu, 8
Night Defensive Position (NDP),
    62, 70, 78, 80, 123—24
Nixon, Richard M., 99, 164
North Viet Nam, 75, 80, 130, 198,
    241

Odysseus, 156
old river road, 107, 209, 215, 219
Old Baldy, 33, 35, 39, 47, 51—52,
    59—61, 65, 73
Old Night, 115
Oregon Trail, 57, 259

Paddylands, 251
Paris, France, 41
Pequod (ship), 94
Pioneer Pad, 18, 20, 104, 106, 153,
    181, 184, 251
Pit, the, 229, 231, 233, 251—52
Playboy pictures, 200
Political commissar (VC), 117—
    20, 127, 130—31, 143, 145, 159,
    163, 180, 209, 216, 222, 224,
    252, 260
Political Section (VC), 75, 78—79
Prometheus, 111, 177, 181, 188
Province Interrogation Center
    (PIC), 13—14, 253n.2
Puerto Rico, 194, 251
Python, 28, 161, 254

Quang Binh province, 245—46
Quang Tri Advisory Team, 105
Quang Tri Citadel Pad, 10, 105,
    183, 200, 247
Quang Tri City, 8, 10, 13, 27, 44,

47, 55, 100, 148, 151, 194—95,
    196, 200, 225, 260
Quang Tri Combat Base, 47, 58,
    181, 184, 188, 252
Quang Tri Province, 6, 174, 198,
    253n.1, 254n.4

Rangers, 56, 66, 88
Red Devil, 106—7, 126, 148, 153,
    182, 185
River Styx, 78
Roman Catholics, 245
Rome plows, 249

S-1, 51, 260
S-2, 16—17, 49, 260
S-3, 18, 50—51, 260
S-4, 51, 260
S-5, 52, 260
Saigon, Viet Nam, 184, 197—98
Sargasso Sea, 22, 83
Satan, 233
Schrödinger, Erwin, 3
Seurat, Georges, 33, 52
Shiva, 181, 234, 260
Sirens, 155
Sisyphus, 215
Snake (serpent), 41—42, 45, 47,
    80, 93—94, 103, 107—8, 111,
    124, 126, 128, 131, 159, 185,
    222—24, 227, 234, 244, 249,
    252, 254n.7
South China Sea, 9, 191
Soviet Union, 130, 243
Spanish, 195, 221
Special Police (ARVN), 10, 13,
    253n.2
Street without Joy, 10
Sulfanilamide, 86, 119—20
Superman, 188

Tacitus, 165
Têt, 55, 96, 145, 151—53, 169,
    238, 246—47
Thach Han River, 8, 20, 47, 61,
    96, 100, 103, 106, 152, 172,
    185, 209, 211
Thach Ma River, 99
3rd Battalion, 1st ARVN Regi-
    ment, 194, 199, 201
Thoreau, Henry David, 2, 46—47,
    57
Thua Thien, 99
Titans, 61, 115, 228
Tonto, 18, 87
Trackers, 53—54, 88, 91, 171
Trail, The, 3, 5, 258
Trans—Siberian Railway, 130
Tree of the Knowledge of Good
    and Evil, 3
Tree of Life, 3, 6, 47
Triêu Phong, 8, 17, 24—26, 33—
    34, 47, 51, 57—58, 61, 65—66,
    74, 82, 91, 100, 145
Truyên Kiêu ("The Tale of Kiêu")
    (Nguyen Du), 110

Ulysses, 155
Underworld (Hell), 78, 86, 191,
    219—20, 228, 233, 242

Valley of the Shadow of Death, 73
Viêt (VC guerrilla): as always
    there, 185; black market activ-
    ities, 192, 196; booby traps of,
    89—90; as "earth god," 251;
    helps Ramos, 208; hides docu-
    ments, 120; hunts rockets,
    248—49; as master of war, 8,
    227; the "new" Viêt, 152; as
    "other," 83; possible mission,

189; as possible VC sapper, 89;
in race with Blunt, 81; in race
with Mao, 207—9; skill at deep-
forest navigation, 83; skill with
U.S. weapons, 30, 75—76; sympathies with VC and North,
198—99; at Têt, 151—52; and
VC women, 87, 89—90
Vietnamese language, 253n.1

Vietnamization, 99—100, 196

Walden (Thoreau), 2
Women, 87, 89—90, 92, 111, 170,
230—31, 236, 238, 250
World, the, 5, 41, 82, 143, 178,
188, 261

Zeus, 109